條約法公約析論

陳治世 著

臺灣 學 生 書 局 印行

序

　　常設國際法院與今之國際法院，皆於其規約第三十八條訂明：法院裁判時首應適用者，爲訴訟當事國間之國際協約。可見國際司法機關論斷是非糾紛時，條約（即國際協約）居法之首位，條約係法院判案之主要法律依據。

　　就常情而言，相關國家簽訂條約，常爲解決國際爭端之上策，亦係預防國際衝突之良方。中華民國政府於民國八十年七月間，與菲律賓政府簽妥海道通行協定後，已消除我方漁民屢遭菲方攔捕之災，亦應可防止日後相同之禍，即屬最近例證。

　　此協定之締結過程，足徵下述至理。即國人支持簽訂條約事宜，訂約者善用談判條約之方法訣竅，又諳熟條約法則，方可於訂約時避免國家受損，進而增進國人利益。故訂約者應習條約法，良有以也。

　　民國五十八年以前，中國學者之中文國際法專書，無論名爲國際法學、萬國公法、國際法入門、國際法概要、國際法大綱、國際法原理、國際公法或國際法，皆於敍述國際協約之章目前，以「締約權」或「條約」爲標題，不用「條約法」等字；討論條約之專書，亦稱爲「條約論」或「條約新論」，而不稱爲「條約法論」或「條約法」。至於以「條約法新論」爲名之專書或爲題之論文，更遑論矣。原因無他，蓋以是年以前，尚無協定之完整國際條約法也。

民國五十八年，條約法公約於維也納締結後，已有名副其實之協定條約法。二十二年以還，泰西學者之若干條約法論著，早已問世，而我國原有之中文條約專書，如吳昆吾先生之條約論（民國二十年初版，六十六年臺一版）、孫希中先生之條約論（民國四十七年版），以及丘宏達教授之條約新論（民國四十八年版），均未見修訂再版，詳敍條約法之新著，尚付闕如，國內一般讀者迄無相關之中文基本讀物，學生更缺應備之適當課本。

筆者講授國際法有年，對條約知識甚感興趣，時加注意，稍有心得，曾於所著國際法（初版原名學生國際法）一書中，列載篇幅頗多之專章，以摘要簡介條約法公約之主要條款，為習國際法者提供條約方面之概念與要義，惜以過於簡約，未作深入析論，難應大學研究生之需。其他中文國際法專書，因限於篇幅，關於條約法之介紹，亦語焉不詳，可謂同有拙著不足之處。

筆者鑒於以上諸種事實，乃乘課餘之暇，從事研究與撰寫，以深入淺出法，用語體文句，分析討論條約法公約各條款，略談舊理論，試述新觀念，偶舉名家見解，旁及學者主張，並作初步評論，冀能助讀者知其然亦知其所以然。

筆者洞悉，口語化之辭句，未能軟化硬性技術性之瑣細條文內容，而增其趣味，而使其輕鬆，讀者或有晦澀乏味之感，然而若能靜心玩味，必可漸入堂奧，體會其中義理也。

條約法公約僅適用於國家間之條約，又不包含國家條約繼承之規條，不足以規範各類條約所涉事項，故聯合國繼續努力，於一九七八年召開國際會議，通過國家條約繼承法公約，復於一九八六年，接受聯合國國際法委員會之建議，經相同程序，簽訂國

家與國際組織間及國際組織間條約法公約。筆者見此二約與條約相關，乍思之初，曾有亦予析論之意，惟經三思之後，因覺一則其一般條款與條約法公約者極似，二則其適用對象不多，且漸減少，三則其實質條款投合專家需要者甚夥，應使一般讀者知曉者綦稀，故姑且暫抑此意，只將其附於書末，以便專家參閱。

　　本書初版，一如所有初版書刊，難免舛誤缺失，懇祈讀者不吝斧正。

陳 治 世 謹識

中華民國八十一年三月二十九日

條約法公約析論

目　錄

索 引

條約法公約析論

前編 緒言 ❶

第一節 什麼是條約？

什麼是條約？這是條約的定義問題。關於這問題，今天仍是衆說紛紜，沒有大家一致的答案。著名傳統國際法學者奧本海（Lassa F. L. Oppenheim）說：「國際條約是創設當事國的法律權利義務的國家或國際組織間的協定」❷。美國哈佛大學條約法研究寫道：「條約是兩個或兩個以上國家建立或圖謀建立彼此在國際法下的關係所協議的正式文書」❸。史沓客（J. G.

❶ 本書第一部分的「前編」二字，用以表示析論公約之前的一編。用這兩個字，也是爲了使本書第一編和公約第一編相配合，並且避免兩者的「編」碼不一致。

❷ Lassa F. L. Oppenheim, *International Law, A Treatise,* 8th ed. by Hersch Lauterpacht, (1958) Vol. I., p. 877. (本定義是本書筆者的中譯文。以下外文的中譯文字，除特別註明的以外，都是本書筆者所譯。)

❸ *Harvard Research in International Law,* Art 1(a), in *American Journal of International Law* (以下簡寫爲 AJIL)，Supplement 686 (1935)。

Starke) 教授認為：「條約可以視爲國際法使用的總名稱，能包括國際組織間或國際組織與國家間的協定」❹。中國外交官學者湯武也寫道：「條約爲國際間或一國與國際機構間成立書面諒解之統稱」❺。一九六九年維也納條約法公約第二條則規定：「稱條約者，謂國家所締結而以國際法爲準之國際書面協定，不論其載於一項單獨文書或兩項以上相關之文書內，亦不論其特定名稱爲何」❻。

　　從上可知，奧本海提到創設法律的權利義務，卻無「依國際法」等字眼；哈佛大學法學院的研究報告，有「彼此在國際法下」等字，卻不包括國際組織爲締結條約者，而且只說正式文書，否定了口頭協定；史杳客顧及國際法、國家、國際組織和條約的關係，卻未說條約是釐定法律權利義務的協定；湯武注意到國家、國際組織、統稱等，卻不承認口頭諒解；條約法公約既不列國際組織，又排除口頭協定。所以這些定義都不能適用於一切形式的條約，什麼是條約的問題，依然存在，沒有令人人滿意的答案。本書爲方便起見，並且爲了幫助行文，姑且採用本公約所下的條約定義。

---

❹　J.G. Starke, *An Introduction to International Law*, 6th ed. (1967) p. 336.

❺　湯武，中國與國際法（臺北：中華文化出版事業委員會（民四六）（三），頁六六八。

❻　一九六九年維也納條約法公約第二條第一項（甲）款。本款中文是中華民國外交部的譯文。本書以下所錄本公約的中文條文，完全抄自外交部譯本。

第二節　條約的名稱

在中國，春秋時代稱條約爲「盟」，盟「卽現代條約之謂，蓋條約爲二國或數國互訂之契約，盟亦二國或數國相締結之契約也。故盟與條約在實質爲一物，第名詞稍有異耳」❼。在英國，一四二七年的 Rolls of Parliament，使用 treaty 一字。自中華民國建立以來，一切國際協定統稱爲條約。分別的稱謂，則因訂約程序的簡或繁，而有換文、公約等五十幾種。現在簡介如下：

(1) 條約 (Treaty)。廣義的條約，包括一切形式的國際協定，一如條約法公約所指的；狹義的條約，則指兩國簽訂的程序最莊嚴複雜的正式條約，例如中華民國與日本國間和平條約、中華民國與美利堅合衆國間共同防禦條約是。

(2) 公約 (Convention)。Convention 又譯爲專約。譯爲公約時，表示約中規定的是許多國家共同的事項，如一九八二年聯合國海洋法公約是。譯爲專約時，是指兩國爲專門性事項而簽訂的協定，如領事專約、引渡專約、劃界專約是。原來 Convention 一字由拉丁字 Conventio 演變而來，其意義是合同，在實質上和條約無異，兩者可互換使用，締結程序多相同，形式也莊嚴隆重。

---

❼　洪鈞培，春秋國際公法（上海，中華書局，民二八；臺灣，中華書局，民六〇），頁二二三。

(3) 憲章 (Charter) 。憲章的形式也很莊嚴，簽訂的程序亦甚複雜，是多邊的國際協定，常用來稱呼國際組織的基本法，聯合國憲章便是一例。

(4) 盟約 (Covenant，美國總統威爾遜提倡使用) 。盟約是許多國家集體締結的文件，用以規定政治守則，並且創設實施守則的機構，國際聯合會 (又譯爲國際聯盟) 盟約就是實例。

(5) 協定 (Agreement)。協定可以是雙邊或多邊的文件，由較少的國際法主體所締結，文件所定事項涉及的範圍較小，其形式不像公約、正式條約那麼莊嚴，比簡化式條約則稍爲隆重，例如在中華民國美軍地位協定是。

以下按各種名稱的英文字母順序列舉名詞。

Accord (協合)。Act (議定書是歐洲協調於一八一五年所創用)。Additional articles (附加條款)。Agreed minutes (同意紀錄)。Aide-memoire (備忘錄)。Armistice (停戰協定)。Arrangement (辦法)。Articles (條款)。Articles of agreement (協定條款)。Barter (軍事協定)。Cease fire (停火協定)。Code (法典)。Communique (公報)。Compact (合同)。Compromis (仲裁協定)。Concordat (敎廷條約)。Constitution (組織法)。Contract (契約)。Declaration (宣言、聲明)。Exchange of letters (換函)。Exchange of notes (照會)。Executive agreement (行政協定)。Final act (藏事議定書或譯爲藏事文件)。General act (總議定書)。Instrument (文件)。Joint declaration (聯合聲明)。Lease (租約)。Mandates (委任統治書)。

Measures （措施）。Memorandum of agreement（協議節略）。Memorandum of understanding（諒解節略）。Minutes（紀錄）。Modifications（修正文件）。Modus vivendi（臨時辦法）。Notes verbals（會談紀錄）。Optional clause（任選條約）。Pact（禁約）。Plan（計畫）。Procés verbal（紀事錄、議事紀錄）。Proclamation（公告）。Protocol（議定書）。Provisions（條項）。Recommendation（建議）。Regulation（章程）。Resolution（決議案）。Rule（規則）。Scheme（清單）。Statute（規約）。Understanding（諒解）。Undertaking（承擔）。當然還有其他名稱未列，應該順此說明。至於兩國締結的雙邊條約、兩國以上簽訂的多邊條約、處分性條約、不平等條約、軍事聯盟條約等，不屬於條約名稱的範圍，是條約分類的用語，本編姑且不予列敍。

第三節　條約簡史

陳顧遠❽、洪鈞培❾、徐傳保❿、甯協萬⓫、馬潤⓬和何炳松

---

❽　陳顏遠，中國國際法溯源（上海，商務，民二六）。

❾　見註❼。

❿　徐傳保，*Le Drait des Gens et la Chine Antigue*

⓫　甯協萬，現行國際法

⓬　馬潤，中國合於國際法論

⑬等中國學者，丁韙良⑭、樓富耳⑮和葛爾士⑯等西方學者，都說中國春秋時代（公元前 722 年至 481 年）已有國際公法，而且「國際間之條約，亦爲春秋國際公法之淵源，……例如春秋時之盟會組織，其初僅包含少數國家；……盟會組織漸漸擴大，大多數國家爲其會員，於是盟會之規約，變爲國際公法。」所謂盟，即現代條約⑰。

在西方國家裏，公元前3100年，Lagash 與 Umma 兩國於 Mesopotamia 簽訂條約，在兩國共同信奉的七位 Sumerian 神前宣誓認證，必予履行。公元前1272年，埃及國王 Ramses II 與鄰國國王 Hittites 克大撒簽訂條約⑱，公元前四一八年，斯巴達與阿哥士締結條約⑲，都是較早的條約先例。

以上所說的條約，雖然是雛形的國際契約，卻表示了一種需要，就是爲了釐訂國家間的權利義務關係，應有具體的文件加以訂明，以便彼此遵循。而以上各學者所述的，如果以雛形的國際

---

⑬　何炳松，中國古代國際法
⑭　丁韙良 (P. Martin), *Revue de droit interational et légis-lation comparé,* Vol. 14, pp. 227-242.
⑮　樓富耳 (Louis Le Fur), *Précis de droit international.*
⑯　葛爾士 (Geles), *A History of Chinese Literature*
⑰　前揭⑦洪著，頁六二、六三。
⑱　A Nussbaum, *A Concise History of the Law of Nations,* rev. ed. New York, 1954., p. 8; J. H. Breasted, *History of Egypt* (1905), p. 437 ff.
⑲　C. Phillipson, *International Law and Custom of Ancient Greece and Rome* (1911), p. 60.

契約爲衡量標準，也是中肯的說法。

　　中國清朝於康熙二十八年（公元一六八九年）與俄國簽訂的
尼布楚條約，劃定黑龍江的中俄國界❷，是中國近代最早最莊嚴
的條約。那年以後，中國簽訂的條約，爲數甚多，刊載於中外條
約大全或中外條約輯編等專輯中。

　　在西洋，被稱爲國際法鼻祖的荷蘭法學家葛羅秀士 (Hugo
Grotius de Groot, 1583-1645) 力倡國際法以後，因爲個人間
的協議形式和國家間的協議形式，相似的地方很多，許多學者便
借用規範個人民事契約法的規則，以發展規範國家民事契約關係
的規則。專制君主訂約承擔的義務，與平民於契約中承諾的雖然
不同，卻都是基於相同的自然法基本原則，而且經常適用這些原
則。到了憲政民主時期，政府須依照憲法規定才能夠設立，國家
訂約便須以公法爲基礎，國家間的協定必是公法性質，與個人間
的以私法爲基礎的契約，在基本概念和性質上，差異就越來越明
顯了。但是許多人士仍然繼續演繹、假借或延伸國內法則爲國際
法則，在簽訂條約時也這樣做。脅迫訂約代表所締結的條約，以
詐欺手段作成的條約，其受害國可以正當拒絕受條約的拘束，就
是移用私法契約規則的兩例。

　　國家與國家簽訂條約，無論是基於自然法的基本理念，或是
移用國內法規則，都因爲事實上的需要，其數目逐年增加。若干
國家爲了減少簽訂同一事項的若干雙邊條約的麻煩和重複，便集
體締結多邊條約，例如普遍適用的所謂立法條約 (Law-making

---

❷　康雍乾道四朝條約，康熙條約，頁一至十一。

treaties)，也不斷出現。葛羅秀士逝世後，一六四八年的衛士發里亞（Westphalia）條約、一八一五年的維也納公會藏事議定書❷、一八三一年和一八三九年的倫敦條約❷、一八五六年的巴黎宣言❷、一八六四年、一九〇六年、一九二九年和一九四九年的改善戰地傷病的四份日內瓦公約、一八九九年和一九〇七年的幾份海牙公約、一九一九年的國際聯合會盟約、一九二〇年的常設國際法院規約、一九四五年的聯合國憲章、一九五八年的四份海洋法公約、一九六一年的外交關係公約、一九六三年的領事關係公約、一九六六年的三份保障人權公約、一九六九年的條約法公約和特種使節公約、一九七八年的國家之條約繼承公約、一九八二年的聯合國海洋法公約等，都各自構成了一般國際法的重要部分。這也表示，條約不但在數目上越來越多，在應用上日益頻繁，而且在促進國際法發展方面，也居於首要地位。

　　原來條約、國際習慣、一般法律原則和司法判例都是國際法的來源。關於這一點，以前的常設國際法院規約和現在的國際法院規約，都在第三十八條第一項規定了，而且都把訴訟當事國明白承認的一般的和特別的規條列於第一位，要求法院決案時首先依據條約（規條），沒有條約可依據時，才依據國際習慣，又無

---

❷　一八一五年六月九日，英國、法國、奧國、葡萄牙、普魯士、俄羅斯、西班牙、瑞典（挪威）等國簽署 The Final Act of the Vienna Congress，規定瑞士為永久中立國、國際河川航行自由、黑奴販賣完全廢止、外交使節為大使公使辦公使及代辦等四級。

❷　該約最重要的具長遠作用的條款，是規定比利時為永久中立國。

❷　該宣言禁止戰時的私掠（Privateering）制度。

國際習慣可依據時，才按一般法律原則，或再參酌判例或學說。而在事實上，常設國際法院和現在的國際法院，常以雙邊條約為判決訟案的依據，以多邊條約為發表諮詢意見的基礎。可見條約在國際司法機關中的地位是多麼的重要。

條約必包含三部分：序文、正文和結語。最早的條約有這三部分，最新的莊嚴條約仍沒有減少。

舊形式的條約序文，往往有禱告語句。禱告語句後列載締約國國名及其元首姓名，再加全權代表職銜姓名，敍明訂約目的，接著說「各代表證書均經校閱，認為妥善，……爰議定條款……。」這裏姑且以中華民國與美利堅合眾國間友好通商航海條約（民國三十五年簽訂）序文為例說。

中華民國
美利堅合眾國 為欲藉適應兩國人民精神、文化、經濟及商務願望之條款所規定足以增進彼此領土間友好往還之辦法，以加強兩國間悠久幸存之和好聯繫及友誼結合，爰決定訂立友好通商航海條約。為此各派全權代表如左：

中華民國國民政府主席特派：

中華民國外交部部長王世杰博士，

中華民國外交部條約司司長王化成博士；

美利堅合眾國大總統特派：

美利堅合眾國駐中華民國特命全權大使司徒雷登博士，

美利堅合眾國簽約全權代表駐天津總領事施參斯先生；

　　雙方全權代表，各將所奉全權證書，互相校閱，均屬
　　妥善，議定條款如左。

條約正文用條碼項碼款碼或段號等，依序列載一般條款、實質條款、特別條款和程序條款。當然，各條款的內容完全針對條約的主旨而定，都是爲了達到主旨而列載細則。程序條款又稱雜項條款，包括條約的有效期間、批准、批准書互換、生效條件、加入方式、所用文字、作準文字、繕謄份數等等。

條約結語部分，則載明代表簽字蓋印，以昭信守，並書明簽署日期和地點。蓋印是中國人簽約的一種習慣，西洋人多以簽姓名爲準，不另加蓋印信。

時至今日，條約序文不復用禱告語句，多數不列締約國國名及其元首姓名，甚至雙邊條約的序文，也都不再列國名和元首姓名。除此以外，條約的其他形式措詞等，沒有大變。例如一九八二年的聯合國海洋法公約，於序文首句就直接了當的寫道：「本公約締約各國 (The States Parties to this Convention)，……（緊接的是一篇長序文）……經協議如下 (Have agreed as follows)：」最後於第三二〇條訂明阿拉伯文、中文、英文、法文、俄文和西班牙文各文字本有同等效力。

英、法、美等民主法治國家，很久以前便編印條約彙編之類的書籍，以利政府人員查考和學人研究。中國最早的條約集，是康雍乾道四朝條約，自有外交部以來，該部先後出版中外條約大全、中外條約輯編等，都以登載中國簽訂的條約爲主；外交部每隔相當時日，視實際需要，以白皮書刊登重要條約，例如上述中美通商航海條約，是於民國四十二年五月，以白皮書第一〇七號刊載其中英文約文、議定書和互換批准議定書。于能模和黃月波合編的中外條約彙編，也屬同一性質。

在西洋國家裏，除政府出版的條約輯以外，還有社會人士刊印的。下列彙編常受研究條約者重視，所以列舉於下，以便參考。

Basdevant, J. *Traités et conventions en vigeur entre la France et les puissances étrangères,* 4 vols, Paris, 1918-1922.

Bernard, J. *Recueil des traitez de paix...et d'autre actes publics...*Amsterdam, 1700.

British Treaty Series, 1892-.

Déak, F. and Jessup, P. C. *Neutrality Laws, Regulations and Treaties of Various Countries,* 2 vols., Washington, 1939.

Descamps, E. E. F., and Renault, L. *Recueil international des Traités du XIXᵉ siècle,* vol. 1. (1801-1825), Paris, 1914.

Descamps, E. E. F. and Renault, L. *Recueil international des Trsités du XXe sièclᵉ,* 7 vols, (1901-1907), Paris, 1904-1908.

Dumont, J. *Corps universel diplomatique du droit des gens,* 8 vols., Amsterdam, 1726-1731.

Dumont, J. *Nouveau recueil des traités...depuis la paix de Munster jusques à l'anné M. DCC. IX,* Amsterdam, 1710.

Dumont, J. *Supplement au Corps du droit des gens,*

by Mr. Rousset, Amsterdam, 1739.

Hertslet, E. *Treaties and Conventions between Creat Britain and Foreign Powers so far as They Relate to Commerce and Navigation*, 31 vols., London, 1840-1925.

MacMurray, J. V. A. *Treaties and Agreements with and Concerning China, 1894-1919*, 2 vols., New York, 1924.

von Martens, G. F. *Recueil des principaux traités d'alliance, de paix, de trêve*...(1761-1801), 7 vols., Götingen, 1791-1801; 2nd ed., 8 vols. (1761-1808), vols V-VIII by K. von Martens, Götingen, 1817-1835.

von Martens, G. F. *Supplement au Recueil des principaux*... (1494-1807), 8 vols., Götingen, 1802-1808.

von Martens, G. F. *Nouveau recueil des traités des principaux*... (1808-1839), 16 vols., V-XVI by K. von Martens and others, Götingen, 1817-1842. *Nouveau Supplements* (1761-1839), 3 vols.

von Martens, G. F. *Nouveau recueil général de traités*...(1840-1874), 20 vols., Götingen, 1843-1875; 2nd series (1876-1908), 35 vols., Götingen and Leipzig, (1876-1908); 3rd series (1907-1942), Leipzig,

1909-1942.

Tresties and Conventions Concluded between the United States of America and Other Powers, Notes by J. C. Bancroft Davis, Washington, 1873.

United States. *Executive Agreement Series,* 1929-1945, Washington.

United States. *Treaties and Other International Acts Series,* 1946-, Washington.

United States Treaty Series, 1908-, Washington.

　以上所列，只是政府和學者出版的主要條約彙編，未能全部列出。自有常設國際組織後，由國際組織集刊的條約已多，其中以國際聯合會（又譯稱國際聯盟，簡稱國聯）和聯合國出版的為最多。國聯依國聯盟約 (Covenant of the League of Nations) 第十八條的規定，自一九二二年至一九四四年間，出版國聯條約彙編 (The League of Nations Treaty Series) 二〇五輯，登載條約四八三四件。聯合國秘書處依聯合國憲章第一〇二條的規定，自一九四六年起至今，出版的聯合國條約彙編 (The United Nations Treaty Series) 將近萬輯，刊登英文或法文作成的條約，以及用英文或（和）法文譯妥的條約。因為條約彙編既多且重，携帶固不方便，典藏亦太佔空間，所以聯合國秘書處已把這些彙編影製成微卷（片），供人購用。

　說到這裏，大致表示了學者政府和國際組織對條約的重視，也稍為說明了重視的一種方式。

第四節　條約法公約的簽訂

　　儘管國際條約已有多年久載的歷史，重要的立法條約不可勝數，學者政府和國際組織都肯定其重要性，但是，向來各國締結條約、履行條約……，都只是依據需要、常理和習慣，並沒有成文法則可資遵循，直到一九六九年，維也納條約法公約 (The Vienna Convention on the Law of Treaties) 簽訂後，才有一套成文的條約法規。

　　原來國聯盟約未訂明國聯應召開國際會議，以締結立法條約，藉以促進國際法的發展。然而國聯中人，認為經由締結條約以使國際法發展，確是十分重要的而且是能做的事情，乃於一九三〇年召開國際會議，列國籍法、海洋法和國家責任法等為議題，於海牙舉行國際法編纂會議，不幸因為各與會代表意見紛岐，會議沒有什麼成果。雖然如此，卻開了常設性普遍性國際組織召開國際立法會議的先河，啓迪了後人的思考。

　　一九四五年，出席聯合國憲章制訂會議的各國代表，深知國際法的重要性，又希望促進國際法的發展，便在憲章第十三條第一項訂明：「大會應作成研究，並作成建議：（子）以促進政治上之國際合作，並提倡國際法之逐漸發展與編纂。」這是全球性國際組織約章以明文作這種規定的創舉，顯示憲章比國聯盟約略有進步，比盟約更重視國際法。

　　聯合國大會遵照憲章的規定，除運用其他方式❷，以謀求國

_____

❷　例如通過決議案，以解釋大會活動的涉及國際法的問題，或以實際行為養成具國際法效力的習慣，或請求國際法院發表諮詢意見，以澄清、確定或宣示某些國際法則。

際法發展外，於一九四七年十一月二十一日，通過第一七四(貳)
號決議案，設立專責機關「國際法委員會」(The International
Law Commission) ㉕，課予發展國際法的任務。委員會雖然
不是憲章明定的機關，卻是大會下的常設單位，設有處理行政事
務的人員。

該委員會從一九四九年起，每年在瑞士日內瓦集會，研討了
國家權利義務宣言、侵略定義等許多問題，草擬了很多公約草
案，其中海洋法、外交關係、領事關係、特種使節、條約法等的
草案，經委員會建議後，由聯合國大會召開國際會議，獲得會議

㉕ 該委員會初置委員十五人，後來隨著聯合國會員國的增加，於一九五
六年擴充爲二十一人，於一九六九年增至二十五人，再於一九八一年
添到三十四人。這名額至今未變。各委員經各國家團體提名，由聯合
國大會選舉產生，任期五年，每五年全部改選，都可以連任。各以個
人條件和資格任職，不代表其國家或政府，但實際情形是名不符實。
一九八〇年五月，該委員會照例於日內瓦開會時，阿富汗政府要求其
卸任大使 Abdul Hakin Tabibi 的原委員席位由其國人接任，只
得一位委員贊成，被拒絕了。該委員會直到現在仍堅持本來原則，卽
各委員應是獨立執行任務的專家，不做任何政府的代表。可是另一方
面，由於各國政府認爲名額應合理分配，委員名額早已依照安全理事
會的五區域制分配：非洲八名、亞洲七名、東歐三名、拉丁美洲六
名、西歐及其他國家（包括美國、加拿大、日本、澳洲、紐西蘭）八
名，二名輪流配給前四區。每當聯合國大會選舉委員時，候選人競爭
相當劇烈，落選者不少，名國際法學者也會失敗，但新興國家的非法
學人士也能當選。中華民國退出聯合國前，徐淑希、劉楷、薛毓麒等
大使曾任該委員會委員。

通過，成爲公約了。本書析論的，就是「一九六九年維也納條約法公約」❷⑥

該委員會於一九四九年初次集會時，便選定了條約法爲許多專題中的一題，指定了專題研究的報告員，同時請聯合國秘書長分別轉請各會員國爲本題目提供相關的法律、命令、條約、外交函件以及其他文書，以供該委員會研究的參考。該委員會以後每年集會時，都對本題特加注意，曾於一九五六年討論其研究報告的初稿，因爲海洋法的草案位次在先，未獲得結果，直到一九六二年，外交關係公約通過後，條約法草案才取得最優先的地位，跟著該委員會每年討論通過部分條文，一九六六年七月十八日，通過決議案，建議聯合國大會儘速召開條約法公約國際會議。大會旋即通過 A/RES 2166(XXI) 號決議案，決定召開各國全權代表會議。會議於一九六八年和一九六九年各舉行一次，經過冗長艱苦的討論與折衷，才於一九六九年五月二十三日，由出席代表三分之二以上表決通過了「維也納條約法公約」❷⑦。

該委員會於一九五〇年研討條約法的範圍，暫先決定應包括換文（照會——exchange of notes）等文書；多數委員贊成

---

❷⑥ 該公約是在維也納舉行的各國全權代表會議中通過的，所以冠上「維也納」三字。

❷⑦ 第二次世界大戰以前，國際會議多採用全體一致的規則，以作成重大的決議，大戰以後，則多採用三分之二的多數原則，以通過重要的立法條約，一九五八年的四份海洋法公約、一九六一年的外交關係公約和一九六三年的領事關係公約等，在投票表決前，都已決定採用這多數決原則。

「條約」一辭的意義應限於「正式文書」（Formal instru-ment），別解釋爲「書面協定」（Agreement recorded in writing），應強調以條約承擔的國際義務的拘束性，又同意國際組織可爲締結條約者。但是各委員對於下列三點，則意見頗不一致：（一）本專題應以一份或數份文件作成？（二）本案的最後形式應爲法典（code）或公約？（三）應分本題爲那幾大部分，以便分配給子題小組專責研擬？英國籍報告員費玆模里士（Sir Gerald Fitzmaurice）認爲，規範條約有關事宜的法律，無需倚重條約，這種法律已經存在，構成了普遍性習慣國際法的一部分，如果把條約法列於多邊條約內，則對於不是該約的締約者的國家和退出條約的國家，會發生解釋上的困難，儘管各國於訂約後仍然應受這習慣國際法的拘束，還會有類似的解釋上的困難。雖然這種形式問題，在實踐上已無多大重要性，只在條約法上，仍是十分重要，因爲條約法是一切條約的效力和效果的基礎。所以，本題的最後形式應是一份法典。

　　可是該委員會於一九六二年決定本題應以公約的形式作成，放棄採用法典的形式，主要是基於下列理由：第一、採用法典形式時，無論訂得怎麼妥善，都由於條約法本質的原因，不能像多邊條約那樣有效地統一這法律，而在這麼多的新興國家加入了國際社會的此刻，統一這法律，旣特別重要，又符合需要；第二、採用多邊條約形式時，可以使條約法成爲法律，也能給這些新興國家直接參與編纂的機會，其參與又可以使法律基礎更廣大更穩固，是大家所最樂見的事情。

　　該委員會決定條約法的最後形式應爲公約後，第一點和第二

點的意見紛岐便迎双而解了。

　　此刻要話說回頭，應該補述一項重要的事實，就是每當報告員提出草案以後，都把草案送交聯合國秘書長，請他分送聯合國各會員國，並請各會員國政府對草案表示意見，各委員參酌各國的意見，再逐部逐條研究討論，最後才把草案定稿，成為建議案。一九六八年和一九六九年國際會議的討論，就是以這種建議案為基礎藍本❷❽。

　　條約法公約採用了一般多邊條約的形式，所以包含序文、正文和結語三部分。正文部分採用編、章、節、條、項、款等標題號誌，以列出一般條款、實質條款、特別條款、程序條款等等。本書便依照公約內容的順序，從學理、國際習慣、先例、國際法委員會中的意見，以及其他方面，逐條作詳細深入的析論。公約的附件一「關於和解委員會的規定」，應融會入適當處加以說明，不予另立段落。至於公約附件二「聯合國條約法會議通過之宣言及決議案」，則因為和條約法本質沒有密切關係，本書不擬加以敍述，更不必析論。

　　本編介紹條約的定義、名稱和簡史以及條約法公約的簽訂後，便可進行析論公約各條款了。如果析論終了時，還有關於條約的一般性問題需要敍明，當於本書最末部分補述。

---

❷❽　本節的內容，是摘述一九五〇年至一九六九年國際委員會歷年報告書 (The International Law Commission Report) 所得的結果。

第一編　公約序文及導言

第一節　序　文

維也納條約法公約序文如下❶：

本公約各當事國，

鑑於條約在國際關係歷史上之基本地位，承認條約為國際法淵源之一，且為各國間不分憲法及社會制度發展和平合作之工具，其重要性日益增加，

鑑悉自由同意與善意之原則以及條約必須遵守規則乃舉世所承認，

確認凡關於條約之爭端與其他國際爭端同，皆應以和平方法且依正義及國際法之原則解決之，

念及聯合國人民同茲決心創造適當環境，俾克維持正義及尊重由條約而起之義務，

鑑及聯合國憲章所載之國際法原則，諸如人民平等權利及自決，所有國家主權平等及獨立，不干涉各國內政，禁止使用威脅或武力以及普遍尊重與遵守全體人類之人權及基本自由等原則，

深信本約所達成之條約法之編纂及逐漸發展可促進憲章所揭櫫之聯合國宗旨，即維持國際和平及安全，發展國際間之友好關係並達成其彼

---

❶　本書所列公約的條款文字，全部照抄中華民國外交部的中譯文，不作任何更改。

此合作，

確認凡未經本公約各條規定之問題，將仍以國際習慣法規則爲準，
爰議定條款如下。

按一般條約的序文，都是說明各締約國的動機、條約的宗
旨、對於條約的期望、立約的具體依據、條約的基本原則、以及
全權代表的證書妥善等項。大致說來，雙邊條約的序文，往往比
多邊條約的簡短，但是相反的實例並非全無。一九一九年的國際
聯合會盟約的中譯序文，只有一○八個字❷，一九八二年的聯合
國海洋法公約的中譯序文，則有五八八個字，中華民國與美利堅
合衆國間友好通商航海條約（民國三十五年簽訂）的中文序言含
二二三個字❸，中華民國與美利堅合衆國間共同防禦條約的中文
序言，亦有二三二個字，但是一九五八年的大陸礁層公約和領海
及鄰接區公約、一九六三年的航空器上所犯罪行及若干其他行爲
公約（在東京簽訂），都沒有說明性的序文，只在正文之前，使
用本公約各當事國議定條款如下等字。從此可知條約序文可長可
短，亦可有可無，條約法公約的序文，屬於較長的一類。

---

❷ 國際聯合會盟約序文

　締約各國爲增進國際間協同行事並保持其和平與安寧起見特允

　　　承受不事戰爭之義務

　　　維持各國間光明平允榮譽之邦交

　　　確守國際公法之規定以爲各國政府間行爲之軌範

　　　於有組織之民族間彼此待遇維持公道並恪遵條約上之

　一切義務

　議定國際聯合會盟約如下

❸ 該約序文已錄入本書前編「條約簡史」節中。

條約序文敍明訂約旨趣時，必集中概述訂約的基本理念、所訂條約的必要性和重要性、以及所訂條約的功用等，所以條約法公約的序文，開宗明義的說，正如本書前編已略提的，早在一千多年前，國家間的良好關係，已經以條約來維持和促進，條約在國際關係上的重要性，固然久已獲得承認和肯定，條約在國際法上的地位，也最優先，又是國際法的主要淵源，常設國際法院規約第三十八條，現在的國際法院規約第三十八條，都訂明條約爲法院判案的首要依據；現在無論是何種憲法何種社會的國家，都以條約來促進其與他國的和平合作。

其次本序文指出，各國已經承認，訂立條約的理念和基準是：自由同意原則、秉持善意原則和必須遵守原則。各國嚴守這三個原則，締結條約的行爲才有意義。

本序文再指出，條約締結後，履行時如果發生關於條約的爭端，便應像解決其他國際爭端一樣，以和平方法並且按照一般正義和國際法原則來解決，不可以使用非和平的方法，也不可以違反正義和國際法原則。

本序文又說，各國要決心創造良好的環境，使我們能夠維持正義，並且能夠尊重條約下的義務。換句話說，如果各國不決心創造良好的環境，或者沒有良好的環境，我們就不容易或不能夠維持正義，不能夠尊重條約義務。

本序文接著說，人民的平等權利、民族自決、國家主權平等、國家獨立、不干涉他國內政、禁止使用威脅、禁止使用武力、各人尊重各人的人權和基本自由、各人遵守各人的人權和基本自由等原則，已是聯合國憲章訂明的國際法原則，本公約各當

事國都牢記住了。

本序文又繼續指出，各當事國深信，本公約所達成的條約法的編纂，所達成的條約法的逐漸發展，都可以促進憲章列明的聯合國宗旨，就是「維持國際和平及安全、發展國際間之友好關係並達成其彼此合作」等宗旨。

本序文最後說，各當事國確認，未在本公約內規定的任何問題，遇到時仍然要依照國際習慣法規則來解決。這一點非常重要，可以說是本序文中最切合需要和實際的文字，因為第一、正如費玆模里士（Fitzmaurice）所說，國際間已有習慣條約法規則，第二、新訂立的條約法公約未必能夠把一切習慣規則盡列無遺，所以公約生效後，有公約未規定的問題發生時，是不是當然應依習慣規則處理？這很可能是一個疑難。現在列載了這一說明，就可以防止這一問題了。

至於本序文最後一句的意義，一如字面意思，用不著解釋。

如果把本公約序文和中美通商航海條約的序文相比，則可以看出下列不同：

第一、後者只用兩國「為欲藉適應兩國人民精神、文化、經濟及商務願望之條款所規定足以增進彼此領土間友好往還之辦法，以加強兩國間悠久幸存之和好聯繫及友誼結合」，以表示雙方的動機和願望，所列的主旨單純，而前者所列的，則很廣泛、很複雜、很抽象、很崇高、很理想化。

第二、後者列載雙方派遣的全權代表及其姓名職銜等，前者則沒有這種列載。不予列載，並不表示無需全權代表。關於這一點，留待下文討論全權證書時，才補充說明。

第三、後者有「雙方全權代表，各將所奉全權證書，互相校閱，均屬妥善」等字，前者則無類似文字。無的原因，也留待下文談全權證書時才說明。這裏只要指出，一九五四年的中美共同防禦條約序文，已不復用「雙方全權代表，……妥善」等字句了。

這些不同，一則表示雙邊條約的和多邊條約的序文，所含內容的性質互異，二則表示由於時代變遷，條約序文的形式也跟著更易。雙邊條約是釐訂兩國的某種權利義務關係，宗旨較單純，序文中的主旨可以用較簡短的文字闡明，而多邊條約（尤其是立法條約）往往牽涉許多當事國的利害，宗旨目標較複雜，序文中的主旨要用較多的文字才能完全表達。

未來的條約，無論是雙邊的或多邊的，序文都益趨簡化，不一定列載全權代表的姓名職銜，也會省略互相校閱全權證書的語句。當然，序文用字多少，還要隨條約性質和範圍而定，也會隨條約草擬者的意見而定。

從以上數例，可以導致下列比擬。條約序文不像專著的序文或導（緒）論，不似中國古籍中的凡例，也許如舉行某專題的一系列演講時的第一場開場白，主持人說明某機構（關）辦理演講會的動機、目的和願望，當時在場者自然聽到，但是從第二場開始聽講者，就不一定注意到這些動機、目的和願望了。因而查閱有序文的條約時，無論是誰，如果只看正文部分，不讀序文，便不易甚至不能體會條約的宗旨、目標和精神。別的暫且不提，先就本公約來說，研究者如果不仔細審閱序文，怎能知道它的宗旨、目標和精神？

若問中華民國憲法的宗旨爲何，便須依據憲法序文，答說是「爲鞏固國權，保障民權，奠定社會安寧，增進人民福利。」若問美國憲法的宗旨爲何，也要照抄下列文字以答：「……in order to form a more perfect Union, establish Justice, insure domestic Tranquility, provide for the common defense, promote the General Welfare and secure the Blessings of Liberty to ourselves and our Prosperity。」若問聯合國憲章的精神和目的爲何，更要按憲章的序文說：「欲免後世再遭今代人類兩度身歷慘不堪言之戰禍，重伸基本人權、人格尊嚴與價值以及男女與大小各國平等權利之信念，創造適當環境，俾克維持正義，尊重由條約與國際法其他淵源而起之義務，久而弗懈，促成大自由中之社會進步及較善之民生。」可見要知道某憲法或某條約的基本精神、目標或宗旨，最迅速的方法就是首先愼讀其序文。

此外，國際法院(The International Court of Justice)於一九五一年在「殘害人羣罪預防及懲治公約保留 (Reservations to the Convention on the Prevention and Punishment of the Crime of Genocide) 案中說，如果條約未規定可否受保留，則並不排除一切保留，只要保留不違反條約宗旨和目標，則接受保留的當事國在條約關係上，可視保留國爲同約的當事國。這一權威性的意見，已被納入本公約第一編第二節。所以今後解釋某條約保留案，約中又無關於保留的條款時，就非先知該約的宗旨目標不可，要是該約有序文，便應先讀序文。

總而言之，研究有序文的條約者，應養成重視序文先閱序文

的習慣。

第二節　導　　言

第一條　本公約適用之範圍

本公約適用於國家間之條約。

在學說上，能夠依國際法享受權利並且擔負義務者，都是國際法人 (International legal person)。在事實上，國際法人中以國家爲最多，最重要，最受人注意。國家，特別是主權獨立的國家，具有締結條約的完整資格和充分能力，其所訂的條約，在國際聯合會秘書處登記的條約中佔絕大多數，在聯合國秘書處登記的條約中屬更大的多數。本公約適用的對象，就是國家簽訂的常佔絕對大多數的條約。

一九四九年，國際法院在「聯合國服務人員損害賠償 (Reparation for Injuries Suffered in the Service of the United Nations) 案中，斷言聯合國組織具有國際人格 (International Personality)，是國際法人，並且有在國際上活動的能力。法院說，因爲國際法的發展已受國際生活的需要所影響，而國家集體行動的增加，又要求若干非國家的實體（例如聯合國組織）從事國際行動；憲章已賦與聯合國權利，也課與它義務，使它在會員國間有其獨立的地位，所以它是國際法主體，可以提出國際索償的請求，以維護其權利。可是法院儘管這樣說了，卻未提及聯合國有沒有締約的資格和能力。

聯合國由於憲章規定和實際需要,且已享受權利負擔義務,而成為國際法主體, 個人是不是也因為已直接享受國際法的權利,又直接擔負了國際法的義務,而成了國際法主體?一九四八年的世界人權宣言、一九六六年的公民及政治權利國際公約、同年的經濟社會及文化權利國際公約、以及一九七九年的反劫持人質國際公約等,都直接保障個人;一九五八年的公海公約和一九八二年的聯合國海洋法公約,都直接禁止海盜行為並且懲罰海盜個人,個人是不是被這些條約視為國際法主體?個人已有締結條約的資格和能力?這兩個問題的答案,在事實上都是否定的,雖然若干學者主張個人應為完整的國際法人,又應被賦與某種國際法上的資格,各國政府卻不許其國民簽訂條約,也不同意其國民和外國私人締結條約。另一方面,公的國際組織(如聯合國及其專門機關中的國際民航組織等),不准許個人加入為會員,國際法院不接受個人為訴訟或諮詢案的當事者,常設國際法院規約訂明惟有國家得為訴訟當事者,現在的國際法院規約第三十四條依舊規定:「在法院得為訴訟當事國者,限於國家。」❹基於這些原因,個人便不能依國際法簽訂條約,本條就當然不能適用於所謂個人間的條約。

誠然國際法院在上述索償案中,不明說一般國際組織有締結

---

❹ 按本條的法文是「Seuls les Etat ont qualité pour se présenter devout la Cour」,英文則為「Only states may be parties in cases before the Court.」。中文條文和英文條文一樣,都是譯自法文原稿,所以中文的「訴訟當事國者」的「國」實在是多餘的。

條約的資格和能力，也未指出聯合國有締約權。可是聯合國早已具有這種資格和能力，用不著國際法院費辭了，因爲聯合國憲章第四十三條授權聯合國簽訂特別協定，以執行安全理事會維持國際和平及安全的決議，憲章第一百零五條復授權聯合國向會員國提議協約。聯合國自成立以來，已分別與美國、荷蘭、瑞士等國訂約❺。這些憲章規定和實際事例，都證明聯合國具有締約資格和能力後，也已多次運用其資格和能力。現在大家旣然承認聯合國是國際組織中最重要的，又知道它以後還會簽訂條約，爲什麼本公約只適用於國家間的條約，不擴大適用於國際組織間的條

❺　一九四七年六月二十六日，聯合國與美國簽訂總會所協定，規定特權及豁免等事項。聯合國大會於同年批准國際法院與荷蘭簽訂的特權及豁免協定。一九四八年，聯合國與瑞士簽訂同性質的協定。聯合國又與伊索匹亞、泰國、瑞士、智利等國訂約，以釐訂設於這幾國的聯合國經濟委員會（Economic Commission）的若干事項（e. g. Agreement Regulating Conditions for the Operation of the the Headquarters of the United Nations Economic Commission for Latin America, Feb. 16, 1953; Agreement Relating to the Headquarters of the Economic Commission for Asia and the Far East, May 26, 1954.）。此外，國際勞工組織（一九四六年）、聯合國糧食農業組織（一九四六年）、國際民用航空組織、國際復興開發銀行、國際貨幣基金（以上三者於一九四七年）、萬國郵政聯盟、世界衞生組織（以上二者於一九四八年）、國際電訊組織（一九四九年）、世界氣象組織（一九五一年）、聯合國教育科學文化組織（一九五二年）、國際金融公司（一九五七年）、國際原子能總署（一九五九年）、海事諮詢組織（一九五九年）、國際開發協會（一九六一年）等都先後與聯合國締結協定。

約呢？或國家與國際組織間的條約呢？或者更縮小範圍，使本公約適用於國家與聯合國間的條約呢？

原來一九五○年國際法委員會的報告說，多數委員贊成把國際組織列入研究範圍內，而且廣泛的初步意見指出，某些國際組織的締約能力是很明顯的，其他國際組織的這種能力，則應留待進一步考慮後才作決定❻。

一九五九年，國際法委員會討論導言編的條文草案。草案第二條（國際協定的意義）說，無論其形式或名稱為何，國際協定必指兩國或兩國以上或其他有締約資格的國際法主體依國際法作成的書面協定❼。這些文字把「其他國際法主體」所締結的條約列入本公約適用的範圍，似乎已消除前文所提的問題。上文說過，國際法院已於一九四九年肯定聯合國組織是國際法主體，所以國際法委員會各位委員（最少也可以說多數委員）同意條約法應對國際組織適用，最低限度也應對聯合國適用。可是該委員會在一九五九年會期中，反復討論後，對於草案第二條的「其他國際法主體」問題，決定延後處理。

一九六○年和一九六一年，該委員會沒有時間處理條約法草案。一九六二年，更改該草案，而於第三條訂明如下：

1. 國家及其他國際法主體皆具有締結條約之資格。

2. 聯邦國各分子締結條約之資格依聯邦憲法之規定。

---

❻ *Official Records of the General Assembly, 5th Sess., Supp.* No. 12, (A/1316)(A/CN. 4/19).

❼ *Ibid*, Supp. 9 (A/4169).

3. 國際組織締結條約之資格依其憲章之規定。

　　草案的這一條文，比原草案第三條具體，適用的範圍也可以說較大。該委員會討論時，雖有委員說明沒有規定締約者資格的必要，多數委員卻主張應予規定，而且應以「其他國際法主體」一詞來包括國際組織、教廷、叛亂團體等。

　　一九六四年，該委員會考慮應否包括國家為其他國家而訂的條約時，或國際組織為其會員國而訂的條約時，一些委員指出後一種和國際組織與其會員國的關係十分密切，難於條約法中處理；又指出，一個國際組織所訂的條約，不專為組織本身，約中有其會員國的名義時，便可能使會員國成為實際的締約國，因而應該列入一般條約法中。該委員會最後決定延後處理這一問題❽。

　　一九六五年，該委員會於年會中提出報告，說條約法草案的許多條文，已經臨時通過的，都是以適用於國家間的條約為基礎，要對國際組織的條約作更多的研究，才可以為這類條約擬訂法則。又說，在編纂國際法的現階段，該委員會的主要任務是編纂條約法的基本原則，如果把草案各條限於國家間的條約，就會有助於基本原則的敘述明顯和簡化，等到草案條文成為法律後，再於適當時機召開會議，專事編纂適用於國際組織所訂的條約，以補充本草案的不足。結果該委員會基於這種考慮，又為了使草案各條首尾一致起見，便決定明白限制本公約只適用於國家間的

---

❽　*United Nations Document* A/C N. 4/173(1964).

條約❾。

一九六六年，該委員會討論條約法草案時，多數委員認為，國際組織有許許多多的特性，如果把其所訂條約列入本草案，便會使問題過度複雜，以致延緩條約法的編纂，所以該委員會再決定把草案適用範圍，以國家間的條約為限，不擴及非國家間的任何條約，並且排除非書面的條約❿。

該委員會經多年多次的詳細深入斟酌後，終於認定以限制條約法的適用範圍為最佳選擇，而且決定把本公約適用範圍列於第一條，藉以顯示本公約的首要著眼點。

然而這裏必須說明，這一限制並不意味國際組織、交戰團體、叛亂團體之類的實體不能締結條約，不否定其所訂條約有效，亦不排除其所訂條約於聯合國秘書處登記，更不否定非書面協定的效力，現在限制的只是本公約各條款的適用範圍而已。

第二條 用 語

---

❾ *U. N. General Assembly, 20th Sess., Off. Rec. Supp.* No. 9 (A/6009) and A/CN. 4/L 110).

❿ U. N. General Assembly, 21st Sess., *Off. Rec., Supp.* No. 9, (A/6309/Rev. 1).一九七四年，國際法委員會企圖把條約法公約的適用擴及國際組織間的條約和國際組織與國家間的條約，直至一九八六年，適用於國家與國際組織間及國際組織與國際組織間的條約法公約才簽訂了，那就是 Vienna Convention on the Law of Treaties between States and International Organizations or Between International Organizations, March 21, 1986, UN Doc. A/CONF. 12915(1986).

一、就適用本公約而言

(甲)稱「條約」者，謂國家間所締結而以國際法為準之國際書面協定，不論其載於一項單獨文書或兩項以上相互有關之文書內，亦不論其特定名稱為何；

(乙)稱「批准」、「接受」、「贊同」及「加入」者，各依本義指一國據以在國際上確定其同意承受條約拘束之國際行為；

(丙)稱「全權證書」者，謂一國主管當局所頒發，指派一人或數人代表該國談判、議定或認證條約約文，表示該國同意承受條約拘束，或完成有關條約之任何其他行為之文件；

(丁)稱「保留」者，謂一國於簽署、批准、接受、贊同或加入條約時所作之片面聲明，不論措辭或名稱為何，其目的在擯除或更改條約中若干規定對該國適用時之法律效果。

(戊)稱「談判國」者，謂參與草議及議定條約約文之國家；

(己)稱「締約國」者，謂不論條約已未生效，同意承受條約拘束之國家；

(庚)稱「當事國」者，謂同意承受條約拘束及條約對其有效之國家；

(辛)稱「第三國」者，謂非條約當事國之國家；

(壬)稱「國際組織」者，謂政府間之組織。

二、第一項關於本公約內各項用語之規定不妨礙此等用語在任何國家國內法上之使用或所具有之意義。

　　正如標題所示，本條列舉了九個常見的用語，並敍明各個用語的涵義，以便利閱讀本公約各條文者，於讀到其中任何一個的時候，都能夠了解，沒有疑惑，無需查詢。這樣列敍，也是為了使全

約的所有相同用語都含相同的意義，使讀者對相同的用語有統一的認知，免致不同讀者因依據不同參考刊物所載的不同註釋，而對本公約某用語有不同的了解。過去的條約，無論是雙邊的或多邊的，大多數不列敍約中用語，曾經引起解釋的困難，例如聯合國憲章，因爲沒有列敍用語的條文，其第十九條的「財政款項」(Financial contributions) 和第二十七條的「程序事項」(Procedural matters) 等用語，曾發生解釋上的爭論。本公約的草議者爲了避免重蹈覆轍，已做了這種列敍。

然而儘管已有這種列敍，所列敍的不過是九個用語而已，並未列盡了全約的用語，已列的只是訂約者當時認爲重要的易引發歧見的罷了，若翻閱下文，便可看見許多用語未列，其重要的程度，未必小於已經列敍的。

本公約草案初稿不列用語的專條，一九六二年的草案才用第一條，稱它爲定義 (Definition) 條，列了條約、簡化式條約、一般多邊條約、簽字、批准、加入、接受、贊同、全權證書、保留和保管機關 (Treaty, treaty in simplified form, general multilateral treaty, signature, ratification, accession, acceptance, approval, full powers, reservation and depository) 等用語。一九六五年，國際法委員會刪去 treaty in simplified form, signature 和 depository 等，增列「締約國」、「當事國」和「國際組織」(Contracting state, party and international Organization) 等。一九六六年，該委員會改「定義」兩字爲「用語」(Use of terms)，並在「當事國」和「國際組織」間加入「第三國」(Third state)。可

見該委員會中各委員對於應列那些用語的意見，彼此不同，先後
有別。還有別的也許是該列而未列的用語，便不在話下了。

　　本條的主旨，一如標題所說，在敍明九個用語在本公約內的
涵義。

　　(甲)「條約」是指國家與國家間一切形式的國際書面協定，
只要協定是以國際法為準，又是國際性的，就不論它是一項單獨
的文書，或是多項相互關連的文書，也不論它被定名為條約、協
定、憲章或規約，都包含在內。因而條約包括簡化式條約，以及
本書前編第二節所列名稱的全部文書。

　　國際法委員會研擬時，最初想用「國際協定」（Intenna-
tional agreement) 一詞，最後決定選用「條約」（Treaty)，
並且採用上述最廣泛的意義，同時排除了非國家間的和非書面的
國際協定。

　　本公約的「條約」既然涵義廣泛，便當然包括「簡化式條
約」，因為它很普通，使用率正在增加中；它和正式的條約，只
在締結的方法上和在生效的程序上有差別，在效力上、施行上、
解釋上的法則可以說完全相同。所以本條所指的條約，不能解釋
為已排除簡化式條約，例如照會、同意紀錄和諒解節略（Ex-
change of notes, agreed minutes and memorandum of
understanding) 等等。

　　早在一九二〇年，常設國際法院規約（The Statute of
the Permanent Court of International Justice) 已於第三
十六條第二項和第三十八條第一項樹立了先例。該第二項說：各
國自願接受法院強制管轄的爭端包括「（子）條約之解釋　（a.

the interpretation of a treaty)」，這一項的條約兩字，顯然不應解釋為只包含名為條約的文書，而排除了使用其他名稱的國際協定。該第一項說：法院裁判時應適用：「（子）不論普通或特別國際協約 (a. international conventions, whether general or particular)」。這些文字中的協約，當然涵蓋一切國際協定，誰也不能阻止法院適用不稱為協約的條約性質的文書，相反的，法院必須適用，而且曾經多次適用了，依上述第二項所作的片面的接受法院強制管轄的聲明，便是實例。

本條「以國際法為準」(Governed by international law) 一語，是用來區別受國際法規範的和受其他法律規範的條約。所謂國際法，是指一般的國際性規律和原則，因而不以這種規律或原則為準的國際書面協定，不屬於本條的「條約」範圍內。

口頭條約的效力被否定，確有先例。一九二七年，羅馬尼亞與匈牙利的混合委員會仲裁庭，在 Kulin 案的裁決中，否認匈牙利所提的載於紀錄的口頭協定的效力。國聯盟約要求登記的條約，必須是書面的。一九二八年泛美各國第六屆會議簽訂的條約法公約第二條訂明：書面形式為條約成立的主要條件⓫。依聯合國憲章第一〇二條的規定，各國向聯合國秘書處登記的條約，也經認定以書面的為限⓬。一九五〇年，國際法委員會報告員布賴

⓫　Article 2, Convention on Treaties, Feb. 20, 1928, *Rep. of the Delegates of the USA to the Sixth International Conference of Americon States,* pp. 197-202.

⓬　但是捷克政府於一九四八年三月一日，依據盟國對羅馬尼亞和約第十六條，以口頭照會通知羅國政府表示應恢復兩國間戰前若干條約，然後把照會向聯合國秘書處登記，秘書處竟照准，只是註明：羅國政府收到這份照會。見 *U. N. Treaty Series,* No. 26.

里 (James L. Brierly) 教授建議說：「條約為兩國或多國或國際組織依國際法在締約各造間建立關係的書面協定」❸。實則口頭條約發生法律效力的實例很少，許多學者對於口頭條約的效力也很懷疑。所以現在的條約應以書面作成，以保障國際關係的確定性和安全度。今天國內的重要契約，都以書面作成，國際協定怎可以不用文書？

但是，這並非謂稱所有條約必須以書面作成。麥乃爾(Arnold D. McNair) 教授曾說：「只要締約代表有合適的資格，則沒有任何規則阻止他們訂約」❹。韋爾遜 (G. G. Wilson) 教授也說：「國家代表可以展示各種符號以締結協定，例如於戰時舉白旗以表示投降」❺。一九二四年十月二十八日，法國總理與蘇聯外長利用電報傳送，確定了兩國間現存條約的地位❻。一九三一年，挪威頒布敕令，兼併東格陵蘭島 (Eastern Greenland) 的一部分，丹麥反對，累經談判無果，乃向常設國際法院訴請判決，所據理由之一是挪威外交部長曾對丹麥駐挪公使承諾，說挪政府對於東格陵蘭主權的承認問題，不會造成任何困

---

❸ J. L. Brierly, *Report on the Law of Treaties*, U. N. Doc. A/CN. 4/23, April, 1950.

❹ A. D. McNair, *The Law of Treaties, British Practice and Opinions.* New York, 1938, p. 47.

❺ G. G. Wilson, *Handbook of International Law,* 3rd ed., St. Paul, 1939, p. 204.

❻ *American Journal of International Law* (以下簡寫為 AJIL) Vol. 29, Supp. 690, Law of Treaties.

難。挪威在法院辯稱，一則其外長無權作這承諾，二則其承諾只是口頭的。法院反駁說，外交部長代表政府所作的承諾，依國際法可拘束其本國，口頭承諾也是一樣⑰。

從上可知，以前的條約，絕大多數是以書面作成，但是，理論和事實都顯示，口頭可以作成條約，其效力正如書面條約的。本公約不否定口頭條約的作成和效力，只是要避免不能克服的編纂上的困難，而規定不適用於口頭條約。

從前的絕大多數條約，常以一項單一的正式文書作成，近年以來，以兩項或多項文書作成一份條約，為數已日漸增加，因而本公約不把一份條約的文書限於一項，准許以兩項和兩項以上文書合成一份條約。不過，這些文書必須是相互關連相輔相成的，才符合本條規定，如果彼此沒有關係，就不可以共同構成一份條約。

「亦不論其特定名稱為何」的意義顯而易見，不敘自明。就是表示，只要是「國家間所締結而以國際法為準之國際書面協定」，無論它名為條約、名為議定書、名為憲章、組織法或規約，或稱做其他東西，都是本公約所定涵義內的條約，本書前編所列的名稱，便當然可用以指涉條約的名稱，反過來說，其中任

---

⑰ Eastern Greenland Case, Permanent Court of International Justice (以下簡寫為 PCIJ), *Judgment, 1933, Series A/B*, No. 53, p. 71. J. W. Garner, "The International Binding Force of Unilateral Oral Declaration," 37 *AJIL* 493(1943).

何一個名稱所指的文書，必是本公約所指的條約。

（乙）「批准」、「接受」、「贊同」和「加入」條約，都是國際行為，國家經由其中一種行為，就足以在國際上表示同意承受條約的拘束。許多國家的憲法，含有其特殊的規定，或訂明條約須經某一（些）機關同意（建議），或要求條約須經立機關一定百分數的立法者批准，然後行政機關或其他特定機關才可以對外表示這種同意。表示的方式，或是互換批准書（雙邊條約所採用），或是寄存批准書（常是多邊條約採用），或是條約所定的國際通知。可是國內法上這些用語的意義，和國際法上這些用語的意義，不一定相同，各國國內法的這些用語的意義也不一致，所以本項強調，對條約來說，批准、接受、贊同和加入，都是「以在國際上確定其同意承受條約拘束之國際行為」。本項並沒有顧及各國國內法規定的涵義，實則沒有顧及的必要，更沒有顧及的可能。

至於以批准、接受、贊同或加入的方式成為條約當事國，在程序上和效力上有沒有差別的問題，則留待下文介紹這四個用語時，才分別說明。

（丙）全權證書是談判條約者、簽署條約者、終止條約者和通知廢止條約者必須具備的文件，十分重要，但這只是指無權代表國家或政府者來說，因為有權代表者無須出具全權證書，只依其職位就可以從事談判、簽署等國際行為。

關於全權證書的其他方面，本公約第七條有進一步的規定，請聽下文分解。

（丁）本公約第二編關於保留的問題，有頗詳的規定，應等到

討論該編各點時，才加以析論，這裏只先漫談條約的保留。

　　本條所稱的保留，是指「一國於簽署、批准、接受、贊同或加入條約時所作之片面聲明，不論措辭或名稱爲何，其目的在摒除或更改條約中若干規定對該國適用時之法律效果。」所以談判條約時的聲明，存放條約時的聲明，在任何其他場合或情勢下的聲明，只要是沒有這種目的，無論是口頭的或書面的，就一律不是保留，無論如何，都不是本公約所定的保留。締約國表示對約中某辭語的了解，或對某條款作解釋，不列入正式文書，又不希望其了解或解釋成爲條約的一部分，便不是保留。許多國家簽署一九二八年巴黎非戰公約時，聲明公約應不妨礙其自衞權的行使。這種聲明，從不被視爲保留。締約國對某情形表示遺憾，也不是作保留。例如蘇聯於簽署一九五二年布魯塞爾國際電訊公約時，發表聲明說：「……國民黨代表實際上不代表中國，故全權代表會議之容許其簽署本公約係不合法。僅有『中華人民共和國政府』委派之代表始有資格代表中國簽署本公約……。」中華民國政府代表針對這聲明，在簽署公約時也聲明說：「出席布諾賽爾國際電信聯合會全權代表會議之中華民國代表團爲該會議中之中國唯一合法代表，並經該會議承認其此項資格。本聯合會若干會員國關於本公約所提之任何聲明或保留，或其附於本公約後之任何聲明或保留，凡與上述中華民國立場背馳者實屬非法，故均無效……」⑬。這些聲明，不涉及該約規定事項，都不構成保留。如果了解或解釋改變或限制了條約規定的事項，就會變成保

---

⑬　丘宏達，條約新論（臺北、撰者，民四八），頁八八。

留。例如中華民國四十一年四月二十八日，日本代表河田烈於簽署中日和平條約前，照會中國代表說：「本代表謹代表本國政府提及貴我二方所成立之了解，即在本條約各條款關於中華民國一方，應適用於現在中華民國控制下或將來在其控制下之全部領土。」中國代表葉公超表示同意這一了解，乃作成雙方同意紀錄，紀錄又附於條約後。像這樣的了解，已涉及條約適用的領土範圍，應視本公約所稱的保留。

　　本項的「摒除或更改」等字，包括了一些國家已採取的行為，因為保留國對條約提具保留時，都是排除或改變約中某(些)規定對其適用的法律效果，藉以減少其在條約下的義務，上述河田烈的了解，便是一例。一九四六年，美國依國際法院規約任選條款作聲明時，摒除國內管轄事項後，再把事項是否屬國內管轄的決定權留給美國。這又是保留一例。

　　在理論上，國家得以提具保留的方式，增加其在條約下的義務，因而增加其在條約下的相對權利。這種增加，依理，其他條約當事國不應反對，因為這種增加不會妨礙彼等在條約下的權利。反過來看，唯有於保留國摒除或更改條約的規定時，才有遭受反對的情形，所以本項對於增加保留國義務的保留，不加以規定，既無規定，又不損他國，自不受限制。

　　增加保留國在條約下的義務的保留，不但在理論可以有，而且在事實上已有先例。荷蘭接受一九三七年的廢止出入口管制國際公約時，片面列舉公約第九條未規定應予廢止的一些管制事項，作為該條選擇權的對象⓳。可是這畢竟是稀罕的例外。

⓳　*LNTS,* vol. 47, p. 393.

　　總括來說，對條約的保留可有四種效果：一是摒除了保留國在條約下的某一（些）義務；二是改變了條約的某一（些）規定事項；三是影響各締國間的某種關係；四是使多邊條約當事國間錯綜互動關係更複雜（第三第四種效果，容後補充說明）。

　　就雙邊條約來說，只會有談判、簽署、批准、互換批准書等程序，不會有接受、贊同或加入的步驟，所以本項的接受、贊同和加入，不是爲了雙邊條約而列載，而是爲了多邊條約而設計的。雙邊條約談判時，任何一方的意見可以隨時向他方表達，如果雙方意見南轅北轍，可能使談判破裂，僵局繼續不變，當然條約不能進入簽署階段，就是簽訂在大兵壓境下的城下之盟，就今天的國際情勢來說，也不一定能有意見極端衝突的情形下的簽約。一九九一年三月三日，戰敗的伊拉克軍事代表與多國聯軍代表簽訂停火協定，接受了聯軍的全部條件，可以說仍是在雙方同意下簽訂的。因此，雙邊條約簽署時提出保留的事例，實不易見。條約簽署後，國內立法機關（例如中華民國的立法院、美國的國會參議院等）審議時，則可能提出保留。一九七八年四月十八日，美國的國會參院同意批准新巴拿馬運河條約時，附上保留，要求得於運河通航受阻時使用武力以維持航行暢通。這是雙邊條約於批准時遭受保留，是國內行爲，也是國內事項。保留須經締約他方接受，才會有下一步驟（即互換批准書），他方如果拒絕接受，訂約事便可能前功盡棄，如果要使已簽署的條約復活，就要重開談判，取得新的協議，達成協議後才會有簽署、批准、互換批准書等情事。在交通困難電訊傳送技術欠精的時代，條約的保留案於互換批准書時方提出，在理論上未嘗是絕無的事情，

但在傳送訊息迅速的今天，則是令人不敢想像的怪事，可以說雙邊條約的保留，只會於批准時提出，或者很偶然的因為新的顧慮而在簽署時提出。

許多國家參與條約談判時，因為各國立場和利益矛盾衝突，往往不能擬具一致同意的約文，以致簽署時，會有談判國提出保留的情事。簽署後，非談判國接受、贊同或加入條約時，更會有提出保留者。若干多邊條約，為了達到發起者的心願，或者為了爭取最廣泛的參與，縱使不以明文表示准許保留，也避免規定禁止一切保留。國聯盟約第一條第一項說：「國際聯合會之創始會員應以本盟約附款內所列之各簽押國及附款內所列願意無保留加入本盟約之各國為度。」這是罕見的先例，代表了傳統的國際習慣。但是，這一規定，只限制了創始會員國不得對盟約作保留，並不當然表示盟約保留國不能成為加（選）入會員國。

締約國意思合致，是條約締結的基礎，沒有這基礎時，除上文所說的被威脅強迫下的不平等條約外，條約不能訂立，更不易履行，所以大致說來，依常理和國際習慣，雙邊條約的保留須經他方同意，多邊條約的保留也須得他國同意，以維持意思合致，使保留依法有效。所以國聯和聯合國的秘書處，於登記並保管多邊條約時，認為國家對條約提出保留，在未獲得其他當事國同意以前，其成為條約當事國的程序不能視為已經完成。

這種認定是否妥善？不規定可否受保留的條約，應不應被保留？如果決定應接受保留，保留國與同意保留國和反對保留國間的關係如何？諸如此類的相關問題，值得重視，現在的國際法院已作了解答。

一九五〇年十月十四日，聯合國秘書處收到一九四八年的殘害人羣罪防止及懲治公約的批准書和加入書二十份，如果這些書都不附任何保留，依公約第十八條第二項的規定，公約便開始生效了，但是，蘇聯、保加利亞、匈牙利、波蘭、羅馬尼亞等國的批准書，附有關於責任和管轄方面的保留，而公約在保留方面則未列隻字，又有締約國反對這些保留，以致秘書長不知如何處理。依照習慣辦理呢？或應採取新的方式處理呢？他無權作主，又不敢貿然決定，只好報告聯合國大會，大會旋卽通過決議，請求國際法院就下列問題發表諮詢意見：

就殘害人羣罪防止及懲治公約而言，一國於批准或加入時，於其批准或加入或作待批准之簽署附上保留，

1、一當事國以上反對保留，其他當事國不反對，保留國可否維持其保留而仍能視為公約當事國？

2、如答曰可，則保留對：

（子）保留國與反對保留國間的效果為何？

（丑）保留國與接受保留國間的效果為何？

3、第一問題的答案的法律效果：

（子）於簽署而未批准公約的國家反對保留時為何？

（丑）於有權簽署或加入但尚未簽署或加入公約的國家反對保留時又為何？

國際法院就第一問題說，國家在雙邊和多邊條約的關係方

面，如不表示同意，便不受拘束，這原則也可適用於條約的保留案。曾被採納的公約完整概念，隱示保留非經全體締約國接受不生效力。但在多邊條約（如殘害人羣罪公約）中，上述概念應視某些情況而作較彈性的適用。有關情況包括聯合國的普遍性、該約預期的廣泛參與的程度、以及對保留有更多的依賴等等。

　　該約沒有關於保留的規定，並不意味禁止保留。可否對該約作保留，端視其性質、宗旨、規條及其準備和作成的方式而定。回顧聯合國大會通過該公約的過程，可知提出保留權已獲得諒解，為各當事國所同意。

　　至於可作何種保留的問題，則必須按該約的特性以求解答。該約的緣起和目標已揭示，其基本原則業經文明國家承認為拘束國家的原則，縱使不負擔該公約義務者，也都受拘束。其次，該公約期求普遍的參加，純為人道和文明的目的，對於達到該公約崇高的宗旨，各當事國都有共同的利益。很顯然的，聯合國大會和各當事國，都期望儘多的國家參加，卻不因而犧牲原定宗旨。換句話說，提出保留和反對保留的自由，必須限於該公約目標和宗旨的範圍內，所以作保留國和反對保留國的準繩，不得逾越該約目標和宗旨的界限。

　　國際法院這一意見，澄清了也確定了一個原則，就是條約沒有關於保留的規定時，如果條約的特性容許，則符合條約目標和宗旨的保留應予接受。這原則和國際習慣的全體一致的傳統原則相違，難怪法院裏有嚴厲的反對，說准許保留已破壞條約的完整性，保留可以不經全體締約國同意便發生效力，更造成條約義務

不平等的情形❷。

這一意見由聯合國大會通過決議案表示接受，秘書處已遵照登記了。至於法院對大會所提問題的答案，則留待下文析論保留問題時，才在適當處摘要說明。

（戊）「談判國」是「參與草擬及議定條約約文之國家」，也可能是談判開始前策動或發起談判的國家。就雙邊條約來說，策動或發起的只有一國；就多邊條約來說，策動並參加談判的國家數目，並無一定標準。一九二八年的巴黎非戰公約，談判並議定條約約文的只美法兩國，一九六三年的禁止在大氣太空及水中試驗核武器條約，只有英美蘇三國，由聯合國國際法委員會建議的公約，參與談判的國家必多。國家全權代表在國際會議中，在通過公約前，是參與談判呢？或是參與條約約文的議定呢？或者參與兩者呢？實在不易分別清楚。無論如何，其中一些人必參與某（些）條款的談判，另外一批人必參與約文的議定，還有一些人參與兩者，全體代表必參加表決。

談判國除參與意見交換、約文草擬和約文議定外，可於約文議定後成為簽署國批准國，而成為當事國。這裏只說「可」，不說「必」，因為約文議定後，國內政局大變，或政策更易，或有其他事故，談判代表不簽署，其本國便不會批准條約而成為當事國。美國英國代表參與「聯合國海洋法公約」的談判，卻不簽署公約。這是新的實例。

---

❷ *ICJ Reports,* 1951, Reservations to the Convention on the Prevention and Punishment of the Crime of Genocide.

（己）「締約國」是同意承受條約拘束的國家。其同意可於條約生效前表示，亦可於條約生效後才表示。因此，締約國可以是談判國簽署國，也可以是未曾參加談判或簽署條約的國家，只是經由接受、贊同或加入的方式，表示了同意承受條約的拘束，表示時如果條約已經生效，其當事國的地位即刻確定，和其他當事國在約中的地位就毫無差別。

（庚）「當事國」是同意承受條約拘束、也同意條約對其有效的國家。承受條約拘束的同意，可採用批准、接受、贊同或加入條約的方式表示，其表示可在條約生效之前，也可以在條約生效之後。同意條約對其有效，則須於條約生效後，才能表示，因爲條約未生效前，不能對任何國家發生法律效力，不能只靠某國同意其有效便眞正依法有效。然而，不管怎樣，任何國家要成爲當事國，都必須一則同意承受條約的拘束，二則同意條約對其有效，而且這兩種同意是同時表示的。

國家既然可用批准、接受、贊同或加入條約的方式成爲締約國，當事國就可以不是談判國簽署國或締約國，只採取接受、贊同和加入的一個步驟，便直接變成當事國。

（辛）「第三國」是條約當事國以外的國家，一般稱爲非條約當事國。它和條約的關係，容後敍述。

（壬）「國際組織」是各國政府間的組織，不指自然人與自然人的國際團體，也不指人民團體和人民團體的國際結合，更不是包括個人會員、團體會員和政府或國家會員的共同體。聯合國組織、國際民用航空組織、聯合國教育科學文化組織等，才是本項所稱的實體，才是本公約所稱的國際組織。

　　一般說來，國際組織是超越國界、立於國家之外、位於國家之間的組織，不是駕於任何國家之上，也不屬於任何國家。在國家之上的是世界政府或超國家，各個國家必喪失其原有的性質。國際組織的成員不像政府下的分子，各可憑自由意志加入或退出，自由表示立場，不受組織的命令，只受組織的約章和決議的約制，一律享受平等的地位和權利。

　　國際組織中，按宗旨分類，可有政治性的（如聯合國）、軍事性的（如北大西洋公約組織）、經濟性的（如國際復興開發銀行）、教育科學文化性的（如聯合國教育科學文化組織）、技術性的（如國際電訊聯盟）、慈善性的（如國際紅十字會）等等。再依其單一性或多重性看，又可分爲專門的（如世界衛生組織）和綜合性的（如聯合國）；如果從其成員的地域分佈看，則有普遍性的（如萬國郵政聯盟）和區域性的（如美洲國家組織）；若依其成員多少來區分，則有多國的（如國際貨幣基金）和兩國的（如美國與加拿大於一九四四年設立的國際聯合委員會）；倘從其成員的法律地位看，則有公的（如非洲團結組織等等）和私的（如奧林匹克委員會等）。本項所稱的國際組織，顯然不包括私的，只以公的爲限，而且只以政府爲成員的爲限，也就是以國家名義單位所構成的組織爲限。

　　在沒有國際立法以統一條約的各個用語以前，各學者使用各個用語時多憑己意，或故創新義，各國立法時也爲所欲爲，或遷就國內的習慣意義，或按立法者的喜愛偏見，採用其所熟悉的用語涵義，終致甲國乙國法律的同一用語，有不同的甚至相互牴觸的意義。本條擬訂者鑒於這一事實，又確知無法統一各國國內法

用語，便定下了今文，以減少將來本公約條文解釋時可能面臨的
困難。

第三條　不屬本公約範圍之國際協定

本公約不適用於國家與其他國際法主體間所締結之國際協定或此
種國際法主體間之國際協定，此一事實並不影響：

(甲)此類協定之法律效力；

(乙)本公約所載任何規則之依照國際法而毋需基於本公約原應適用於
　　此類協定者，對於此類協定之適用；

(丙)本公約之適用於國家間亦有其他國際法主體為其當事者之國際協
　　定為根據之彼此關係。

　　如上文所說，本公約各條款只適用於國家間的協定，不適用
於非國家間的任何國際協定，或國家以外任何國際法主體間的協
定，或任何非書面協定。所謂「其他國際法主體」，依傳統國際
法，是指梵諦岡城國（State of the City of Vatican），交
戰團體（Belligerenency）等；又依國際法院在「聯合國服務
人員損害賠償案（Reparation for lnjuries Suffered in the
Service of the United Nations, 1949）的意見，聯合國組
織也是國際法主體，因而本公約不適用於交戰團體或聯合國所締
結的國際協定。

　　非書面的協定，通常指口頭協定，不以文字作成的協定。

　　在事實上，現在已經有許多非國家間的協定、國家和非國家
間的協定、以及其他國際法主體間的協定，以後還會繼續增加。

因此，如果本公約不列入本條的規定，便會引起誤解，被誤爲本公約不顧及這一事實，或被誤爲本公約生效後，非國家間的協定就不再有合法的地位，就沒有可以適用的條約法，或推論非國家間的條約關係便需改變了。

本條的主旨很明確，訂明了三點：(一)任何國際法主體間的協定，無論是書面的或非書面的，只要具有法律性質，不牴觸國際法的絕對軌範，它的法律地位就不因本公約生效而受影響；(二)規範任何國際協定的規則，本來就無須基於本公約的規則，也不受本公約的影響；(三)國家間的協定，兼有其他國際法主體爲當事者時，其彼此間據以建立的現存關係，亦不受本公約的影響。

本公約於訂明不適用於非國家間的條約後，如果不規定繼續承認那些條約的效力，就會使那些條約下的國際關係動搖，自然引發嚴重後果，陷世界於混亂狀態。有了本條，已可避免由於這原因的混亂狀態。

第四條　本公約不溯既往

以不妨礙本公約所載任何規則之依國際法而毋須基於本公約原應適用於條約者爲限，本公約僅對各國於本公約對各該國生效後所締結之條約適用之。

本條的意旨，正如標題所示，在訂明本公約的效力不溯及以前的任何條約，依照國際法，原應適用於條約的本公約列載的規則，縱使沒有本公約，也仍應對那些條約適用，不受有或無本公

約的影響。至於本公約所列載的規則對於本公約締結時才締結的
條約,則要等到本公約生效後始可適用,也就是說,本公約規則
的開始適用,須有兩種情況:一是本公約已發生效力,二是本公
約當事國於公約生效後締結了條約。換句話說,本公約和過去的
條約規範不發生任何關係,本公約不追問往日的條約。

第五條　組成國際組織之條約及在一國際組織內議定之條約
　　本公約適用於爲一國際組織約章之任何條約及在一國際組織內議
定之任何條約,但對該組織任何有關規定並無妨礙㉑。

本條文字意義十分淺顯,容易了解,只是說:構成國際組織
基本法的條約,任何國際組織依其議事規則所議定的條約,都是
本公約適用的對象,也就是說,都在本公約適用的範圍內,適用
時不妨礙有關國際組織的內部規則。例如聯合國憲章 (Charter
of the United Nations) 是一份條約,是聯合國組織(United
Nations Organization) 的約章,是本公約適用的對象,適用
時不妨礙聯合國內的任何有關規則 ,例如「大會議事規則」、
「安全理事會議事規則」 和 「 經濟暨社會理事會議事規則」
(Rules of Procudure of the General assembly, Rules of
Procedure of the Security Council and Rules of Proce-

㉑　按「並無妨礙」四字,是原條英文 without prejudice to 的中譯
　　文字,如果把「但」字以下的文字改爲「而不妨礙該組織任何相關規
　　則」,就會比較流暢順口。又本條三個「一」字都以刪去爲較符中文
　　使用的習慣。

dure of the Economic and Social Council) 等。

　　乍看之下，因爲本條規範國際組織的約章，似乎和本公約第一條相矛盾相牴觸，實則這兩條相互爲用，毫無相互排斥的含義，理由是這種約章的當事國，全是國家，沒有「任何其他國際法主體」，而且本條所稱的國際組織，是本公約第二條所定的國際組織——政府間的組織。

　　國際組織內的規則，多數是依照其約章的授權而制定的，不像其約章那樣經過各會員批准的莊嚴程序，例如聯合國的大會、安全理事會和經濟暨社會理事會的議事規則，是分別依聯合國憲章第十一條第三十條和第七十二條的規定，各自制定的，只經過這些機關在其會議中投票表決通過，通過時未必是全體一致贊成；這三個機關的成員，只有大會的包括聯合國全體會員國，安全理事會的原來只包括十一個（現在是十五個）會員國，經濟暨社會理事會的原來只包括十八個（現在是五十四個）會員國，縱使於通過規則時獲得出席會員國全體一致同意，通過後無須經任何會員國批准，便可在各機關內生效施行，所以這類規則的位階在聯合國憲章之下，其他國際組織內部規則的位階，也必在其組織約章之下。由於本公約須經規定數目的國家批准後，才能開始適用，適用於國際組織時，如果和國際組織內的規則相牴觸，則按兩者的位階順序，當然應以本公約的條款優先，才可以消除牴觸的問題。這樣一來，便很可能引起有關國際組織內部秩序的紊亂。爲了預防這種紊亂，本條乃規定：本公約適用於國際組織的約章時，和適用於它議定的條約時，不妨礙它內部的規則。

第二編　條約之締結及生效

第一節　條約之締結

第六條　國家締結條約之能力

每一國家皆有締結條約之能力。

　　本公約已於第一條訂明：「本公約適用於國家間之條約」，又於第五條訂明適用於國際組織的約章，再於本條規定「每一國家皆有締結條約之能力」。可見訂約的主體和訂約的客體，都是條約法要首先訂明的要項。

　　本條訂明國家有訂約的能力，不意味只是國家有這能力，更不暗示其他國際法主體無這能力，也就是本條不否認國際組織、屬國、被保護國、聯邦的分子國、交戰團體等的締約能力。本條為了明白又簡潔的目的，並且配合本公約第一條起見，僅明文直接列載「每一國家」。

　　「締結條約之能力」 (Capacity to conclude treaties)，不指締結條約的權力。這能力是國際法的要求，唯有完整的國際法人才符合這要求，以充分行使締約的權利；這權力是國內法的規定，行憲國家於憲法中訂明由那一（些）機關行使，多數現代民主國家是由行政和立法機關共同行使，常是先由行政機關談判

簽署條約，後由立法機關審議表示是否同意批准條約。例如中華民國政府的行政院先交付外交部談判簽署條約，後由立法院審議表示意見。又如美國先由總統派員談判簽署，經國會參議院同意後，才正式批准條約。這一國內的規定如何，國際法不過問，國際法所要求的，只是國家於締結條約時具有本公約所定的能力。

本條所定的能力爲何？條文上沒有說明，因而必須從「每一國家」(Every state) 中「國家」的含義內探求，才可以知道。

前文已經說過，遠在中國的春秋時代，各國已行使締結條約的權利；公元前一二七二年，埃及有締結條約的事實；一八一五年維也納公會以後，國家締結的條約不可勝數。所以國家有締結條約的能力，是多年久載的廣泛事實。常設國際法院也說，締結國際協定的權利是國家主權的特性❶。

一九三三年蒙地維多公約 (Montevideo Convention) 第一條訂明：「國家要成爲國際法人，應具備下列條件：(一)常住的人民；(二)固定的領土；(三)政府；(四)和他國發生關係的能力。」本條所稱的國家，顯然是指蒙地維多公約所列的和常設國際法院所提的國家。

以前世界各地有許多屬國和被保護國，現在都已變成獨立國，或已和他國聯合，或已併入他國，原來的地位完全改變了，所謂屬國和被保護國幾乎全是歷史名詞，在現實國際政治上和當代國際法上，不復有重要性了。印度是英國的屬國時，於一九一

---

❶ The Wimbledon, *P.C.I.J., Judgment,* 1923.

九年簽署國聯盟約，又於一九四五年簽署聯合國憲章；突尼西亞為法國的被保護國時，於一九二二年簽訂簡化海關手續公約，又於一九三〇年締結燈船協定❷；埃及仍是英國的被保護國時，與英國簽訂尼羅河水資源分配協定❸。這些實例顯示，屬國和被保護國也有締結條約的能力。

聯邦分子國有沒有締結條約的能力？這問題的答案端視聯邦憲法的規定而定。美國是聯邦國，其聯邦憲法不許任何州和外國簽訂正式條約；瑞士也是聯邦國，其憲法第七條和第九條規定，各邦可與外國訂約以釐定非政治性事項；另一個聯邦國德意志聯邦共和國，准許各邦在其立法權範圍內並經聯邦政府同意後，與外國締結條約。可見聯邦分子國亦有訂約的能力，但是並非所有聯邦分子國都有。

本公約不直接明示國際組織的締約能力，只以「在國際組織內議定之任何條約」等字作暗示，間接承認國際組織創制條約的能力。實則國際組織的這種能力，用不着本公約作承認的表示，早已有公約訂明了。一九四五年，聯合國憲章第一〇五條訂明，世界各國旋即確認，聯合國組織有締結條約的能力；聯合國憲章又於第四十三條和第六十三條分別授權安理會簽訂特別協定，准許經社理事會與各專門機關締結協定。而且在事實上，自聯合國成立以來，聯合國曾與美國、瑞士等許多國家訂約，經社會已與國際勞工組織等許多專門機關締結協定。可見聯合國和各專門機

❷ *League of Nations Doc. A, 6 (a) 1934 V. Annex*, pp. 31, 38.

❸ 93 *LNTS* 44.

關在法律上和事實上都具有訂約能力，已是無可置疑的事情。其他國際組織的這種能力問題，現在還沒有通則加以規範，要看各別的基本法規定才可以解答。

交戰團體經甲國承認後，可與甲國訂約，但是不一定可與不承認它的國家訂約，因為其他國家常不認為它有訂約的能力，它的本國政府更不願承認它具有。例如中華民國政府視中共政權為叛亂團體時，於中共與英國簽訂香港九龍歸還中國的協定後，聲明中共不能代表中國行使這一締結條約的能力，雖然許多識者曉得，這聲明是法律性的國際行為，也是政治性的公開表示，實質上不一定能對那協定發生正面或負面的作用。無論如何，這實例表示交戰（叛亂）團體的締結條約的能力，少為其本國政府所承認。

梵諦岡城國的前身是教皇國（Papal state），原有領土約四萬平方公里，約有人口三百萬之眾，是完整的國際法人；一八七〇年，領土被義大利兼併了，直至一九二九年，教皇才能夠和義大利締結拉特朗條約（Lateran Treaty），於約中確定梵諦岡城國有締結條約的能力。其所訂的條約，叫做康科德（Concordat），已獲得全球各國承認，包括一九九一年以前無神論的國家蘇聯。

第二次世界大戰後，出現了四個分裂國家：中華民國——「中華人民共和國」（中共）、大韓民國（南韓）——朝鮮民主主義人民共和國（北韓）、越南共和國（南越）——越南人民共和國（北越）、德意志聯邦共和國（西德）——德意志人民共和國（東德），都分別與其友邦簽訂條約，雖然獲得其他友邦承

認，卻未獲得與其無邦交的國家接受，例如西德曾與英美法等國簽訂北大西洋公約，東德曾與蘇聯等國簽訂華沙公約，南韓和美國簽訂安全保障條約，中華民國曾與許多友邦締結了許多條約（包括中美共同防禦條約），中共也和許多國家訂約。這些條約都被同一國家的另一「國」認為無效，訂約「國」都堅稱具有代表全國簽訂條約的資格。所以分裂國家的締約資格問題，全由各國按政治考慮而下結論，自作抉擇。南越已於一九七五年由北越

❹　東德與西德於一九九〇年八月三十一日簽訂建造德國統一條約（The Treaty on the Establishment of German Unity).

Article 11

Treaties of the Federal Republic of Germany

The Contracting Parties proceed on the understanding that international treaties and agreements to which the Federal Republic of Germany is a contracting party, including treaties establishing membership of international organizations or institutions, shall retain their validity and that the rights and obligations arising therefrom, with the exception of the treaties named in Annex 1, shall also relate to the territory specified in Article 3 of this Treaty. Where adjustments become necessary in individual cases, the all-German Government shall consult with the respective contracting parties.

Article 12

Treaties of the German Democratic Republic

(1) The Contracting Parties are agreed that, in connection with the establishment of German unity, international treaties of the German Democratic Repub-

兼併，南越所訂的條約幾乎全被否定。東德於一九九〇年十月三
日和西德合併，東德已簽訂的條約正在逐漸處理中❹。到現在爲

---

lic shall be discussed with the contracting parties
concerned with a view to regulating or confirming their
continued application, adjustment or expiry, taking into
account protection of confidence, the interests of the
states concerned, the treaty obligations of the Federal
Republic of Germany as well as the principles of a free,
democratic basic order governed by the rule of law, and
respecting the competence of the European Communities.

(2) The united Germany shall determine its position
with regard to the adoption of international treaties of
the German Democratic Republic following consultations
with the respective contracting parties and with the
European Communities where the latter's competence
is affected.

(3) Should the united Germany intend to accede to
international organizations or other multilaieral treaties
of which the German Democratic Republic but not the
Federal Republic of Germany is a member, agreement
shall be reached with the respective contracting parties
and with the European Communities where the latter's
competence is affected.

該約文見 30 INTERNATIONAL LAW MATERIALS,
471-72 (1991). 該約又規定：

Article 3 of the Unification Treaty provides that,
upon accession (of the German Democratic Republic
to the Federal Republic of Germany in accordance
with Aricle 23 of the Basic Law) taking effect (on
October 3, 1990), the Basic Law of the Federal Republic

止，關於分裂國家統一後的條約處置，還沒有一定的法則。

至於特殊的政治實體，例如利克天士泰 (Liechtenstein) ❺、一九九一年八月前的烏克蘭和白俄羅斯❻、流亡政府❼、戴高樂將軍 (General Charles de Gaulle) 領導的自由法國運動 (The Free French Movement) ❽和叛亂團體等等，也

---

of Germany shall enter into force in the *Länder* of Brandenburg, Mecklenburg-Western Pomerania, Saxony, Saxony-Anhalt and Thuringia, and in that part of Land Berlin where it has not been valid to date, subject to the amendments arising from Article 4 (of the Unification Treaty), unless otherwise provided in the Unification Treaty

Section I of Chapter I of Annex I lists the treaties that are excepted from validity in the territory set out in Article 3, in accordance with Article 11. Paragraph 10 reads:

10. Exchange of notes of May 4, 1988, between the Federal Republic of Germany and the Union of Soviet Socialist Republics regarding inspections in relation to the Treaty of December 8, 1987, between the United States of America and the Union of Soviet Socialist Republics for the Limitation of Intermediate and Short-Range Missiles, with Order of May 30, 1988 (BGBI. 1988-II, F. 534)—Order Regarding Inspections under the INF Treaty.

一九九一年四月二十二日，美國與德國簽訂議定書一份，於書中訂明，除須經專家詳加研議的三份協定外，所有美國與東德締結的協定，自德國統一的當天起一律終止，並以附表列舉經同意終止的十三份協定。見 Dept. of State File No. p. 91 [0064-0625/0628.

都有締結條約的能力問題。學者對於這問題的主張很紛歧，本公約未加規定，又未見其他公約予以訂明，所以問題依然存在。好在本公約已提到，未於約中訂明的事項，全依國際習慣處理。

---

❺ 利克天士泰於一九二〇年申請加入國聯爲會員國，被拒，審查委員會雖然承認它是主權國，卻認爲它沒有履行盟約義務的能力，因爲它既無軍隊，又委託外國代辦海關、電報、電話、郵政、外交等業務，某些訟案也由外國作最終審判。參見 H. Green Hackworth, *Digest of International Law* (1944), vol. I. pp.48-49.

❻ 聯合國憲章是一份極端重要的條約，這已爲全世界人士所肯定。五十一國簽署憲章，烏克蘭和白俄羅斯也是其中簽字國，所以成爲聯合國創始會員國。蘇聯雖然於一九四三年修改憲法，准許各加盟共和國與外國締結條約，但在實際上，蘇聯政府堅決禁止各加盟共和國一切外交行爲，簽署聯合國憲章，純粹是在史丹林命令下進行，以便蘇聯在聯合國大會增加兩個投票權。

❼ 合法政府於戰時遷至友邦境內，繼續統治本國人民，或其人士在盟邦境內建立新組織，以行使本國政府的部分權力，執行部分的國家任務。這類機構統稱爲流亡政府。第一次世界大戰時，波蘭國家委員會最高執政團(The Supreme Political Authority of the Polish National Committee) 獲得協約國承認爲具有自治權的盟國，可在倫敦執行國家的任務。比利時、捷克、盧森堡、挪威、荷蘭、波蘭、南斯拉夫、希臘等國，在第二次世界大戰期間，國土被德軍佔領後，取得英國同意，遷移政府到倫敦，繼續制訂法律、頒布命令，互換使節，締結條約。一九四五年五月七日，德國無條件投降，同月二十九日，荷蘭政府於倫敦與中華民國政府簽約，放棄荷蘭在華治外法權。

❽ 第二次世界大戰時，法國本土大部分被德軍佔領，維琪政權（The Vichy Régime）投降，戴高樂在法國海外屬地從事反德復國運動，接受盟國的承認、政治的支持和軍事的援助。另一方面，維琪政府和美國維持微妙的關係，直至德國投降時止。

第七條　全權證書

一、任一人員如有下列情形之一，視爲代表一國議定或認證條約約文或表示該國承受條約拘束之同意：

(甲)出具適當之全權證書；

(乙)由於有關國家之慣例或由於其他情況可見此等國家之意思係認爲該人員爲此事代表該國而可免除全權證書。

二、下列人員由於所任職務毋須出具全權證書，視爲代表其國家：

(甲)國家元首、政府首長及外交部長，爲實施關於締結條約之一切行爲；

(乙)使館館長，爲議定派遣國與駐在國間條約約文；

(丙)國家派往國際組織會議或派駐國際組織或該國際組織機關之代表，爲議定在該會議、組織或機關內議定之條約約文。

　　本條可以說只是照述國際習慣，不是創立新制，因爲（一）持有適當全權證書（full power）的人員，或從某人本國習慣看，就可以知道其本國政府有意委派他擔任訂約代表，依照國際慣例，都可以代表其本國議定條約約文、認證約文或表示同意承受條約拘束；（二）國家元首、政府首長和外交部長等，都已經各國承認可以代表其本國締結條約；使館館長雖然不具備這種權力，也可以不另經授權，就議定或認證其本國與駐在國間條約的約文；派駐國際組織或其機關或派往國際會議的代表，也可以無需另獲授權，就議定該組織、機關或會議內的條約約文。（三）以上各種人員，持有全權證書者出示證書後，可免除證書者證明本人身分後，其所從事的行爲必有法律上的效力。

　　國家元首、政府首長和外交部長，過去曾有親自談判條約的事例。國家元首兼爲政府首長的美國總統威爾遜（Woodrow

Wilson)，參加一九一九的巴黎和平會議談判與簽約。身為政府首長的英國首相喬治 (Lloyd George) 和法國總理克里孟梭 (Georges Clemenceau) 等，也參加該和約的談判和簽署。中華民國外交部長葉公超，簽署中日和平條約前，負責該約的談判。這些人員既可免除出具全權證書，其所談判簽署的條約，便不在序文中提其本人的全權證書等字樣。

全權證書是證明持用者經合法授權以談判條約、或議定約文或認證約文或簽署條約或互換條約批准書的文書，由國家元首、政府首長或外交部長頒發都屬有效，究竟應由誰頒發，則須視條約的性質和重要程度而定。以美國為例，美國外交服務規則訂明：「代表美國簽署需經批准之國際條約時，簽署者全權證書應由總統頒發。」

古代的全權證書，形式複雜，歐洲國家的常以拉丁文作成，有冗長的序文，保證必定批准條約，約定互換批准書的事項，授予談判代表廣泛的權力。十九世紀以後，證書形式由繁變簡，但其格式和文字，各國使用的並未一致。不過，無論怎樣，其內容必須明確表示數點：(一)持用者姓名及（或）職銜；(二)持用者已獲法定的授權；(三)其權限範圍；(四)有權頒發者；(五)頒發日期及地點。如果內容欠明確，則會被視為不妥善，無效。例如中國代表與日本代表談判馬關條約時，因為清廷頒發的全權證書說有事「須向總理衙門請示行事」，而且只授權給代表商議，未授權給他簽署或訂約，更不提及批准的相關字樣，日本代表指出不夠妥善，便加以拒絕。又如日本代表河田烈提出的全權證書的中譯文為「日本國政府茲任命河田烈為出席關於日本國政府與中

華民國政府間終結戰爭狀態及恢復正常關係之會議之全權代表，並畀以與中華民國之全權代表商議，以及代表日本國政府簽名蓋印於該會議中所訂之一切文件之全權。」因爲證書不提及簽訂和平條約事，中國代表葉公超認爲不夠妥善，便要求日本代表作成下列紀錄說：「中華民國代表聲明其所奉全權係與日本國全權代表商訂與簽署和平條約，日本全權代表聲明彼亦經日本政府授與該項權限，惟該權限之如何行使，則係另一問題。兩全權代表玆證實上述紀錄。」❾

　　全權證書的文字，二十世紀時仍有拉丁文的。例如出席一九一九年巴黎和平會議的奧國代表，其全權證書是以拉丁文作成的。現在的一般情形，則是先用代表的本國文字作成，然後譯成當時當地適合使用的文字。在國際會議中，通常是用會議的通用文字，在聯合國召開的會議中，中文英文法文西班牙文俄文和阿拉伯文都可使用，在締結雙邊條約時，如果兩國同文，就都用其國文，如果不同文，就以協議所決定的第三國文字譯妥其全權證書。

　　全權證書中是否必須有「條約將來如經〇〇〇〇〇政府批准，定予實施」等字，則沒有定規或定論，因爲莊嚴的條約，大多數須於批准後才能生效實施，縱使簽約代表的全權證書沒有這些文字，其所簽條約還是非經批准不能實施。

　　一八五二年倫敦會議時，普魯士和奧地利的代表，等到簽署文件前夕才收到全權證書。一九一〇年，美國代表先在一九〇七

❾　湯武，**中國與國際法**（臺北、中華文化事業出版社，民四六），第三冊，頁六九二。

年國際捕獲法院規約修改議定書上簽署，後來收到全權證書時才
向荷蘭外交部補送。近來因為交通方便，電訊傳送迅速，條約談
判代表於談判開始時未具備全權證書的情形，幾像鳳毛麟角了。
何況代表本國政府所頒發的公開訓令，也可作為締約權限的根
據，必要時得展示以證實已有的權限。

　　中華民國的代表全權證書，以前由國民政府主席頒發，現在
則由總統頒發。所用格式如下：

　　　　　中華民國總統為發給證書事，茲因中華民國與○○○
　　　○國商訂○○○○○條約，特派
　　　中華民國○○○○○○○為全權代表。
　　　　　所有該代表以中華民國名義締結之條約，將來如經中
　　　華民國政府批准，定予施行。
　　　　　　　　　　　　　　　　　總統○○○（簽署）
　　　中華民國○○年○月○日

　　各代表的全權證書都經審閱確認為妥善後，才可以開始執行
其所奉任務。審閱的方式，就多邊條約在國際會議中的情形來
說，可有五種：(一) 通知 (Communicating)。一八九九年第
一次海牙和平會議採用這方式。(二)交換 (Exchanging)。一
九一九年巴黎和平會議採用這方式。(三)寄存 (Depositing)。
這是一九○七年第二次海牙和平會議時的方式。(四) 展示 (Ex-
hibiting)。即展示上述的政府的公開訓令，為一九二三年洛桑
(Laussane) 會議所採用。(五)提示 (Presenting)。一九四

七年談判對義大利、保加利亞、芬蘭、羅馬尼亞、匈牙利等國的
和平條約時，都用這一方式。

　　以上五種方式的任何一種，都是兩國以上的代表參加時的審
查方式，現在仍被採用。很多代表參加時，則常組成委員會，以
互責審查。雙邊條約的代表全權證書，仍用互相校閱的方式，例
如中華民國三十四年八月十四日簽訂的中蘇友好同盟條約，其序
文末句說：「雙方全權代表，各將所奉全權證書，互相校閱，均
屬妥善，議定條款如左。」

　　現在必須特別指出，近代簡化式的條約很多，都以照會（換
文）方式作成。依照一九六一年外交關係公約第三條第一項第三
款的規定，使館館長可與駐在國政府談判，無需另備全權證書，
就可以簽訂條約。這一較早的公約規定，已納入本條文，乃是顯
然的事情。有了這些規定後，使館館長固然免除提具全權證書，
便可進行訂約事宜，就是在沒有外交關係公約之前，使館館長已
經這樣行事，例如中華民國四十年一月三十日和二月九日，中華
民國外交部和美國駐華大使館以照會方式，決定了美國軍事顧問
團的相關事項，包括團中美方人員享受使館人員的同等待遇。這
樣重要的決定，也可用簡化式條約作成，雙方代表無需備具全權
證書。現在一般說來，當有關各造同意時，可以免除證書，例如
一九三六年十一月二十一日，美國與希臘簽訂條約，希臘外交部
常務次長代表希臘簽署時，無全權證書，僅通知美國代表說，其
職位使其有足夠權力簽署該條約❿。可見有關國家同意，也是可

---

❿　H. Green Hackworth, *op. cit.*, p. 40.

以免除全權證書的決定性因素。

第八條　未經授權所實施行為之事後確認

關於締結條約之行為係依第七條不能視為經授權為此事代表一國之人員所實施者，非經該國事後確認，不發生法律效果。

本條的目的，在使無權訂約者的訂約行為無效，其所訂條約，除非嗣後經其本國確認，不發生拘束其本國的法律效果。

無權簽訂條約的人員，會從事訂約的行為，眞是稀有。但是由於微妙的原因，並非不可能有。一九〇八年，美國駐羅馬尼亞公使完全未經授權，便簽署了兩份公約⓫。一九五一年，關於乳酪命名公約在史楚列撒（Stresa）簽署，代表挪威和瑞典兩國簽署者同為一人，實則他只經挪威一國授權⓬。一九三九年，美國駐賴比瑞亞公使於無全權證書時，與賴國簽訂調解條約，美國國務院認為這是不完善的條約，命令他收到全權證後，和賴國另訂條約。還有一種情形是，訂約代表已經獲得授權，但他不依權限行事，擴大了權力範圍，例如波斯〈卽現在的伊朗〉代表於國聯理事會中討論時，聲稱波斯代表互換一八四七年艾色藍條約批准書時，已經越權接受了一項解釋性的備忘錄。現在的波斯代表，竟企圖以這藉口為理由，否認該項條約⓭。

⓫　H. Green Hackworth, *op. cit.*, Vol. IV, p. 467.

⓬　H. Green Hackworth, *op. cit.*, p. 42.

⓭　同註⓬，頁32。

顯然的，無權的或越權的代表所訂的條約，其本國當然可以否定該條約的任何效力。這是本條的意旨。但在另一方面，也很顯然的，其本國如果於事後承認其所爲，同意承受其所訂條約的拘束，而加以確認，則該約就有法律效力。此外，其本國縱使不作明示的確認，如果援引約中的條款，從事該約要求的行爲，或有視其代表所爲有效的具體表現，也可以解釋爲其本國已隱含（默示）同意承受該約的拘束。

第九條　約文之議定

一、除依第二項之規定外，議定條約約文應以所有參加草擬約文國家之同意爲之。

二、國際會議議定條約之約文應以出席及參加表決國家三分之二多數之表決爲之，但此等國家以同樣多數決定適用另一規則者不在此限。

本條規定如何表決條約約文，規定條約的形式、內容和文字都擬妥後，以全體一致或三分之二多數表決。談判國把條約各條款擬妥，又逐一校對後，便可以確定條約的文字、形式和內容，由參加草擬的國家代表投票表決。這表決的結果，只是確定形式、文字和內容無訛，不意味參加表決的國家因而受條約拘束，因爲承受條約拘束的同意還要經由其他方式表示。

本條第一項只說「議定條約約文」，不分多邊的或雙邊的條約約文，就它和第二項的關係看，可知是指多邊和雙邊條約的約文，雙邊條約的約文必須由兩國代表參加草擬，也須經兩國代表

同意，才可以議定。這是無需特別指出的事情。

　　從前多邊條約約文的議定，常需談判國全體同意，適用全體一致規則是常態，採用多數決原則是例外。第一次世界大戰後，多數決原則才逐漸增加採用，國際組織紛紛成立，國際會議召開的次數越來越多，而且規模愈來愈大，與會代表來自背境十分歧異的國家，任何決議要取得全體同意，幾乎等於緣木求魚，而且在某些事項上，也無爭取一致同意的必要，如果爭取，就是不切合實際。所以本條第一項的規則，只可適用於雙邊條約和少數幾個國家間的條約。許多國家參加談判的條約，則須採用不同的規則。當然，全體代表都認為必需而且適當時，不但可以而且必須適用全體一致規則，這一適用可於事前決定，也可以臨時協議。

　　本條第二項的適用對象有二：一是多國參加的國際會議，二是國際組織的大會。這兩者議定條約約文時，須有出席並且參加投票的三分之二的國家同意。獲得這種多數的國家同意後，以後實施就可有較好的效果。少於三分之二的表決原則，通常是過半數原則，就是百分之五十加一原則，採用這原則以議定的條約約文，恐怕不能獲得更多的國家批准或簽署，終使多邊條約的宗旨不能達成。

　　本公約的草擬者為什麼決定於約中訂明三分之二原則？這是不易答覆的問題。也許除了受前段的考慮所影響外，還顧及聯合國憲章的規定、一九五八年海洋法會議、一九六一年外交關係公約會議和一九六三年領事關係公約會議等的先例。憲章第十八條第二項規定，大會之重要問題應以出席並參加投票會員國三分之

二同意決定之。上述會議作成的公約，都是經出席並參加投票代表三分之二表決通過的。

為什麼放棄全體一致原則後，不採用四分之三或五分之四原則？因為三分之二原則適用時，已經不易獲得積極的結果，要是改用四分之三或五分之四原則，任何國際會議和國際組織通過條約案的可能性就一定更小。一九六〇年，第二次海洋法會議的領海寬度議題，表決時只因一票之差，未達三分之二同意票，以致功虧一簣，令人嘆惜。

不過本條第二項富有彈性，參加草擬約文的國家，可以經由三分之二的表決，放棄三分之二原則，改用其他表決原則，包括五分之四、五分之三、四分之三、過半數等原則。

第十條　約文之認證 (Authentication)

條約約文依下列方法確定為作準定本：

(甲)依約文所載或經參加草擬約文國家協議之程序；或

(乙)倘無此項程序，由此等國家代表在條約約文上、或在載有約文之會議藏事文件上簽署、作待核准之簽署(Signature ad referendum) 或草簽。

為了使談判國最後確知條約的形式、文字和內容為何起見，約文的認證是必需的。經認證後，各談判國已經協議的草案，便變成定稿的約文，不得未經再度協議就更改，所以認證是定稿約文的確定過程，是證實約文無訛又真實的過程和行為。

二十世紀以前的法學家，通常不說認證是締結條約過程中的

獨立步驟，因爲他們把簽署視爲認證約文的一般方法，而且認爲
簽署是另一種程序的初步表示，即批准、接受或贊同條約或國家
同意承受條約拘束的預示，於是把簽署條約和認證約文的兩種功
用混合了。但是近來已有認證約文的其他方法，方法之一是把未
經簽署的約文併入外交會議的㢱事文件中；方法之二是在國際組
織內，由會議主席或其他有權人員簽署，以認證條約約文；方法
之三是把條約載於國際組織的決議案中，藉以認證約文。這些作
法，逐漸使各國締結公約時，在程序中採用認證步驟。此外，一
份公約無論以一種或一種以上文字作成，都可能有一種以上不同
文字的譯本，也要加以認證。這種種事實，已使認證約文成爲締
結多邊條約的必需步驟。

依照本條的規定，認證約文的程序，常於約文中訂明，或由
談判國協議決定，如果未經訂明，又沒有協議，則由各談判國以
簽署、作待核准之簽署或草簽，或把約文併入㢱事文件中，以表
示認證行爲。

如上文所說，今日的條約約文認證，採用國際組織某機關的
決議案形式，或由其內部有權人員簽署。這種認證行爲，並非不
尋常。但是這種形式和行爲，是屬於國際組織內通過條約的作
法，已於本公約第五條加以規範，現在無需贅及了。

可是這裏仍須強調，條約約文一旦依本條的規定認證了，約
中的內容、條碼、形式、文字、符號等等，便是最後確定了，不
得再由任何談判國或簽署國更改，如果作任何更改，就非依約中
所定程序處理不可。但是，因爲抄錄造成的錯誤或遺漏，則不是
更改，而是校正或勘誤，抄錄者可以隨時更正。

第十一條　表示同意承受條約拘束之方式

一國承受條約拘束之同意得以簽署、交換構成條約之文書、批准、接受、贊同或加入，或任何其他同意之方式表示之。

本條綜列國家同意承受條約拘束的各種表示方式，包括簽署、批准、接受、贊同、加入、交換構成條約的文書等。至於其他任何方式，只要各談判國同意，也都可以採用，同樣有效。

原來十九世紀以前，各國締結條約時，無論依照國際習慣法，或依照協定法，都不必遵守一定的程序規則，締約國同意承受條約拘束時須作鄭重的表示，與其說是基於法制，不如說是出於禮制，所以締約國應於何時表示這種同意，應以什麼方式作這種表示，諸如此類的問題，沒有定則或定論，全由各締約國事前或臨時商定，就是到了今天，已有本公約的規定和本條的定則，國家表示同意承受條約拘束時仍可自由選擇其他方式，可以選定其認爲最適合的一種，而且只用一種即可，無需用一種以上。

十九世紀以前的國家間的條約，往往是一經簽署，簽署國便當然受條約拘束，因爲在君主專制時期，君主代表國家，以君主或國家名義締結的條約，只要君主同意了，條約便可以開始履行了。民主政治制度逐漸推行後，演變至今，國家的代表簽署條約後，不能立刻履行條約義務，要等到條約經一定國內程序批准後，國家才能採取國際行爲，正式表示同意承受條約的拘束，而表示的方式，除習用多年久載的簽署外，現在已有交換構成條約的文書等等，比從前複雜多了。

簽署、批准等方式的詳細說明，留待下文介紹第十二條第十

三條第十四條第十五條和第十六條時，才分別進行。

　　　　　第十二條　以簽署表示承受條約拘束之同意

一、遇有下列情形之一，一國承受條約拘束之同意以該國代表之簽署
　　表示之：

　　（甲）條約規定簽署有此效果；

　　（乙）另經確定談判國協議有此效果；

　　（丙）該國使簽署有此效果之意思可見諸其代表所奉之全權證書或
　　　　已於談判時有此表示。

二、就適用第一項而言：

　　（甲）倘經確定談判國有此協議，約文之草簽構成條約之簽署；

　　（乙）代表對條約作待核准之簽署，倘經其本國確認，即構成條約
　　　　之正式簽署。

　　本條只規定以簽署表示同意承受條約的拘束，不涉及其他表
示方式。

　　「簽署」兩字作動詞用時，是中文常用的簽字或簽名（英文
是 to sign 或 signing）；「簽署」兩字作名詞用時，是中文常
用的署名或蓋章（英文是signature），都是相當正式的行為。
就締結條約的程序來說，簽署是談判代表於獲致協議後，在已達
成的結論或決議的文件上，所作的肯定表示，或是非談判國代表
在條約上所作的具體表示。簽署的效果，按不同的情況而有分
別。簽署條約的最普通效果，是簽署者轉請其本國政府批准條
約，一如前述中華民國全權證書末句所說：「將來如經中華民國

政府批准，定予施行。」這就表示，簽署條約是批准條約的前奏曲，先有簽署，然後有批准，有簽署才會有批准，雖然簽署後不一定有批准，簽署國在一般情形下也無批准的法律義務，而需經批准才能生效的條約，則絕大多數都經過簽署的手續。但這只是通例，並不是沒有例外。國際勞工組織通過的勞工公約，向來是直接送請各會員國批准，不先由各會員國代表簽署。一九四六年二月十三日，聯合國大會通過聯合國特權及豁免公約後，亦無簽署程序，便逕送各會員國。

　　條約談判結束後，約文又經過認證時，通常就由各國代表簽署，例如聯合國憲章內容等等都確定時，於一九四五年六月二十六日由參加談判或前已簽署聯合國宣言的五十國代表簽署。但也有下列情事：(一)不參加談判的國家代表待後可以補簽，補簽後仍稱為簽署國 (signatory)，例如波蘭於一九四五年十月十五日才簽署聯合國憲章，仍被准許為聯合國創始會員國❿；(二)條約訂明從某日起到某日止，在甲地接受非談判國的代表簽署，另一期間在另一地點接受各國的代表簽署，例如一九八二年的聯合國海洋法公約第三〇五條第二項訂明：「本公約應持續開放簽字，至一九八四年十二月九日在牙買加外交部簽字，此外，從一九八三年七月一日起至一九八四年十二月九日止，在紐約聯合國總部簽字。」這規定和聯合國憲章的規定不同，准許非談判國的國名留存條約上，和一九二五年二月十九日簽訂的鴉片公約先例

❿　聯合國其他會員國後來加入時，不被要求、邀請或准許簽署憲章，是所謂「加入會員國(admitted members)」，有別於「創始會員國(original members)」。

一樣，未嘗不可以說是一種進步的作法。

在條約約文確定時簽署也好，持續開放一段期間簽署也好，簽署代表都不一定是同約的談判代表，儘管在事實上談判代表常是簽署代表，簽署條約者多是參加條約談判者，而且在通常的情形下，談判代表所奉的全權證書授予其簽署條約的權限，可是各國仍然可以換人，另派簽署代表。另派的原因很多，原談判代表公忙、患病、職位變動、死亡或新的身分不宜擔任簽署代表，或政府首長更迭，都是常見的原因。

另一方面，國際習慣法和協定法雖然不要求談判代表任簽署代表，更不排除談判代表任簽署代表，卻如前文所說，除簡化式的條約外，都要求簽署者出示全權證書，除非依例依協議或本公約規定，他是無需由他人授權的代表，如國家元首、政府首長等。

雙邊條約的末尾條文中，往往有「簽字蓋章，以昭信守」等字，例如上文提及的中美通商航海條約的尾語說：「為此，雙方全權代表爰於本約簽字蓋章，以昭信守。」⑮這些文字表示，雙方代表簽字之後，還蓋印章。中華民國四十一年的中日和平條約，中國代表葉公超和日本代表河田烈，都在約中簽名後再蓋印，又是一例。

簽署雙邊條約，常由雙方代表在同時同地進行，但亦可有例外，例如一七八五年美國與普魯士間條約、一九〇二年美國租用

---

⑮ 約中英文是 In witness whereof, the respective plenipotentiaries have signed this Treaty and have affixed hereunto their seals.

古巴煤站軍港條約，都是各在其本國首都簽署。

　　簽署雙邊條約，有所謂輪署制（Alternat），就是各代表先簽其本國保存的約本，後簽對方保存的約本，因此，中文本的條約上，先簽者的姓名在前，後簽者的姓名在後，在文字橫書的約本上，先簽者的姓名在上，後簽者的姓名在下。不論約本以一種兩種或三種以上文字作成，也不問以其中一種或兩種文字本作準，簽約代表都可以只簽其本國文字的姓名，也可以另簽外文譯出的姓名，例如中華民國代表於聯合國憲章上簽中文姓名，中國代表王世杰於上述中美通商航海條約中，簽中文姓名後再簽英文譯名，美國代表於該約互換批准議定書中簽 J. Leighton Stuart，又簽「司徒雷登」四字。

　　國際會議的藏事文件（議定書），如果列載會議作成的條約和各種相關文件，則簽署藏事文件（議定書），就等於簽署了條約和各種相關文書。一九二八年泛美二十一國國際會議藏事議定書，就是這樣簽署的一例。但這一實例仍不能作為通例的證明，如果待簽字的議定書不以明文規定，則簽約代表還是要分別簽署各項文件。

　　近代條約，尤其是多邊條約的末端，代表簽署後，不復有蓋印情事。一九四五年的聯合國憲章只說：「為此聯合國各會員國之代表謹簽字於本憲章，以昭信守。」❶❻一九八二年的聯合國海洋法公約只說：「為此，下列全權代表，經正式授權，在本公約

---

❶❻ 該句的英文是 In faith whereof the representatives of the Governments of the United Nations have signed the present Charter.

上簽字，以資證明。」❶都不再有蓋印等文字，而且不像從前的大國代表必先簽，小國代表的殿後，以示尊卑，更不採用輪署制了。在絕大多數的公約中，現在改按英（法）文國名第一字母順序排列，由各國代表依次簽字，所以聯合國憲章上的簽名順序是 Argentina, Australia, Belgium, Bolivia,…Chile, China,… Union of South Africa, Union of Soviet Socielist Republics, United Kingdom of Great Britain and Northern Ireland, United States of America,…Yugoslavia.

　　本條所稱的簽署，不是簽字代表必轉請其本國政府批准條約的簽署，亦非認證約文的簽署，而是其本國已同意承受條約拘束的正式表示，所以和其他作用的簽署不同。簽署要有這種法律效果，就必須(一)所簽的條約已規定簽署有這種效果，或(二)經由各談判代表協議決定，簽署發生這種效果，或(三)從簽署代表所奉的全權證書中，可知證書有意使簽署發生這種效果，或(四)談判代表已於談判時作同樣的表示。

　　本條第二項說，經談判各代表協議後，草簽可以等於簽署。所謂草簽，就是中文的簽花押、簡簽或畫稿，只寫名字或只寫名的一個字，不寫姓，更不寫全姓名，例如簽署者是「張李趙」，只寫「趙」或「李趙」，不寫「張李趙」。草簽的英文字是 initialling，草簽時只寫姓和名的第一字母，例如 Theodore Roosevelt, Flanklin D. Roosevelt, John F. Kennedy 等

---

❶　該句的英文是 In witness whereof the undersigned plenipotentiaries, being duly authorized thereto, have signed this Convention.

人的草簽是 T.R., F.D.R. 和 J.F. K。草簽不是正式的簽署，唯
於各談判代表協議草簽等於正式簽署時，才有簽署的同樣效果。
一九二五年的羅卡諾 (Locarno) 條約，於十月十六日在羅卡諾
草簽，於同年十二月一日才在倫敦正式簽署，便是一例。但是另
一方面，符合下列兩條件的草簽，也可有正式簽署的效果：㈠由
於草簽者所任職位而有實際權力可用簽字以拘束其本國，㈡草簽
者有意使其簽字發生正式簽署的效果（這種情事雖然曾經發生，
但是可以說少而又少，而且草簽者的意思唯有從整套文件或相關
情況推想才可以知道）。總之，草簽在其他情況下，是認證約文
的行為，沒有其他作用，不當然變成簽署。

　　締結條約的程序中，又有「暫簽」。暫簽就是代表所作的簽
署，要等到其本國政府確認後，才發生正式簽署的效果，所以本
條第二項（乙）款稱為「待核准之簽署」 (Signature ad referendum)。一九三四年的「泛美限制最惠國條款之適用協定」
第三條訂明：「……任何國家得先作暫簽，俟依其憲法程序提存
批准書後 ， 始對該國生效。」這是「 待核准之簽署」的較早規
定。這規定的優點是，在場的談判代表可以立即簽署，以後如果
其本國政府不批准其所簽的條約，簽署就沒有效果，如果批准該
約，只要提存批准書 ， 便使簽署和條約生效 ， 無需另派代表簽
署，其本國不但是該約當事國，而且是簽署國。

　　草簽和暫簽的主要分別如下：(一)草簽基本上只是認證約文
的行為，而暫簽於約文未經認證時原是認證行為，於約文已經認
證時則為「待核准的簽署」；(二)草簽永遠是草簽，性質和作用
不能改變，而暫簽則可經確認後變為正式的簽署；(三)簽署代表

本國政府的確認，有追溯既往的效力，使暫簽行為的當日成為簽署日，而草簽之後，正式的簽署則沒有溯及既往的效力，不能使草簽日成為簽署日，計算條約期間仍以簽字當天為簽署日期。

採用草簽和暫簽的情況也不相同。草簽可為各種目的而採用。一是認證談判時某階段的約文，以便把約文讓各有關國家作進一步的考慮；二是談判代表雖經授權進行談判，卻未具有（或當時還未取得）簽署條約的授權。現在締約代表收到全權證書前，可用電報的或傳真的授權證明，以證明其所奉的簽約權力，各國已接受這種證明有效了，所以草簽的需要愈來愈少。有些時候，代表因為某種原因，雖然未經授權，亦主動的採取行為，便對約文先行草簽。在上述情況下，暫簽也會被採用。但是現在許多政府認為固然應該對約文有所行動了，卻不願即時承受正式簽署所隱含的拘束，所以命令其代表暫簽，以保留從長計議的餘地。

一般說來，草簽和暫簽的規定，可適用於雙邊條約和多邊條約、國際會議通過的公約和國際組織內通過的公約。

第十三條　以交換構成條約之文書表示承受條約拘束之同意

　　遇有下列情形之一，國家同意承受由此種交換之文書構成之條約拘束，以此種交換表示之：

　　（甲）文書規定此種交換有此效果；或

　　（乙）另經確定此等國家協議文書之交換有此效果；

本條所指的文書（Instrument）是指任何書面的文件。只

要文件上規定，構成條約的文件一經兩國或兩國以上交換，各國便受條約拘束，就是交換發生了表示的效果 —— 承受條約拘束的同意。這種效果，可於交換的文書中規定，也可由相關國家協商決定。

嚴格說來，以後採用這方式的需要不會多，因為締結雙邊條約時，談判代表可以直接了當的在約文中訂明如何使條約生效；締結多邊條約時，談判代表也可於約文或所附議定書上訂明條約生效的條件，以避免各國交換文書的麻煩。條約生效後，締約國才受條約拘束。這是各國公認的規則，現在已經用不着以任何其他文件訂明了。

不過必須在這裏指出，如果交換的文書是條約批准書，則自當別論，因為締約國互換批准書，早已是締約程序中司空見慣的常規，例如前述中美通商航海條約第十三條第一項訂明：「本約應予批准，批准書應在南京儘速互換。」依照這訂明，該約批准書於第二（民國三十六）年十一月三十日在南京交換了。

第十四條　以批准、接受或贊同表示承受條約拘束之同意

一、遇有下列情形之一，國家承受條約拘束之同意，以批准表示之：

（甲）條約規定以批准方式表示同意；

（乙）另經確定談判國協議需要批准；

（丙）該國代表已對條約作需經批准之簽署；或

（丁）該國代表作須經批准之簽署之意思可見諸其代表所奉之全權證書，或已於談判時有此表示。

二、一國承受條約拘束之同意，以接受或贊同方式表示者，其條件與適用於批准者同。

本條規定同意承受條約拘束的三種表示方式，就是批准條約，接受條約和贊同條約。

先敍批准條約。

批准條約是國家或政府對其代表所簽國際協定的最後確認，是國家或政府的正式國際行為，具有最終的確定性。

公元五六一年，羅馬的查士替尼元 (Justinian) 帝和波斯國王抽士勞士 (Chosroes) 訂約，列有須經批准的條款，以後這種實例頗多，例如一二九六年，英王愛德華一世 (Edward I) 和佛蘭德 (Flander) 伯爵訂約，一三○三年英國和法國所締結的條約，都規定應經批准手續。

可是十八世紀以前，所謂條約須經批准，只是指條約議定後，主權者確認並且最後證實其原來的授權，檢視其談判代表所簽的協定，主要是從事形式的事情，不是核定協定的內容，所以君主已授予全權給談判代表簽約，便有批准條約的義務。一七八七年，全球第一部成文憲法（美國聯邦憲法）通過施行，規定行政機關（總統）簽訂的條約，須經國會參議院勸告及同意後，總統才可以批准。其後許多行憲國家，要求行政首長的締約權受立法機關節制，批准條約的程序便變成了控制的手段，條約批准制發生了基本的性質改變，逐漸形成了新的制度，就是條約須經談判代表或簽署代表的本國政府正式批准，其本國才受拘束，或者才能開始發生效力。除簡化式的國際協定外，當條約採用莊嚴形式時，批准制更受重視，必定採用，而且以明文規定採用，這樣就很自然的孕育了一種公意：批准是條約有拘束力的根據，批准是普遍的規則。二十世紀的重要公約，如一九一九年巴黎和平

條約、一九四五年聯合國憲章、一九六九年條約法公約、一九八二年聯合國海洋法公約等，都訂有批准條款，其他條約縱使有例外，也是稀奇的例外，條約只對批准國有拘束力，這已是一般原則。至於條約也對非締約國有拘束力，則是罕見的例外。

以上演變，使條約發生拘束力的條件益趨複雜。關於拘束力的爭論，儘管是理論性的⓲，也無法對抗真正的事實，比較莊嚴的文書，都以明文規定須經批准，甚至換文（照會）或其他簡化式協定，也偶有相同的規定。

批准要在國際層面發生效力，必須先經過國內程序。批准條約的程序，各國的規定很不一致。那些條約須經批准？由什麼人或什麼機關批准？如果由機關核定，核定的程序是怎樣的？各國給予這些以及相關問題的答案，或是大不相同，或大同小異，或是大異小同。

在中華民國，簡化式條約（Treaties in simplified form）

⓲　關於條約應否經批准後才生效的問題，有兩學派的理論，古典學者中，有人認為締約全權代表似私法的代理人，在代理權限內締結的條約應拘束其本國，除約中有特別規定或代表越權外，條約無須經過批准便可生效，葛羅秀士、瓦泰耳、馬廷士、布倫齊利(Grotius, Vattel, Martens, Blunchli) 等屬這一派。主張應經批准者，現在已佔絕大多數，其理由是：㈠民意政治要求條約簽署後，由人民代表再加以審查，以確定是否違反民意，以貫徹憲法的規定；㈡條約可能涉及國家重大利益，應於簽署後有再作縝密考量的機會；㈢條約如果於簽署後須經批准，則可於有基本的情況改變時設法應變；㈣批准條約時可以確定締約代表是否越權、被脅迫或被詐欺；㈤締約代表與其本國只有公法上的關係，沒有私法上的代理權。

如照會 (Exchange of notes)、換函 (Exchange of letters) 等，由外交部或其他主管部簽報行政院，由院長交付院會討論通過，就算是批准了❶，或由外交部長核定就行了，無需由行政院諮請立法院審議並且通過。在美國 ，行政協定 (Executive a-greements) 、換文、換函等簡化式條約，也可不經國會參議院表示意見，便生效施行。在英國，多年久載的傳統是，內閣有締結條約的全權，雖然勞工黨 (The Labor Party) 於一九二二年初次執政時，宣稱以後締結的重要條約應取得國會同意，方予施行，但是在事實上，只是口說而手不動，現在無論是保守黨或勞工黨，還是依照傳統行事，換文、議定書、臨時辦法、宣言、商約、仲裁協定、邊界協定等，都可免經國會同意批准。從此可知，什麼條約須經批准的問題，各國的實踐有別❷。

須經批准的條約，應由國內何人或何機關批准？中華民國憲法第五十八條規定，各部會首長應將條約案「提出於行政院會議議決之」。第六十三條又訂明，立法院有議決條約案的權力。所以名為條約、專約、公約、憲章、盟約等的國際法律文書，不但要由行政院會議議決，而且要經過立法院議決同意批准，方可由總統簽署，完成我國同意承受條約拘束的國內程序。美國憲法第

---

❶ 例如中華民國八十年七月的「中華民國與菲律賓間海道通行暨農漁業合作協定」是。

❷ Arnold D. McNair, *The Law of Treaties, British Practice and Opinions,* New York, 1938, pp. 85-87. 英國一如其他國家，亦不要求戰地指揮官在其職權範圍內所簽的停火或換俘協定、以換文作成的協定等須經國會批准。

二條第二節第二項規定，總統有經參議院勸告及同意後締結條約的權力。因此，總統和外國簽訂的具條約性質的國際法律文書，除上述行政協定、換文之類的文件外，必須送請國會參議院審議，取得同意後，總統才可以簽字批准，以終結締約的國內程序❷。以上兩例表示，立法機關行使條約批准的同意權，條約未經同意不得批准。

　　至於立法機關行使同意權的程序，各國略有不同。就中華民國來說，條約簽署後，由主管部（多是外交部）簽請行政院核可，由行政院轉請立法院同意。立法院收到條約案時，通常是先交程序委員會。該會審查該案的提案手續是不是完備，再看它是不是屬於立法院審議的權力範圍內，如果都是，便送由相關的委員會（多是常設的外交委員會）審查，列入議程提報院會，院會同意後，指定委員會（通常又是外交委員會）審查。涉及其他部會機構職權的條約，該會必會同相關的其他委員會舉行聯席會議，以該會召集人爲主席，例如通商航海之類的條約，必與經濟、財政、交通甚至國防等委員會開聯席會議。立法院外交委員會和司法委員會聯席會議，於民國八十年三月二十一日通過「中華民國與多明尼加共和國間引渡條約」，便是舉行聯席會議審查條約案的近例。開會時邀請有關部會機構代表列席說明備詢，必要時亦得邀請學者專家社會名流提供意見。無論是由一個委員會單獨審查，或由聯席會審查，都要有法定出席委員的過半數同

❷　這裡應該指出，條約如果不涉及撥款或預算，只由參議院勸告及同意，就可以批准，不必徵求國會衆議院的意見。換句話說，衆議院沒有過問條約的憲法所定的權力。

意，才能通過條約案，提報院會，建議院會通過。負責審查的委員會或聯席會議，於贊成提報院會的委員不超過半數時，條約案便告擱置了。條約案送達院會後，院會須有委員總額七分之一出席，才得開議，有出席委員過半數同意，才能通過，可否同數時取決於主持院會的主席。英美等國家的立法機關是國會，中華民國的國民大會、立法院和監察院，雖然經司法院大法官會議解釋為共同相當於西方的國會，但國民大會和監察院並無憲法上的權力，以分享條約批准的同意權。又因為立法院議事規則所定的表決規則，只有過半數制，沒有三分之二制，所以條約案獲得法定開議委員數二分之一加一委員贊成，便是同意批准，總統便可以簽字，完成訂約的國內程序❷。

美國國會參議院通過條約批准案的程序，比中華民國立法院的程序更困難。條約案由美國總統送達參議院後，通常是像立法案一樣，分配給外交委員會 (Committee on Foreign Relations) 負責審查。該會處理時，必先請國務院 (Department of State) 和相關部會機構代表列席說明備詢，必要時舉行公聽會（英文名詞為 hearing, 又中譯為聽證會），以探悉學者專家各界各行業要員的意見，然後在委員會裏表決，須有過半數委員出席及同意，才能通過，附保留或不附保留，通過後提報院會，建議院會通過或不通過。院會表決時，須有出席議員（不是法定議員總額）三分之二（不是過半數）贊成，才可以通過。這三分之二數比過半數的取得，真很困難，因為參議員任期六年，每兩年

❷　請參閱楊國棟著，**中華民國條約與協定的批准制度**（臺北、商務、民六二）。

改選全體議員三分之一，自美國兩大黨制定型以來，無論是民主黨或共和黨，都未曾於選舉中贏得參議院三分之二席位，總統的條約案縱使有其本黨參議員一致支持，還要有反對黨若干參議員贊成，才可以通過，反對黨如果堅決反對總統的條約案，則只需要全體議員或出席議員三分之一加一人，就能夠粉碎總統的希望，所以兩百多年來，條約案通過時附有保留的很多，被擱置的亦不少㉓。

　本書不能也無需再舉其他國家的作法。讀者從上述說明，已知各國關於批准條約的規定和習慣，固然不盡相同，一般國際法和本公約也不置喙，完全由各國自作選擇㉔。

　國際組織締結條約，也有批准的行為。聯合國自一九四六年起和美國簽訂關於總會所協定，和瑞士、奧地利簽訂聯合國辦

㉓　一九七七年巴拿馬運河條約，是附有保留的近例。一九一九年巴黎和平條約，是附上許許多多保留後被擱置的名例。

㉔　英國的締約權屬於王座(The Crown)。王座得談判簽署批准條約，某些條約縱使訂明須經國會同意，王座仍是決定性因素。但是改變國內法律、更動國民實質權利、割讓領土和由國庫付款的條約，國會的贊成必視為十分重要，所以聯合國憲章、北大西洋公約等，都送請國會兩院審議通過。其他一般條約，總是先由內閣單獨決定談判，然後由王座批准，不送請國會表示意見。

　又有所謂「默示的批准」，就是簽署國不以文書表示批准條約，便開始履行條約。又有所謂「間接的批准」，例如一九一九年巴黎和平條約第二九五條說：「未批准一九一二年鴉片公約之締約國，其批准本和約應視為亦批准該公約。」但是這兩種批准，都不是本公約所指的批准。

事處協定，都經由聯合國大會投票表決通過，正式批准。聯合國各專門機關 (Specialized agencies) 和其會所地國簽訂的協定，如國際民用航空組織、聯合國糧食農業組織、國際勞工組織 (International Civil Aviation Organization、Food and Agriculture Organization of the United Nations、International Labor Organization) 等，分別和加拿大、義大利、瑞士締結的會所協定，都各經其大會投票表決批准。國際組織批准條約的規則，幾乎是一致的，都由組織的大會投票決定是否批准。

　　本條主旨，在規定以批准條約等方式，表示同意承受條約的拘束，不涉及批准條約期限，也不隱含規定期限的意思。如果從本公約第八十二條的文字看，就可知道本公約的草擬者連本公約的批准，也不限期。該條說：「本公約須經批准。批准書應送請聯合國秘書長存放。」本公約其他條款，並不提到批准條約應有期限。因此，除非有關條約明訂批准截止期限，批准是可以無限期的。但反過來說，條約規定批准須於某期限前作成，亦非國際法所禁止，締約國如不依限行事，當可視爲拒絕批准。另一方面，儘管條約使用「本約應儘速批准」等彈性文字，或對批准事隻字不提，各締約國也應該在合理期間內，予以批准，合理期間過後，亦可被視爲拒絕批准。所謂合理期間，確是很有彈性，究竟多少歲月的期間才算是合理？這要看條約性質和各國情況而定。條約內容重要又複雜，則需要較長的時日以批准，國會議員改選或政府首長更迭，都可能有批准的拖延。

　　談判國於簽約後有無批准的義務？從本公約的精神和各條款

觀察，可見這已是理論的問題❷，因爲一則某條約是否必須經過批准，多以明文規定，二則勉強要求簽字國或談判國批准條約（如聯合國憲章生效前的若干和平條約），未必能夠達到目的，何況現在已禁止國家對外國施行強迫，三則簽約國不批准條約的事例，屢見不鮮。然而如果訂約代表沒有越權，簽約後沒有使條約不能履行的原因，國內不發生情況的基本改變，再詳加考慮後又不認爲條約必損害國家重大利益，則多數國家仍是在無批准的法律義務下，批准已簽署的條約。

國家批准條約可發生兩種效果：(一)如果該約規定須某數目的國家批准時才於若干日後生效，該國的批准書在那時候送達該約保存者，湊足了條約生效所需的國家數，則批准有使該約生效的效力；(二)於批准書送達保存者的時候，批准國不但須受條約拘束，而且須履行該約所定的義務，也和其他當事國發生該約所定的法律關係。

要是批准不符合國內程序，那批准是不是有效？對於這疑問的說法有三種：一說以爲有國際層次的效力，正如前段所列的效果，批准國須受條約拘束而履行其義務；一說強調等於未批准，那所謂批准的行爲無效，沒有前段所列的效果；還有一說採折衷

---

❷　古典學派 Grotius, Vattel, Bynkershoek 等說，爲維持國家的國際信用，國家受其代理人談判簽字代表行爲的拘束，簽約國便有批准條約的義務。近代學者則認爲，國家的談判或簽字代表非私法上的代理人，國家如果必須批准，則批准流於形式，民主政治要求立法機關監督行政機關的行爲，可以撤銷談判或簽署條約者的行爲，所以國家絕無批准其代表所簽條約的義務。

立場,認爲縱使那批准不符合國內法規定,批准國也應擔負國際責任,不得主張其批准無效而且免受拘束,如果因批准程序違法,使條約不能履行,造成其他締約國的損害,就要負責賠償。這些說法現在已經沒有實質意義了,因爲幾乎所有須經批准的條約,都訂明各締國依其法定程序予以批准,互換或交存批准書後,條約才開始生效,例如聯合國憲章第一一〇條規定:「一、本憲章應由簽字國各依其憲法程序批准之。」一九六三年東京「航空器上所犯罪行及若干其他行爲公約」第二十條訂明:「本公約應由簽署國依其憲法程序批准之。」有了這樣明確的規定時,簽署國便不會作違憲的批准,卽令約內沒有類似的文字,批准條約者也會避免違憲的行爲,

其次談以接受和贊同表示同意承受條約的拘束。

接受 (Acceptance) 和贊同 (Approval) 都可以有兩種用法:一是未經事前簽署便表示同意承受條約拘束,二是作了無拘束性的簽署後所作的批准。兩者的主要差別,全在締約國的意圖上,都可以適用批准條約的全部規則。

在締結條約的程序中,「接受」經由各國實踐逐漸獲得確認,是最近五十年內的事情。在新程序中,「接受」有兩個名稱,一個類似批准,一個類似加入,所以與其說「接受」是訂約方法的創新,不如說「接受」是術語的增添。如果條約規定開放給「須經接受的簽署」(Signature subject to acceptance),則「接受」在國際層次上的程序,就像「須經批准的「簽署」(Signature subject to ratification);條約如果規定開放給未作事前簽署的「接受」,則這程序就像加入。所以條約使用

「接受」一詞，或者使用「批准」一詞，常視約文中的措辭而定，以致在兩種不同的程序上，有相同的名詞出現。另一方面，「接受」現在確有兩個形式了，一是確定一國簽署後同意承受條約拘束的行爲，一是確定一國未曾簽署便同意承受條約拘束的行爲。

　　「須經接受的簽署」，在締約實務上利用，主要是爲了提供「批准」的簡化形式，以便某類條約依某國國內法雖然無須經過批准，其政府仍有再度審酌該約的機會。因此，無論就條約的形式或主旨看，在許多國家內都要依憲法程序批准的條約，必定避免採用「須經接受的簽署」。然而在國際實踐上，爲了盡量方便各國容易訂約起見，多在約文訂明可用批准或接受的方式，以表示同意承受條約的拘束，而且現在已廣泛承認，「接受」通常是用以表示「批准」的簡化程序。

　　關於「接受」的上述說明，大致可准用於「贊同」。贊同用在「須經贊同的簽署」（Signature subject to approval）的較多，條約開放給非簽署國批准時，則少見這一詞語。實則在這兩種情形下，都可以使用「贊同」。

　　爲什麼在締約的新程中，增添「接受」後，又加了「贊同」？此中原因，實不能知，大概是因爲若干國家批准條約的憲法程序上，或其習慣上，使用了「贊同」一詞，影響了國際上的用語和程序。

　　依照本條第二項末句的涵義，同意承受條約拘束的表示方式，無論是接受或是贊同，都必須符合關於批准方式的各種條件，也就是(一)條約已規定可以選用接受或贊同；(二)另經確定

談判國已有協議，各國可以選用接受或贊同；(三)有關國家的代表已在條約上表示「須經接受的簽署」；或(四)這種簽署的意思已載於代表所奉的全權證書，或者他在談判時已作這一表示。

第十五條　以加入表示承受條約拘束之同意

遇有下列情形之一，一國承受條約拘束之同意，以加入表示之：

(甲)條約規定該國得以加入方式表示此種同意；

(乙)另經確定談判國協議該國得以加入方式表示此種同意；

(丙)全體當事國嗣後協議該國得以加入方式表示此種同意。

加入 (Accession) ❷⑥ 是非簽署國在某些情況下成為條約當事國的傳統方式。情況之一是條約規定某國家可以加入，或某類國家可以加入；情況之二是依條約規定原無資格成為當事國的國家，後來經各當事國同意邀請加入。

條約生效前，可否依法加入？以前曾有正反兩說。反對者認為條約生效前，前途未卜，可能永遠不發生效力以拘束任何國家，變成一紙具文，怎可以接納任何國家加入為締約國❷⑦？但是

---

❷⑥ 本公約英文本以 accession 一字表示加入，不用 adhesion(介入)、adherence (選就)，更不用 signature differée (補簽)，因為加入、介入和選就，現在已無差別，補簽通常是適用於談判國，只有偶然的例外。

❷⑦ James L. Brierly's second report on the law of treaties, *Yearbook of the International Law Commission*, 1951, Vol, II, p. 73; Sir Gerald Fitzmaurice's first report on the law of treaies, *Yearbook of the International Law Commission*, 1956, Vol. II. 125-6.

大多數新條約的實例顯示，於規定准許加入時，如果不明定條約於生效前就得加入，便是默許交存加入書，加入書亦計入使條約生效所需的締約國數目中。國際實踐已經有了這樣的發展，本條於是不訂明條約須於生效後才准許加入。

　　表示加入條約的文書，偶有包含「須經批准」字樣的。有這些文字的加入書是否有效？本條不訂明它無效。一九二七年，國際聯盟說，除有相反的明白表示外，加入書具有最後的確定性，這是聯盟旣不鼓勵也不阻止的事情❷。現在聯合國採取相同的做法，就是秘書處收到含有這些文字的加入書時，暫不把它列入擬加入爲締約國的名單中，也不通知其他締約國這一事實，等到收到具最後確定性的加入書時，才予登列，才發通知。因此，本條不提及這種加入書，雖然似乎有所遺漏，卻方便了聯合國秘書處依慣例處理。不過在非由聯合國秘書處保存的條約加入書中，如果含有上述文字，有關條約又無可適用的處理條款時，又該怎麼辦呢？這仍是個疑問。

　　加入條約，是非談判國的行爲❷。條約訂明准許加入，是爲了接納不參與條款議定的國家爲當事國。無論有無明訂，加入國

---

❷ *Official Journal of the League of Nations,* 8th Ordinary Session, Plenary Meetings, p. 141.

❷ 從前曾有加入條約的其他方式，如另訂條約、發表加入聲明、發出通知等。加入國提出加入文件（Act of accession），由全權代表送給條約當事國，經當事國以接受書（Act of acceptance）表示接受後，便重新訂約；加入國的聲明經條約當事國允諾後，加入的程序便告完成。這兩種加入方式，現在幾已被廢棄。至於單方發出通知的方式，則留下文敍述第十六條時補行說明。

必須完成批准、接受或贊同條約的相同步驟·而且依照本條的意旨，須有下列的一種情況才可以加入：(一)條約或其修正條款規定它可以加入；(二)另經確定談判國有意接納它加入；(三)各當事國後來協議同意它加入。(一)和(三)兩種情況，乍看之下，似乎都是修改條約，實則只有(一)的情況是修改條約，(三)的情況雖然有修約的可能，並不一定是修約。

　　無論是經由談判國或全體當事國協議，以准許或邀請某國、某些或某類國家加入條約，那協議都很可能是政治考慮的結果，例如北大西洋公約的當事國，當年決議邀請希臘和土耳其加入前，無疑曾作了深入的政治分析。准許或邀請加入條約既是政治事項，便非法則所能規範，所以本條對於怎樣達成協議的問題，避而不提。

　　多邊條約的主旨，或是釐定某些國家間的權利義務關係，或是澄清、確定、創立國際法則，或是設立國際組織。一國以加入的方式表示同意承受前兩種條約拘束後，只要履行條約，應無旁生的枝節。加入設立某國際組織的條約後，是否當然自動成為該組織的會員國？這問題的答案顯然是否定的。例如批准聯合國憲章的國家，須自行申請並通過憲章所定的入會程序，才能夠變成聯合國會員國。其他國際組織約章的規定，大致相同，也就是一國加入某國際組織為會員國，固然以加入某約章為前提，但加入其約章並不當然成為其會員國。

　　加入條約等於締結條約，加入國的權利義務，除經以保留摒除的以外（關於保留問題容後補敍），和原談判簽署國的相同；除國際組織約章中關於入會的限制外，加入國的地位不因加入時

間的先後而有差別，例如聯合國的選入會員國，於一九五〇年加入的，並不優先於一九八〇年加入的。

除已經履行條約後才申請加入的情形外，加入國自依法加入後才受條約的拘束，也就是在其加入書經收受保存日或加入書生效日起，加入國才成爲條約當事國。

加入條約的國家可否退約？一般說來，因爲情況的基本改變或特殊重要的原因，取得其他當事國同意後、應該可以退約。假如不可以，勉強留它爲當事國，它也許已沒有履約的能力，它固然沒有繼續留爲當事國的需要，其他當事國亦得不到利益，所以總是以准許退約爲原則。可是加入條約和談判後締結條約一樣，如果條約是立法性的，例如本公約所定的全是一般規則，加入本公約的國家，仍以不許退約爲合理。

第十六條　批准書、接受書、贊同書或加入書之交換或交存
　　　　除條約另有規定外，批准書、接受書、贊同書或加入書依下列方式確定一國承受條約拘束之同意：
　　（甲）由締約國互相交換；
　　（乙）將文書交存保管機關；或
　　（丙）如經協議，通知締約國或保管機關。

依照本條規定，任何國家把批准書、接受書、贊同書或加入書作下列的一種方式處理後，其承受條約拘束的同意就告確定了：（一）和同約任何一個締約國交換這些書的一種；（二）把這些書的一種交存保管機關；（三）向其他締約國或保管機關致送已批

准（接受、贊同、加入）的通知。通知的方式，必須經過協議，才可以採用。

就往例說，締結雙邊條約時，才有互換批准書這回事，締結多邊條約時，則不採行這一方式。締結雙邊條約的程序中，無所謂接受、贊同或加入，只要互換了批准書，條約就可以生效。多邊條約的締結程序中才有接受、贊同和加入，而且批准書、接受書、贊同書和加入書多是交存保管機關。保管機關收到後，把這事實通知各有關締約國。

這種交存的方式，有其優點，就是省事、減去了互換的麻煩、易於計算已收到的文書件數、各有關國家易知條約已否生效。

保存機關可以是一個談判國的政府機關，也可以是訂約國際會議地主國的政府機關，由國際組織主持簽訂的條約，則常以該組織的秘書處爲保管機關。例如聯合國憲章的保管機關爲美國政府，本公約的各種文書由聯合國秘書處保管。

交存保管的方式，可能有令人疑惑的時候。只要有了交存行爲，交存國和其他締約國的法律關係就當然發生了？或者要等到保管機關發出通知時才發生？一九六一年外交關係公約和一九六三年領事關係公約，都規定公約生效後的批准書，於交存聯合國秘書處第三十日起，公約對交存國發生效力，不要求等到秘書長通知時才可以生效。原來談判國爲了方便起見，決定以交存批准書爲參加條約的確定性因素，所以其他締約國雖然在交存後若干日，才知道交存的事實，因爲原已同意交存行爲有這種效力，便不得以知道較晚爲理由，而否定這種效力。執行這規則時，如果

在特殊情況下遭遇困難，就唯有讓當事國依個案善加處理了。好在自從聯合國秘書處執行條約保管的任務以來，還沒有任何締約國企圖否定這種效力，秘書處也未曾遭遇想像中可能發生的困難。

　　承受條約拘束的同意，以通知締約國或保管機關的方式表示，現在確實少見了。雖然少見，並不是絕對沒有。偶然有的時候，也只是用於文書互換的簡化式，或文書交存的簡化式（Simplified form of exchange of instruments or Simplified form of deposit of instrument），當其他締約國收到通知時，通知國和被通知國間的法律關係便告確立，也才能開始有這種關係。通知如果送給條約保管機關，則當保管機關收到通知時，通知國和其他締約國間的法律關係便告建立，正和交存批准書的效力一樣。

第十七條　同意承受條約一部分之拘束及不同規定之選擇

　　一、以不妨礙第十九條至第二十三條爲限，一國同意承受條約一部分之拘束，僅於條約許可或其他締約國同意時有效。

　　二、一國同意承受許可選擇不同規定之條約之拘束，僅指明其所同意之規定時有效。

　　有些條約以明文規定，准許締約國只同意承受條約某部分或幾部分的拘束，或准許締約國排除條約某部分，同時准許締約國只批准、接受、贊同或加入條約的一部分。這就是通稱的准許保留。沒有這類規定的條約，依照確立了的規則，任何國家批准、

接受、贊同或加入條約時，都必須包含全約各條款，雖然可依第十九條對可選擇的規定作成保留，卻不得只同意承受其所選部分的拘束。所以本條第一項說：「在不妨礙第十九條至第二十一條」關於多邊條約的規定下，一國同意承受條約一部分的拘束的表示，只於條約許可或各締約國許可時有效，如果沒有這種許可，就無效。

本條第二項規定，各國得從條約的不同規定中作選擇，同時得以其指明的規定為其承受條約拘束的範圍。這種條約絕無僅有，這樣的規定以後也許會由條約保留的程序所代替，因為希望對條約的規定作保留的國家，往往可以從條約的全部規定中作選擇，選定其願受拘束的規定。

現在多邊條約迅速增加，而且擬訂或策畫多邊條約者，也許希望絕大多數國家成為締約國，以求約中規則能夠普遍或廣泛施行，發生普遍性國際法則的效力，因而大開方便之門，讓各國容易變成其所擬條約的締約國，准許各國只受條約一部分規定的拘束，又訂明各國可以承受條約不同規定的拘束。這樣一來，一份條約的不同締約國所負擔的義務便可以大不相同了。

因此，本條的兩項規定，只是針對多邊條約而列的，不涉及雙邊條約的任何一點，不會也不能適用於雙邊條約，假如適用，那是不可思議的事情，因為雙邊條約的任何一邊，如果不願承受約中部分條款或任何條款的拘束，都可以和對造談判，以達成協議，把那部分或那條款刪除，無需援引本條的規定，要是不能達成協議，就只有作罷了，簽訂條約事須等待來日了。

第十八條　不得在條約生效前妨礙其目的及宗旨之義務

一國負有義務不得採取任何足以妨礙條約目的及宗旨之行動：

(甲)如該國已簽署條約或已交換構成條約之文書而須經批准、接受或
　　贊同，但尚未明白表示不欲成爲條約當事國之意思；或

(乙)如該國業已表示同意承受條約之拘束，而條約尚未生效，且條約
　　之生效不稽延過久。

　　任何國家簽署條約後，或交換構成條約的文書後，還沒有明
白表示不想成爲條約締約國的意思以前，縱使其簽署或文書必需
其本國政府批准、接受或贊同，在誠信原則下，也負有義務以
避免可妨礙條約目標和宗旨的行爲。這早已是獲得普遍接受的原
則，非本公約的創意，而且許多國家也遵守施行了，因而學者認
爲，假如簽署國或交換國不遵行，便是濫用權利，違反國際義
務。本公約生效後，公約締約國不遵守，就是違反條約義務。

　　一國表示同意承受條約的拘束後，卽令條約還沒有發生效
力，只要條約的生效不拖延過久，該國在條約生效以前，就已有
義務以避免足以妨礙條約目標和宗旨的一切行爲，也就是說，該
國雖然無需開始履行約中各條款，卻不得破壞條約，譬如甲國於
簽署交換某島的條約後，便不得以任何方法使該島沈沒，甚至不
得准許、縱容或容忍任何人破壞該島，以致交換該島的目標不能
達成。

　　本條第一項所指的簽署，可以適用於雙邊條約和多邊條約，
適用於雙邊條約時，以「須經批准」的爲限；而「須經接受或贊
同」的簽署和文書，只會適用於多邊條約，不會於締結雙邊條約

時有適用的必要。至於第二項的規定，則於締結雙邊和多邊條約時，都有援引的可能，因爲生效所需的批准國數目很多的多邊條約，往往稽延十幾年才能生效，甚至一些雙邊條約也於簽署後多年久載才生效，這兩類條約，永不生效的實例，爲數不少，所以有「條約之生效不稽延過久」的規定。這一規定，確有必要，其理由是：甲國於簽署某條約後，如果因乙國或其他國家故意拖延，以致條約生效遙遙無期或希望渺茫，甲國繼續避免某些行爲的義務，就應予解除，否則違背情理。從另一方面看，這一規定的彈性頗大，不能有確切的解釋。多久才是「過久」❸❶？這眞是無適切答案的問題，所以遇到爭執時，唯有按個案的各種相關情況以謀求答案。一般說來，內容十分複雜的條約，影響各國利益廣泛而長遠的條約，牽涉重大問題的條約，以及締約國特別多的條約，拖延開始生效的歲月必較長，其他條約則可於較短時日內生效。

　　適用「須經批准、接受或贊同」的簽署或構成條約的文書，以締結多邊條約時的頻率較多，簽訂雙邊條約時機會極少。這兩類條約開始生效的日子距離簽署的日子，多邊的常較長，雙邊的往往較短，因而本條第二項的規定，可以說多爲符合締結多邊條約的需要而列載的。

第二節　保　　留

---

❸❶　本條的「不稽延過久」等字是英文同條「…not unduly delayed」的譯文，也可以中譯爲「不合適的稽延」。

第十九條　提具保留

一國得於簽署、批准、接受、贊同或加入條約時，提具保留，但有下列情形之一者不在此限：

(甲)該項保留為條約所禁止者；

(乙)條約僅允許特定之保留而有關之保留不在其內者；或

(丙)凡不屬(甲)或(乙)兩款所稱之情形，該保留與條約目的及宗旨不合者。

所謂保留，依本公約第二條的規定，是指國家在簽署、批准、接受、贊同或加入條約時所作的片面聲明，以排除或更改約中某規定對其適用時的法律效果，無論聲明的措辭或名稱為何。這定義的意思已於前文敍明，不予重述。

對雙邊條約提具保留所引起的問題，比較單純，也較易解決。對多邊條約提具保留所引起的問題，則往往很複雜，不易處理。

兩個國家有意締結條約時，在一般情形下，不應有提具保留這回事，但是這情事並非不能發生。在談判階段，任何一方有新意見時，都可以提出，爭取對方接受，經對方接受後，便無需於簽署時提具保留，如果對方堅決拒絕了，便不會進入簽署程序，所以說簽署雙邊條約時不應有提具保留的情事。然而在民主國家裏，負責談判條約的是行政部門，行政部門已表示完全同意的條約規定，送請立法部門表示意見時，立法部門可能有不同的看法，於是提出保留，例如美國總統於一九七七年與巴拿馬簽訂了新巴拿馬運河條約，送請國會參議院勸告及同意，參議院表示同

意批准時提出保留❸。

　　雙邊條約簽署後，簽署國因其立法機關決議或其他原因對該約提具保留，就等於提出新意見，可由兩國針對新意見重開談判，對方接納新意見，或保留國後來放棄新意見，都可以完成締約程序❸，如果保留被對方拒絕了，又未經撤回，則談判失敗，締約的希望必須放棄，或締約的程序必須停頓，以待來日了。

　　對多邊條約提具的保留，或有不能克服的困難。甲國所提的保留，獲得乙國同意後，可能遭遇丙國反對，也許只被丁國作有條件的接受，而未見其他締約國表示立場，以致保留是否有效的問題發生了。多邊條約牽涉許多國家的時候，困難的程度勢必增加，所以多邊條約的保留問題，於一九四〇年代就受注意和重視，聯合國大會在一九五〇年代也多次考慮❸，國際法院也曾就條約保留案發表諮詢意見❸。這諮詢意見發表後，關於條約保留的效力問題，才獲得權威性的解答，以前存在多年的疑問，於本公約締結後才告消除了。

---

❸　該約訂明美國應於二〇〇〇年把運河和兩岸領土管轄權移歸巴拿馬共和國。參議院的保留大意是：運河由巴拿馬管理時，如果通航自由受到妨礙，美國得以武力恢復並維持這自由。

❸　上註所敍的保留，於美國和巴拿馬重開談判，獲得巴拿馬同意後，該條約終於由雙方批准生效了。

❸　例如於一九五一年討論關於對殘害人群罪防止及懲治公約的保留問題，於一九五七年討論關於政府間海事諮詢組織公約的印度保留案問題。

❸　該案是 The Reservations to the Convention on the Prevention and Punishment of the Crime of Genocide.

　　聯合國國際法委員會，於草擬條約法公約前，對於條約保留問題，不但要加以注意和重視，而且必須作詳細深入縝密的研究，以便提出具體的條文。在聯合國大會裏、國際法院裏和該委員會裏，絕大多數人員都認爲，多邊條約的保留的效力問題，在怎樣的情形下才有效力的問題，是根本性的問題，但是他們對於保留的其他方面，意見十分歧異，莫衷一是。

　　在理論上，曾有反對准許對條約作保留者，也有贊成者。反對者說，准許作保留時，締約國可以摒除其認爲不利的規定，會使條約各條款的一貫統合性被割裂，又造成各締國權利義務的不平等。贊成者說，保留案須經其他締約國同意，則不利其他締約國的保留不能生效，不會因而產生各締約國權利義務不齊一的情形，何況只對約中次要條款作保留，應可使較多的國家成爲締約國。在事實上，則有受保留的和未被保留的多邊條約，國際聯盟主持簽訂的多邊條約，一九三一年以前遭遇二五九件保留，聯合國憲章未曾有任何條款被保留，就憲章的精神和宗旨看，其條款是不允許任何會員國保留的，正如國聯盟約一樣，申請加入聯盟的國家，必須無保留的批准盟約。

　　像本書第二編介紹用語時所敍的，一九五一年，國際法院在殘害人羣罪防止及懲治公約保留案中，沒有法官堅稱任何條約都不應准許保留，只有四位法官認爲，全體一致的傳統原則已被普遍接受爲習慣法則，所以條約的保留須經保留國以外的全體締約國同意才能有效，但是多數法官不敢苟同，雖然承認這原則具有不必爭論的價值，卻反對它已變成法則的見解，並就聯合國大會所提的問題，作如下的答覆：

一、一國提具並堅持的保留遭受一個或多個公約締約國反對，不被其他締約國反對，如果保留與公約目標和宗旨相容，則保留國得被視為公約締約國，如果不相容，則保留國不得被視為公約締約國。

二　(a) 認為保留與公約目標和宗旨相違而反對保留的締約國，得在事實上視保留國為非公約締約國；

　　(b) 認為保留與公約目標和宗旨相容而接受保留的締約國，得在事實上視保留國為公約締約國。

三　(a) 已簽署但未批准公約的國家對保留表示的反對，惟有在該國批准後才有上述第一題答案的法律效果，在批准前只有向他國通知其最後態度的作用。

　　(b) 具有簽署或加入公約資格但未簽署或加入的國家對保留表示的反對沒有法律效果❸。

法院發表上述意見時，說明這是就本案而論，不是就一般條約保留創立規則。可是儘管法院這樣說，法院實已敘明了一些一般性的觀點如下：

(一)在條約關係上，國家非經同意不受拘束，所以對條約所作的保留，非經其同意不能對其有效。

(二)保留非經全體締約國一致接受不發生效力的傳統概念，

---

❸ 除載於 The International Court of Justice, *Reports of Judgments, Advisory Opinions and Orders* (以下簡寫為 I.C.J. Rep.) (1951) 以外，又見於 *Official Records of the General Assembly,* 6th Sess., Supp. No. 9 (A/1858) Par. 16.

如果於談判時已經說明那是必需的，則有毋庸置疑的價值。

（三）但是廣泛參加像殘害人羣罪公約般的多邊條約的國際實踐，現在已有較大的彈性，保留愈多就愈容許默示的同意保留，保留雖然爲某些國家反對，保留國仍被視爲接受保留國所承認的締約國。

（四）在當代國際實踐上，不能因爲某條約沒有關於保留的規定，便推定締約國不得提具保留。該約的性質、宗旨、條款、準備的經過、通過的方式等因素，在沒有明文規定保留問題時，可參酌據以考慮或決定該約是否准許保留。

（五）基於條約完整原則，保留須經全體締約國明示的或默示的同意。現在仍不能證明這已經成爲習慣法則。

以上一般性觀點，當時的國際社會還不能完全接納。聯合國大會收到法院的諮詢意見後，請國際法委員會就多邊條約的保留表示意見。委員會說，法院的與條約目標和宗旨相容的準則，會受主觀見解所左右，普遍適用於多邊公約時必受反對，所以委員會指出，法院的意見只就殘害人羣罪公約保留案而發，不是包括一切情形的妥善規則，於是向大會建議，保留須經全體締約國同意才能生效，保留國才可以成爲締約國。可見多數委員拒絕接受法院的意見，不願修正傳統的全體一致原則。

聯合國大會辯論條約保留問題時，與會者分爲兩派，一派贊成全體一致原則，其中有傾向於三分之二原則者；另一派反對全體同意主義，堅持彈性原則，主張由各國自行決定接受或反對保留，認爲這樣可以保障少數免受多數票壓倒，可以使條約獲得最廣泛的參加。但是另一派又辯稱，彈性原則不宜普遍適用，僅可

適用於像泛美聯盟那麼單純的共同體 。由於各代表意見這麼 紛 岐，大會只能作成決議，請秘書長遵守法院意見，建議各會員國接受法院意見的指引，決定以後聯合國策畫締結條約時以秘書長為條約保管者，應要求其遵照：

（一）繼續擔任含有條約保留或反對保留的文書保管者，而不對這類文書的法律效力表示意見；

（二）把這類關於保留或反對保留的文書全文通知有關國家，讓各國從通知推斷出其法律的結論。

一九五一年以後，國際社會成員迅速增加，可能參加多邊條約的國家日多一日，減少了全體一致原則的適當性和可行性，聯合國秘書長在上述指引下，保管新條約時亦採用彈性原則，把收到的文書轉知各有關國家，不加註意見，把附保留的文書交存國計入足以使條約生效的締約國數目中。此外，許多國家表示反對全體一致原則 ，國際法院又已經指出該原則未成為習慣規則 ，所以許多對保留緘默的國家，在實踐上已承認保留國是公約締約國。

由於國際情況的顯著改變，十一年後（一九六二年），國際法委員會才能達成下列共識：條約規定保留事宜者，依規定處理；明文或默示規定禁止的保留，無效；明文或默示許可的保留，有效；條約未規定保留事宜者，保留和反對保留的正當性標準，是其是否與條約目標和宗旨相容 。委員會已注意到：這一「相容」標準，在無解釋條約的法庭或經授權的其他機關的情形下，施行時因受主觀考量的影響，會有不能克服的困難，因而以為締約國數極少的條約，如果未規定保留事宜，則可用全體同意原則

以處理保留問題；至於締約國很多時怎樣處理呢？仍然沒有答案。

　　國際法委員會還有其他考慮。締約國很多的條約，其保留應經相當多締約國接受才有效？保留不符條約宗旨，又只得一國或很少國家接受，保留國就可以成爲締約國？這顯然不妥善。談判時因爲妥協或後來准許破壞條約宗旨的保留，由於不表示反對者被視爲默示同意，以致雖有某國（或少數國）的強烈反對，保留國仍可成爲締約國，和若干國家發生條約關係。這也是要預防的事情。所以有委員主張保留須經某數（譬如三分之一）締約國接受，或於保留撤回後，保留國才可以成爲締約國。

　　又有委員覺得，本公約的完整固然重要，其最大可能的彈性也不可缺少，其他條約亦如此；大多數保留只涉及保留國不能容忍的枝節，只是稍爲減損了條約的完整性，或者縱使涉及條約的重要規定，如果保留國只有幾個，那減損也甚少；如果保留國衆多，又涉及條約的重要規定，就表示條約本身須經進一步考慮了，但是，無論如何，那完整性被減損的條約，仍然是其他締約國間的重要協議。於是追求條約效用和條約完整時，便要爭取足夠的締約國，使其接受約中多數條款。

　　委員會也不贊同另一意見，即條約的普及性要求准許保留，以便接受保留的國家和緘默的國家與保留國維持條約關係。而在事實上，准許保留的條約，會使某些國家較易參加，較易擴大其適用範圍，因爲可以作一個或一個以上保留時，那些國家才能夠參加，否則寧可不參加，也不願撤銷其保留。

　　今天由聯合國策畫的條約簽訂會議，參加談判的國家，爲數

必在一百個以上，其政治、經濟、文化情況都很不相同，爲了爭取其中絕大多數爲締約國，就要考慮給予提具保留的機會，免致因爲一國或數國反對而排除了那些保留國；其次，談判國如果不採取必要的步驟，以吸收較多的國家參加多邊條約，則會阻礙經由條約以發展國際關係，另一方面，如果從寬准許保留，則不當地減損條約完整性的程度也會較小。在兩害相權取其輕的原則下，委員會便認爲，在當前對傳統概念挑戰的時代，預料能取得共同協議的最廣泛接受的法則，應是最投合國際社會目前需要的法則。

委員會再定下列兩個規則，以保障締約國的實質利益，並且避免作保留國和不作保留國間的不平等：

(一)在合理時間內表示反對保留的國家，得視條約不在其與保留國間發生效力；

(二)接受保留的國家，得反對保留國把本身已免除的條約義務加諸接受國。

在實踐上，保留國和不作保留國能不能完全平等？不能，因爲不作保留國面對其他不作保留國時，應遵守條約全部規定，包括保留國已經摒除的規定；被摒除的規定，保留國不受拘束，不作保留國則仍有履行的義務。然而另一方面，也不因而增加不作保留國的義務，因爲在正常情形下，作保留的國家，最少要受條約最低限度的拘束，不作保留國對著其他不作保留國，橫豎要遵行約中各項規定，不受有無締約國作保留的影響。被保留的規定，不作保留國如認爲最重要，可以強烈反對，使條約不在其與保留國間生效。另一種情況是：不作保留國未參加條約前，知道

其他國家是面對著那些保留而參加的，就會索性拒絕參加。所以堅決反對保留的國家，參加談判時，盡力爭取以明文禁止保留並且維持全約完整性，才是保護己身的適當途徑，爭取不成時，唯有置身度外了。

委員會反覆計議後，終於採用保留彈性制，讓各國自行決定是否接受保留，由其決定是否視保留國爲同約締約國；委員會也決定，彈性制適用於極少和極多締約國的多邊條約❸ 。

本條的規定，便是基於以上多年多次的研議而作成，並經由維也納國際會議折衷改進後通過的。

本條規定條約得准許保留 ，除條約禁止者外 ， 保留可於簽署、批准、接受、贊同或加入條約時提出；不屬於條約明定准許範圍內的，違背條約目標和宗旨的，都應無效。這種規定的利弊得失，已於上文敍明，用不著重述。這裏只指出，本條不意味或暗示保留可於談判時提出，談判時的保留是不許可的，因爲談判時條約的實質內容、形式、文字等未定，有特殊主張或要求的國家，可以提出作爲談判事項，不必保留，而且其主張或要求一經提出，就不能視爲或稱爲保留了。

簽署條約時提具保留，效果應該比較好，因爲其他國家於簽署或批准同一條約時，就表示接受或反對那保留，例如中華民國代表反對巴黎和平會議處理山東省問題的決定，於一九一九年五

---

❸ *Yearbook of the International Law Commission,* 1962, Reports of the International Law Commission on the Work of Its Thirteenth Session, Commentary to the Present Article.

月六日聲明，要對和平條約中關於山東省部分提具保留，和平會議秘書長通知中國代表說，會議不同意這一保留，中國代表於和約簽字前三小時又聲明說，中國代表團的簽署應不阻止中國要求將來再考慮山東省問題。這一保留又被拒絕後，中國代表便不簽署和約。

批准條約時提具保留，所得反應不如簽署時提具的那麼迅速，其他國家如果還未批准條約，就要等到其批准時才知道其如何反應，如果已經批准，就要等到其收到關於保留的通知時，才會有反應（卽接受保留、反對保留或默示接受而不作任何表示）。對雙邊條約的保留，通常是附於批准書上，交給締約對造，於對造同意後，再把同意事實記載於書後。現在交通方便，電傳迅速，締約此方有意提出保留時，如果有彼方使節駐紮此方京都，則立刻通知他（她），由他（她）請示本國政府是否接受已提出的保留，如果沒有這一使節，也可以經由其他方式探悉對方立場，要是對方反對保留而願再談判，當卽重開談判，談妥後再簽署和批准，所以先在批准書附上保留的做法，眞正少見了。至於對多邊條約的保留，依照當代的習慣做法，都是在批准書附上保留後，送交保管國（機關），由保管國（機關）把保留通知有關各國，接到通知的國家把表示接受或反對保留的文書送達保管國（機關）。默示接受保留的國家，當然可以不作書面表示。若有必要，保管國（機關）再分別通知各有關國家。

接受、贊同和加入，都是同意承受多邊條約拘束的表示方式，只適用於多邊條約，不能移用於雙邊條約。然而僅由兩談判國完成的某種條約，雖然可能最初只是雙邊條約，但因有使其普

及的必要，開放給各國加入，終於變成了多邊條約，一九二八年
巴黎非戰公約便是一例。在這特殊的訂約程序中，加入等等方式
自可適用了。

　　無論如何，一國接受、贊同或加入多邊條約時提具保留，都
必須經過其國內的程序，而且只於符合本條規定的情形下才能成
爲締約國。國際聯盟秘書處負責保管條約時，認爲加入國如果提
具保留，則其保留未取得其他締約國同意前，其加入手續視爲未
完成。可是自一九五一年以後，尤其是本公約生效以後，聯合國
秘書處已把提具保留的加入國列入可以使條約生效所需的國家名
單中。

　　　　　　　　第二十條　接受及反對保留

一、凡爲條約明示准許的保留，無須其他締約國事後予以接受，但條
　　約規定須如此辦理者，不在此限。

二、倘自談判國之有限數目及條約之目的與宗旨，可見全體當事國間
　　適用全部條約爲每一當事國同意承受條約拘束之必要條件時，保
　　留須經全體當事國接受。

三、倘條約爲國際組織之組織約章，除條約另有規定外，保留須經該
　　組織主管機關接受。

四、凡不屬以上各項所稱之情形，除條約另有規定外：

　　(甲)保留經另一締約國接受，就該另一締約國而言，保留國卽成
　　　　爲條約之當事國，但須條約對各該國均已生效；

　　(乙)保留經另一當事國反對，則條約在反對國與保留國間並不因
　　　　此而不生效，但反對國確切表示相反之意思者，不在此限。

　　(丙)表示一國同意承受條約拘束而附以保留之行爲，一俟至少有

　　另一締約國接受保留，卽生效力。

五、就適用第二項與第四項而言，除條約另有規定外，倘一國在接獲
　　關於保留之通知後十二個月期間屆滿時，或至其表示同意承受條
　　約拘束之日爲止，兩者中以較後之日期爲準，迄未對保留提出
　　反對，此項保留卽視爲業經該國接受。

　　本條第一項的意義，一望可知，旣明白，又確切，規定除條
約有相反的規定外，明示准許的保留（這必然排除所謂隱含的准
許），經提具後，用不着其他締約國表示接受，也不問是於批
准、接受、贊同或加入條約時提具的，無論條約已否生效，保留
必自動生效。

　　一九六二年，如前文提過的，國際法委員會放棄「一小羣國
家締結的條約」的概念，因爲許多政府評論委員會的報告時，認
爲「一小羣國家」的涵義不確定，不宜用於彈性的普通（一般）
規則。可是委員會於一九六七年的概念，仍和以前的略同，只改
以「談判國之有限數目」爲標準，於本條第二項規定，「自談判
國之有限數目及條約目的與宗旨」，可見全約規定適用於全體當
事國是各談判國同意承受條約拘束的必要條件時，保留非經全體
當事國接受，不發生效力。反過來說，如果談判國不重視或不主
張這一條件，保留就可以不經全體當事國同意而發生效力。這時
候應請注意，「談判國之有限數目」，正如「一小羣國家」，涵
義模糊，無法確定，究竟多少國家才不是「有限數目」（Limited
number）？實在有解釋上的疑問，直到現在還沒有權威性的解

釋❸。至於條約的目標和宗旨，如果已於約文中明確昭示了，把條約對照保留案，便可知道有沒有經全體當事國接受的必要。另一方面，從這一項的文字看，就知道全體一致同意原則並未完全放棄。自本公約生效施行後，遇有不規定保留事項的條約時，這傳統原則雖然不一定自動適用，如果適用，就如一九五一年國際法院少數法官所說的，適用以維持條約的完整和各締約國權利義務的平等，但其適用須受很大的限制──唯有於談判國一致協議時，才有適用的機會，如果談判國沒有協議，就無須適用。

　　本條第三項所列的是特殊規則，只適用於國際組織的組織約章，規定對約章的保留，須經有關組織的有權機關接受，才能生效。一九五九年，印度發表聲明，接受政府間海事諮詢組織 (Inter-Governmental Maritime Consultative Organization) 公約，重提保留問題。該聲明送達諮詢組織後，又轉送到聯合國秘書處。因為聯合國大會再度確認前已給予秘書長的指示，並且擴大該指示的範圍，以包括聯合國主持締結的一切條約，不以一九五二年以前締結的為限，所以秘書處說，印度的聲明必須轉送有權解釋該公約的機關❸，以致國際組織約章的保留問題，當時仍然未得解答。

　　國際法委員會則認為：國際組織約章的完整，究竟可以從寬

---

❸　「談判國之有限數目」的英文原文是「limited number of the negotiating states」。其草擬者究竟着眼於「有限數目」或意指「少數談判國」？實在不能代為辨明，如果着眼於談判國，不把重點放於「有限數目」上，則中文以譯為「少數談判國」較佳。

❸　海事諮詢組織公約，亦是聯合國策畫下的產物，所以也在聯合國大會給予秘書處的指示所包括的範圍內。

解釋被削減到何種程度的問題，必須由其會員於有權的機關中集體作決定，即令約章中沒有關於保留的規定，也要經集體的決定。例如聯合國憲章沒有規定是否准許保留，在事實上，又沒有國家申請加入聯合國時，對憲章提具保留，所以這憲章是否准許保留的問題，至今仍然存在。至於其他以國家爲會員的普遍性國際組織，如國際勞工組織、國際民用航空組織、國際復興開發銀行、世界衞生組織等等，其約章可否受保留的問題，雖然沒有任何國家正式提出，卻在理論上還是疑問。

本條第四項包括三種（第一至第三項以外的）情形。在這些情形下，如果不受條約規定的限制，就會：（一）只要有一國接受保留，條約又已對保留國和接受保留國生效，接受國就得視保留國爲條約當事國，兩國便發生條約關係；（二）反對保留國必須明白表示否認條約在其與保留國間發生效力，條約才不對其有拘束力，否則在其與保留國間發生效力，因爲有些國反對某一（些）保留，只是基於政策或原則，而無意使條約不在其與保留國間發生效力；（三）保留最初最少也要有一個締約國接受時才發生效力，不是在提出時生效；另一方面，保留只要有一個締約國接受就生效，無須有兩國以上接受才開始生效。保留一經生效，保留國就受條約拘束。這表示保留國受條約拘束的開始時間，和第一個接受國接受保留的時間相同。

本項又准許締約國就條約某些規定只和某些國家發生條約關係，不要求全體締約國就條約全部規定和其他全體締約國發生條約關係，所以甲締約國可就條約第一至第十條的規定和乙丙丁三國發生條約關係，乙締約國可就條約第五至第九條的規定和戊己

庚辛等國發生條約關係，戊已庚辛四國如果不願就第一至第四條
及第十條的規定和甲乙丙或丁國有這種關係，便可於甲乙丙或丁
國提出關於這五條的保留時，表示反對，並聲明約中這幾條不在
其與甲乙丙丁國間生效。

　　本條第五項的主旨，在訂明締約國表示接受或反對保留的期
限，以免保留經提具後，長遠不能確定有沒有締約國接受或反
對。這一點不確定，便不能知道保留國已否成了條約當事國、條
約已否在保留國和反對國間生效、何國已免除條約所定的某項義
務、以及何國已捨棄條約所給予的某項權利。

　　依照本項規定，締約國須在接到關於保留的通知後十二個月
內，或在表示同意承受條約拘束的當天，表示接受或反對已提具
的保留。如果十二個月期限截止日期在表示同意承受條約拘束的
日期之後，則以截止日期為限，如果截止日期在前，則以表示這
種同意的當天為準。譬如甲國的保留提出後，各締約國接受和反
對的截止日期為一九九二年一月一日，乙國表示同意承受條約拘
束的日期，如果是一九九一年十二月三十一日，則其接受或反對
保留須於第二天表示，如果是一九九二年一月一日或隨後任何一
日，都必須於一月一日或隨後任何一日表示。截止日期終了後，
不表示接受或反對的締約國視為已默示接受保留。

　　十二個月的表示期限，是過長或過短或適中呢？這是難答的
問題。過去有定為三個月的❸，有定為六個月的❹，還有定為九

----

❸　例如一九五二年便利商品樣本及廣告材料輸入國際公約 (Interna-
　　tional Convention to Facilitate the Importation of Com-
　　mercial Samples and Advertising Material)。
❹　例如一九二九年禁止偽造貨幣國際公約 (International　Conven-

十天的❹。現在國際社會成員眾多，多邊條約的締約國也必多，其內容也可能是錯綜複雜，因而給予締約國十二個月的期限，以對多邊條約的保留表示立場，可以說是恰當的。

上述公約都規定，在截止日期終了時，不表示反對保留者，就視為已經接受。一九五九年美洲法學家委員會 (Inter-American Council of Jurists) 第四屆會議，於其最後議定書中建議，締約國如於收到關於保留的通知一年內不答覆，就應假定其不反對。可見默示接受保留的概念，早已存在。國際法院於殘害人羣案中，也曾宣示這概念已在國家實踐上獲得接納，並已取得國際上的承認，所以本條採默示接受主義，實非偶然。

第二十一條　保留及對保留提出之反對之法律效果

一、依照第十九條、第二十條及第二十三條對另一當事國成立之保留：

(甲)對保留國而言，其與該另一當事之關係上照保留之範圍修改保留所關涉之條約規定；及

(乙)對該另一當事國而言，其與保留國之關係上照同一範圍修改此等規定。

二、此項保留在條約其他當事國相互間不修改條約之規定。

---

tion for the Suppression of Counterfeiting Currency).

❹　例如一九五〇年失蹤人死亡宣告公約 (Convention on the Declaration of Death of Missing Persons) 和一九五七年已婚婦女國籍公約 (Convention on the Nationality of Married Women)。

三、倘反對保留之國家未反對條約在其本國與保留國間生效，此項保留所關涉之規定在保留之範圍內於該兩國間不適用之。

　　本條第一項所指的，是以條約已生效為前提，依照本公約第十九條第二十條和第二十三條對另一當事國成立了的保留。保留成立後，保留國和該另一當事國間的關係所涉及的條約規定，便須依照保留的範圍來改變，改變後可以適用的規定必減少了。譬如甲國提具保留，乙國接受了，乙國便是另一當事國，保留卽在甲乙兩國間成立，兩國關係所牽涉的條約規定，就要按照保留的內容加以修改，修改後，約中規範兩國關係的規定當然減少了。這種保留，對於不提保留國與其他不提保留國間的條約原有規定，不發生影響，不促使其改變，也不使其有改變的必要，因為這些國家間的條約關係，不以接受保留為條件，和保留沒有關連。

　　本條第三項是為反對保留國留餘地，也是一種彈性的規定。依照這規定，一國反對某國的保留時，雖然不反對條約在其與該國間生效，被保留的約中規定卻不對其與該國適用。國際法院在殘害人羣案中曾說，「認為保留與公約目標和宗旨相違而反對保留的締約國，得在事實上視保留國為非公約締約國。」本條第三項，所以是補充了法院的意見，使反對國固然可以視保留國不是當事國，也可以視其為條約當事國，雖然保留範圍內的規定不對兩國適用。這無疑是國際法委員會的一項進步和發展，比法院的意見有更大的彈性。

　　第二十二條　撤回保留及對保留提出之反對

一、除條約另有規定外，保留得隨時撤回，無須經已接受保留之國家同意。

二、除條約另有規定外，對保留提出之反對得隨時撤回。

三、除條約另有規定或另經協議外：

（甲）保留之撤回，在對另一締約國之關係上，自該國收到撤回保留之通知之時起方始發生效力；

（乙）對保留提出之反對之撤回，自提出保留之國家收到撤回反對之通知時起方始發生效力。

雖然偶然有人說，保留一經另一國接受，便建立了保留提出國和保留接受國間的條約關係，所以保留非經接受國同意，不得撤回。這一意見不但有其理由，而且有其先例。一九一一年，英國批准保護海獺公約時提具保留，聲明該約第三條須由英國取得各自治領同意後才對英國生效。這一保留後經各締約國同意，已發生效力，再後來，這一保留經各自治領同意，又獲得公約各當事國同意，才被撤回了。但是，儘管這樣，本條第一項還是規定：除條約有相反的規定外，保留可以不經接受國同意就撤回，而且可以隨時撤回，沒有期日上的限制。這是基於各締約國的一致熱切期望，期望保留國儘早放棄保留，趕快重新參與條約全部規定的施行。依照這一項的規定，撤回保留可以：（一）無時間的限制，（二）不以保留接受國同意為前提，和（三）不負擔因保留而增加的任何責任。

反對保留的締約國，本來希望保留國放棄保留，希望保留國和全體當事國共同履行全約的規定。對保留提出反對後，保留國可能放棄保留，也可能堅持保留。保留繼續維持，則反對未達目

的。保留一旦撤回，則反對失去對象。本條第二項於是規定，對
保留提出的反對可以隨時無條件的撤回，正和撤回保留一樣。

　　保留國對條約的規定既作了保留，則於撤回保留時有通知條
約其他當事國的責任，使其與彼等的關係恢復條約原定的狀態。
由於撤回後要發通知，這種撤回不是立刻生效，除條約有相反的
規定或另經協議外，要等到其他當事國收到通知時，才發生效
力。這種規定會使撤回的生效期日不確定，可能有甲國收到後數
十日乙國才收到的情形，無疑是一個缺點，應設法避免。怎樣設
法呢？改定撤回行為發生後若干日生效？如果這樣改，若干日應
該是多少天？改為撤回的通知發出後若干日撤回便自動生效？這
若干日又應為幾日？這些日數總是沒有絕對標準的，同樣會引起
爭論。所以規定通知收到時生效，是不得已的決定，也是缺點較
少的抉擇。

　　撤回對保留提出的反對，於保留國收到撤回的通知時就生
效，立刻使保留國和反對國間的條約關係恢復條約原定的狀態。
只就這一點說，撤回對保留提出的反對和撤回保留有相同的法律
效果。

　　論者或說，一國收到撤回的通知後，無論那是關於保留的或
反對保留的通知，都應有一段日子，以便適應，不應於通知抵
達時撤回就立刻生效，因為已依照條約規定在國內採行的某些措
施，須假以時日作調整，例如修改法律、頒布命令或添置人員，
才能夠適應那撤回所造成的新情勢，而本條卻未顧及這種需要，
未免是一個缺點。好在這種需要既不重大，又不常有，只要有關
國家誠信相處，困難應可迎刃而解。譬如撤回國先透露即將撤回

的決定，若干日後才正式發出撤回的通知，其他有關國家便不會有措手不及的窘境。

總觀上文所敍關於條約保留的各點，可知條約保留的情狀眞是複雜無邊。條約有未經任何當事國提具保留的（如聯合國憲章），有只經一國提出一項保留的，有經一國提出二項以上保留的，有經多國提出一項或多項保留的。保留的內容有相同的，也有互異的，依國際法院規約第三十六條第二項（所謂任選條款）所作聲明中的保留，就有這種情形。條約的保留中，一些獲得其他當事國全體接受，一些獲得其他當事國多數接受，一些只獲得少數國家接受。可是因爲一國收到關於保留的通知十二個月內不表示立場，便被視爲已接受保留，所以無論各項保留的內容怎麼複雜，各締約國對於保留的反應只能有兩種，就是接受和反對，跟着就各當事國和保留國的關係說，僅有接受國和反對國的區分。每一項保留遭遇的接受國和反對國不同，接受國和反對國的數目不一，其接受和反對的表示日期參差，其撤回反對和保留國撤回保留的日期不齊，以致保留國、接受保留國和反對保留國受條約不同規定拘束的時間有別，所以要確定甲當事國與乙當事國在子條約下的法定關係，就非查明上述種種相關事實不可，而且非以查證時的事實爲基準不行，因爲早晚事實有變，變是常態，不變只是偶然而已。

前文說過，撤回保留和撤回對保留提出的反對，都無需經接受保留國或保留提具國同意，便可生效。這一規定的目的，在便利這兩種撤回。就短期的事實看，這只是一種期望，就遠程想像，將來能不能達到目的的一部分呢？現在還言之過早，不敢蠡

測。但是，就經驗說，國家的國際行為，完全以其利益為前提，
需要經過容易或艱難的程序，常和其行為或不行為無關。所以在
長遠的將來，這目的仍是可望而不可卽。

第二十三條　關於保留之程序

一、保留、明示接受保留及反對保留，均必須以書面提具並致送締約
　　國及有權成為條約當事國之國家。

二、保留係在簽署須經批准、接受或贊同之條約時提具者，必須由保
　　留國在表示同意承受條約拘束時正式確認。遇此情形，此項保留
　　應視為在其確認之日提出。

三、明示接受保留或反對保留係在確認保留前提出者，其本身無須經
　　過確認。

四、撤囘保留或撤囘對保留提出之反對，必須以書面為之。

　　本約所稱的程序，是國際層次的，不是國內的。國內的程
序，隨不同的國家而有差別，非常複雜，不能在這裏綜述，這裏
也沒有綜述的必要。

　　本條訂明：條約的保留、明示接受保留和明示反對保留，三
者都必須以書面作成，口頭的保留、接受或反對，都不符合規
定。三者依照規定作成後，還要送給各締約國和有權成為條約當
事國的國家。所謂「有權成為條約當事國的國家」，是指已正式
簽署條約的國家、可經由接受或贊同條約而成為條約當事國的國
家，以及被邀請加入條約的國家。

　　所謂致送，就是把保留的文書、接受保留的文書或反對保留

的文書傳給上述三大類國家。至於經由何種途徑致送，則沒有規定。依照前文有關的說明類推，致送的途徑應該是：關於雙邊條約保留的文書，由此方逕送彼方；關於多邊條約保留的文書，則在特殊情形下，或條約已有規定時，由保留提出國、接受國或反對國分別送給各有關國家；在普通情形下，並且按照聯合國成立後的實例，由於國際組織策畫主持下締結的多邊條約，都訂明條約保管機關，所以關於這些條約保留的文書，都是先送達保管機關，再由保管機關分別致送各相關國家，而其保管機關常是聯合國秘書處。由一（數）國發起推動完成的多邊條約，如果訂明該國負責保管條約，則關於該約保留的文書，先送達該國政府，然後由該國政府分別轉知各相關國家。由保管機關（政府）轉送的程序，可以減少不必要的文書手續，是一大優點。

　　一國簽署須經批准、接受或贊同的條約時，可以提具保留。簽署時提具的保留，必須於該國以批准、接受或贊同的方式，表示同意承受條約拘束時加以確認，才算有效，因為該國批准、接受或贊同條約的日期，不但在簽署的日期之後，而且可能距離簽署日期很久，該國經過這段期間後，或已決定放棄原已提具的保留，所以本條第二項要求該國於批准、接受或贊同條約時，正式確認其已提具的保留。簽署條約和確認保留的日期，一在前，一在後，都涉及保留，究竟以那一個日期為保留提出的日期呢？本條規定以確認的日期為保留提出的日期，不追溯簽署的日期。

　　為什麼要確定保留提出的日期？因為法律文書的作成，固然需要標示日期，和那保留有關的國家間的法律關係，也須自所定日期起建立。條約的保留，涉及保留提出國、接受國和反對國間

的條約關係，而這關係的確定，必須以保留提出的日期爲基準。譬如甲國於子日提出保留，乙國於子日表示接受，則乙國在事實上視甲國從子日起爲條約當事國，兩國便在摒除被保留的條款或規定事項的情形下，當天便建立了條約關係。又譬如丙國於丑日提出保留，丁國於同日表示反對，同時聲明不願條約在丙丁兩國間生效，則從丑日起，丁國不視丙國爲同一條約當事國，因而確定了丙丁兩國沒有該條約的法律關係。從此可見，保留提出的日期確有加以確定的必要。

　　在保留經正式確認以前，對保留的明示接受、對保留的明示反對，兩者都無需經過確認，唯有於經正式確認的保留內容主旨改變時，這接受或反對才須經確認。譬如原來提具的保留目的是東上，被確認時已改變爲西下，這時候，以前表示的接受和反對，都可以改變，當然也可以不改變，改變或不改變，全可由原表示國自行決定，因爲嚴格說來，保留的內容主旨改變時，已使原保留成爲新的保留，經保留國正式確認後，各締約國便可依新的保留重行考慮，不爲已表示的接受或反對所限制，亦無作任何表示的義務。

　　撤回保留和撤回對保留提出的反對，也要以書面作成，因爲附於雙邊條約的保留，經撤回後，須把撤回的文書送給保留國的他造，以便他造採取必要的措施；附於多邊條約的保留，經撤回後，通常須把撤回書送請條約保管機關（國家）登記，保管機關（國家）再轉知各有關國家。撤回對保留提出的反對，在事實上也需要辦理同樣的手續。

　　對條約的保留一經提出後，除可有上述的反對外，也可有上

述的接受。而接受，一如上文所說，除明示的以外，還有默示的。默示的接受已被各國承認，也爲國際法院所肯定。默示的接受本來自始就沒有書面的表示，所以撤回時不應有也無需有具體的表示，假如要有，就是因爲原有的保留內容主旨變更了，或者因爲默示接受國的立場改變了，由接受換爲反對了。由於本公約和國際習慣都不承認默示的反對，所以其反對必須以明示的方式表示，也就是必須以書面作成。

保留的明示接受，也應該可以撤回。可是本條只提及撤回保留和撤回對保留提出的反對，要用書面作成，不說撤回對保留的接受，亦應以書面作成。何故？這是令人費解的問題，本公約擬訂者也許是疏忽了。無論依本公約或國際習慣，明示接受條約保留的國家，可以隨時撤回已表示的接受，其接受原是明示的，撤回時便須以書面表示，若說可用默示的方式表示，可以達到撤回的目的嗎？撤回國和保留國間的條約關係需不需要跟着調整？如果沒有撤回國的書面通知，又根據什麼作調整？爲了解答這些問題以及實際需要，撤回對保留的明示接受，必須以書面作成。

不過這裏仍應一提，但願本條未提及上述撤回須以書面作成，不是由於本公約擬訂者的疏忽，而是故意支吾含糊，留給有關國家自行決定，希望其別作這種撤回。

第三節　條約之生效及暫時適用

第二十四條　生　效

一、條約生效之方式及日期，依條約之規定或依談判國之協議。

二、倘無此種規定或協議，條約一俟確定所有談判國同意承受條約之拘束，卽生效力。

三、除條約另有規定外，一國承受條約拘束之同意如係由於條約生效後之日期確定，則條約自該日起對該國生效。

四、條約中爲條約約文之認證、國家同意承受條約拘束之確定、條約生效之方式或日期、保留、保管機關之職務以及當然在條約生效前發生之其他事項所訂立之規定，自條約約文議定時起適用之。

　　條約規定生效方式和生效日期的，當然依照規定的方式和日期開始發生效力，如果沒有這種規定，就必須由談判國協議，以決定條約生效的方式和日期。這種協議，唯有談判國才有權達成，而且應於條約未簽署前達成，以便非談判國批准、接受、贊同或加入條約，所以非談判國沒有機會參與協議，也不應邀請非談判國參與協議。本條只訂明由談判國協議，不提及非談判國，就是基於此理。而在事實上，只有談判國決定條約生效的方式和日期，條約沒有規定時，固然由談判國決定，條約如果已有規定，也是談判國的主意和協議，沒有協議，約中就沒有規定。

　　其次，卽令沒有關於條約生效的方式和日期的規定，又沒有談判國的協議，條約還是可以生效。那就是，能夠確定各談判國同意承受條約拘束時，條約便當然生效。這裏必須注意，本條第二項用「所有談判國」等字，不用「過半數」或「大多數」等字，就是要求須於全體談判國的意思經確定時，條約才開始生效。因此，某一條約如果沒有規定生效的方式和日期，其談判國又無協議，則於簽署後，很可能要等到談判國最後一個表示同意承受條約拘束時，才符合本項的規定而生效。今後爲使多邊條約

儘早生效計，應在約中規定生效方式和生效日期，如不能做到，
也應訂明生效所需數目的批准書、接受書、贊同書或加入書交存
保管機關（政府）時生效，正如近年來若干公約所訂明的。

條約生效後，某國才表示同意承受該約的拘束，如果該約沒
有相反的規定，則在該國的同意被確定的當天，該約便對該國生
效，在該日以前，該約不對該國有拘束力，只對其他當事國有
效。這就是條約「非經同意不受拘束」的基本原則。

本書已在前編裏提及，條約包括序文、實質條款和程序條款
等。實質條款常涉及締約國的權利義務，依條約「非經同意不受
拘束」的基本原則，非等到締約國表示同意承受條約拘束時，不
能開始適用。但這只是就條約的實質條款立論，關於程序條款所
列的一些事項，卻不受這原則限制，必須於約文議定時、條約生
效前、締約國表示同意承受條約拘束前，就開始適用，否則很難
達成締結條約的願望。這些事項是：（一）約文的認證；（二）國家
同意承受條約拘束的確定；（三）條約生效的方式；（四）條約生效
的日期；（五）條約的保留；（六）條約保管機關的職務；（七）條約
生效前發生的其他事項。

上述（一）至（六）的事項，前文已經分別敍明，用不着重述。
（七）的其他事項，究竟指什麼事項呢？大體說來，專就雙邊條約
看，可以指互換批准書的地點、是否再簽議定書等事項；就多邊
條約看，可以指締約國的特殊聲明、形近保留而無保留實質的文
書等事項，甲國表示不因批准條約而有承認乙締約國或其政府的
效力等，便屬於這類事項。

本條第四項的規定，不是一項創制，而是歸納沿襲多世紀以

來的國際習慣。許多國家和國際組織，締結條約時都已依本項
規定處理。例如前述中華民國與美利堅合衆國間友好通商航海條
約，在第十三條規定：「一、本約應予批准，批准書應在南京儘
速互換。二、本約自互換批准書之日起發生效力，並自該日起在
五年期限內，繼續有效。」又如一九四五年制訂的聯合國憲章，
於第一百一十條規定：「一、本憲章應由簽字國各依其憲法程序
批准之。二、批准書應交存美利堅合衆國政府。該國政府應於每
一批准書交存時通知各簽字國，如本組織秘書長業經委派時，並
應通知秘書長。三、一俟美利堅合衆國政府通知已有中華民國、
法蘭西、蘇維埃社會主義共和國聯邦、大不列顛及北愛爾蘭聯
合王國與美利堅合衆國、以及其他簽字國之過半數將批准書交存
時，本憲章卽發生效力。美利堅合衆國政府應擬就此項交存批准
書之議定書並將副本分送所有簽字國。四、本憲章簽字國於憲章
發生效力後批准者，應自其各將批准書交存之日起爲聯合國之創
始會員國。」本公約於一九六九年定稿，距離一九四五年已二十
四年，足證本項規定受了先例的影響，非新創的制度。

第二十五條　暫時適用

一、條約或條約之一部分於條約生效前在下列情形下暫時適用：

　　(甲)條約本身如此規定；或

　　(乙)談判國以其他方式協議如此辦理。

二、除條約另有規定或談判國另有協議外，條約或條約一部分對一國
　　之暫時適用，於該國將不欲成爲條約當事國之意思通知已暫時適
　　用條約之其他各國時終止。

　　此刻首先應該說明，條約暫時適用，和條約不經批准便生效施行，兩者頗不相同。前者是指條約須經批准才能生效施行，但在未經批准前，由於事實需要，又具緊急性，談判國便協議條約應暫時先行適用，以待來日批准。後者是指無需經過批准便可生效施行的條約，或因條約所定的事項無須經過批准（例如互設領事館的條約，多數國內習慣是不必經立法機關同意或政府首長批准），或因必須高度保密，或因儘速爭取時間，談判國便協議條約於簽署時就生效施行。

　　條約的暫時適用，又和本公約第二十四條第四項的適用不同。暫時適用的條約規定，於條約一旦生效時便無再援引的必要，因爲條約生效後，各締約國可以正式依規定適用，無需暫時適用了。第二十四條第四項，是適用於訂約的程序事項，如約文的認證、條約生效日期等，沒有條約生效前生效時或生效後的區別，固然可於條約生效前適用，亦可於條約生效後長遠適用。

　　要暫時適用條約的規定，便要在條約的全部或一部分生效以前，依照條約的規定辦理，或按照談判國已達成的協議辦理。沒有條約規定時，必須有談判國的協議。旣無規定，又缺協議，則不得暫時適用。

　　條約的適用旣是暫時的，就不得永久適用於全體締約國，也不能永久適用於某一締約國，所以除非條約有相反的規定，或談判國有不同的協議，則無論是全約或其部分對某國暫時適用，都於該國通知同約其他締約國，說明其無意成爲該約當事國時，對該國的暫時適用便立刻終止。這時候，該國如果依照條約的規定，因條約暫時適用而仍有應盡未盡的義務，當然應該按誠信原

則，**繼續**履行完畢。

　　爲了使條約全部或一部分規定能夠暫時適用，可以在約中列載達到這目的的條款，可以在條約外另立議定書，也可以用照會或其他方式表示。本條不規定爲此目的的表示方式，各談判國可以自由抉擇。

　　條約規定的暫時適用，向來稀少，偶見於雙邊條約，多見於多邊條約。多邊條約的規定，要暫時適用的情形，比雙邊條約的何止倍蓰。

第三編 條約之遵守、適用及解釋

第一節 條約之遵守

第二十六條 條約必須遵守

凡有效之條約對其各當事國有拘束力,必須由各該國善意履行。

條約有現行有效的,有經廢止的,有已逾期無效的。本條所稱的條約,是指有效的 (In force)。只要條約是有效的,就屬於本條的範圍,即令它已因故暫停施行,不是現行的 (in execution),也視為現行有效的。

國家採用某方式表示同意承受某條約拘束後,就成為該約的當事國,在該約有效期間,當然受該約拘束,有善意履行該約的法律義務,不履行,就違反「條約必須遵守」原則 (The Principle of Pacta sunt servanda),引起相應的國際義務。

條約必須遵守,是條約法的基本原則,指有效的條約必拘束其當事國,各當事國必須善意 (Good faith) 履行。這原則的重要性,不言可喻。早在一八七一年,各國簽訂倫敦宣言時,已明白確認條約對其締約國有拘束力。一九二八年,義大利實證法

學家安士樂提 (Dionisio Anzilotti) 在其名著中寫道：

　　　　每一法律秩序包含許多軌範，而軌範又從直接或間接
　　相關的一個基本軌範獲得拘束性。這基本軌範決定那些軌
　　範，以構成一個法律秩序，並使全體統一；國際法律秩序
　　由一項事實來辨別，那就是在這秩序裡「條約必須遵守」
　　無需倚賴更高的軌範，在國際法上，它本身就是最高的軌
　　範。「國家必須遵守其所訂的條約」規則，便構成了區別
　　其他軌範的正式標準，並使全體〔軌範〕統一。所有軌
　　範（也只有軌範）倚賴這原則為其拘束性的必需和專屬的淵
　　源。」❶

安士樂提視「條約必須遵守」原則為國際法最高軌範，說它無需
倚賴其他軌範而有拘束力。這已獲得普遍的接受，本條也完全容
納了他的主張。

　　善意履行條約，也是基本原則。一九一○年北大西洋漁權仲
裁案中有言：「…條約造成一種必需的關係，以便英國訂立管理
規則以行使主權權利，但這權利以在善意訂立規則並且不違反條
約為限。」❷ 聯合國憲章先於序文中呼籲善鄰之道，再於第二條
訂明：「各會員國應一秉善意 (in good faith)，履行其依本憲

---

❶ D. Anzilotti, *Corso di Dirito Internationale,* 3rd ed. (1928), Vol.1, p.43.

❷ 1910 *Reports of International Arbitral Awards,* Vol. X1, p.188.

章所擔負之義務。」在國際司法機關中，善意原則本身亦已是法律原則，已構成「條約必須遵守」原則的不可分的一部分。例如國際法院在「摩洛哥境內美國人權利案」中說：「估價權屬於海關當局，但這權力必須合理的並且善意的行使。」❸

善意原則既是「條約必須遵守」原則的構成部分，「條約必須遵守」原則又是條約法的最高最基本軌範，則拋棄或背離了這軌範，條約法便沒有堅實的基礎，締結條約的一切努力會盡付東流。這是現代學者和政府官員的共識，無人置疑了。

本條條文有「有效之」三字，有人以爲這三字會引起解釋的麻煩，又會削弱這規則的氣勢。但是，如果把關於條約的生效、暫時適用、條約生效前簽字國的某些義務、條約的無效和終止等條款同時列入考慮，就會覺得有這三字較嚴謹，較妥善，可適用於暫時有效的條約、經確定有效的條約等等，而且不妨礙大原則的力量。

本公約序文已說，善意原則和「條約必須遵守」原則已獲得普遍的承認，本條重提這兩原則，並且明列專條，足證本公約擬訂者多麼的寄予重視，又可見這兩原則在條約法中居於何等重要的地位。假如這些原則只是口號，這條規則只是虛文，那麼，不但國際法不能隨條約法所定規則而有進展，就是正常的國際關係也不能維持，世間的法律秩序必蕩然無存。

第二十七條　國內法與條約之遵守

一當事國不得援引其國內法規定爲理由而不履行條約。此項規則

❸　*I. C. J. Rep.*, 1952, p. 212.

不妨礙第四十六條。

本公約第四十六條的意義，等到討論該條時才加以敍明。這裏只先指出，該條牽涉訂約權限，如果當事國政府越權表示同意承受條約的拘束，則應依該條的規定辦理。

依照本條規定，條約當事國同意承受條約拘束，承擔了條約義務後，就必須善意履行，不得以其國內法禁止或限制為理由而不履行。該國所承擔的條約義務，如果與其舊的國內法牴觸，則依一般法理「後法優於前法」看，該國在條約下的義務應居優先，該國沒有不履行條約義務的藉口。該國已承受的條約義務，如果與其新的國內法衝突，或與其國內的最高法（憲法）牴觸，就是確有履行條約義務的障礙，不能按原定程序履行。這時候，該國必須經由其他程序，採取一切可行的措施，克盡其在條約下的義務，例如可用金錢賠償的義務，就應先行賠償，可用道歉使受損者滿足的，就應道歉。

本條只禁止條約當事國以國內法規定為理由而不履行條約義務，並不意味其受新的國內法阻礙而不能履行時，不得採取其他行為，以解除其不能履行的義務。在一般國際法下，該國可以採取的其他行為包括：（一）要求修改條約（本公約第四十一條所定事項），（二）要求暫停施行條約（本公約第四十七及第四十八條所定事項）及退出條約（本公約第五十四條第五十六條所定事項）等。

在理論上，本條的規定，也許會引發舊的疑問：「國際法和國內法孰應居優先？」這一個老問題，曾招致熱烈的爭論，至今

仍難說已有人人接受的定論。一元論的層次學派,說法律規則的效力和拘束力來自高一層的規則❹,國內的最高層是憲法,憲法的拘束力則是一個基本假定,國際法的拘束力則基於「條約必須遵守」原則,國內法和國際法共同的最高層規則,則是一個基本理念——管理人類行為的實際需要。二元論者則認為,國家意志有最高權力,國際法是為國家而釐訂,非經轉化為國內法,不能於國內法院適用,遇有國際法和國內法的優先次序問題時,當然由國內法居先❺。

在事實上,國際司法機關常優先適用國際法。例如常設國際法院在希保社區 (Greeco-Bulgarian Communities) 案中說:「在締約國雙方的關係間,國內法的規定,不能優於其條約的規定。」❻該院在法瑞自由區 (Free Zones of Upper Savoy and the District of Gex) 案中又說:「法國不得以本國立法來限制其國際義務範圍。」❼該院又在波蘭國民待遇(Treatment of Polish Nationals in Danzig) 案的諮詢意見中,指出當事國不得援引其憲法,「以規避其在國際法或有效條約下所負之義務。」❽聯合國憲章第四十八條規定:「執行安全理事會為維持

---

❹　請閱❸的引句。

❺　請參閱陳治世,國際法 (臺北,商務,民七九) 第三章「國際法的性質與根據」,藉以比較各家學說。

❻　P.C. I. J. *Series B*, No.17(1930), p.32.

❼　P. C. I J., *Series A/B*,No. 46(1932), pp.12,96.

❽　P. C. I. J., *Series A/B*, No.44(1932), p.24; Manley O Hudson, 2 *World* Court Reports 788, 804(1935).

國際和平及安全之決議所必要之行動，應由聯合國全體會員國或
由若干會員國擔任之，一依安全理事會之決定。」這也表示憲
章的規定優於各會員國的決定，縱使其決定是經由立法程序作成
的。

因此，本條所定的規則，是以國際法（尤其是條約）優於國
內法的先念爲出發點，使國際習慣法法典化，澄清了一項國際法
則，只是澄清，不是創新。

第二節　條約之適用

第二十八條　條約不溯旣往

**除條約表示不同意思或另經確定外，關於條約對一當事國生效之
日以前所發生之任何行爲或事實或已不存在之任何情勢，條約之規定
不對該當事國發生拘束力。**

各談判國認爲妥善又有必要時，可使條約各條款或部分條款
有追溯旣往的效力，不受國際法限制，也沒有任何人能藉任何理
由加以阻止。一般原則是訂約純以各談判國的意思爲準，不設定
條約有溯及旣往的效力。因此在一般情形下，條約不溯及旣往，
只於各締約國有相反的意思時，才承認相關條約有這種效力，而
各締約國的意思，或可從條約約文中看出，或可用其他方式確
定，一經確定，條約的溯往效力，便可依約發生。

國際司法機關重視一般原理，不輕易承認條約有溯往的效
力。在安巴細埃羅案（The Ambatielos Case）中，希臘在先

決抗辯階段時辯稱：希臘依據一九二六年希英條約，有權請求英國於一九二二年和一九二三年的行爲負責賠償，因爲一八八六年希英條約載有類似一九二六年希英條約的條款，所以英國應爲其一九二二年和一九二三年的行爲負責。國際法院駁斥說：一九二六年希英條約訂明，各條款於批准時立刻生效，約中並無特殊目標或特別條款使條約溯及既往，法院不能推定約中任何條款於條約批准前已經生效❾。這意見也明確表示，除非條約特別訂明，任何條約都沒有追溯既往的效力。

條約生效前的行爲、事實或情勢 (acts, facts or situations)，於條約生效後如果仍然繼續發生或存在，就應由條約列入而加以規範。條約生效時才開始的事項，不得假定爲條約生效前已經開始，以致妨礙條約不溯既往原則。條約生效前已經開始的事項，於條約生效後繼續發生或存在，又經條約訂明列入，則關於該事項的條約規定，當可對各當事國發生拘束力，因爲旣於約中訂明列入，就是約中事項。

本條使用「除條約表示不同意思」(Unless a different intention appears in the treaty」等字，不使用一般用語「除條約另有規定外」(Unless the treaty otherwise provides)。爲什麼？簡單地說，就是一份條約的效力是否溯及既往，不完全根據約中特殊規定，主要是根據條約的性質和條約所表示的意思，而加以判斷。那意思顯示要使條約有溯往的效力，它才可以有這效力。

---

❾ *I.C.J. Rep.,* 1952, p.40.

從上可知，條約生效前的行為、事實和情勢，通常不是條約適用的對象，而已失效的條約，則可能和條約施行時的行為、事實或情勢有某種關係。那一種關係？且待介紹條約的失效時分解。

第二十九條　條約之領土範圍

除條約表示不同意思或另經確定外，條約對每一當事國之拘束力及於其全部領土。

本條中文的「領土」，是英文的「territory」。按這一英文字可中譯為「土地」、「地方」、「地域」、「領土」、「版圖」、「範圍」、「屬地」（美國習用）、「領域」等等，所以其意義不以土地為限，應解釋為國家所管轄的領域，而國家所管轄的領域，則包括在國家主權下的領陸領水和領空。

不涉及適用空間的條約，沒有通常意義的領域範圍問題，適用於一定領域的條約，才有領域範圍問題，必須有明確的規定，以免引起條約適用時的爭執。有些條約規定適用的領土或地區，例如 一九二〇 年十月 二十一 日條約，承認挪威享有史匹子柏梗 (Spitzbergen) 的主權❿，一九五九年十二月一日南極條約，訂明各當事國從事科學研究的南極地區⓫。另一方面，引渡條約

---

❿ *League of Nations Treaty Series* （以下縮寫為 *LNTS*），*Vol.* 11, p.8.

⓫ *United Nations Treaty Series* （以下縮寫為 UNTS），Vol. 402, p.71.

之類的判決執行條款，則多不限制其效力可及的領域範圍，因為如果加以限制，便不易達到執行的目的。

　　多年久載的國家實踐、國際司法機關的法理、以及許多法學家的著作，都支持一個意見，就是除非條約表示不同的意思，條約必適用於各當事國的全部領域。而依照本條的規定，條約對每一當事國的拘束力，除條約本身表示相反的意思，或經由其他方式確定條約有不同的意思外，一律及於當事國的全部領土。這就表示，無論如何，一定可以完全按締約國的意思，以列載或排除條約適用的空間。而這裏所稱的全部領土，當然是在其主權下的領土，也就是在其專屬管轄權下的領域。

　　十九世紀以前，國際社會分子稀少，國際法適用的對象簡單，締結條約時需要顧慮的情況，也不如今天的複雜，條約的拘束力幾乎全被視為必及於當事國的全部領域。可是現在締約國認為那不是當然的事情，可於必要時規定條約的拘束力只及於其部分領域，尤其是像英國這樣的締約國，可能常常以為有這種必要，因為英國仍是國協 (The Commonwealth of Nations)的一員，又是國協的首領。在大英帝國時期，英國有許多自治領（如加拿大、澳洲等）和殖民地（如馬來西亞、牙買加等），自治領和殖民地在英國法律上的地位不同，在國際法上的地位也有差別。各自治領分別獨立有其主權後，和英國組成不列顛國協 (The British Commonwealth of Nations)，以英王為共戴的國家元首，各有英王任命的總督代表英王行使國家元首的職務，所以英國和外國締結條約時，常於約中訂明適用的範圍，訂明對英國本土和海外屬地一律適用，或僅適用於大不列顛與北愛

爾蘭聯合王國 (The United Kingdom of Great Britain and Northern lreland)，如果條約涉及其國內事項，則一定訂明只適用於聯合王國本土，不適用於海峽島嶼和曼島（The Channel lslands and the lsle of Man)。

條約適用於當事國領域以外、國家繼承是否涉及這種領域外適用的條約等問題，不屬於本條的範疇，這裏不予敍述，留待下文有關部分作說明。

第三十條　關於同一事項先後所訂條約之適用

一、以不違反聯合國憲事第一百零三條爲限，就同一事項先後所訂條約當事國之權利與義務應依下列各項確定之。

二、遇條約訂明須不違反先訂或後訂條約或不得視爲與先訂或後訂條約不合時，該先訂或後訂條約之規定應居優先。

三、遇先訂條約全體當事國亦爲後訂條約當事國但不依第五十九條終止或停止施行先訂條約時，先訂條約僅於其規定與後訂條約規定相合之範圍內適用之。

四、遇後訂條約之當事國不包括先訂條約之全體當事國時：

(甲)在同爲兩約之當事國間，適用第三項之同一規則；

(乙)在爲兩約之當事國與僅爲其中一條約之當事國間彼此之權利與義務依兩國均爲當事國之條約定之。

五、第四項不妨礙第四十一條，或依第六十條終止施行條約之任何問題，或一國因締結或適用一條約而其規定與該國依另一條約對另一國之義務不合所生之任何責任問題。

聯合國憲章第一百零三條訂明：「聯合國會員國在本憲章下

之義務與其依任何其他國際協定所負之義務有衝突時，其在本憲章下之義務應居優先。」所以聯合國會員國過去現在已訂的條約和將來締結的一切條約，無論性質、範圍和名稱爲何，發生條約義務的衝突時，都必須先履行其在憲章下的義務，不得以任何藉口爲理由而不履行。憲章旣有這樣的規定，聯合國全體會員國又已批准憲章，以明確表示同意承受憲章的拘束，因而從今以後，縱使沒有本條的規定，也必須遵行憲章的規定。

　　然而條約法的適用，不以聯合國會員國爲限，亦包括非聯合國會員國。兩個或兩個以上非聯合國會員國，如果就同一事項先後訂約而有解釋條約的岐見時，本條第一項怎樣適用？先後締結的多邊條約，如果當事國包括聯合國會員國和非聯合國會員國，本條第一項是否亦可適用？雖然現在國際社會的成員幾乎都已是聯合國會員國，這些問題眞正發生的可能性小而又小，但是單從理論看，這些問題仍然潛存。另一方面，聯合國各會員國爲了預防或消除前後條約義務衝突的困境計，當一致認定有必要時，或者會援引憲章第二條第六款，以促使非聯合國會員國接受憲章第一百零三條的規定。

　　本條規定，如果符合憲章第一百零三條的意旨，則各當事國就同一事項先後締結的條約所含的權利義務，可依下列各項規則處理：

　　第一、若干國家就甲事項訂約後，往往再就甲事項訂立新約，或於甲事項的條約簽訂後，有其他國家加入，或於其加入後又另訂新約，新約訂妥後再有不同的國家加入。這是很複雜的條約關係，也是很可能發生的情形。另一種情形是：子丑兩國參加

一份許多國家締結的條約後，在該約許可的範圍內就丁事項簽訂雙邊條約，使該多邊條約在兩國間施行時更爲便利。一九六三年領事關係公約第七十三條第二段，准許各當事國互訂條約，在不違反該公約的範圍內履行新約及公約的義務。這是一個明確的實例。

若干條約訂明：本約不妨礙（或不牴觸）各當事國在其他特定條約下的義務。在國際聯盟時期，一些條約訂明不得視其任何條款使當事國違反盟約下的義務。現在則有一些條約說當事國的義務不得牴觸其在聯合國憲章下的義務。這又佐證了一個原則，就是前約優於後約，多邊條約優於雙邊條約。因而當條約訂明受甲約限制，或訂明不得認爲牴觸甲約時，則該甲約應居優先，也就是當條約訂明不得違反先訂的或後訂的甲約，或訂明不得視爲和先訂的或後訂的甲約牴觸時，則甲約的規定應居優先。

第二、同一批國家就子事項訂約後，無論是希望改變全約或只希望修改該約，都有權就子事項締結新約，以達到其希望，不會遭遇法律上的困難，締結新約時，除有相反的規定外，新約如果牴觸舊約全部條款，則表示其有意終止舊約，新約如果只牴觸舊約部分條款，則視爲修改舊約，所以於舊約全體當事國都是新約當事國，新約不訂明終止或停止施行舊約，新約舊約的規定不一致時，則各當事國的權利義務以規定一致的爲限。

第三、舊約的當事國不包括新約的全體當事國，兩約的內容又不全同，則同爲兩約當事國的國家須受兩約拘束，僅爲舊約當事國者只受舊約拘束，僅爲新約當事國者只受新約拘束，新約不得剝奪舊約當事國的權利，締結新約者如果於新約列入與舊約相

悖的條款，以剝奪舊約當事國的權利，則犯了侵權行為，非法律所容許。有些條約為了預防這種行為，便以明文規定各當事國不得共同或與第三國簽訂牴觸本條約的文件。例如關於中華民國的九國公約（The Nine-Power Pact of 1922 with Respect to China）第二條規定：「各締約國同意不相互不個別不集體與任何一國或若干國簽訂會侵犯或妨害第一條所列原則之任何條約、協定、辦法或諒解。」⑫ 沒有這種禁止規定的條約，可由各當事國相互集體或個別與第三國或自行訂新約、予以修改或廢止。

　　第四、條約可以規定自立性的義務⑬，也可以定下互依性的義務⑭。一國所訂新約牴觸其在舊約下的自立性義務，有什麼責任？或牴觸其在舊約下的互依性義務，又有什麼責任？兩者的性質有什麼不同？是不是兩者都使新約不能發生效力？或者牴觸互依性義務的新約仍可發生效力？如果新約全體當事國明知有這種

---

⑫　*LNTS*，Vol. 38, p. 281.

⑬　自立性的義務是：義務的有效性是顯而易見的、絕對的、每一當事國固有的、不以其他當事國履行相對義務為條件的。換句話說，不受任何外在因素影響的義務，就是自立性的義務，例如殘害人群罪公約、人權公約、國際勞工公約、一九四九年日內瓦戰俘公約等所列的義務，都是自立性的。

⑭　互依性的義務是指各當事國的義務以其他各當事國都履行相同義務為前提，只要一當事國違反其義務，條約所定制度對於其他全體當事國的施行便受妨礙，該國和其他當事國的關係也受妨礙，例如裁軍、禁止試驗核子武器的條約，只於一當事國違約時，裁軍或禁試制度便會被破壞無遺。

牴觸，又應怎樣處理？規定自立性義務的條約規則，不具有絕
對規律 (Jus cogens) 或絕對最高軌範 (Absolute supreme
norm) 的性質，規定互依性義務的條約規則，就不用說了，所
以這些新約和牴觸絕對規律或絕對最高軌範的條約不同，因為後
者自始無效 (Invalid ab initio) ，而前者則未必無效。就本公
約看，未見有視為新約無效的規定。

　　新約牴觸當事國在其舊約下的義務時，依本公約的意思，並
不當然無效，那麼，當事國應怎樣履行其在舊約下的義務呢？因
為其已違反國際義務，便有國際責任，必須依處理國際責任的法
則處理，所以本條第五項作如下的規定：㈠本條第四項不妨礙關
於條約修改的第四十一條；㈡同項不妨礙關於終止條約的第六十
條的問題；㈢同項不妨礙依第六十條停止施行條約的問題；㈣同
項不妨礙國家因訂新約而違反其在舊約下的義務所應負擔的國際
責任問題；㈤同項也不妨礙國家因適用甲條約而牴觸其乙條約下
的義務所應負擔的國際責任問題。這些規定綜合表示一點，就是
國家因訂後約而違反其在前約所定義務時，必須依國際法擔負國
際責任，如有爭執，應按國際責任法規來解決。

　　最後，條約當事國因其他當事國違約而受損害時，可以請求
補救，可以停止施行該約，在某些情形下，也可以終止該約。多
邊條約的兩個當事國間，締結新約以修改該公約的施行，如果違
反這兩國對其他當事國的義務，則是本公約所准許的，最少可以
說未被本公約禁止。

第三節　條約之解釋

第三十一條　解釋之通則

一、條約應依其用語按其上下文並參照條約之目的及宗旨所具有之通常意義，善意解釋之。

二、就解釋條約而言，上下文除指連同弁言及附件在內之約文外，並應包括：

　　(甲)全體當事國間因締結條約所訂與條約有關之任何協定；

　　(乙)一個以上當事國因締結條約所訂並經其他當事國接受爲條約有關文書之任何文書。

三、應與上下文一併考慮者尚有：

　　(甲)當事國嗣後所訂關於條約之解釋或其規定之適用之任何協定；

　　(乙)嗣後在條約適用方面確定各當事國對條約解釋之協定之任何慣例；

　　(丙)適用於當事國間關係之任何有關國際法規則。

四、倘經確定當事國有此原意，條約用語應使其具有特殊意義。

　　任何一本完整的國際法課本，都介紹條約通論，而且提及條約解釋的原則、方法或規則。可是究竟有沒有條約解釋的原則或規則或準則？如果有條約解釋的國際法規則，那（些）規則有沒有任何功用？若干學者懷疑有，有些學者認爲有，卻對那（些）規則的強制性（拘束力）採取很保留的態度。就是肯定那（些）規則或準則的學者，對於下列三點也有不同的意見：㈠解釋時應

著重於作爲意思眞正表示的約文？㈡解釋時應著重於約文外當事國主觀成分的意思？或㈢解釋時應著重於經宣告的或明顯的條約目標或宗旨？贊成㈠者，強調約文爲解釋條約的首要基準，只應顧到當事國在約文以外表示意思的東西，並且審酌條約目標和宗旨。贊成㈡者，注意條約締結前的準備工作和一切足以顯示當事國意思的證據。贊成㈢者，則著眼於目的論的原則，對於普遍性的多邊條約，解釋時往往會越出甚至脫離約文所載的當事國的原本意思。時代演進迅速，自本公約誕生後，各學者的觀念受到影響，現在已可以說，大多數學者願探擇上述㈢的主張。

在事實上，在國際方面，國際司法機關裁判了若干案件，涉及條約解釋，提及許多條約解釋的原則或準則。在國內，法院也曾適用不少原則和準則，以解釋國內的法規和契約，很多外交部也曾援引一些原則或準則，以解釋國際協約。可見現在確有條約解釋的通則了。

旣有條約解釋的通則，又有以明文規定通則的必要，便應於本公約中列載。但是仍有人認爲，已有的原則準則，只是邏輯上的理性的產物，有助於探悉當事國已在約文中表示的意思，那些原則準則還缺乏強制力。究竟應在什麼情形下適用呢？這就須視解釋文件者的領悟、字與句的特殊位置、字句的相互關係、文件各部分的相互關係、文件的通性與作成的情況等等而定；那些原則準則，卽令已有適用的時機，還要看解釋者據以領悟特殊情況的理念爲何；其領悟左右其決定是否適用，而時機並不當然使那準則或原則自動適用。換句話說，那些原則準則的適用，是隨意的無強制性的，文件的解釋，可以說是藝術，不是嚴格的科

學。所以列載普遍適用的全部原則準則，無異徒步上青天。

然而無論如何，必有可以列出的原則 —— 可普遍適用的原則，最少有下列三個基本原則：

第一、條約應依法以善意解釋，使條約必須遵守原則具有意義。

第二、使條約約文在解釋時有其明確的地位，並使其是當事國意思表示的記載。

第三、注意條約的明文規定，並顧及隱含的當事國意思。

其他原則，例如不應修改或補充條約、特別規定優於一般規定、直接的意義優於間接或隱含的意義、明列一物或一人即排除他物或他人 (Expressio unius est exclusio alterius) 等原則，無疑都值得參考。雖然也有人主張，先分條約為立法的和非立法的，然後據以擬定解釋的規則，但是這主張顯然不可行，首先遭遇的困難，無法克服，那就是根本不能把條約作這樣的準確區分，因為一切條約都立法，多邊條約為三個以上國際法主體立法，雙邊條約為兩個主體立法，不可以稱為「非立法的」。

依照本條所列通則，解釋條約時，首先就應該假定約文是當事國意思的真正記載，所以第一步是澄清約文上已載的意思，不是探究約文外的當事國意思，如果探究，便會擴大解釋的功能。國際法院認為，以約文為主的解釋步驟，已是確定的法則，而且解釋的功能不是修改條約，不是把約文不明示或隱含的東西輸入約中❺。該院也曾說，法院受付託以解釋並適用條約的規定時，

---

❺ 例如在 the United States Nationals in Morocco 案中所說的。見 *I, C. J. Rep.*, 1952, pp. 196-199.

首要責任是盡力按上下文的文字自然而通常的意義，使文字有效果⑯。此外，當然任何文字或語句的意義，也以適合序文和各條款的目標與宗旨的爲可取。

用不著說，條約序文是條約的一部分，正如附於一份文書的附件是文書的一部分。現在要問的只是：爲了解釋條約的目的，那些附件可以視爲或應該視爲條約的一部分？依照本條的規定，以下列兩類附件爲限。第一類是全體當事國於締結條約時所達成的協議，第二類是締結條約的相關文書，已獲得其他當事國接受爲相關文書者。第二類是片面性的，所以不但要和條約的締結相關，而且要取得其他當事國接受後，才可以成爲條約的一部分。

本條列舉了兩類附件，並不意味兩類都必然是條約的構成部分，只是表示一點，就是爲了澄淸約文的不明處或難解處，可以參酌那些附件，以求得約文字句自然而通常的意義。至於這兩類附件是不是條約的構成部分，則須視個案而定，尤其要依各當事國的意思而定。

各締約國於簽訂條約後，如果作成關於該約解釋的協議，則於解釋該約時，當然應視該協議爲不可或缺的依據。而各締約國在談判時就某條文的意義作成的諒解，是不是後來解釋該協議的基礎呢？這是事實問題，不能按一般理則答覆，如果答案是正面的，該諒解就應視爲解釋條約的基礎部分。

各締約國於簽訂條約後，如果有履行條約的習慣或實例，確

---

⑯ 例如在 Competence of the Genenal Assembly for the Admission of A State to the United Nations 案中所說的。見 *I. C. J. Rep.*, 1950, p.8.

定了各當事國對於某（些）條款的了解，則那習慣或實例當然應與條約上下文一併考慮，因為那習慣或實例已以事實證明那些條款的意義為何，而且已由各當事國以行為表示接受了。雙邊條約的兩當事國間的履約行為，固然是顯示條約規定的兩造同意的意義，就是多邊條約的兩當事間的履約習慣或實例，只要不違反其對其他當事國的義務，又可以投合其要求，則解釋該約時應重視那實例或習慣，假如多邊條約的全體當事國有相同的習慣或實例，則解釋該約時更應刮目相看，而解釋的結論必更易適用。從另一方面回頭看，又可見那習慣或實例不一定是也無需是全體當事國共有的。

　　本條第三項丙款說：「適用於當事國間關係之任何有關國際法規則。」也應該和條約上下文一併考慮。這一款所稱的規則，是以解釋條約的為限，和條約解釋無關的國際法規則，一概不是本款所稱的規則。其次，本款所稱的只是適用於當事國間關係的國際法規則，不包含任何不得適用於這種關係的規則。符合這兩點的任何規則，不受時間的或空間的限制，於解釋條約時，應與條約上下文共同考慮，以澄清約文字句的意義。

　　解釋條約的準則中，有所謂內證法 (Intrinsic evidence) 和外證法 (External evidence)。內證法就是按約文以求義的方法，從條約的序文、條文、和構成條約一部分的附件、以及條約的目標、宗旨和精神等，以探悉正待解釋的條款意義。外證法就是利用條約以外的資料，或根據當事國間的協議，或追查訂約時的情況，或參酌訂約國以前締結的條約，參考談判條約的紀錄等文書，審察當事國於訂約後履約的慣例或行為，或注意各當事

國於訂約後所締結的其他法律文件，藉以辨明或證實或確定各當
事國的意思。

文字有自然的通常的專門技術的和特殊的意義。同樣的文
字，用於專門技術性的文件時，應先採用其專門技術上的意義，
用於特殊情況時，應先採用其特殊的意義，用於一般條約時，應
著眼於其自然而通常的意義。本條第一項規定，解釋條約時應依
照約文用語的自然而通常的意義，本條第四項准許採用特殊的意
義，但是採用時必須先確定當事國原已採用特殊的意義，否則不
應按照特殊的意義，仍須採用自然而通常的意義。

本條四項的規定，都是解釋條約的通則，包括了學者所稱的
內證法和外證法，可以說是普遍適用的公認規則。

第三十二條　解釋之補充資料

為證實由適用第三十一條所得之意義起見，或遇依第三十一條作
解釋而：

(甲)意義仍屬不明或難解；或

(乙)所獲結果顯屬荒謬或不合理時，為確定其意義起見，得使用解釋
之補充資料，包括條約之準備工作及締結之情況在內。

依照一般法理和司法機關的先例，解釋條約時，如果覺得
約文字句自然而通常的意義足夠明顯，那意義又符合上下文的旨
趣，就無需使用條約以外的資料，以資補充。以資補充的資料
中，最常見的是記載條約的準備作業和締約時的情況。國際法院
在核准國家入會之條件 (Conditions of Admission of A

State to Memdership in the United Nations) 案中說：

「本院認爲公約約文已夠清楚，所以不覺得應該捨棄常設國際法院前後一貫的慣例，就是如果公約約文本身已夠清楚，就無需使用準備作業的資料。」這也表示，必須認定約文爲各當事國意思的眞實記載，澄淸其意思才是解釋條約的初衷，不應於開始解釋步驟時，便探究其在約文以外的意思，臆測其已於約文外所表示的意思。

本公約第三十一條已經訂明，依照條約用語的通常意義、條約約文、條約目標和宗旨、一般國際法規則、以及當事國對條約的解釋等，都是解釋條約的首要標準。本條進一步訂明，唯有在下列兩種情形下，才可以使用上述各標準以外的資料：第一、已經適用第三十一條以解釋條約後，以其他資料證實解釋所得的意義；第二、依照第三十一條以解釋條約後，正待辨明的意義還是不明確或者難解，或者解釋所得的結果顯然荒謬或不合理。如果沒有這兩種情形，就不應使用補充資料。如果依照條約用語的通常意義以解釋後，約中意義仍然不明確或費解，或者解釋結果顯然荒唐背理，便應拋棄用語的通常意義，採用上述首要標準以外的資料所證實或確定的意義。所以本條標題使用「補充資料」等字，藉以表示本條所列資料，不是解釋條約的首要資料，只是於首要資料不足以達到解釋條約的目的時，才可以或者才需要採用的資料。

什麼是準備作業 (Preparatory works, traveaux préparatoires)？本條沒有加以界定，實則不易界定，也不必界定。簽署條約前的各種文書、紀錄、函件等等，都屬於準備作業的範

圍。作業無論已經或未經印行，都以當事國曾參與的部分為限。
這一部分才可用以辨明當事國的意思。當事國如果未參加談判，
只以接受、贊同或加入的方式成為當事國，則不能利用準備作業
來確定其意思，因而準備作業用於雙邊條約的解釋比較合適，用
以解釋多邊條約的機會比較少，用於許許多多國家為當事國的條
約解釋，必然機會更少，儘管準備作業在條約解釋的程序上，可
以維持其極不重要的地位。

第三十三條　以兩種以上文字認證之條約之解釋

**一、條約約文經以兩種以上文字認證作準者，除依條約之規定或當事
國之協議遇意義分岐時應以某種約文為根據外，每種文字之約文
應同一作準。**

**二、以認證作準文字以外之他種文字作成之條約譯本，僅於條約有此
規定或當事國有此協議時，始得視為作準約文。**

三、條約用語推定在各種作準約文中意義相同。

**四、除依第一項應以某種約文為根據之情形外，倘比較作準約文後，
發現意義有差別而非適用第三十一條及第三十二條所能消除時，
應採用顧及條約目的及宗旨之最能調和各約文之意義。**

　　近代各國締結條約時，以兩種或兩種以上文字認證約文，已
是十分普通的情形。自聯合國成立以來，一般多邊條約以五種或
六種文字（中文、英文、法文、西班牙文、俄文或阿拉伯文）擬
妥或最後定稿的，為數頗多。以多種文字認證作準的條約，可能
於解釋時有各不同文字本的地位問題，可能是各本有其真正約文
的地位，或者其中一種兩種只是「正式約文」（Official text）。

談判國已簽署而未接受爲「權威的」（Authoritative）約文，各國、各政府或國際組織譯妥的約文「正式譯本」（official translation），都不能視爲作準約文。任何文字的譯本，必須於獲得其他當事國接受後，才可取得作準約文的地位。

　　現在比較莊嚴的條約，無論是多邊的或雙邊的，大多數以明文規定其不同文字本的地位，或訂明其中那一（幾）種文字本爲作準本，只有極少數條約沒有這種規定。沒有這種規定時，就按普遍接受的規則，以作成條約的各種文字本作準，解釋時每一種都具有「權威性」。換句話說，除有相反的規定外，各種文字平等，各種文字本同一作準，效力一致，沒有優先順序或重輕比對的問題。有些條約訂明，僅以某一（些）文字本爲權威性的，例如第二次世界大戰後，盟國與義大利、保加利亞、匈牙利等國間的和平條約，都以英文本、法文本和俄文本作準，而義文本保文本匈文本只是正式譯本，不具權威性質❸。有些條約以某一種文字本爲某些國家間的作準文本，並以另一種文字本爲其他國家間的作準文本，一九一八年 Brest-Litovsk 條約❹第十條的規定便是一例。

　　本條所稱的文字，是指用以認證作準的文字，不指用以草擬約文的文字。本公約第十條，已規定認證約文是締約的一個步驟，也是締約程序的重要階段。本條規定以認證約文的文字爲

　❼　*I.C.J. Rep.*, 1948, p. 63.

　❽　對義和約第十九條、對保和約第三十八條、對匈條約第四十二條、對羅馬尼亞和約第四十條、對芬蘭和約第三十六條都有相同的規定。

　❾　該約是列寧領導的俄國政府與德國簽訂的和平條約。

準，是爲了配合第十條的意旨。

以多種文字認證作準約文的條約，可以訂明於不同文字的約文意義有歧異時，以其中某一約文本爲準；當兩國訂約，一方不甚熟悉對方文字，或雙方不願承認對方文字的優越性時，可用第三國文字訂約，並且訂明該種文字本爲消除約文歧義的作準約本。一九五七年日本與依索匹亞間的友好條約，用日文、安哈律文（Amharie）和法文作成，於第六條訂明以法文本作準⓴，便是近例。至於採用那一種第三國文字，則由談判國以協議決定，雖然聯合國的官方語文包括中文英文法文西班牙文和俄文，而且英文和法文曾經多次被採用爲第三國文字，但是英文或法文並非非採用不可。

第三國文字作準的約文，或指定某一種文字作準的約文，是不是自動適用？是不是於兩種文字的約本有極微小的歧義時便當然適用？換句話說，歧義達何種程度時，適用作準約文才算正當？應否先使用全部解釋的首要資料，或應先使用一些首要資料，以確定歧義是否存在，如果存在，才適用作準約文？這些問題沒有斬釘截鐵般的答案，可由條約的相關當事國決定。

某一種文字的約文本，儘管未經訂明爲作準約文本，亦可以具有權威性，成爲消除約文歧義的文書，只要有關國家同意接受，歧義便歸於烏有。

以多種文字作準的條約，經協議採用的約中用語都一律具權威性，同時具有多重性，而多重性則常造成解釋條約的需要，也

⓴　*UNTS*, Vol. 325, p. 300.

是解釋條約的背景因素。但是，這多重性和約文與約文間的歧義，並不能改變一個事實，就是依法只有一份條約，只有一套經各當事國接受的用語，只有一個關於各用語的共同意識。所以解釋條約者的任務，是在一份條約中找到各當事國接受的用語共同意識。

　　一份條約的條文無論多少，以多種文字作準時，總難免不同文字的約文間有歧義。各種文字的不同特徵、相同事物間缺乏完全相同的表徵、無充分時間校對各約文本，都是各約文本間有歧義的可能原因，而條約的多重性則是用語含糊或文字艱澀的主要額外根源。同一用語在甲約文中的意義含糊，在乙約文中的意義卻很可能十分明白，而能夠令人相信是各當事國的共同意思。所以用兩種或更多種文字以認證作準約文，可能簡化也可能繁化約文的解釋，也就是說，條約以多種文字作準，有方便處，也有缺點。

　　以多種文字認證作準約文的條約，解釋時比較各不同文字的約文，又適用本公約第三十一至三十三條，才不徒勞無功。條約雖然已用多種文字表示意思，卻只有一套用語和一套當事國的共識，所以統一全約的用語意義，是解釋條約時的重要步驟。視同一用語在各種文字的約文中的意義一致，再視各認證作準約文的權威相同，才可以使用語的意義統一，確保各不同文字的約文本平等。在同一用語的不同意義中作選擇之前，必須爲各約本找到共同的意義，無論那歧義的根源是用語在各約文本中含糊或難解，或是在甲約文本中含糊或難解，而在另兩種約文本中卻意義明確，都應運用條約解釋的標準規則，以探求各當事國附於各用

語的原本意義，不得只選用一種文字的約文，而不按照條約目標、宗旨、準備作業、訂約時的情況、訂約後的履約慣例等等，以消除含糊或艱澀，應採用這些首要的和補充的資料，以調和各約文，並且判斷各當事國的原本意思。

因此，本條第三項訂明：「條約用語推定在各種作準約文內意義相同。」又在第四項規定，除依照本條第一項必須以某約文爲根據的情形外，如果比較各種不同文字的約文，便發現有歧義，非運用首要資料不能消除那歧義時，就應抉擇顧及條約目標與宗旨又最能調和各約文的意義。這是從嚴原則（The principle of restrictive interpretation）。遇到用語意義含糊時，這原則可否適用呢？答案要看條約性質和相關的上下文而定，如果只於不同文字的約文中有含糊處，仍不能推定這原則應不應適用❷。

本公約規範的條約，以書面作成的爲限，不涉及口頭協定，所以本節談條約解釋，亦不提及口頭協議的解釋問題。

本節只列三個條文，分別訂明三點：條約解釋的通則、條約解釋的補充資料和以兩種以上文字認證的條約的解釋。三條包含的各項，無疑都是很重要的。但是，這不等於說已包含所有的要點。嚴格說來，關於條約解釋的要點還有很多，這裏應該補述其中一部分，以便利一般讀者參考。

條約的締結，以締約國意思合致爲基礎（不平等條約和城下

---

❷ 以上三個條文的析論，曾參考 *Reports of the Intennational Law Commission*, 17th and 18th Sessions, 1964, Commentaries on the Articles Concerning Interpretations of Treaties.

之盟的和平條約屬於例外）。履行條約時，約中規定的意義如果不清楚，便不能確定何國應履行什麼義務或可享受什麼權利。不幸由於種種原因，條約的條款意義往往不易確定。第一、締約時各國代表同意使用的文字和用語，因為歲月推移環境變遷而意義變更，以致履約時約中文字和用語的意義發生疑問；第二、各國文字辭句是其文化特徵的一部分，以兩種以上文字認證作準約文的條約，縱使於締約時有充分的時間，仔細校閱不同文字的約文譯本，相同條款在不同文字的約文中，仍然可能有不完全相同的涵義；第三、以多種文字作成的條約，如果不明定其中某一種文字本作準，或以多種文字本為準，則如前所說，更容易發生條款相同而意義互異的情形；第四、可能是因為談判國間的政治經濟或其他原因，不能選用人人同意的盡善最佳的用語或文字，而勉強使用含糊的辭語。無論是由於那一個原因，只要遇有條款意義不明確，當事國間發生爭執時，便有解釋條款的必要。

　　國內的法院和其他法定機關（例如中華民國的司法院大法官會議、法國的憲法委員會），對於憲法、法律和條約所作的解釋，可拘束其本國政府、自然人和法人。條約的解釋，不專屬締約國單方的國內管轄，一締約國國內程序下的解釋結果，不能拘束他國，也不一定獲得相關外國接受。條約解釋究竟由誰或何機關擔任，解釋的結果才可以拘束各有關國家呢？許多條約明訂解釋機關，以消除這一疑問。例如前文提及的中美友好通商航海條約，於其第二十八條規定：「關於締約兩國政府間，因本約解釋或適用所發生之爭執，不能經由雙方外交調整者，除雙方同意其他和平方法解決外，應予送達國際法院。」本公約第六十六條也

訂明提請國際法院解釋條約。列載這種條款的條約，於需要解釋時，沒有應由何人或何機關解釋的問題。當事國很多的多邊條約，如果沒有這種條款，要各當事國臨時協議以決定解釋人員或機關，若非不可能，亦必曠日費時，困難重重。好在自從國際法院成立以來，許多條約訂明該院為解釋機關，而且若干條約的疑難，已由該院發表的諮詢意見消除了，雖然那些相關條約並未規定由該院解釋，也可以送請該院釋疑解紛。

解釋條約的目的，在找出當事國訂約時的本意，藉以排難解紛，使相關當事國享受其應有的權利並且履行其應有的義務。如果已有完善的解釋法則，解釋條約的任務容易完成，解釋的目的迅速達到，立竿見影，即時收效。可惜像上文所敍的，許多人還在懷疑已有一套法則，那一套法則已經完善的說法，就不用提了。本公約所列的條約解釋的條文，為數固少，內容亦簡，似乎只是聊備一式而已。然而儘管有這種懷疑和弱點，一些權威學者仍然認為，若干原則和準則應予重視。例如奧本海（Lassa F. L. Oppenheim）於本公約締結前，雖然說沒有關於條約解釋的習慣或協定的國際法規則，卻列舉了下列原則和準則：

（1）所有條約按照其合理的相對於字面的意義加以解釋。

（2）條約所列的用語，如果它不顯然採用了專門技術的意義，或者在上下文中的意義不明顯時，必須按照其日常生活語文的通常意義加以解釋。

（3）締約國當然做合理的、不牴觸普遍承認的國際法原則的、不違反其對第三國舊條約義務的事情，所以條款的意義如果含糊，則採用合理的意義，捨棄不合理的意義；或採用較合理的

意義，捨棄只合理的意義；或採用符合國際法則的，捨棄牴觸國際法則的意義；或採用不違反舊約義務的，捨棄違反舊約義務的意義。

(4) 對於任何條款的意義有疑問時，要考慮全約；除斟酌條約字句外，還要顧及條約宗旨、締約動機和締約時的一般情況。

(5) 減輕負擔原則必須適用。如果用語的意義曖昧，便採用義務國負擔較少的意義，或較少干預當事國領土主權的意義，或限制當事國較寬的意義。但是採用時必須注意擔負義務是訂約的首要宗旨，所以通常必推定各當事國有意使條約有效果，並且避免使條約無效果。

(6) 為澄清某條款的意義起見，可以把相同的當事國先訂的條約和其中一國與第三國簽訂的條約相比較。

(7) 如果約中某條款可有兩種意義，則採用提議該條款的當事國當時所知的是接受國所選定的意義。

(8) 如果約中某條款可有兩種意義，則採用因該條款而受惠的國家受惠較少的意義。

(9)「明列一物或一人卽排除他物或他人」。這原則已由許多國際法庭用以解釋條約。

(10)一國堅持某用語的意義，取得他國接受後，該國和他國締結的條約中列有該用語時，應以被堅持的意義為準。

(11)約中某條款的意義曖昧，如果一當事國在爭執發生前公開其所主張的該條款的意義，其他當事國旣不表示異議，又不提議必要步驟以謀求該條款的權威性解釋，則於爭端發生後解釋者應堅持該意義。

(12)各當事國當然有意使條約各條款有某種效果，無意使任何條款沒有意義，所以不應採用條款無效果或無意義的解釋。若無充分的效果是因各當事國不能就充分的效果的程度達成協議所致，則解釋時應牢記這種情形。

(13)所有條約的解釋，必須排除詐欺，使條約施行符合善意原則。

(14)國內各法院通用的解釋國內法的規則，援引以解釋條約（特別是所謂立法條約）時，以已是法律的一般規則為限，不得援引僅為某國國內法採納或國內法院適用的規則。

(15)兩種文字的不同約文本的意義如果有差別，則除有明文作相反的規定外，各當事國只受其本國文字約本的拘束，不得主張其他文字約本中的利益。

(16)當事國訂約後的行為，在若干情形下可以作為解釋條約的資料，適用該資料於該國行為所承認的相關義務上，尤具價值。

奧本海教授列上述各項後，繼續說明：訂約的談判紀錄、訂約大會及各委員會實錄、各份條約草稿等，都是解釋條約的參考資料，從談判到簽署的各階段討論，以及報章新聞，往往是有價值的證明資料[22]。

以上所敍奧本海教授的意見，和本公約所訂的規則，有幾點雷同，似有異曲同功之妙。奧本海的意見，比公約早數十年，

---

[22] L. F. L. Oppenheim, *International Law: A Treaties,* 8th ed. by H. Lauterpacht, Vol. 1, pp. 951-958.

可能對於本公約草擬者發生某種程度的影響，也就是受到他們的
重視，因而今天的讀者對於奧本海的主張，也應該注意㉓。

　　從各種論著和司法機關的宣示可知，解釋條約還應有下列概
念：

　　(1) 不應修改或補充條約，因為修改條約的內容，或補充條
約的不足，都是條約當事國權力內的事情，不是條約解釋者的任
務。

　　(2) 應認定各當事國不因為訂約而減損其基於主權的行動自
由和意志自由。

　　(3) 訂明懲罰的條約優於不訂明懲罰的條約。

　　(4) 訂明懲罰較重的條約優於訂明懲罰較輕的條約。

　　(5) 特別規定優於一般規定。

　　(6) 禁止的規定優於命令的和容許的規定。

　　(7) 不許延遲的規定優於可寬延的規定。

　　(8) 命令式的義務先於許可式的義務。

　　(9) 一國負有兩種義務，不能同時履行時，可由權利享受國
選擇，選擇的意思不明時，推定其選擇較重的義務。

㉓　關於條約解釋的問題，許多學者詳加討論，例如註㉒所舉專書頁九五
　　一至九五八所列的書刊論文，很值得參閱。比較新近的論著，只研討
　　準備作業的文章，如 Herbert W. Briggs, "The Traveaux
　　préparatoires of the Vienna Convention on the Law of
　　Treaties," 65 *AJIL* 705（1971），很可以幫助了解本公約給予準
　　備作業的地位。至於 traveaux préparatoires（preparatory
　　work）一詞，外交部的中譯文是「準備工作」。本書筆者認為譯成
　　「準備作業」，較接近原文意義，所以在本書中使用「準備作業」。

(10)通常的意義優於特殊的意義。

(11)經各當事國接受的特殊意義優於一般意義。

(12)直接而明顯的意義優於間接的或隱含的意義。

(13)給予用語例外的意義時，必須嚴格證明用語確有例外的意義。

(14)符合國際法的和違反國際法的意義並存時，採用符合國際法的意義。

(15)採用合理的意義，摒棄不合理的意義。

(16)兩種意義都合理時，採用訂約時各當事國明知的意義。

(17)兩種意義都有害時，採用爲害較少的意義。

(18)有利的和有害的意義並存時，採用受益國得利較少的意義。

(19)各種意義都有利時，採用對各當事國最有利的意義。

(20)條約給予權利時，必許可採取行使該權利的手段。

儘管列述了很多關於條約解釋的準則和原則，還有漏列的，則是勢所難免。無論如何，現在已可知道，解釋條約，首先要辨明各當事國的意思，然後按照法理或常理，審度各種相關情況，以確定各當事國的權利和義務。

第四節　條約與第三國

第三十四條　關於第三國之通則

條約非經第三國同意，不爲該國創設義務或權利。

什麼國是第三國？正如本公約第二條第一項 h 款所定，第三國是指非條約當事國的任何國家。

兩個國家或更多的國家簽訂的條約，對於第三國究竟有怎樣的間接效力？關於這一問題，傳統國際法向來沒有明確的答案，也就是沒有規範這問題內涵的規則。學者對於這問題，也只有見仁或見智的說法❷。一九二三年，常設國際法院在東卡略利亞地位 (Status of Eastern Carelia) 案中，宣告第三國不得主張條約上的權利❷。一九二六年，該院在上細列細亞之德國某些利益 (Certain German Interests in Upper Silesia) 案中說：波蘭既不是第一次世界大戰停戰協定的當事國，便沒有援引該協定的權利❷。一九三三年，仲裁庭在中央羅道皮亞森林（The Forests of Central Rhodopia) 案中說：希臘不是君士坦丁堡 (Constantinople) 條約的當事國，沒有以該約相關規定為基礎的法律根據，提出賠償的請求❷。這又表示，第三國不得主張享受條約上的權利。

一般法律原則，肯定說條約只對締約國生效，不對非締約國（即第三國）有任何效力。法諺也說：「條約不給予第三國權利

---

❷　半世紀以前，已有學者討論這一問題，例如 R. F. Roxburg，在其所著 *International Conventions and Third States* (London, 1917) 中，已作深入的析論。

❷　*PCIJ, Series* B, No. 5 (1923), pp. 27-28.

❷　*PCIJ, Series* A, No. 7, (1926) pp. 27-29.

❷　*Annual Digest and Reports of International Law Cases,* 1933-1934, Case No. 39, p. 92.

與義務。」(Pacta tertiis nec nocent nec prosunt)。這就是對一般法律原則的確認。

本條的規定，顯然是採納了上述原則，使原則變成國際法規則。國際法的基礎，是國家主權和國家獨立，沒有這兩個觀念者，心目中不可能有國際法。這兩個觀念逐漸導致一個原則，就是國家非經其同意不受拘束。時至今日，這原則已為國家實踐、國際裁判和學者著作所承認、接受與確定。

專就常理來說，條約猶如一般契約，契約所定的權利或義務，如果可以由第三者享受或負擔，則甲某可能在意外中獲得利益，乙某會無端受害，以致有非訂約的甲某乙某間的爭執，人人隨時有意外的災殃，不知怎樣防範。所以為社會安全計，法律應要求契約只對當事的訂約者有效，不對第三者發生拘束力。同理，為國際社會的安全計，國際法要求條約只為當事國創設權利義務，不對第三國發生效力。

本條所用的文字，是斬釘截鐵般的肯定，不是模稜含糊，是一個通則，不准許例外，唯有於條約訂明賦予第三國權利時，第三國才可以享受條約所定的權利。

第三十五條　為第三國規定義務之條約

　　如條約當事國有意以條約之一項規定作為確立一項義務之方法，且該項義務經一第三國以書面明示接受，則該第三國卽因此項規定而負有義務。

現代國際關係常有多面性，條約關係又會有錯綜複雜的牽

連。許多國家共同簽訂的條約，尤其是所謂立法條約，例如特種使節公約、聯合國海洋法公約等，其締約國於談判簽署時，往往在有意或無意中，使條約直接影響或損益非締約國（即第三國），使條約的效力能課予第三國義務，或賦予第三國權利，以致第三十四條所定的原則發生例外。

第一次世界大戰後，國際組織的約章中，已有使前述原則接納例外的規定。國際聯合會盟約第十七條訂明：

一、若一聯合會會員與一非聯合會會員之國，或兩國均非聯合會會員，遇有爭議，應邀請非聯合會會員之一國或數國承受聯合會會員之義務，照理事會認為正當之條件，以解決爭議。此項邀請如經承受，則第十三條至第十六條之規定，除理事會認為有必要之變更外，應適用之。

二、前項邀請發出後，理事會應即調查爭議之情形，並建議其所認為最適當最有效之辦法。

三、如被邀請之一國拒絕承受聯合會會員之義務，以解決爭議，而向聯合會一會員以戰爭從事，則對於取此行動之國即可適用第十六條規定。

四、如相爭之兩造被邀請後，均拒絕承受聯合會會員之義務，以解決爭議，則理事會可籌一切辦法並提各種建議，以防止戰事，解除紛爭。

這些規定已使盟約課予第三國（非聯合會會員國）義務，包括和

平解決爭議的義務和不得違反盟約以作戰的義務。

聯合國為貫徹其宗旨與原則起見，於憲章第二條第六款規定：「本組織在維持國際和平與安全之必要範圍內，應保證非聯合國會員國遵守上述原則。」上述原則是指主權平等原則、善意履行憲章義務原則、以和平方法解決國際爭端原則、不在國際上使用武力或威脅原則、盡力協助聯合國依憲章所取行動原則等。可見本是重要條約的憲章，也課予第三國義務，一如國際聯合會盟約所標示的。

這些國際組織約章課予第三國義務，只有片面的決定，並不徵求第三國同意，畢竟是很特殊的情形。一般國家間的條約，尤其是普通雙邊條約，如果課予第三國義務，則依一般道理和法律原則，仍須取得第三國接受，未經接受前，課予義務的條款就不能生效，最少也可以說不得要求第三國履行義務。只有在強凌弱大欺小的時代裏，那類條款才有發生效果的可能。列強用秘密條約課予第三國義務，強迫第三國接受，曾有先例。其中之一是，一九四五年，美國羅斯福總統、英國邱吉爾首相和蘇聯史大林元帥簽訂雅爾達（Yalta）密約，要求中華民國租借旅順、大連等地給蘇聯。自聯合國憲章生效後，尤其從一九六〇年代以來，以條約把義務無理的加諸第三國的作法，為國際輿論所指摘，為國際社會所唾棄，為多數國家所反對，所以於一九六九年，本公約締結時，在第三十五條明訂：條約當事國要使第三國承擔義務，就要先在約中以明文規定，又要獲得第三國以書面表示接受，該國才須負擔義務。這就是說，不以書面表示接受的任何第三國，得拒絕負擔條約所定的義務，條約的規定不能對該國發生作用。

這和國際聯合會盟約及聯合國憲章的規定大異旨趣，未改變早已確立的國際法原則 —— 國家非經同意不受拘束。

基於國家獨立和國家平等的概念，條約如果要拘束第三國，就必須取得該國明示的同意，不得只憑默示的同意。取得明示的同意之前，還需要確定各當事國有課予義務的意思。有這意思，又經該第三國明示的同意後，該國雖然不是締約國，卻和各當事國間達成間接的協議，依這協議而受條約相關規定的拘束，應履行規定的義務。

這裏必須強調，條約以其條款課予第三國義務時，非經相關的第三國同意不爲功，正如常設國際法院在自由區 (The Free Zones) 案中說：無論如何，因爲瑞士不是凡爾賽條約締約國，該約第四百三十五條便不能拘束瑞士，如有拘束，亦以瑞士已接受的範圍爲限；那範圍定於一九一九年五月五日瑞士行政委員會的照會中；只在照會中所列的條件和保留範圍內，瑞士政府默認了第四百三十五條的規定❷❸。這案例表示，課予第三國的條約義務，必須經該國接受才能夠生效，義務範圍以其明示接受的爲限。

第三十六條　爲第三國規定權利之條約

一、如條約當事國有意以條約之一項規定對一第三國或其所屬一組國家或所有國家一項權利，而該第三國對此表示同意，則該第三國因此項規定而享有該項權利。該第三國倘無相反之表示，應推定其表示同意，但條約另有規定者不在此限。

---

❷❸ *PCIJ, Series A,* No. 22 (1929), pp. 17-18; *ibid, Series A/B,* No. 46 (1932), p. 141.

二、依第一項行使權利之國家應遵守條約所規定或依照條約所確定之條件行使該項權利。

條約賦予第三國或其所屬的一組國家或所有國家一項權利，實例頗多。最普通的實例，是於條約內列載最惠國待遇條款 (Most favored-nation clause) 的結果。甲國與乙國簽訂的通商航海條約中，如果含有這種條款，以後與丙國締結同性質條約時，把未給予乙國的優惠條件給予丙國，則乙國無需與甲國另訂新約，便可依據甲丙兩國間已訂的前約中最惠國待遇條款，當然可以享受甲國給予丙國的相同優惠條件，雖然乙國不加入甲國與丙國所締的條約，也就是說，乙國只是該約的第三國，仍可享受該約的特定權利❷。這種條款，第一次世界大戰以前，許多國家（特別是外貿航海發達的國家）訂約時列載，以造成不平等條約的結果，受損國的經驗教訓，已使近代的訂約者注意，避免重蹈覆轍，所以含有這種條款的條約少而又少了。也就表示，用這種條款給予第三國權利的情形已不多見了。

一八八一年，阿根廷與智利簽訂邊界條約，賦予所有國家船舶通過麥哲倫海峽 (Strait of Magelan) 的權利。一八八八年的君士坦丁堡條約，規定蘇以士運河 (Suez Canal) 應開放給各國商船軍艦通行。一九〇一年的美國與英國的 (Hay-Paun-

---

❷ 最惠國待遇條款的規定，可有三種不同的形式。一是規定締約國民在與第三國國民同樣條件下享受優惠條件；二是規定締約國國民可以無條件的享受優惠條件；三是只規定締約國國民可以享受優惠條件，不提及何種條件或在何種情形下可以享受。

cefote） 條約和一九〇三年的美國與巴拿馬的條約，訂明准許各國公私船舶通過巴拿馬運河 (Panama Canal)。這些都是條約賦予第三國權利的名例。丹麥和瑞士，都不是凡爾賽和約的當事國，但該約第一百零九條給予丹麥權利，第三百五十八條第三百七十四條賦予瑞士權利。第二次世界大戰後的一些和約，也分別給予某些非當事國權利。聯合國憲章第三十五條訂明，任何非聯合國會員的國家，都有權把爭端提交聯合國安全理事會或大會處理。這些都是條約給予一些或所有第三國權利的實例。

　　創設客觀存在的法律地位的條約給予第三國的權利，尤其是建立政治或領土制度，如割讓領土或保證某國中立的條約，設定國際地役的條約，其所規定的義務和權利，第三國都應予尊重。專就國際地役來說，縱使權利行使對象的領土有主權移轉的事實，該第三國仍可繼續行使原有權利。例如一八五六年英法俄三國的阿蘭島 (Aaland Islands) 條約，禁止俄國在島上恢復設防禦工事；一九一九年，阿蘭島併入芬蘭。一九二〇年，芬蘭與瑞典發生爭議，請國際聯盟理事會解決；理事會交法學家委員會研究，委員會判定瑞典有權利主張芬蘭不得在島上設防，俄國已承擔的不設防義務，雖然不是由於國際地役的結果，仍不受領土主權移轉的影響。一九四〇年芬蘭與蘇聯的條約，一九四七年芬蘭與各盟國簽訂的和平條約，都確認不得在該島設防的義務。

　　因為有了以上的例外，又為了以後的例外，本條便規定：條約當事國如果有意給予一個、一批或所有第三國一項權利，該第三國又表示同意享受該項權利，便因該項規定而享有該項權利，如其不作相反的表示，則推定其同意享受，但是條約另有規定

時，不在此限；第三國行使該項權利時，應遵守條約規定的或依照條約所確定的條件。

條約為第三國創設權利後，一個一組或全體當事國，未經該第三國同意，可否撤銷或變更該項權利？已表示同意享受權利的第三國，可否直接要求當事國履行該項權利的相對義務？或者須由一個當事國代為要求？對於這些問題，各方意見紛紜。或說第三國可以享受的只是利益，不是法律上的真實權利，不得要求條約當事國履行所謂權利的相對義務，當事國可以撤銷或變更該項「權利」，無需取得該第三國同意。或說第三國經賦予權利後，得請求當事國履行關於該項權利的規定，非經其同意，條約當事國不得撤銷或變更該項權利。或說於有關條約有效期間，條約未終止或修改前，已表示同意行使權利的第三國，享有法律上的真實權利，得請求履行關於其權利的條約規定，但各當事國得隨時撤銷或變更該項權利，無需經該第三國同意。

常設國際法院判決自由區 (The Free Zones of Upper Savoy and the District of Gex Case) 案時，可以說已涉及上述三種意見。原來一八一五年拿破崙戰爭結束後，歐洲列強締結了幾份協定，瑞士不是其中任何一份的當事國。其中一份為了日內瓦的利益，在自由區內設立關稅自由制度，使瑞士獲得利益。一九一九年凡爾賽和約第四百三十五條把自由關稅區撤銷，引起了法國與瑞士間的爭議。法國認為瑞士依據一八一五年的條約，固然已取得權利，但是於有關條約廢止後，瑞士便喪失了權利。這是上述三種意見的第一種。瑞士則堅稱，一八一五年有關條約的簽訂背景和經過，都確證各當事國有意賦予瑞士法律的真

實權利，須經瑞士同意，已由條約創設的關稅自由區才可以撤銷。這是上述三種意見的第二種。法院則在判詞中說：就一八一五年條約簽訂的經過、當時的情況和履行條約的實際情形看，各當事國確有意給予瑞士真實的權利，所以關稅自由區須經其同意才可以撤銷。法院又說：旨在創設第三國真實權利的條約規定，不得輕易推定為已被接受；主權國家如果有意創設這種權利，並且於約中規定使那意思能發生權利的效果，便沒有阻止它發生的理由，所以一國是否根據他國的條約而取得權利，須視個別情形而定，決定時須辨明當事國是否有意創設第三國的真實權利，並且確定該第三國已否依約接受❸。這是上述三種意見的第三種，最具權威性，現在已獲得廣泛的接受。

　　在事實上，給予第三國條約規定的權利，有些可不經相關的第三國同意，便予以撤銷或變更，有些則不可以。前者例如聯合國會員國可經修改憲章的程序，以撤銷或變更憲章已賦予第三國的權利，後者例如一九一九年巴黎和約給予捷克等國自行獨立的權利，非經捷克等有關國家同意，任何國家都不得撤銷或變更。還有一種情形，享受條約權利的第三國，不一定可以直接要求當事國履行條約相關規定，例如土耳其是享受一八五六年巴黎條約權利的第三國，不得要求當事國英國法國或奧國履行該約規定，使用武力以對抗土耳其的獨立或領土遭受的威脅。但凡爾賽和約第三百八十六條規定，與德國維持和平關係的第三國，於其在基爾運河 (Kiel Canal) 的自由通航權，因德國違反第三百八十

---

❸　*PCIJ, Series A/B* (1932), No. 46.

條至第三百八十六條而被妨礙時，得請求常設國際法院判決。這又表示，以條約給予第三國的某一權利，是否須經該第三國同意才可以撤銷或變更，權利國可否請求履行條約規定，都要視條約如何規定和權利性質等因素而定。

條約內關於賦予第三國權利的規定，第三國表示同意的行為究竟是什麼性質？換句話說，那是訂約性質？或是確認性質？一說認為授予權利的條款是契約法所稱的要約，第三國表示接受的行為，等於與條約當事國訂立新約的行為，行為國成為新約的締約國，依新約行使原約所定的權利。這是畫蛇添足般的說法，沒有法理或事實的依據，因為私法上利益契約的說法，今天在國際事件上已被摒棄，而且條約所定的權利必須先存在，第三國才可以行使，如果說第三國表示接受的行為是締約行為，就是等於說先行使權利，然後訂約以取得該項權利，那是本末倒置之論；如果那是締約行為，請看曾有其所訂條約向國際聯盟或聯合國秘書處登記嗎？何況條約當事國自始無意與任何第三國訂約，只有意創設第三國的權利，訂約後，沒有任何一個當事國為該項權利與任何第三國締結條約。例如一九○一年的美英條約和一九○三年的美巴條約，其第三國不是任何特定國家，而是汎指所有國家，沒有任何第三國專為巴拿馬運河通航的權利，而與美國、英國或巴國另行訂約。還有一說認為，第三國表示同意條約的規定，只是對既存權利的確認，不是與條約當事國訂立新約，其權利和條約同時開始存在，不是從虛擬的所謂新約中產生；而且第三國的確認，大多數是以默示的方式表示，也就是以行為表示，具體的說，就是把船舶依運河管理法規從運河通過，不對有關條約作任

何表示。

　　本公約對於上述性質問題，未曾提及，只於第三十七條訂明：依公約已使第三國享有權利時，如經確定其原意為非經第三國同意就不得撤銷或變更該項權利，則條約當事國不得撤銷或變更。這一規定，把條約當事國的原意作為決定性因素，十分恰當。

　　條約賦予第三國的權利，既然須經第三國表示同意接受，則該國享受該權利前，就應作同意的表示。但是，某國故意不表示或因疏忽而未表示，是不是不能行使該項權利呢？依照本條的規定，不問該國因何緣由而不表示，只要其不作反對的表示，就推定其同意接受。前述麥哲倫海峽、蘇以士運河、巴拿馬運河等的通航權，許多國家未曾表示同意或反對接受，而在事實上行使了。

　　本條訂明第三國行使條約權利的條件，較難，前條訂明第三國擔負條約義務的情形，較易，因為權利範圍甚廣，條約當事國不能把權利強加於第三國，如果強加，第三國可以拒絕，卽令勉強接受，也可於接受後放棄。所以本條規定，第三國表示同意接受才可以受益，最少也要不作相反的表示，才可以行使條約所賦的權利。

　　第三國行使條約所賦的權利，縱使無需擔負配合權利的相稱義務，也須遵守條約所定的條件，或遵守依照條約以確定的條件，以免當事國在約中的權利因第三國行使權利而化為烏有，或因第三國不遵守已定條件而難以行使。本條對於這種可能的情事，已作防範性的規定，而於第二項要求第三國遵守已訂明或經確定的條件。至於那些條件的問題，則留待各談判國決定。

原來防範性的規定，早已有了先例。一八八八年君士坦丁堡條約訂明：蘇以士運河於平時戰時對各國商船軍艦開放，永遠不得封鎖；不得於運河建築永久性防禦工事；任何國家都不得在運河內或運河港口三浬內交戰；交戰國軍艦應盡速通過運河，非有絕對必要，亦不得在蘇以士港或塞德港 (Port Suez or Port Said) 停留超過二十四小時；兩交國的軍艦進入運河航行，須相隔二十四小時；軍火軍隊和其他作戰物資，不得在運河內或運河港口裝卸；軍艦不得在運河內停泊；非交戰國才可以各在蘇以士港和塞德港停泊軍艦兩艘。雖然以上只是關於戰時使用蘇以士運河的限制，未提及運河平時的管制，實則管制運河使用的規則固不可缺，亦已有之，例如限制船舶噸位、入河時間、應繳規費、安全保證等等，自不在話下。總而言之，條約當事國必共同希望於條約開始施行時就享受條約所定的權利，因而都有資格要求第三國行使約中權利時，必須遵守其所定的條件。所有條約與第三國的權利關係都是這樣，君士坦丁堡條約只是一例而已。

第三十七條　取消或變更第三國之義務或權利

一、依照第三十五條使第三國擔負義務時，該項義務必須經條約各當事國與該第三國之同意，方得取消或變更，但經確定其另有協議者不在此限。

二、依照第三十六條使第三國享受權利時，倘經確定原意為非經該第三國同意不得取消或變更該項權利，當事國不得取消或變更之。

條約各當事國依照第三十五條使第三國擔負義務，該第三國

表示同意後，就當然負有條約所定的義務，雖然不因承受義務而成爲該約當事國，卻已正式承擔義務，而應該遵守承諾。條約各當事國要求第三國擔負義務，又獲得其同意承受，便也應該尊重其意思，所以如果有意取消或變更那義務，就應該取得其同意，反過來，如果其主動取消或變更那義務，亦須經各當事國同意，才使雙方地位平等，否則是不平等的關係。但是這種規定並非全無例外，例外之一是條約當事國與第三國有不同的協議。另有協議時，就當然應該按照協議的程序處理。例外之二是聯合國憲章的規定。憲章第二條第六款要求非聯合國會員國遵守憲章所定的原則，憲章是極重要的多邊條約，非聯合國會員國除退會者外，都不是該約的當事國，而是該約的第三國。憲章使第三國擔負遵守憲章原則的義務，並不依照本公約第三十五條的規定辦理，未曾經由第三國以書面表示接受，而且根本就沒有徵求第三國的同意，所以聯合國憲章當事國取消或變更這義務時，可以不經任何非憲章當事國同意，就能夠達到目的。

如上所述，條約當事國有意給予第三國權利時，縱使未以條文明定非經該第三國同意不得取銷或變更，各當事國也不一定可以隨時任意取消或變更。依照本條規定，於條約要求須經第三國同意時，固然應徵求同意，以其他方法確定須經第三國同意時，也應於取消或變更那權利之前，獲得其同意，才算合法。

兩類問題可能跟着發生：第一、誰有權確定取消或變更那權利？條約部分當事國？各當事國和相關的第三國？全體當事國？全體當事國和全體第三國？兩個全體一致或幾分之幾？或全體當事國和幾分之幾第三國？由各當事國確定，必比較容易作成結

論，很可能確定各當事國的原意是無需第三國同意，發生對第三國不利的結果。第二、依照第三十六條的意旨，第三國中，或有同意接受權利而尚未作任何表示的，試問依照本條約的規定作決定時，要不要邀請這類國家參與決定的程序？如果邀請，有什麼法律依據？這些問題，現在還沒解答的實例，仍然存在，希望只是理論上有，在實際上永遠沒有這類問題。

第三十八條　條約所載規則由於國際習慣而成為對第三國有
　　　　　　拘束力
　　　第三十四條至第三十七條之規定不妨礙條約所載規則成為對第三國有拘束力之公認國際法習慣規則。

本條規定條約所訂明的規則，可以變為國際法習慣規則，不受本公約所列載的規則的限制，特別是不受第三十四條至第三十七條各條所定規則的限制，而且於任何條約所載的規則變成公認的國際法習慣規則後，可以對第三國發生拘束力。如所周知，國際法習慣規則拘束一切國際法人，老早已是事實，為各國和所有國際法學者所接受，所以雙邊的多邊的條約規則，一旦變成了國際法習慣規則，便當然可以拘束第三國，已是毋庸爭議之論，而可能引起爭議的問題只是：「某條約規則已否獲得絕大多數國家承認而且接受為習慣法則？」

某條約規則，除原來已是多年久載的國際習尚（International usage）的以外，要變成國際法習慣規則，真是戞戞乎其難。一九六九年，國際法院於北海大陸礁層（The North Sea Continental Shelf Case）案中說，一九五八年大陸礁層公約

(The Convention on Continental Shelf) 的等距離原則 (The principle of equidistance) ，歷時未久，還未成爲劃定大陸礁層界線的國際法習慣規則，不能對德國發生拘束力，德國不是該公約當事國，也沒有遵行那原則的義務。從一九五八年到一九六九年，只有十一年的時間，那原則固然未被國際法院視爲習慣規則，就是歷時更久的國家行爲，已是許多國家屢行不變的行爲，多數國家已視爲具有法律意味的習慣，其國際法習慣規則的地位，也會受到質疑。例如領海寬度三浬制，於一九三〇年以前，海運發達的國家，固然宣稱那已是國際法習慣規則，許多其他國家亦不堅決反對，可是到了一九三〇年，國際聯合會舉行國際法編纂會議，討論領海寬度三浬制時，各說紛紜，莫衷一是，卒使海洋法規則不能訂立，一九五八年和一九六〇年的兩次國際會議，都不能就領海寬度取得共識，相反的，只否定了三浬制已是各國承認的國際法習慣規則。

　　然而無論如何，把條約的規定適用於第三國，擴大各當事國所定的適用範圍，其後各當事國和其他國家的實踐則扮演一個很重要的角色，這是公認的事情，用不着例證。某些國家以條約訂立某一個規則或制度後，由第三國普遍接受而成爲習慣，進而變成拘束其他國家的規則或制度，海牙公約的陸戰規則，便是一例。所以編纂現行習慣規則的多邊條約，是普遍接受的習慣規則滙輯，當然對非締約國有拘束力。

　　儘管這樣，仍然不能說這種多邊條約本身對第三國有法律效果，因爲這些條約並不建立各當事國與第三國間的條約關係，只是第三國也承認約中規則已是有拘束力的習慣法則，使條約對第

三國發生了法律效果。換句話說，就第三國而論，條約規則具拘束力的根源不是那條約，而是遵行那規則的習慣，因而本條訂明，本公約第三十四條第三十五條第三十六條和第三十七條，不管其規定爲何，都不妨礙任何條約的任何規則變爲國際法習慣規則，只要已變爲習慣規則，便可對所有第三國發生拘束力。

　　從國際法發展史看，本條不含一點兒創意，只是把過去的演進實況作一綜述，以文字描敍了現況，使各國和學者已接受的規則更富有法律意味了。

第四編　條約之修正與修改

　　本第四編不分節，只列第三十九條第四十條和第四十一條等三個條文，先訂條約修正的總則，次訂多邊條約的修正，然後規定關於只在若干當事國間修改多邊條約的協定的規則。雖然第三十九條的通則可適用於雙邊條約和多邊條約，但是，從本編整體看，着眼點是放在多邊條約上，實則雙邊條約的修正修改問題較少，也較容易處理，多邊條約的修正修改問題較複雜，也較難解決，因而要求本公約訂立較詳細的規則。

第三十九條　關於修正條約之通則

　　條約得以當事國之協議修正之。除條約可能另有規定者外，此種協議適用第二編所訂之規則。

　　近代國際組織發展迅速，數目不斷增加，多邊條約則不但數目頻添，內容也益加複雜，而國際組織的創立，又非有多邊條約作為其組織規章不為功。這些事實，對於條約修正修改的程序，必發生衝擊的作用。現在多數修正多邊條約的行為，直接牽涉國際組織，因為當條約是國際組織的章程時，尤其是在條約（例如國際勞工公約）為組織內的機關所擬訂的情形下，該組織和條約修正的關係更加密切。由國際組織發起並主持而簽訂的多邊條

約，如果規定該組織的秘書處為條約保管機關，條約修改或修正時和該組織的關係也密不可分，因為草擬修正或修改條款和文字的任務，必由該組織本身或其秘書處擔任。這樣一來，就保障了各締約國參與約條修正的權利，由其於審定草案時行使這權利。

多邊條約的簽訂愈頻繁，多邊條約的數目愈衆多，就愈增加訂約者的經驗，愈使其多所顧慮，使其於約中規定的重要事項可於日後修正。現在於條約訂明其修正和修改程序的條約，已屢見不鮮，條約當事國要修正或修改這種條約時，就不會有程序上的爭議了。當然實質內容上的歧見，不會因為避免了程序上的爭議而消除或減少了，因為這兩種爭議沒有因果關係，也不一定相互影響。

參加同一多邊條約的國家數目，也隨國際社會成員的數目增加而益多。有百數十個當事國的條約，要於修正或修改時取得各當事國一致同意‧然後才能使修正或修改案生效，幾乎已是完全不可求了。談判多邊條約者洞燭機先，或在約中規定這種案件的生效，無需經全體當事國同意，或在約中訂明，這種案件可在同意國間生效，原約仍在其他當事國間繼續施行，不予改變，這樣的作法，已逐漸形成一種國際實踐。一八六四年的日內瓦改善戰地軍人傷害狀況公約 (The Geneva Convention of 1864 for the Amelioration of the Condition of Soldiers Wounded in Armies in the Field) ，於一九〇六年修正時，訂明修正部分經批准後，在批准國間取代一八六四年條約的相同部分，原約仍在不批准修正案的國家間繼續適用。一九〇七年海牙公約，修正一八九九年陸戰規則時，附上類似的程序約款。聯合國成立

後，也曾以議定書修正一些國際聯盟所訂的公約，讓修正部分與
原約並存。

　　關於多邊條約的修正，雖然已有上述實踐，多邊條約所列載
的修正條款，至今仍有多種形式。其中綜合訂明修正的法律層次
的，爲數極少。多數訂明得建議修正案的條件而不提及談判程
序，或訂明修正案生效的條件，或要求修正案須經全體當事國同
意才能生效。因此，今天還不能從過去的多邊條約修正實例，演
繹出一套國際法習慣規則。

　　基於以上所述，本條規定條約得由各當事國協議修正，除條
約有相反的規定外，修正時須受本公約第二編各條規定的限制，
舉凡修正案的作成和生效等項，都不得違反規定。又鑒於近代國
際實踐，已是以新的多邊條約修正舊的多邊條約時，都訂明修正
部分只在批准國間生效，本條便不要求修正案須經全體當事國同
意才能生效，只盡量保障各當事國參與修約的權利，准許各國所
協議的方式，甚至容許其採用口頭方式，包括國家適用條約的行
爲所證實的默示協議方式，以使修約能夠達到目的。總之，在條
約沒有相反規定的情形下，各當事國可採用其所喜歡的任何方式
以修正條約。

　　最後必須指出，有些條約的個別條款改變時，學者稱爲修正
（Amendment），條約的全部條款調整時，則稱爲改正（Re-
vision），使其和許多國家內的用語相同，藉以避免混淆。可是
本條的修正一詞，包含了上述的條款改變和調整，和那些國內用
語的含義不盡相同，而本條約的修改（Modification），則用以
表示兩個和更多當事國改變其在同一多邊條約下的關係，修正一

詞則用以表示全體當事國改變其在同一條約下的關係。所以本條的修正和修改兩詞的含義，在實質上互不相同，和許多國家的國內法用語也不盡一致。

第四十條　多邊條約之修正

一、除條約另有規定外，多邊條約之修正依下列各項之規定。

二、在全體當事國間修正多邊條約之任何提議必須通知全體締約國，各該締約國均應有權參加：

　　（甲）關於對此種提議採取行動之決定；

　　（乙）修正條約之任何協定之談判及締結。

三、凡有權成爲條約當事國之國家亦應有權成爲修正後條約之當事國。

四、修正條約之協定對已爲條約當事國而未成爲該協定當事國之國家無拘束力，對此種國家適用第三十條第四項（乙）款。

五、凡修正條約之協定生效後成爲條約當事國之國家，倘無不同意思之表示：

　　（甲）應視爲修正後條約之當事國；並

　　（乙）就其對不受修正條約協定拘束之條約當事國之關係言，應視爲未修正條約之當事國。

　　研討本條時，首先應該注意，本條只提多邊條約的修正，不涉及雙邊條約的調整。雙邊條約僅有兩個當事國，如果需要修正，則由兩國直接談判，達成協議，作成決定，就可以達到目的。本公約第二編各條的規定，足以規範雙邊條約的修正事宜。一般說來，各當事國應基於誠信善意原則，對於修正條約的提

議，作善意的回應，免致提議國認爲對造無故不理，而走向片面宣告廢約的路上，使兩國邦誼受考驗，兩國實質利益受損害。

本條規定多邊條約的修正事宜，以便條約各當事國有意修正條約時，有可遵循並應遵守的規則。各當事國以新的協定來改變多邊條約的規定，並且對全體當事國生效，則和僅對部份當事國生效的協定，顯然不同。各當事國開始談判修約事宜時，或許預定新的協定對全體當事國生效，可是不幸因爲一些當事國不予批准、接受、贊同或加入那協定，結果的事實是只能對部分當事國生效而已。雖然可能有這種情形，本條的規定仍以全體當事國受拘束的條約修正爲限，而把僅在若干當事國間生效的修正多邊條約規則，移到第四十一條列載。這樣處理，應可避混亂難解的情形。

本條第一項很清楚的說明，關於多邊條約的修正事宜，如果被修正的條約已列有修正條款，就必須依照那（些）條款辦理，唯有於條約沒有修正條款時，才可以適用本條約的規定。換句話說，條約所載的條款，常爲主，常居先，本條的規定，常爲副，常居次。而在事實上，許多多邊條約的草擬者，因爲預料條約日後有修正的需要，又希望條約能被修正，更要使修正過程順利，便在條約內明訂修正的程序。這也就是爲什麼本條開宗明義的說，條約的修正依條約的規定進行。

依照本條第二項的規定，所有預定對全體當事國生效的任何修正建議，當事國或條約保管機關處理時，必須通知並且邀請每一當事國參與談判及決定，每一當事國都有權參與建議案的任何行爲。無論過去條約修正的做法是怎樣的，本公約生效以後，涉

及條約全體當事國的修正案，如果不遵守這一項的規定，便是顯然不合法的，除非有非常特殊的情形，例如排除一個經聯合國宣告的侵略國，不通知不邀請它參與條約的修正程序。在本公約簽訂以前，聯合國憲章於一九六三年修正時，已依照本項的規定辦理。

本條第三項規定，有權成爲當事國的國家，都有成爲修正後條約當事國的資格，曾參加談判仍未成條約當事國的國家，對於條約的修正案，往往有更大的興趣，或有參與修正程序的願望，但是由於它不是當事國，不具有參與的權利，它從旁表示的意見，在修正過程中，受重視或被忽視，被採納或遭拒絕，都難預卜。它如果要成爲當事國，就須等到條約修正後，採用批准、接受、贊同或加入的方式，那時候，它也只能夠在接納各修正條約的情形下，成爲當事國，要是它對那些條款有所不滿，又決心設法修正，就唯有尋覓適當時機，推動再修約的程序了。

本條第四項規定，修正條約的協定，只對同意修正條款的原當事國有拘束力，不對其他原當事國生效，對其仍適用本公約第三十條第四項（乙）款的規定，也就是「在爲兩約之當事國與僅爲其中一條約之當事國彼此之權利與義務依兩國均爲當事國之條約定之。」現在就條約修正的情形來說，同意修正和反對修正的原當事國間的權利和義務，仍須依照未修正前的條約規定處理。此外，按條約不課予第三國義務的一般原則，縱使沒有本項的規定，反對修正的原當事國也不應受修正後條約的拘束。然而制訂本公約時，如果不列入本項的規定，則會讓人猜想經修正的條款，必對反對修正的原當事國有或多或少的法律效力，因爲近代

若干多邊條約訂明，除反對修正的當事國作明確的反對聲明外，都受修正後條約的拘束。

　　本條第五項規範比較複雜的事項。一份條約業經修正並且已在若干原當事國間生效後，某國才成為原約當事國。這時候，它和條約各當事國的關係是怎樣的？這無疑是比較複雜的情形，因為一份修正條約的協定，只獲得一部分原當事國批准，確是很常見的情形，這情形使一份條約有兩類當事國，一類是修正後條約的當事國，另一類是原約和修約協定兩份文書的當事國，按一般意義，都是條約當事國，同有該約下的相互關係，但是，修正後條約的當事國間的相互關係，只是原約當事國間的相互關係，這兩類當事國間的相互關係，同是原約和修約協定當事國間的相互關係，其與上述兩類當事間的相互關係，本來已是錯綜複雜，再於條約修正後，又有原約的新當事國，當然使各當事國間的關係更複雜了。不過仍然可以指出，只是原約的當事國僅受原約規定的拘束，同是原約和修正後條約的當事國須受修約協定下的條約的拘束，至於條約修正後的原約新當事國的地位，則有待商榷。它當然應是原約和修正後條約的當事國？或在它不作相反的表示時才是？它當然只是原約的當事國？或在不作相反的表示時，才可以推定它只是原約當事國，不和修約協定當事國發生條約關係？當普遍性多邊條約修正時，這些問題不只具有理論性，而且必有實然性，因為許多國家表示同意承受條約的拘束時，往往不透露其關於修約協定的立場，以致條約保管者（機關）收到批准、接受、贊同或加入條約的文書時，推定送交文書國的意旨包括原約和修正條款。但是這樣的推定結論，未必符合該國的意

旨，甚至與其原意相違。

　　本公約擬訂者，顧及當事國有不表明意思的情形，便於本項定下規則。這規則基於兩個原則，一是國家於成為條約當事國時，有權抉擇只為原約的當事國、為原約和修正後條約的當事國、或只為修約協定的當事國，二是於該國不作任何表示時，採用能使最多國家發生同約相互關係的方法，以推定該國的意思。所以本項規定，修約協定生效後，原約的新當事國不表示相反的意思時，便㈠視其為修正後條約的當事國，㈡它和反對修正的當事國間的關係上，視其為原約的當事國。

　　原約當事國參加修約協定的草擬後，由於某種原因（例如需經立法機關同意的修約案，不幸被立法機關拒絕），竟未成為協定的當事國。它可否以任何理由（假如以其權利被剝奪為藉口），反對協定在其他當事國間生效？雖然本條對於這一節未加規定，沒有權威性的法律性的答案，但按常理說，它如果真的表示反對，那是不可思議的事情，也是於法無據於理不通的反對。

　　第四十一條　僅在若干當事國間修改多邊條約之協定

一、多邊條約兩個以上當事國得於下列情形下締結協定僅在彼此間修改條約：

　　（甲）條約內規定有作此種修改之可能者；或

　　（乙）有關之修改非為條約所禁止，且：

　　　　（一）不影響其他當事國享有條約上之權利或履行其義務者；

　　　　（二）不干涉任何如予損抑卽與有效實行整個條約之目的及宗旨不合之規定者。

二、除屬第一項（甲）款範圍之情形條約另有規定者外，有關當事國
　　應將其締結協定之意思及協定對條約所規定之修改，通知其他當
　　事國。

　　本條各項的規定，不像本公約第四十條，不規範涉及全體當事國的修約，而是如本條標題所示，規範「僅在若干當事國間修改多邊條約之協定」，所規範的修改，只在某些當事國間生效，不影響其他當事國在條約上的權利或義務。修約國也許自始無意讓其他當事國參與修改，不邀請其參與，拒絕給予其參與的機會，所以這種修約，和自始便邀請全體當事國參與的情形大不同，而且在修改後，原約的目標或宗旨可能被改變了。改變條約的目標或宗旨，在一般情形下，非經全體當事國同意不可，因而本條針對可以修約的情形，作詳細確實的規定。

　　本條第一項規定，首先要判定條約內規定有作所提修改的可能，其次是所提修改未為條約所禁止，再次是所提修改不影響其他當事國的條約權利或義務，最後是所提修改不違反條約的宗旨或目標。換句話說，必須符合下列幾個條件，少數當事國才可以經由修約途徑，以改變其在條約下的義務（或權利）。第一、不妨礙條約目標或宗旨的有效完成；第二、不牴觸條約的禁止規定；第三、不影響其他當事國的權利或義務；第四、所提修改是可能的。這些條件同時全部符合了，才可以進行修改程序，只符合其一其二或其三，或符合了其中三者，仍然不符合本條的規定。其中第一個和第二個條件，難免稍有重疊，因為背離條約的目標或宗旨，可以說也是條約隱含禁止的，只是為了使隱含的禁

止變爲明示的禁止，並且排除兩者的隱隱約約的牴觸，才把兩者並列。

本條第二項要求修約國通知其他當事國，通知須列示所提修改的內容。這種要求的目的，在防範修約逾越條約許可的範圍，保障反對非法修約的當事國，避免條約被輕率的修改。有關當事國的通知，可否分批發出？可否在發出的時間上間隔多日？可否內容不完全相同？本項對於這些枝節問題未作規定，可由修約國商定答案。修約國把「其締結協定之意思及協定對條約所規定之修改，通知其他當事國」，就符合本項的目的了。誠然用不着說，通知應該以書面作成。

以上所敍的，是以文書修改條約的程序。在事實上，條約的修改也可以經由習慣。條約簽訂後，各當事國適用約中某條款時，雖然不符該條款於訂約時談判者的意思、簽署者的意思、批准者的意思、或自然而通常的意思，但是各當事國不察覺、不重視或明知而接受，已按共同認識接受的意思以履行該條款，而且反覆照樣履行，履行多次，無人否認履約行爲的合法性和正當性，養成了符合各當事國利益的習慣，無形無意中修改了條約，發生了以文書修約的相同效果，甚至更具體更切合需要的效果。例如聯合國憲章第二十七條第三項訂明：「安全理事會對於其他一切事項❶之決議，應以七理事國之可決票包括全體常任理事國

---

❶ 安全理事會議處理的事項，分爲程序的事項和其他一切事項。所謂「其他一切事項」，就是通稱的實質事項或非程序事項。某事項是不是實質事項的問題，視爲非程序事項，表決時常任理事國得行使否決權，也就是得反對其爲程序事項而投票，那反對票發生否定多數贊成票的效力，使該事項再於會中提付表決時，該反對國得再投反對票，使該事項最終被否決。這是俗稱的安全理事會常任理事國的雙重否決權。

之同意票表決之」❷。顯然的，常任理事國於表決時所投的應是同意票，不是於表決時缺席，也不是於表決時棄權（說是不投票或投空白票或於舉手表決時不舉手表示贊成或反對），唯有於全部可決票中包括五個常任理事國的同意票，議案才可以合法表決通過。可是現在安全理事會已有一個習慣，就是任何議案提付會議表決時，只要有九個❸或更多理事國贊成，沒有常任理事國反對，即令有五個常任理事國棄權或缺席，亦可以通過。這一演變，無疑是出了憲章草擬者意料之外，不符現行憲章第二十七條文字的通常而自然的意義，可以說已修改了條約（即憲章），只因有關各國早已默認這是好的改變，對各國並無不利，對國際社會必定有益，所以大家接受，無人表示反對，結果是以習慣修改了憲章。

　　重大的情勢變遷，往往會導致條約修改，因為重大情勢變遷原則 (The principle of rebus sic stantibus) 曾被引以為修改條約的理由。所謂重大情勢變遷，是訂約時的情勢發生了極大的改變，不只是已有微小的不同，而且那情勢是訂約的主要誘因與基礎，誘因與基礎已變，難免要使條約配合改變，那條約可以是雙邊的，也可以是多邊的，可能於訂約後不久便發生那改變，改變又可能是突發的或逐漸累積的結果，都引起重大情勢變

---

❷　一九四五年的憲章第二十七條第二項，原定應為七個理事國，一九六三年修改憲章，把安全理事會理事國由十一國增加為十五國，並把該項的「七」字改為「九字」。該項的其他文字未變，現在未見任何人倡議，理事國數目應隨聯合國會員國的增加而增加。

❸　請閱註❷的說明。

遷原則可否適用的問題。

　　若干學者認爲，每一條約都隱含着這一原則的適用，或說訂約時的情勢發生了改變，便是修改條約的正當理由，或說這簡直是終止條約的有力根據，因爲當事國訂約時相信當時不損害其重大利益，以爲訂約可以增進其福祉，現在旣已有始料未及的惡劣變化，如果必須繼續履行條約義務，就必定造成嚴重後果，甚至妨害其生存，阻礙其發展更不用說了，所以原當事國應有權援引上述原則，要求修改條約、解除條約義務或宣告終止條約。

　　本公約不排除重大情勢變遷原則的價值和適用，所以把它列入專條，詳加訂明，以預防濫用它所帶來的弊端。至於有那些弊端的問題，留待下文析論第六十二條「情勢之基本改變」時，才作說明。

第五編　條約之失效、終止及停止施行

第一節　總　　則

　　本編的內容，包括條約的失效、條約的終止和條約的停止施行，於第一節總則中談條約的效力和連續有效原則、國際法所加於締約國的義務、條約規定的可分性，以及締約國援引條約失效等理由的權利喪失，於第二節敍明國內法與締結條約的權限、國家表示同意的權力限制、錯誤、詐欺、對代表的賄賂和強迫、對國家的武力使用或威脅、以及與絕對法的牴觸等，於第三節列載諸如終止和退出條約、廢止條約、暫停施行條約、不能履行條約等的規則，於第四節訂明條約失效等的程序、司法與公斷及和解的程序、以及應使用的文書，然後於第五節詳訂條約失效、條約終止、條約暫停施行等的後果。所以本編可以說是爲了防止簽訂條約時節外的瑕疵，收拾條約的殘局，減少當事國的無可避免的損害。

　　第一節標題是「總則」，因其所列四條條文，可適用於雙邊條約、多邊條約、退出條約、終止條約等等，不會有例外的情形，不涉及特殊的規則，所以又可以叫做通則。

第四十二條　條約之效力及繼續有效

一、條約之效力或一國承受條約拘束之同意之效力僅經由本公約之適用始得加以非議。

二、終止條約、廢止條約、或一當事國退出條約，僅因該條約或本公約規定之適用結果，始得為之。同一規則適用於條約之停止施行。

　　各國締結條約時，總是希望先釐定彼此間的權利和義務關係，然後遵循約中所定的規則，以享受權利履行義務，並且希望這種關係正常穩定。所以本條訂明，條約的效力，國家表示同意承受條約拘束的效力，在常態下，都是連續不斷的，非經由本公約各有關規定的適用，不得否定，換句話說，各當事國必須遵守本公約的規則，不得持異議。唯有這樣，才可以維持條約效力的持續和穩定，各當事國才願依賴條約的規定，繼續依照條約內容以享受權利和盡義務。同理，任何當事國要終止條約、廢止條約或退出條約，如果不是適用本公約規定的結果，又不是適用相關條約規定的結果，就不得終止、廢止或退出條約。

　　所謂「本公約之適用」，是指本公約所列載的規定的適用，而規定則包括一切相關的規定，連同使特定條款生效的規定，不以關於條約失效或終止的特別條款為限，例如作為國際組織的構成基石的條約、條約可分性等的規定，必須連同其他相關條款加以考慮。簡單說來，本公約的適用，是指約中所有相關規定的適用。

　　本條有「僅經由本公約之適用」和「僅因該條約或本公約規

定之適用」兩詞。兩詞都表示，除特殊條約明白規定的以外，本
公約所列條約失效、終止條約、廢止條約、退出條約的理由，是
完全而充分的，要終止、廢止或退出條約的國家，不得以其他理
由爲藉口，企圖達到其目的。已經過時、長久不予適用或施行、
顯然已無用處，都是條約失效的原因，當事國可據以進行談判，
協議終止或廢止條約。專就雙邊條約來說，兩造都不再適用條約
時，該條約便自然無用了，也就是有了失效的眞正原因。再就多
邊條約來說，一個當事國喪失國際人格時，條約便少了一個當事
國，因而產生的後果，只以減少一個當事國爲限，不引起其他問
題。但是，由於喪失國際人格、退出條約或其他原因，當事國繼
續減少時，減到何一程度，才會引起其他問題？等到下文析論第
五十五條時，才針對這問題的相關各點加以敍明。

　　條約的暫停施行問題，已由本公約第五十七條、第五十八
條、第五十九條及第六十條作詳細的規定，任何當事國暫停施行
條約時，依照本條第二項末句的規定，亦須因該條約或本公約規
定的適用結果，才可以暫停。

第四十三條　無需基於條約之國際法所加義務

　　條約因本公約或該條約規定適用結果而失效、終止或廢止，由當
事國退出或停止施行之情形，絕不損害任何國家依國際法而毋需基於
條約所負履行該條約所載任何義務之責任。

　　依照本條的規定，條約失效、條約終止或條約廢止，是適用
本公約結果，或因爲適用相關條約的規定所致，因當事國退出或

停止施行而產生的情形，完全不減少❶當事國依國際法應擔負的責任（就是無需由於該條約的規定而有的責任），各當事國必須善意履行該條約所載的全部義務，絕不得減少；只要依照國際法，彼等仍應繼續履行各項義務的責任，絕不受條約失效、終止條約、廢止條約、當事國退出或停止施行條約的影響。

本條所稱的國際法 (International law)，因為沒有冠上特別的或區域的之類的限制字，所以應可解釋為各種國際法，包括區域的特別的普遍的國際法 (Regional, particular and universal international law)，當然也就包括國際法的習慣規則(Customery rules) 和協定規則(Conventional rules)，而協定規則有現行的和非現行的，本條的國際法所含的規則，便應以現行的為限❷。

第四十四條　條約之規定可否分離❸

一、除條約另有規定或當事國另有協議外，條約內所規定或因第五十

---

❶　「減少」是本條條文中的「損害」。按「損害」是譯自英文的「im-pair」一字，而 impair 則有「損害」、「減損」、「減少」等意義。用以說明本條的涵義時，譯為「減少」比較符合中文的用法。

❷　本公約提到國際法時，不訂明國際法的定義，對於某些讀者或會引起疑問。請注意，有疑問時，應採其廣義。

❸　本標題是「條約之規定可否分離」，不夠妥善，又不明確，究竟是可分離或是不可分離？只從標題看，其本身也是疑問。這標題的英文是「Separability of treaty provisions」，譯為「條約規定之可分性」，才符合英文原義，也符合中文的習慣用法。本書不改原用文字，只順此註明。

六條所生之當事國廢止、退出或停止施行條約之權利僅得對整個條約行使之。

二、本公約所承認之條約失效、終止、退出或停止施行條約之理由僅得對整個條約援引之，但在下列各項或第六十條所規定之情形下不在此限。

三、倘理由僅與特定條文有關，得於下列情形下對各該條文援引之：

(甲)有關條文在適用上可與條約其餘部分分離；

(乙)由條約可見或另經確定各該條文之接受並非另一當事國或其他當事國同意承受整個條約拘束之必要根據；及

(丙)條約其餘部分之繼續實施不致有失公平。

四、在第四十九條及第五十條所稱情形下，有權援引詐欺或賄賂理由之國家得對整個條約或以不違反第三項為限專對特定條文援引之。

五、在第五十一條、第五十二條及第五十三條所稱之情形下，條約之規定一概不許分離。

前文於析論第十九條第二十條第二十一條第二十二條和第二十三條的內涵時，提及對條約的保留，本條則專談條約規定的可分離性。對條約的保留和條約規定的分離，在基本觀念上是彼此互異，沒有相互的關係，更沒有因果關係。但是，一份條約的各項規定如果可以分離，則締約國對其可分離的規定作保留，只就其餘規定承受拘束，便不引起可否提出保留的問題，其選擇的結果不會違反條約。

原來自有簽訂條約的行為以來，沒有可以分割條約各項規定的觀念，也沒有條約規定可受分割的理論，必視約中各項規定為

一整體，各項密切相關，缺少其中之一，條約便失其完整性，甚至刪除其中某項時，會使其餘各項不能履行或喪失作用。最原始的雙邊條約，固然爲這一不可分割的觀念所囿，就是最早的多邊條約，也不准許分割約中條款。時代進入本世紀後，終止條約的權利，基於該約已牴觸另一條約的理由，才能夠獲得承認，但以根據這一理由的權利爲限。第一次世界大戰以後，若干權威學者承認條約規定可分割的原則，認爲處理條約失效案和戰爭對條約的效果案時，應注意這原則，盡量避免使相關條約的全部規定無效。他們主張在某些情形下，可以刪除或暫停施行約中某項規定，刪除或暫停施行並不當然牽動其餘規定所確立的權利義務的平衡。毫無疑問的，縱使在理論上，可以說一份條約內的某一規定可與另一規定分離，但在實踐上，要確定其可分性，卽令不是絕不可能的事情，也會招致嚴重的爭議。甲某認定某兩（若干）項規定可分離，但乙某堅持相反的認定。所以國際法院對殘害人羣罪防止及懲治公約保留案發表意見時，多數法官承認不違反公約目標與宗旨的保留有效後，少數法官指出，違反與不違反的標準無定，會受主觀考慮左右，多數法官的意見於是不可取。從此可見，解釋條約時採用分離規定的原則，處斷條約失效或條約終止時適用分離規定的原則，兩者的難易度是很不相同的。

無論是關於條約失效或當事國終止、廢止、退出或暫停施行條約，約中如果只訂明當事國有權分離條約的規定，不訂明如何行使這權利（就是不訂明怎樣分割各項規定），解釋該條約時，就應該讓各當事國自定行使這權利的條件。當事國如果不特別指出只廢止或終止約中一部分規定，就推定其有意針對全部規定行

使權利。所以本條第一項說，條約所定的一項權利，除該約另有規定或各當事國另有協議外，只能對全約一切規定行使。所謂「另有規定」和「另有協議」，是指得不對全約行使那權利的規定和協議，可以針對著約中一項或某些項行使那權利的規定和協議。

在一般情形下，維持一份條約的各項規定的完整，是各締約國的首要意圖，也是訂立條約的基本原則。多邊條約各締約國的期望是這樣，雙邊條約的談判者尤其如此。所以本條第二項訂明，使條約失效的理由，以及終止、退出或暫停施行條約的理由，爲本公約所承認的，只可以對整個條約援引，不得對約中部分規定援引，也就是說，不得依據其中理由使條約的部分規定失效，或只終止、退出或暫停施行約中部分規定。這一規定，能否有助於維持條約的完整呢？還在未定之天，仍須拭目以待。只從理論方面看，答案應該是正面的。

本條要求維持條約的完整，是一般原則，遇有本公約第六十一條所規定的情形時，則可以有例外，不受本條規定的限制。那些例外，留待敍述該條各項規定時才列舉。

本條第三項的意旨是：援引條約失效的理由，或援引終止、退出或暫停施行條約的理由時，涉及的規定如果顯然可以從約中其餘規定分離出來，接受被涉及的規定又不是同約其他當事國同意承受全約拘束的必要根據，而且該約其餘規定的繼續施行不產生不公平的情形，就可以對各項特定的有關條文援引那理由，不受條約完整原則的限制。在這情形下援引後，不受影響的其他條文繼續有效。至於接受那（些）相關規定是不是其他當事國同意承

受全約拘束的必要依據的問題，則要按條約的內容來解答，或用別的方法加以確定，應參照各條文所定事項、該相關規定和其餘規定的關係、訂約前各種準備作業、訂約時的情況等等，以求得解答或確定。至於把條約的某一（些）相關規定分離後，繼續施行其餘規定時，有沒有不公平的情形，則是事實問題，唯有根據個案的實情才能找到答案。

　　本條第四項指涉第四十九條規定的詐欺和第五十條規定的賄賂，旨在訂明：准許受害國援引被詐欺或其代表受賄賂爲理由，以使條約全部無效，並且准許受害國使全約中特定條文無效，只要全約或該特定條文和那理由有關，受害國的抉擇就是合法的。

　　本公約第五十一條規定代表受強迫，第五十二條規定國家受強迫，第五十三條規定牴觸絕對法的條約。本條第五項的意旨，在排除前兩條規定下的情形，也就是訂明，在代表或國家受強迫下締結的條約，各條款都絕對無效，任何條款都不許分割，理由是強迫一個國家或其代表訂約，違反了一般國際法強制規律（絕對法），所有違反這種規律的條約無效，無效的條約內各條款就不許分割，縱使只是約中某一（些）條款違反了，全約仍是無效，各條款仍然不許分割，各當事國如果還要使條約有效，就唯有修正條約，把牴觸這種規律的條款刪除，重訂新約，如果不重訂新約，便應維持這規律的特性，置條約於規律之下，才符合本項的意旨。

第四十五條　喪失援引條約失效、終止、退出或停止施行條約理由之權利

一國於知悉事實後，而有下列情形之一者，即不得再援引第四十六條至第五十條或第六十條及第六十二條所規定條約失效、終止、退出或停止施行條約之理由：

(甲)該國業經明白同意條約有效，或仍然生效或繼續施行；或

(乙)根據該國行爲必須視爲已默認條約之效力或條約之繼續生效或施行。

在國際法上，善意原則和公正原則的基準之一，是不許締約國因其前後不一致的行爲而受益。換句話說，締約國在後的行爲和在先的行爲相互矛盾時，不得從矛盾中選擇於已有利的結果，同時排除於已不利的解釋。這一基準在國際法上的妥適性，不但已受學者重視，而且獲得了普遍的承認。從一般道理看，也唯有堅守這基準，才能夠維持善意原則和公正原則，所以無需特別強調這基準了。

在條約法中，善意原則和公正原則尤其重要，因爲使條約失效，終止條約、廢止條約、暫停施行條約的理由，本來就隱含著些許被浮濫引據的危險。甲締約國明知約中有實質的錯誤或乙締約國已違約……等情事，卻不作任何表示，只繼續履行條約，儼若不知有這些情事，等到對其有利的時機成熟時，希望藉別的理由以終止其在條約下的義務，才提起實質錯誤或乙國違約，作爲其終止條約的理由。這無疑是終止條約理由的濫用，是上述原則的考驗，所以本條要限制締約國的權利，免致權利被濫用以使條約失效或終止（廢止、退出或停止施行）條約。

本條(甲)款規定，甲當事國明知已有理由以使條約無效，或

有理由終止（廢止、退出或停止施行）條約時，如果仍然「明白
同意條約有效或仍然生效或繼續施行」，就必須視其已經放棄援
引這種理由的權利。要是還援引，便是濫用權利，依照本款的規
定，是違法的行爲。

一個當事國已經注意到某一事實，可援引爲使條約無效或終
止（廢止、退出或停止施行）條約的理由時，如果仍然繼續採取
某行爲，該行爲又足以視爲已表示默認條約的效力、條約繼續生
效或條約繼續施行，而且足以使其他當事國認爲已有這種默認，
該當事國便喪失了援引這些理由的權利。要是還援引，便是本條
(乙)款所禁止的行爲。

然而從另一方面看，當事國如果不注意到可以行使這種權利
的事實，或者雖然注意到，卻不能夠自由表達意志或者不能行使
這些權利，則自當別論，不受本條規定的限制，所以本條排除了
第五十一條（對一國代表之強迫）、第五十二條（以威脅或使用
武力對一國施行強迫）所列的情形，准許當事國援引這些理由，
以使其代表或國家被強迫簽訂的條約無效。這裏說這種條約無
效，表示當事國有權使它無效，只是就訂約國的權利來說。若就
現代一般國際法而論，強迫代表或以威脅或使用武力對締約國施
行強迫下所締結的條約，便違反了公認的絕對法，自始無效，用
不著受害的當事國使它無效。

第二節　條約之失效

第四十六條　國內法關於締約權限之規定

一、一國不得援引其同意承受條約拘束之表示爲違反該國國內法關於
　　締約權之一項規定之事實以撤銷其同意，但違反之情事顯明且涉
　　及基本重要性之一項規則者，不在此限。
二、違反情事倘由對此事依通常慣例並秉善意處理之任何國家客觀視
　　之爲顯然可見者，卽係顯明違反。

　　在實行憲政民主的國家裏，締結條約的權限多由憲法規定，
少由習慣規範。以憲法限制締約權的行使，也各有不相同的方
式，而且把這權限分屬行政和立法機關，由兩者共同行使。有些
憲法規定，非經立法機關事前同意，行政機關不得締結條約，或
者不得締結特殊種類的條約（這是屬於極少數的規定）；有些憲
法規定，非經立法機關同意，不得批准條約（如中華民國憲法）；
有些憲法規定，非經立法機關某單位經特定程序表示同意，條約
不能成爲有效的國內法（如美國憲法）；還有一些國內特別法，
限制行政機關的締約權，而且該法的修改須經修憲的特別程序。
可見各國憲法關於締約權行使的規定，五花八門，各投所好。但
是，從大處看，無論其規定怎麼複雜，仍可以歸納爲兩類，一類
以憲法限制政府的締約權，影響政府的實質權力，另一類要求條
約須經立法機關同意，未經同意前不得施行，影響行政機關施行
條約的權力。不管是那一類，都屬於國內法範疇。這些限制對於
國家代表所表示的同意，對於國家代表似乎已獲得授權才表示的
同意，在國際法上究竟可以有怎樣的影響？

　　大家知道，同意承受條約拘束的決定，這一同意由什麼機關
負責表示，以及按什麼程序以對外表示，全由各國選擇自主，國際
法從不過問。旣不過問，於考慮某國簽署、批准、接受、贊同或

加入某條約，須確定那簽署、批准、接受、贊同或加入的國際行
為有沒有拘束該國的效力時，便應知道該國憲法的相關規定，把
限制國家機關締約權的國內法，視為國際法的一部分，以避免該
國不依其憲法規定，而在國際上表示同意承受條約拘束，或使其
同意可以撤銷。此外，違反憲法規定而使其國家受拘束者，無論
依照國內法或國際法，都絕無從事這種行為的資格。以上是一派
學者的說法。依照這一說法，誰也不能完全信賴表面上有權使國
家承受條約拘束的權威人物，如國家元首、行政首長（總統、院
長、首相、總理等）、外交部長等，各國必須依個別案件，以查
證相關外國未違反其本國憲法的規定，不然，就會冒條約後來被
宣告無效的危險，而使自己的全功盡廢。

　　以上一派堅持把憲法併入國際法，被稱為併入派，其主張若
經採納，又對多邊條約的保管者(機關)實施，便會面臨不能克服
的困難。每當收到一份批准、接受、贊同或加入條約的文書時，
是否必須先查證批准（接受、贊同或加入）的決定適憲？又要確
實表示那決定的程序合法？如果答說「必須」，保管者(機關)怎樣
完成或進行？當然還需要考慮其他許多問題和困難，無法避免的
困難。因而另一派學者認為，可以把憲法併入國際法，以保障條
約的安存，預防條約簽訂者白費功夫，但是必須修正併入原則，
只併入顯明的憲法限制，同時排除不顯明的憲法限制（就是盡力
辨識仍不能察覺的限制），只容許當事國援引顯明的憲法規定，
以辯護其關於條約效力的立場，所以顯然違憲的簽署、批准、接
受、贊同或加入條約，在國際法和國內法上都當然無效。如果以
這一說為準，正如完全併入說一樣，會遭遇重重困難，無法克

服。怎樣的憲法規定是顯明的或不是顯明的？有些憲法規定的含義，常隨解釋者主觀理念而變化，例如政治性條約，或特別重要的條約，須經特定程序處理等措詞，意義含糊，可含多種不同的意義，那一種條約是政治性的？那一份條約特別重要？都隨解釋者的主觀意志而變更，也可能因時空更易而變化。近來簡化式條約愈來愈多，其內容的彈性越來越大，其處理是否違反憲法所定程序的問題，常由行政機關依政治考慮作判斷，那判斷後來可能受立法或司法機關挑剔，因而在許多情況下，很難肯定說某條約是適憲的產物，更不能斷言某條約的某當事國法院會判決該國憲法規定是顯明的。換句話說，修正併入派的主張也不可行，須再加以修正。

　　再修正派的法學家強調，締約意志的形成和決定的機關與程序，各國得自由作主，不屬於國際法的範疇，國際法只管那意志在國際上對外國的表示，不過問各國可以自行作主的事情，又規定各國表示同意承受條約拘束時應具備的條件，以及應遵循的程序，再規定何機關和人員有以國家名義完成那程序的資格，因而符合這資格者，經由既定程序以國家名義行為，表示同意承受條約拘束後，就可以斷定該國依國際法應受該條約拘束，縱使其行為違反國內法，使條約在國內法下無效，他並且要受法律所定的處分，只要他已依照國際法（也就是條約法公約）所定的權能從事那行為，他的違法（憲）便不影響條約在國際法上的效力。這是再修正派的主要說辭，特別著重於本公約規定的效力，如果還進一步強調，說其他當事國明知他違反國內法，或者他缺乏憲法規定的行為權限很顯明時，即視為已明知，則這一種主張的原則

最妥善可行。在這原則下，各當事國有權推定某代表依國際法有權做了應做的事情，唯有於其應該能夠知道他無權，或於其必須依法推定他無權，或者他只在某一案中無權，各當事國才可以否定他的行爲能發生國際法上的效力。

　　常設國際法院在東格陵蘭案 (Legal Status of Eastern Greenland Case) 中說，挪威外交部長伊蓮 (M. Ihlen)，依其職權對丹麥代表所作的承諾，當然對其本國挪威有拘束力；法院只依國際法所定的他應有的權限下判斷，而不追查伊蓮依挪威法有沒有使挪威受拘束的權力❹。法院在這一案中，雖然不直接提到條約，卻間接顯示法院只就國家代表的國際行爲以論斷問題，何況多人已視伊蓮已締結了口頭條約，口頭條約和書面條約一樣，能夠拘束締約國。

　　回顧往昔，不見何國以其代表違憲爲理由，撤銷了其承受條約拘束的同意，亦少見條約保管機關處理過這種案件。直到今天，締約代表相互校閱全權證書、簽署、互換批准書或交存接受書時，只注意這些文書的形式和內容是否妥善，不進一步追查各代表的行爲是否違反其本國法。如果追查，便可能有干涉內政的嫌疑。雖不追查，也未曾發生弊端。

　　本公約已規定批准、接受、贊同和加入等方式，任由各國選用其一，以成爲條約當事國，任何一國在決定選用那一方式以前，有時間，也有充分自由，依其憲法所定程序作決定。談判條約、草擬約文者，可以顧及各國締約權限的差異，簽署一經簽字

---

❹ *P. C. I. J., Series A/B* (1933), No. 53, pp. 56-71 and p. 91.

即行生效的條約者，如果當時未獲得授權，一則可以臨場說明，二則可以立刻請示本國政府應否簽署，三則可以作待核准的簽署，所以已用批准或其他方式成為當事國者，日後以已違反國內法為理由，要求撤回承受條約拘束的同意，雖然不敢說不會有，卻可以斷言必是鳳毛麟角了。至於簡化式的條約，必定以簽署表示批准，批准就使條約生效，可能因為一時疏忽，有不符國內法規定的情形。但是無論如何，政府總是有控制簽署行為的方法，若不盡力控制，讓條約開始生效，便應擔負應有的國際責任。條約當事國面臨憲法上的困難，又知困難的真正所在時，通常可經由國內的行為，或爭取其他當事國從寬考量，以消除困難。唯有採取這種態度，才可以避免更大的國際責任 —— 違反條約的國際責任。

　　話說回頭，本條第一項的規定，是不是過度僵硬？國家元首明知違憲以訂約，或因疏失而違憲訂約，訂約後自行擔負一切責任，其政府後來可否要求撤銷其已作的承諾？若依本條第二項的規定，則除非締約國違反其國內法的情事，按照一般慣例，又以善意客觀的態度研議，必可看出那顯然是事實，則任何國家都不得援這事實作為理由，以撤銷原已表示的同意。反過來說，只要那是顯然的事實，當事國便可以援引。不過這種說法，仍未解答「是不是過度僵硬」的問題❺。現在姑且認定那確是過度僵硬，唯有依照本條第二項的規定處理，才是合法的。

---

❺　關於第四十六條的析論，曾參考 International Law Commission Reports (1962) 的相關評論部分。

第四十七條 關於表示一國同意權力之特定限制

如代表表示一國同意承受某一條約拘束之權力附有特定之限制，除非在其表示同意前已將此項限制通知其他談判國，該國不得援引該代表未遵守限制之事實以撤銷其所表示之同意。

國家的代表，依照國際法和國內法，除因其職位而當然有權者外，須經充分授權，才可以從事使其國家受拘束的行爲。他的權力受特定的限制，他卻不遵守這限制，在缺乏應有的權能時，越權從事那行爲，便會招致麻煩。那行爲如果是簽署一經簽字即時生效的條約，困難會即刻發生，如果是簽署須經批准、接受或贊同的條約，則其本國政府詳加考量後，可以決定是否批准、接受或贊同。假如作否定的選擇，便是否定其代表的行爲，使越權的行爲沒有效果，假如作肯定的選擇，便是使其代表的行爲獲得效果，補救了缺乏權力的缺陷，消除了法律上的困難。

缺乏應有權力的代表，一旦簽署了條約，縱使所簽的是即時生效的條約，其行爲的效力和權力充分者的簽署效力相同，如果他不在談判時或簽署前向其他代表說明權力不足，其本國應受其行爲所帶來的拘束。如果他及時說明了，其他代表也知道了，其本國便沒有受拘束的原因了。

總之，國家對其代表的權力加以限制，只能對其代表有效，不能影響他國代表的考慮，因爲國際法只要求各代表須有充分的權力，以書面證明其權力，各代表自動提出全權證書就行了，用不著任何人向代表的本國查證，國際法不課予代表任何責任，以查證其他代表的權限，也不使代表自動肩負這責任。所以本條規

定，國家代表表示同意承受條約拘束的權力，若受特定的限制，
又不及時把這限制通知其他談判代表，則其本國不得以其代表越
權爲理由，撤銷其已表示的同意，以解除其受條約的拘束

第四十八條　錯誤

**一、一國得援引條約內之錯誤以撤銷其承受條約拘束之同意，但此項
錯誤以關涉該國於締結條約時假定爲存在且構成其同意承受條約
拘束之必要根據之事實或情勢者爲限。**

**二、如錯誤係由關係國家本身行爲所助成，或如當時情況足以使該國
知悉有錯誤之可能，第一項不適用之。**

**三、僅與條約約文用字有關之錯誤，不影響條約之效力。 在此情形
下，第七十九條適用之。**

本條所稱的錯誤，包括一國單方所犯的錯誤和兩國以上共犯
的錯誤，也就是適用時，不區分錯誤爲單方的和共犯的，對於一
國的兩國的和多國的錯誤一律適用。

錯誤有關於事實的， 如某物於某日置於某地 ； 有關於情勢
的，如某日某國向某國發出最後通牒❻；有關於法律的，如條約
內某款是否牴觸某國憲法。依照本條第一項的規定，當事國得援
引關於事實的和情勢的錯誤爲理由，以撤銷其承受條約拘束的同

---

❻　最後通牒又稱哀的美敦書，是英文 Ultimatum 的中譯名，是強國
發出的一種威脅性的最後警告和要求， 顯示情勢已極端嚴重，爭端
不能經由談判等和平方式解決了，通常以四十八小時或更短的時間爲
限，對方如果不於時限內接受那要求，便必定遭受武裝的攻擊或其他
危害。

意，不得爲了這目的而援引關於法律的錯誤。

　　無論是關於事實的錯誤，或是關於情勢的錯誤，縱使都是實質的錯誤，如果不關涉重要事項，那（些）事項又不是當事國同意承受條約拘束的必要根據，當事國便不得援引該錯誤爲理由，以撤銷原已表示的同意。其次，依本條第一項而撤銷的效力，只及於原來的同意，並不使條約無效，唯有依本公約各項相關規定撤銷了同意，條約才是自始無效。

　　依國內法訂立契約，依國際法締結條約，都可能犯錯，但前者的錯誤較多，後者的錯誤很少，因爲簽訂條約的過程，通常有很多人參與，時間又較長，先經談判代表和行政機關的相關人員斟酌，再由立法機關的議員和專家審議，能夠做到集思廣益，避免錯誤，而訂立契約的時間常較短，參加的人員也較少，沒有兩批人員反覆推敲的情形，以致較易犯了錯誤，簽訂簡化式條約，通常參與的人員不多，時間較短，程序也相對的單純，犯錯誤的可能性似乎和訂立契約的相若，但是因爲簡化式條約所涉的事項，總是較小較單純，所以犯錯誤的可能性，在理論上是較多，在事實上則較少。然而較少不等於零，仍應定下規則，以便偶有條約上的錯誤時遵循。

　　條約上的錯誤，屬於地理性的較多，地圖上的更多。國家間的疆界圖，從前因爲交通不便、測量法不準確、製圖術欠精密等原因，造成界線錯誤的地圖，經發覺後，引起關係國家間的爭端，如果不能另訂界約，又不能經由公斷（仲裁）或司法解決，便會嚴重妨害邦交。經由國際司法解決的涉及地圖錯誤的實例，前有常設國際法院的論斷，近有國際法院的判決。前者在東格陵

蘭 (Legal Status of Eastern Greenland) 案中，駁斥挪威的
地圖錯誤的主張，說挪威外交部長對丹麥代表所作的答覆，是確
定的無條件的，不像他已想到的這事情有任何相關的錯誤❼。這
是否定地圖錯誤的一例。一九六一年，國際法院在普里維希廟案
(Case Concerning the Temple of Preah Vihear) 中說：
「這一種類的任何錯誤〔地圖錯誤〕，顯然已是法律性的錯誤，
但是無論如何，本院不認為本案的爭議處是真正的錯誤；其次，
確有錯誤，錯誤又在司法上有重要適切性時，可以影響推定為事
實上已表示的同意❽。」一九六二年，該院又說，儘管泰國反覆
聲稱錯誤，本院卻認為不但法律上沒有錯誤，原來締結的條約也
沒有錯誤，兩國已在條約上有協議，就是某特定區域的國界是某
一分水線；劃界的結果，所得地圖上的界線和協議不一致，這錯
誤後來經泰方接受了；依照已確立的法律規則，當事國的行為導
致錯誤，是其能夠避免的錯誤，或者如果當時情況足以使其知道
有錯誤的可能，該國便不得援引錯誤為理由，以撤銷其已表示的
同意❾。不准許引據自犯的錯誤以取得利益，這又是一例。以上
兩例顯示，條約上不容易有錯誤，即令有小錯誤，條約也不因而
無效，唯有重大錯誤確實存在又非當事國自犯的，才可據以撤銷
承受條約拘束的同意。這也就是本條約第一項的主旨，也是本條
第二項的規定。

---

❼　*P. C. I. J., Series A/B* (1933), No. 53, pp. 71-91.

❽　*I. J. Rep.* 1961, p. 30.

❾　*Ibid,* 1962, p. 26.

本條第三項的意義非常明確，訂明只是條約約文用語的錯誤，不但不會使條約無效，而且不應改變約中任何規定的內容，一旦錯誤被察覺了，只要依照本公約第七十九條的規定，把錯誤更正就行了（該條延後析論）。

第四十九條　詐欺

倘一國因另一談判國之詐欺行為而締結條約，該國得援引詐欺為理由撤銷其承受條約拘束之同意。

什麼是詐欺？或問什麼行為是詐欺行為？答案可能隨不同的法律體系而不同，因為各個法律體系雖然有詐欺的概念，卻各有不同的範圍。在國際上，既無先例，又無國際司法機關的法理，更無習慣可供參酌，以確定國際詐欺行為的範圍。所以本條對於這種範圍不加以規定，留給國際司法機關就個案作考量。

大致說來，故意作不真實不正確的事實陳述，或以其他欺罔的方法，使他人相信為真正的事實而陷於錯誤，以達到謀取不當利益的目的，就是詐欺行為。譬如張三把當代仿造古鼎一具，向愛好古董的李四說：「這是漢代古鼎」，使李四信以為真而以不合理的高價買了該鼎，張三於是獲得不當的厚利。這是一般國內法所稱的詐欺行為，在國家間採取這種行為能否達到目的？難有定論，按常情看，故意使用詐欺以達到誘使他國締結條約的情形，確是很少。

詐欺和錯誤不同。錯誤是清白善意的不正確陳述，犯了錯誤時，並不當然使條約無效，可依本公約第四十八條關於錯誤的規

定處理，而詐欺則是惡意的行爲，行爲結果可能在根本處妨害條約，影響受欺當事國同意承受條約拘束，摧毀締約國互信的整個基礎。可是本條仍然規定，詐欺行爲的效果，並不當然使條約無效，只是給予被詐欺國一種權利，那就是於其認爲必需而且願意時，得援引被詐欺爲理由，以撤銷其已表示的承受條約拘束的同意。這一規定，不僵硬，有彈性，讓被詐欺國自由決定是否擺脫條約的拘束，如其知悉被詐欺後認定仍以受拘束爲宜，就可以繼續維持其同意，享受權利，擔負義務。

第五十條　對一國代表之賄賂

倘一國同意承受條約拘束之表示係經另一談判國直接或間接賄賂其代表而取得，該國得援引賄賂爲理由撤銷其承受條約拘束之同意

賄賂是給予或許以財物或其他不正當利益，使接受者不行爲或從事一定內容的行爲，行賄者因而達到不法的目的。賄賂談判國代表的行爲，旨在影響其考慮和決定，誘使其締結條約或同意列入特定條款，所以有別於詐欺行爲和強迫行爲。行賄者的目的既是違法的，其手段又是給予不正當的利益，而且是要求受賄者作弊，所以談判代表贈予或收受小禮物或小紀念品，不是行賄或受賄，因爲這種贈予和收受行爲，都與賄賂的動機、意旨、性質完全不同，都是合法合情的事情。

條約當事國察覺其代表受賄後，依本條的規定，得援引其代表受賄爲理由，以撤銷其已表示的承受條約拘束的同意。本條只說「得援引」，不說「應援引」，所以縱使代表受賄的罪過十分

嚴重，當事國仍然可以決定是否援引，以解除或維持其與條約的關係，如果援引，則必可達到解除那關係的目的，不應遭遇不能克服的阻礙，如不援引，亦應受鼓勵，不會有外來的強制。至於是否處罰受賄者的問題，則是國內事項，本公約和一般國際法都不追問。

本條「另一談判國直接或間接」等字，只是表示代表行賄的事實；一方的談判代表行賄，另一方的談判代表不接受，或接受後不影響其本國對條約的立場，換句話說，其本國表示同意承受條約拘束，和代表行賄受賄的行為無關，則其本國不得援引賄賂為理由，以撤銷那同意；只於賄賂的行為結果，可以直接或間接歸責於「另一談判國」時，當事國才可以援引賄賂為充分的理由，立刻撤銷原已表示的同意，解除條約的拘束。

第五十一條 對一國代表之強迫

一國同意承受條約拘束之表示，係以行為或威脅對其代表所施之強迫而取得者，應無法律效果

以威脅方式施行強迫，可以針對着一個國家，也可以針對着國家的代表。本條所規範的，是對代表所施的強迫。

對談判代表的人身施加強迫或威脅，使其簽署條約，或對其他人員施加強迫，使其批准、接受或贊同條約，其簽署、批准、接受和贊同的行為，一概無法律效果，這是毫無疑問的，也是大家公認的。

對國家使用威脅或武力的實例，史不勝書，對國家代表施加

強迫的事實，相對的少，雖然強制談判者簽署條約，強令立法者批准條約，也曾有其事，但是有些強迫行為，究竟是對國家施加的，或是直接對國家代表施加的，則往往不易辨別。一九三九年，德國領袖希特勒（Adolf Hitler）對捷克總統哈察（Hacha）施予強迫，使其簽署條約，把波希米亞（Bohemia）和摩拉維亞（Moravia）兩地變成德國的保護地。論者不能分辨這是對國家的強迫，或是對國家代表的威脅，因為希特勒的行為不但是對哈察人身的，也是對捷克的強迫。然而無論怎樣，還是要把這種強迫分開看待，以便本條只規定以行為或威脅所施的強迫。

本條的規定，包括針對代表個人的各種威脅方式，破壞其名譽、傷害其身體、恐嚇其家屬，諸如此類，都是威脅方式，以威脅的任何方式，強迫國家代表作同意承受條約拘束的表示，不問他是國家元首、行政首長、外交部長、簽署代表或談判代表，那表示都一律沒有法律效果，而且是自始無效，不是其本國政府對強迫國抗議或拒絕履約時，可以宣告無效。

這一規定，現在已是條約法的規則，實則這早已是普遍國際法的規則，久經公認為習慣法則，所以即令沒有本條的規定，國家代表被強迫的同意承受條約拘束的表示，自始無效。

第五十二條　以威脅或使用武力對一國施行強迫

條約係違反聯合國憲章所含國際法原則以威脅或使用武力而獲締結者無效。

中國在春秋戰國時期，戰爭頻仍，罄竹難書，城下之盟，如

恆河沙數；泰西古國的戰爭與和約，並無不同，而城下之盟應無法律效果的觀念，則中西一樣，並不存在。十七世紀初期，國際法鼻祖葛羅秀士 (Hugo Grotius) 於其戰爭與和平法一書中，只分戰爭為合正義的和不義的，不主張禁止一切戰爭，也不認為以使用威脅或武力強迫締結的條約無效。一六四八年的魏士發利亞條約 (The Westphalia Treaty)、一八一五年的維也納公會 (The Congress of Vienna)、一八九九年的第一次海牙和平會議，都未宣示被武力強制下簽訂的條約為非法，海牙和平會議通過和平解決國際爭端公約外，還訂立許多戰時法則。一九一九年的國際聯合會盟約，其第十五條第六項仍說：「如行政院（又中譯為理事會）報告書，除相爭之一造或一造以上之代表外，該院會員一致贊成，則聯合會會員約定彼此不得向遵從報告書建議之任何一造從事戰爭。」這間接表示了一點，就是強迫訂約未被宣告為違法。直至一九二八年，巴黎非戰公約(The 1928 Briand-Kellogg Pact of Paris) 簽訂時，才禁止以戰爭為推行國家政策的手段，否定國家具有侵略性的戰爭權，不復允許戰勝國強制戰敗國簽訂屈辱性的和平條約。這一禁約的功效不彰，多人懷疑仍應繼續努力訂立同性質的約法。一九四五年的聯合國憲章制訂者，於憲章第二條第四款規定：「各會員國在其國際關係上不得使用威脅或武力……」。於是在國際上使用威脅或武力，除了自衛或依照聯合國的決議以外，全是違反聯合國法了，以威脅或武力強迫簽訂條約，也被禁止了。

　　禁止在國際上使用威脅或武力以前，國際法在國際關係上的一種功能，是維持國際法律秩序的穩定，解決某些國際爭端，減

少國家間的武裝衝突，藉以取得局部的或全面的國際和平與安全，只祈求安定，不強調正義或公平，推行兩害相權取其輕的原則，因而承認一切條約有效，秘密的片面的不平等的被強迫簽訂的種種條約，只要一經正式簽訂，便一律有效，不問締約國在怎樣的情況下簽署，更不管簽署代表是在斧鉞壓頸下動筆，條約的效力都不受影響。巴黎非戰公約，否定被強迫締結的條約依法有效，逐漸形成一股國際輿論與潮流，只惜於一九三〇年代全遭遏抑。聯合國憲章力挽狂瀾，使仁人志士的觀念轉而傾向正義之法，一九四六年的紐崙堡（Neurenburg）國際軍事法庭，依其規約把德國戰犯繩之以法，才在國際實踐上加強國際法的發展，使各國接受一個新的法則。一九六九年，這法則法典化的時機成熟，成爲本條所定的規則。

使用威脅的方式很多，不易列舉，也不必列舉。本條只訂明「係違反聯合國憲章所含國際法原則以威脅或使用武力」。這原則就是「各會員國在國際關係上不得使用武力」，除爲個別或集體自衛或執行聯合國決議外，爲其他任何目的（當然包括訂約）而威脅或使用武力，已在禁止之列。可是遍閱聯合國憲章，只見禁止和准許使用武力的文字，不見例示威脅方式的文字，因而斷絕某國在其國際河川上的水源、摧毀某國的經濟資源、在某國境內經常協助恐怖活動等行爲是否已被禁止？在這類威脅下同意簽訂的條約是否有效？諸如此類的問題，不能依照理論預作解答，須於解釋憲章時就個案案情以求答案。

禁止使用威脅，禁止使用武力，是憲章所列的現行國際法，聯合國各會員國負有嚴格遵守的義務，違法以強迫簽訂的條約，

就是本身沒有法律效果，無需被強迫國以任何行爲使它無效。本條爲了表達這一意義，不採用「違反聯合國憲章」等字眼，選用了「違反聯合國憲章所含國際法原則」等字，而且直接明說這類條約「無效」，不說它是「可使無效的」。這些文字凸顯了強調了「無效」的絕對性，未留下絲毫彈性。因爲聯合國憲章第二條第六款規定，「本組織在維持國際和平及安全之必要範圍內，應保證非聯合國會員國遵行上述原則。」所以聯合國會員以外的國家，於締結條約時使用威脅或使用武力，致有危及國際和平及安全的可能，或其所簽訂的條約內容有這種危險，那條約本身也是無效的，何況本條並不區分締約國爲聯合國會員國和非聯合國會員國。

依照聯合國憲章第二條，使用威脅和使用武力被禁止了。這一禁止的規則確定後，才有被強迫簽訂的條約絕對無效的規則，在禁止的規則之前，絕對無效的規則未具有普遍性，甚至可以說未經接受爲現行法則，所以違反憲章第二條所列原則的條約絕對無效性，早已獲得各國確認，不因本條的規定而強化了，只因本條而具體化了。

在違反憲章的情況下締結的條約，自始無效，本來不能生效，不在任何時間內有片刻的法律效果，無需締約國援引憲章以挑剔，使它喪失效力，正如違反絕對軌範的其他條約，自始無效，用不着訂約後的任何行爲使它無效。

聯合國已有一六六個會員國，未加入聯合國者只有幾個國家。所有會員國已經批准聯合國憲章，所以憲章所含的國際法原則，已獲得普遍的接受，以致隨憲章第二條第六款而來的本條所

立的規則，現在固然已是普遍國際法的規則，而且早在憲章生效施行時，已可以毫無保留的適用了，儘管在憲章生效前，適用這規則時有所疑慮，在憲章生效後，尤其在一九九〇年代，沒有人再懷疑這規則的權威性了。第二次世界大戰結束以來，沒有違反這規則的實例。戰敗國義大利、保加利亞、匈牙利、羅馬尼亞、日本等國與各盟國分別簽訂的和平條約，無人指稱已違反了憲章原則；所謂韓戰和越戰停火後，沒有簽訂和約；印度和巴基斯坦間的武裝衝突，不因簽訂和約而停止；埃及和以色列於一九七九年締結條約，不是使用威脅或使用武力的直接結果；伊朗和伊拉克苦戰八年後，烽火熄滅了，未見有和約的締結；一九九一年二月的波斯灣戰爭，因伊拉克接受聯合國安全理事會的決議，而宣告結束。因而本公約生效以來，本條所定的規則還未經考驗，沒有國家引據本條以申訴，沒有仲裁庭處理過關於適用本條的爭端，沒有本條可能隱含的疑難送請國際法院論斷。本條究竟能夠發生怎樣的效用？還須拭目以待，等待事實驗證。

第五十三條　與一般國際法強制規律（絕對法）牴觸之條約

　　條約在締結時與一般國際法強制規律牴觸者無效。就適用本公約而言，一般國際法強制規律指國家之國際社會全體接受並公認為不許損抑且僅有以後具有同性質之一般國際法規律始得更改之規律。

　　何謂一般國際法？就是前文所提的普遍國際法。嚴格說來，兩者的內涵不盡相同，前者指國際社會多數成員已接受的法律，後者則指國際社會成員幾乎已全體接受的法律，但是現在許多學

者把兩者視爲內涵相同，而輪換使用，未曾引起誤解。

什麼是「一般國際法強制規律（絕對法）」？自有國際法以來，尤其在二十世紀上半期，這問題曾引發喋喋不休的爭論，反對者說根本沒有國際法的強制規律，不必作這種虛擬，贊成者強調不但有絕對法，而且必須有，沒有就不能建立國際法的起碼體系。本公約的擬訂者，也許是有鑑於這種爭論，便爲絕對法下了定義。依照這一定義，一般國際法強制規律須具備三個要件，一是那規律已被國際社會全體國家成員接受了；二是都認爲那規律不可加以損抑；三是那規律只可以由後來同性質的法規予以變更。任何規律，缺少三要件中的一個，就不具強制性，可由各締約國變更，而無需國際社會全體國家成員接受。

所謂「國家之國際社會全體」，是指由國家形成的國際社會成員全體，儘管國際組織中的聯合國，業經國際法院宣告爲具備國際人格的國際法主體，可以成爲國際社會的一員，仍不屬於國家的國際社會，所以這社會的全體，不包括聯合國。而所謂「全體」，也不應解釋爲所有國際法人（主體）或所有國家，應解釋爲就整體來看的大多數國家，縱使極少數國家是例外的，這大多數國家已足以代表全體，並且在國際法上可視爲全體了。假如解釋「全體」爲包括全球每一個國家，不能有一個例外，則在事實上做不到，也就不能有任何一個強制規律，連「條約必須遵守」這麼重要的規律也被否定了。聯合國憲章第二條所定的原則，現在由一六六個國家接受了，國際社會的成員中，還有哈薩克、亞美尼亞、亞塞爾拜占等未加入聯合國爲會員國，以正式表示其接受憲章，因此，如果把上述「全體」解釋爲「一個都不能少」，

無疑是誤會了本公約擬訂者的本意，違反了務使條約有效的條約解釋準則。

所謂「以後」（Subsequent），是指本公約生效後的任何時間。本公約生效後，「同性質之一般國際法規律」一旦形成了，便可以更改現在的強制規律，因而現行規律何時為新規律所取代，無法預知。本條採用「以後」兩字，便排除了「以前」，也就是以前締結的條約，不在本條的適用範圍內，只有於本約生效後，又在條約締結時，牴觸強制規律，條約方無效。只要牴觸，就一定無效，無論牴觸是由於無知或疏忽，或出於故意，都一律無效。

依照本條的規定，就沒有永遠不得更改或不能更改的絕對法，只是絕對法更改十分困難，不得由少數國家以締約或其他方式予以更改，必須符合前述三個要件，才由新的取代現行的絕對法。從當代國際法發展的趨勢蠡測，新強制規律的形成，很可能是經由國際會議通過公約，再由各國加以批准的程序，也就是經由國際立法的程序，不復由國際習慣以形成。

關於某國際法規則是不是強制規律的問題，如果引起爭議，就應由公正人士或機關解答。某條約是否因牴觸絕對法而自始無效的疑問，更應由第三者公斷或法庭判決，正和解決一般法律爭端一樣，謀求客觀公正的論斷。

第三節　條約之終止及停止施行

第五十四條　依條約規定或經當事國同意而終止或退出條約

在下列情形下，得終止條約或一當事國得退出條拘：

（甲）依照條約之規定；或

（乙）無論何時經全體當事國於諮商其他各締約國後表示同意。

多數現代的條約，都列載程序條款，以訂明條約的有效期間、條約的終止日期、條約的終止條件或事件、通知廢止的權利、通知退出條約的權利等等，所以要終止條約時，可以完全依照條約的規定辦理。如果沒有關於這些事項的規定，則何時可以終止條約、如何通知有關當事國的問題，就要按條約的性質或適用，或利用條約的解釋，以求得解答，條約如果是雙邊的，縱使沒有這些事項的規定，因為受牽涉的只有兩國，不難使它終止，如果是很多當事國的公約，便會有較大的困難。

條約可以列載的終止條約的程序條款，五花八門，不勝枚舉。許多條約規定於連續不斷的特定年歲期間內有效，或有效到某特定日期或特定事件發生日止。一些條約則訂明由各締約國商定條件，以終止條約。各條約所列的特定期間，長短不一，很多是在一年和十二年之間，長到二十年五十年或九十九年的也有。很多當事國為方便計，採用彈性的規定，只定一個較短的五年或十年的首期，同時訂明於期滿後即時連續有效，但各締約國可以行使止約或退約權，這樣一來，可使條約連續無限期的有效，或延長條約若干年，在延長的期間未屆滿前，准許各當事國於六個月或十二個月前，行使通知止約或退約的權利。還有一些條約，不提有效期間，只訂明終止條約或退約的權利，並且列載發出止約或退約通知的最長期間。偶有極少數的條約，只規定五年或十

年的單一有效期，准許於這期間內止約或退約。以五年爲期的條約，通常是貿易協定、學術合作學人交換協定、科學技術協定等。

　　一般說來，不管條約怎樣規定終止條約的事項，當各當事國全體同意時，必可撇開原有的規定，隨時終止條約。其次，儘管曾有不同的說法，說終止條約必須採用訂約時已用的程序，就是簽署、批准、互換或交存批准書等手續，但那是某些國內法要求的做法，不是國際法的規則。實則各當事國達成協議時，可以採用任何方式以終止條約，協議止約前，也許難免要顧及某（些）當事國的國內程序，但這不是基於國際法的原因，因爲國際法只問各當事國是否同意終止條約，不追查任何國內的規定。

　　依照本條的意旨，終止條約時，如果不採用條約所定的方式，就非經全體締約國同意不可，不得像修改條約，只有若干締約國同意就行了。這一要求全體同意的主旨無他，在保障各締約國的權利而已。如果不作這一要求，任由一國或少數締約國達到終止條約的目的，則條約的安全和締約國的權利，常可由一國掌握了。

　　條約締結後，可不可以隨時終止？是不是必須經過若干歲月後才可以終止？這類問題可有如下的籠統答覆。條約如果規定某一年月後才可以終止，就不得隨時終止它，非等到那特定年月過後不可。條約如果沒有這種規定，則只要全體締約國一致同意，便可以隨時終止條約，因爲獲得全體締約國一致同意，以終止條約，固然是一件難事，也符合常理，法律更不應予禁止❿。

---

❿　關於條約失效與終止的依據問題研討，下列一文值得參考：S. E.

第五十五條　多邊條約當事國減少至條約生效所必需之數目以下

除條約另有規定外，多邊條約並不僅因其當事國數目減少至生效
所必需之數目以下而終止。

　　本條所規範的，是多邊條約，不涉及雙邊條約。

　　多邊條約，除約中有明文禁止者外，大多數規定當事國可以
廢止或退出，或規定當事國減少到某一數目以下時，條約便自動
終止。這數目是三、是五、是六、是十或十以上，完全可由談判
國決定，沒有國際法規則提供任何標準。

　　大多數多邊條約訂明，須經某一數目以上的國家批准、接
受、贊同或加入，才能開始生效，例如聯合國憲章第一一○條第
三項訂明，於中華民國、法蘭西、蘇維埃社會主義共和國聯邦、
大不列顛及北愛蘭聯合王國、與美利堅合衆國，以及其他簽字國
的過半數將批准書交存時，本憲章即發生效力。又如本公約第八
十四條第一項訂明，於第三十五件批准書或加入書存放之日後第
三十日起發生效力。因此，下列問題可能發生：無論是由於當事
國廢止條約或退出條約，當其數目減少到上述數目以下，憲章和
本公約是否一定跟着終止？依照本條的規定，這問題的答案應是
否定的，因爲談判國如果認爲條約一定跟着終止，已可於約中以
明文作這一表示。從前雖然曾有一些條約，依照這一類明文的規
定，自動終止了，但是這一類規定，還沒有演進到已成通例。現

Nahlik, "The Grounds of Invalidity and Termination of
Treaties," 65 *AJIL* 734 (1971).

在究竟一份多邊條約起碼應有多少當事國才能開始生效？還沒有定則可循，繼續履行條約所必需的國家數，也仍無鐵則可資參考，所以條約可以不因當事國減少到其生效所必需的數目以下而自動終止。當事國少於這數目時，不退約和不廢約的國家，仍然可以繼續享受條約權利，同時履行條約義務，如果認為已經無法行使權利盡義務，則可以通知退約或宣告廢約，達到其目的。

因此，本條為消除疑問計，已作如下的明確規定：除非條約有相反的規定，多邊條約發生效力後，縱使當事國減少到條約生效所必需的數目以下，也不當然自動終止。

最後還應略提，當事國減到只有兩個的時候，條約仍然可以繼續存在，減到只有一國的時候，條約就非終止不可了。

第五十六條　廢止或退出並無關於終止廢止或退出規定之條約

一、條約如無關於其終止之規定，亦無關於廢止或退出之規定，不得廢止或退出，除非：

(甲)經確定當事國原意為容許有廢止或退出之可能；或

(乙)由條約之性質可認為含有廢止或退出之權利。

二、當事國應將其依第一項廢止或退出條約之意思至遲於十二個月以前通知之。

本條所列「條約」兩字，未加上限制詞，可以指雙邊條約、多邊條約、莊嚴的條約、簡化式條約等等。但是雙邊的和簡化式的條約的任何一造，於認為必須廢約或退約時，可以隨時和他造談判，以修改條約或另訂新約，或以其他方式達到目的，用不着正式逕行廢約或退約，所以本條在實際上只可適用於多邊條約。

　　既不訂明有效期限又不列載終止條款的條約，不提廢約或退約權利的條約，不可勝數。姑就一些較新的來看，一九五八年的領海及鄰接區公約、公海公約、捕魚及養護公海生物資源公約、大陸礁層公約，一九六一年的維也納外交關係公約，一九六三年的領事關係公約，一九六九年的本公約和特種使節公約，一九八二年的聯合國海洋法公約等，都不提到有效期限、終止廢止或退出條約的事宜。這些多邊條約可否由當事國通知廢止或退出？若可，是否須經其他當事國全體同意？可否視個別當事國在某種情形下，有退約的潛在（隱含）權利？這些都是有待解答的問題。

　　在原則上，這些問題的答案須視個別條約的性質而定。某種性質的條約，其簽訂者無意准許當事國退出或廢止，排除了退出或通知廢止的可能情形，例如結束戰爭的和平條約、劃定國界的條約、交換領土的條約等，都不容許廢約或退約。某些多邊條約，例如一九五九年的南極條約(The Antarctic Treaty)，其少數當事國退出或通知廢止條約，不會違反條約主旨。至於多邊條約不以明文規定退約或廢約時，可否視為排除當事國個別退約或廢約的權利？學者對於這問題有兩種意見。一種強調必須約中有退約或廢約的規定，或經其他當事國全體同意，才可以退約或通知廢止。另一種辯稱，縱使條約不提到退約或廢約事項，其中一些可有當事國在某些情況下退約或廢約的隱含權利。姑不論各種意見如何，條約談判國的用意才是決定性因素，於其有意包含這種權利時，當事國就可以行使，否則不得行使，而談判國的用意為何，則是事實問題，應按事實來確定有無這種權利，查證事實時，不但要參照條約的性質，而且應顧及個案的各種情況。總

之，依事實以發現談判國是否給予當事國退約或廢約的權利。

　　依照本條的意旨，條約不規定終止、廢止或退出事宜時，當事國不得退出或廢止該約，除非「經確定當事國原意爲容許有廢止或退出之可能，或由條約之性質認爲含有廢止或退出之權利。」所以除了本條第一款所定的談判國的用意外，還須注意條約的性質、退出或廢止的可能。

　　本條又訂明，任何廢約退約權利的行使，應受於合理期間內通知其他當事國的限制。終止條約，通常須於六個月前發出通知。可以更新的條約，通常也准許於更新時或更新前發出廢約通知。條約無限期有效又容許廢止者，即令不硬性規定通知事宜，廢約通知通常也須於十二個月前發出。所以本條明確規定，這事前通知的期間不得少於十二個月，藉以使其他當事國的權利獲得充分保障，並且減少廢約國與其他當事國間的爭議。

第五十七條　依條約規定或經當事國同意而停止施行條約

一、在下列情形下，條約得對全體當事國或某一當事國停止施行：
　　(甲)依照條約之規定；或
　　(乙)無論何時經全體當事國於諮商其他各締國後表示同意。

　　本條所稱的停止施行 (Suspension of operation)，是指暫停施行，不具終止施行的意思，所以如果把原英文本所用的 Suspend 中譯爲「暫停」，就會使中文讀者更易了解。

　　暫停施行一份條約，乍看之下，近似終止一份條約，因爲暫停施行後，假如不幸不恢復施行，便似把條約終止了，雖然各當

事國決定暫停施行時，沒有終止條約的意思，未料到竟發生了終
止條約的結果。

有些條約訂明，在某些情況或條件下，約中全部規定或若干
規定可以暫停施行。有了訂明，要暫停施行時，只按訂明辦理就
行了。沒有訂明的話，如果全體當事國都同意，也可以暫停施
行，而且可以隨時暫停施行全部或若干規定。同理，全體當事國
一致同意時，亦得暫停施行某一條約或某些條約，藉以消除履行
條約義務的臨時困難。當然，可以暫停施行的條約，包括雙邊的
和多邊的。

依照本條的規定，暫停施行條約可以依照條約的規定辦理，
也可以經全體當事國同意❶後進行，可以對全體當事國生效，亦
可專對某一個當事國實施，誠如上文所說，可以包括全約條款，
可以只針對部分條款，如果暫停施行某一份條約，則暫停的效力
及於該約全體當事國，如果暫停施行一份條約的部分條款，則暫
停的效力及於全體當事國，也可以只及某一個（些）當事國。簡
單地說，各當事國都同意時，可以控制條約的一切變化。

一份多邊條約可否僅經部分當事國同意便暫停施行？這是第
五十八條包含的問題，且待下文分解。

第五十八條　多邊條約僅經若干當事國協議而停止施行

----

❶ 本第五十七條第二款的英文原文爲：「at any time by consent of
all the parties after consultation with the other contracting states. 如中譯爲：「經全體當事國於任何時間諮商其他各締
約國後一致同意」，或更接近原義。

**一、多邊條約兩國以上當事國得暫時並僅於彼此間締結協定停止施行
　條約之規定，如：**

　　(甲)條約內規定有此種停止之可能；或

　　(乙)有關之停止非爲條約所禁止，且

　　　　(一)不影響其他當事國享有條約上之權利或履行其義務；

　　　　(二)非與條約之目的及宗旨不合。

**二、除屬第一項(甲)款範圍之情形條約另有規定者外，有關當事國應
　將其締結協定之意思及條約內其所欲停止施行之規定通知其他當
　事國。**

　　和上文指出的一樣，本條所稱的停止施行，原意是指暫停施
行。

　·暫停施行一份或多份多邊條約，不是終止條約，所以不像終
止條約的程序，無需全體當事國同意。

　　許多多邊條約的締約國，彼此在條約關係上，以雙邊的爲最
多，也最重要，採取集體行動才能行使權利盡義務的情形，少而
又少，所以暫停施行多邊條約的規定，可以不要求需經全體當事
國同意。

　　基於以上考慮，本條容許兩個或更多當事國暫停施行條約，
同時訂明停止施行須受下列限制：第一、有關當事國應締結協
定；第二、暫停施行只是暫時性質；第三、協定只於有關當事國
間有效；第四、條約內規定其所提的暫停施行確有可能；第五、
該暫停施行不是條約所禁止的；第六、該暫停施行不違反條約的
目標和宗旨；第七、該暫停施行不妨礙其他當事國依條約享權利
盡義務；第八、除條約另有規定外，有關當事國應把下列兩點通

知其他當事國：(一)其締結協定的意思，(二)擬暫停施行的條約內的條款。依照往例和實際需要，通知應是書面的。

本條對於發出通知的時間一節，未加以訂明。究竟應否迅速及時通知原約其他各當事國？依照本條第二項的意旨，有關當事國只須於締結協定前發出通知，不必於協定締結後再行通知，如果原擬暫停施行的條約內的規定，於最後談判協議更換了，其他各當事國不被通知，則會背離本第二項的意旨，所以就一般常理說，有關當事國應再發適當的通知，或向聯合國秘書處登記其協定，以使該新協定為眾所周知，尤其是使原約其他各當事國詳悉。

有了本條所列的八項限制，條約各當事國如果善意遵守的話，則縱使容許若干當事國暫停約中某一（些）規定有缺點，那缺點亦屬輕微了，即令所涉的是集體安全條約（以前常以同盟條約為名），例如一九四九年的北大西洋公約（North Atlantic Treaty）⑫，在事實上也不能有暫停施行某一規定的弊端了，因為一則暫停施行其任何規定，非經集體決定不可，再則該約第五條規定，對任何一個或幾個當事國的武裝攻擊，都認定為對全體當事國的攻擊，每一當事國應個別的或與其他當事國一致採取必要行動，包括使用武裝部隊，以協助恢復並維護北大西洋地區的安全。這就使兩個或幾個當事國不能暫停施行其規定，而該約

---

⑫ 該約於一九四九年四月四日在美國首都華盛頓簽署，比利時、加拿大、丹麥、法國、冰島、義大利、荷蘭、挪威、葡萄牙、英國和美國十一國為簽署國。該約於同年八月二十四日生效，後來據以組成北大西洋公約組織。希臘、土耳其和德意志聯邦共和國已加入為會員國。

第五條規定的協助自衞，又是其最主要宗旨，違反條約宗旨的情
事，已是本條所禁止的。

第五十九條　條約因締結後訂條約而默示終止或停止施行

一、任何條約於其全體當事國就同一事項締結後訂條約，且有下列情
形之一時，應視爲業已終止：

　(甲)自後訂條約可見或另經確定當事國之意思爲此一事項應以該
　　　條約爲準；或

　(乙)後訂條約與前訂條約之規定不合之程度使兩者不可能同時適
　　　用。

二、倘自後訂條約可見或另經確定當事國有此意思，前訂條約應僅視
爲停止施行。

　　一份條約的當事國，就該約的相同事項另訂新約，不訂明要
終止該約或暫停施行該約，新約的規定又牴觸該約的規定。在這
情形下，如果兩約的當事國完全相同，便可以視該約已被廢止，
因爲於其一致同意時，得廢止該約。縱使兩約的當事國不完全相
同，於該約全體當事國亦爲新約當事國時，亦得廢止該約，因爲
於其一致同意時，旣可廢止該約，就當然可與他國家廢止該約。
這一節已是沒有爭論餘地的事情。仍待解答的問題只是：在怎樣
的情形下，可以視爲默示終止了該約？或默示暫停施行該約？這
就要先確定各當事國的意思，看其有無維持該約效力的意思，如
果有，便是默示了，如無，則否。所以解答這問題，純是兩約的
解釋事項。

　　本條 第一項 的意旨 ， 在訂明各當事國締結牴觸舊約的新約

時，得視其有意廢止舊約，於是規定(甲)自新約可見或另經確定當事國有意就舊約的事項，另行規定，並以新規定為準，或(乙)兩約的規定相互牴觸，而且牴觸程度很嚴重，兩約不可能同時適用，便可以視其已默示終止了舊約，儘管新約沒有提及終止條約一事。換句話說，本項只規定默示的條約終止。

本條第二項的意旨，在訂明各當事國另訂新約後，自新約中可以看出，或另從各種相關因素考量後，確定各當事國無意終止舊約，只有意暫停施行舊約，縱使兩約的規定相互牴觸，甚至嚴重的牴觸，仍是暫停施行。所以依照本項的規定，新舊約的規定即令彼此牴觸，舊約未必即被終止，只是暫停施行而已。

原來本公約第三十條，已規定相同事項的先訂和後訂條約的適用範圍，而本條則訂明後訂條約的事項，與先訂條約的事項相同時，是不是被視為默示終止了先訂條約。

第六十條　條約因違約而終止或停止施行

一、雙邊條約當事國一方有重大違約情事時，他方有權援引違約為理由終止該條約，或全部或局部停止其施行。

二、多邊條約當事國之一有重大違約情事時：

(甲)其他當事國有權以一致協議：

(一)在各該國與違約國之關係上；或

(二)在全體當事國之間，

將條約全部或局部停止施行或終止該約。

(乙)特別受違約影響之當事國有權援引違約為理由在其本國與違約國之關係上將條約全部或局部停止施行。

(丙)如由於條約性質關係，遇一當事國對其規定有重大違反情
　　事，致每一當事國繼續履行條約義務所處之地位因而根本改
　　變，則違約國以外之任何當事國皆有權援引違約爲理由將條
　　約對其本國全部或局部停止施行。

三、就適用本條而言，重大違約係指：

　　(甲)廢棄條約，而此種廢棄非本公約所准許者；或

　　(乙)違反條約規定，而此項規定爲達成條約目的或宗旨所必要
　　　　者。

四、以上各項不妨礙條約內適用於違約情事之任何規定。

五、第一項至第三項不適用於各人道性質之條約內所載關於保護人身
　　之各項規定，尤其關於禁止對受此種條約保護之人採取任何方式
　　之報復之規定。

　　　大多數國際法學者同意，雙邊條約的當事國，於另一當事國
違約時，有權廢止該約，也有權暫停履行該約所定的義務，因爲
違反條約義務，正如其他任何義務，使其他當事國作適度的反
應，針對違約國的權利作報復，或以其他非武力的方法行使本身
的權利。這就是違約權。雖然關於這權利的範圍爲何、行使這權
利的條件爲何等問題，各學者的意見仍然莫衷一是，這權利的存
在，卻無人置疑了。一派學者認爲，現在還沒有國際機關有效的
使各當事國守約，守約國應有廢約權，藉以制裁違約國，所以國
際法應無條件的賦予守約國一般性的廢約權。另一派學者不以爲
然，指出其缺點說，如果守約國有絕對的廢約權，就會小題大
做，藉故廢約；我們爲預防弊端起見，應限制廢約權，規定只於
重大違約或基本違約時，才可以行使廢約權，而且行使必須經由

一定的程序。

怎樣確定廢約權行使的範圍？妥當行使的條件是什麼？罕有先例可援引以解答這些問題。從前的廢約者，或先發制人，責怪他方，或說他方已違約，或辯稱其他理由，作爲自己行爲的遁詞，避免認眞深入討論廢約所涉的法律原則，他方反駁時，通常是提出未曾違約的事實，而不強調法律的理由，偶爾提到廢約爲不合法時，也不過是抗議廢約國單方任意的宣告而已。當然的，一方明知自己有重大違約情事時，並不否定他方有廢約權。

國內法院和國際司法機構都承認下列原則，卽一方的違約，給予守約他方廢約權。這原則可能發生嚇阻作用，使條約當事國避免輕率的違約。一九四五年的中華民國與蘇維埃社會主義共和國聯邦間友好同盟條約，於蘇方嚴重違反後，中方宣告予以廢止，免使中方重大利益繼續遭受損失。這一宣告，也是一種隱示的警告，其他條約的當事國，應引以爲鑑。這種廢約的權利旣獲得國內和國際的承認，守約國於國內和國際方面，便不引起責任問題。可惜過去的國內法院，常於其行政機關認爲需要廢約後，認可那廢約權，並不覺得應徹底檢討行使廢約權的條件。

一般說來，違約情形無論多麼嚴重，都不當然使條約終止，因爲守約的其他當事國也許認爲並不嚴重，而可以忍受，或者認定容忍嚴重的違約，較廢約爲有利。一個當事國推定某當事國已嚴重違約，也不可以宣告條約已廢止，因爲那推定可能是純主觀的不妥善的。不過，在另一方面，大家都贊成，在某種範圍內和若干限制下，守約國援引違約爲理由以終止或暫停施行條約的權利，應予承認。

　　本條的主旨，便是針對上述情形，設定可因違約而廢止條約或暫停施行條約的條件。

　　本條第一項訂明，雙邊條約一方嚴重違約，便予他方權利，以援引違約為理，終止條約或暫停施行條約，而且可以自由決定只包括約中部分規定或全部規定。「援引……為理由」只意味依照本條規定而有的權利，不給予守約國絕對的權利，以任意宣告終止條約。因此，他方如果辯稱不違約，或否認已嚴重違約，便發生兩方的爭端。爭端當事國在一般國際法和聯合國憲章下的義務，就是採用和平的方法，以解決這爭端。當一方認為他方已嚴重違約，他方又不辯駁時，守約一方才可以援引違約為理由，以廢止或暫停施行條約的部分或全部規定。

　　援引違約為理由而採取行為的權利，不是基於一般國際法承認的報仇，而是來自本條的規定，本條的規定是按照一個明顯的基本原則，即當他方違約不履行條約義務時，不能要求此方履行同一條約的義務，應該給予此方權利，包括廢止條約或暫停施行條約、提出國際索償、要求他方擔負違約的責任等。

　　本條第二項訂明關於違反多邊條約的規則、各守約當事國集體行為的權利、受害當事國個別行為的權利等。第一款規定：守約各當事國得以一致的協議，暫停施行條約或終止條約，而且暫停施行或終止條約，只可以適用於其與違約國間的關係，也可以適用於所有當事間的關係。受害當事國單獨行為時，便近似雙邊條約當事國的行為，無論是暫停施行全部或局部條約，其權利行使的效力只及於其與違約國的關係，不影響其他各當事國與違約國間的關係，而且不得終止條約，因為任何當事國個別行為時，

必須顧全守約各當事國的權利，不得未經其同意而終止條約。在一般情形下，停止施行條約的權利，是爲特受影響的當事國提供足夠的保護，違約情事確使其受害時，其能暫停施行條約，就是一種保護，提出國際索償、要求違約國擔負違約責任等，也是保護。

本條所稱的多邊條約，包括一般的條約和所謂立法的條約，所以任何當事國固然不得單獨終止一般的條約，更不得因某當事國違約而終止所謂立法條約。

本條第二項第三款規定，違約情事造成嚴重的根本的情勢改變時，上列同項第一款第二款便不能給予特別受害國充分的保障，如果在改變後的新情勢下，該國暫停施行條約，便會違反其與其他當事國間的條約義務，如果不暫停施行條約，又不能自保，所以第三款規定：「如由於條約性質關係，遇一當事國對其規定有重大違反情事，致每一當事國繼續履行條約義務所處之地位因而根本改變，則違約國以外之任何當事國皆有權援引違約爲理由將條約對其本國全部或局部停止施行」。所謂「根本改變」，雖然只限於當事國的地位，不直指一般情勢，卻和下文討論的「情勢之基本改變」有近似的地方，應順此說明，並請注意比較。

前文已指出雙邊條約的一造違約，即給予他造終止條約或暫停施行條約的權利。究竟怎樣的違約才給予這種權利？從前有些權威人士認爲，對條約任何規定的任何違反，都使廢止條約爲合法。本條不採納這種主張，規定只有嚴重的違約情況可以給予廢約的權利，於第三項使用「重大的」（Material），以代替「基

本的」（Fundamental），希望能夠避免誤解，因爲「基本的」
違反，會被了解爲僅直接觸及條約中心宗旨條款的違反，而「中
心宗旨」常是被視爲條約最基本的東西，但是，也許某些當事國
認爲，有效履行條約的實質條款，才是誘使其參加該約的主要條
款，縱使這些條款屬輔助性，亦被其視爲主要的。這樣的規定，
把違約限於重大的，同時把輕微的違約排除了，只有「非本公約
准許的」廢棄條約，違反「爲達成條約目的或宗旨所必要」的條
約規定，才是重大的違約。援引重大違約爲理由以廢止條約，才
是合法的，換句話說，藉其他理由以廢約，便不是本公約所容許
的。

　　本條第四項說，遇有違約情事時，如該約有關於違約的規
定，就必須優先適用，不受本條規定的影響，也比本公約其他規
定優先。這是特別法優於普通法原則。

　　本條第五項進一步訂明，本條第一項至第三項的規定，不適
用於保護人身的條約或人道性的條約（例如殘害人羣罪防止及懲
治公約）。也就是說，當某一當事國嚴重違反這類條約時，其他
當事國不得援引爲理由，以廢止或暫停施行其全部或局部規定，
更不得藉任何理由，以限制、終止或暫停施行關於禁止報復其所
保護者的規定，因爲這類條約直接保護個人和人羣，不是保護任
何國家或政府。要是當事國得援引違約爲理由以廢止或暫停施行
這類條約，便會背離簽訂該約的初衷，也正中了違約者的詭計。

第六十一條　發生意外不可能履行

一、倘因實施條約所必不可少之標的物永久消失或毀壞，以致不能履

行條約時，當事國得援引不可能履行為理由，終止或退出條約。
如不可能履行係屬暫時性質，僅得援引為停止施行條約之理由。
二、倘條約不可能履行係一當事國違反條約義務或違反對條約任何其
他當事國所負任何其他國際義務之結果，該當事國不得援引不可
能履行為理由，終止、退出或停止施行條約。

　　一份條約簽訂時，如果規定了履行條約的要件，該要件是某
標的物的存在，或是某標的物完整無缺，則於該標的物消失或毀
壞，以致不能繼續履行條約時，當事國可以援引不可能履行為理
由，以終止、退出或暫停施行條約。標的物如果永久消失或永久
毀壞，就可以正式終止或退出條約。在標的物暫時消失或暫時毀
壞的情形下，只可以暫停施行條約。標的物永久或暫時消失或毀
壞，不同於情勢的基本改變，應加注意。因為第六十二條規定情
勢的基本改變，所以容後析論該條時，才敍述其不同的要義。

　　標的物永久消失，在理論上固然是可能的，在事實上也會發
生，雖然先例並不多見，立法時卻須意料。海島沈沒、湖泊乾
竭、河川缺水、水庫崩倒、電廠傾塌，使以其為標的物的條約不
能繼續履行。海島沈沒是標的物永久消失，水庫崩倒是標的物永
久毀壞，湖泊乾竭是標的物暫時毀壞，或是永久毀壞。無論是永
久或暫時性質，都會使條約不能履行。

　　儘管條約已不能履行，卻不因標的物消失或毀壞而自動終
止，當事國也不當然終止了或退出了條約。只是當事國可以援引
這一事實為理由，宣告終止、退出或暫停施行相關條約，其他當
事國如果認為理由正當，就可以表示同意，如果認為不正當，則

可以反對那宣告。被反對時，便發生爭端，有關當事國應依解決國際爭端的途徑處理。這是本條第一項隱含的意義。

條約不能履行，由不可抗力 (Force majeure) ⑬ 造成的，當事國據以宣告終止、退出或暫停施行條約，乃是合法的，如果是其違法或過失所致，則其不但不得援引這一事實爲藉口，甚至須擔負違法或過失的責任。所以本條第二項規定：倘條約不能履行，是一當事國違反條約義務的結果，或是一當事國違反其對同約任何其他當事國所已承擔的任何其他國際義務的結果，該國就不得援引這一事實爲理由，以宣告終止、退出或暫停施行條約。這一規定的作用，顯然在防止條約當事國任意找藉口廢約，或減少其惡意破壞條約的機會。

條約生效實施後，各當事國正在履行條約義務時，假如某當事國已因其他當事國的履約而獲得利益，該國終止、退出或暫停施行條約時，應否盡某些義務，以使其他當事國獲得近似的利益？對於這一方面，本條未加規定。一般說來，按公道原則和國交常理，答案應是肯定的。至於雙邊條約的一個當事國消滅，就當然使條約不可能履行。本條沒有提及那一情況，因爲那情況出現時，會有國家繼承的問題，必定包括條約繼承事項，應由關於國家繼承的法則加以規定，不必於本公約內訂明。

---

⑬ 不能抵抗的自然界原因，不能意料、預防或阻擋，沒有人爲因素，全是天然現象，結果造成嚴重災難，如地震、暴風、巨雷、閃電、洪水等天災。這種原因，中文稱爲不可抗力，英文稱爲 act of God, 法文稱爲 force majeure.

第六十二條　情況之基本改變

一、條約締結時存在之情況發生基本改變而非當事國所預料者，不得援引爲終止或退出條約之理由，除非：

(甲)此等情況之存在構成當事國同意承受條約拘束之必要根據；

(乙)該項改變之影響將根本變動依條約尚待履行之義務範圍。

二、情況之基本改變不得援引爲終止或退出條約之理由：

(甲)倘該條約確定一邊界；或

(乙)倘情況之基本改變係援引此項理由之當事國違反條約義務或違反對條約任何其他當事國所負任何其他國際義務之結果。

三、倘根據以上各項，一當事國援引情況之基本改變爲終止或退出條約之理由，該國亦得援引該項改變爲停止施行條約之理由。

本條標題爲「情勢之基本改變」(Fundamental change of circumstances)，實際上和常用詞「重大情勢變遷」的涵義相似，所以本條的意旨，可以說是從「重大情勢變遷原則」(Principle of rebus sic stantibus) 演變而來。

上文所敍的修正條約的通則、多邊條約的修正、僅在若干當事國間修改多邊條約、條約失效終止和暫停施行等項，都是爲了維持條約的穩定和功能，並且使訂約者有所期望和遵循。而依照本公約的規定，締結條約須有各締約國的意思合致，意思合致又是基於各締約國所認知的當時情勢。條約締結以後，無論是因爲人爲的原因，或是由於不可抗力的作用，當時的情勢已有變化，在國內或國外，都今非昔比，如果這變化傷及某當事國的立國基礎或重大利益，仍要求其繼續照常履行條約義務，就是顯然不公道不應該的事情，所以維持條約效力的概念中隱含一個條

件，即「條約繼續存在應以情勢依舊爲條件」(Conventio omnis intelligitur rebus sic stantibus)，這條件演變結果，使人承認締約時情勢發生重大變遷後，當事國得終止或暫停施行條約，而牴觸「條約必須遵守」原則。

原來歐洲自然法學者自十三世紀起，爲了補救羅馬法和日耳曼法的過度剛嚴和僵硬，曾主張使用情勢變遷條款 (Clausula sic stantibus)，以避免當事國受不合理的束縛。二十世紀第一次世界大戰後，國際聯合會盟約第十九條規定：「大會可隨時請聯合會會員重行考慮已不可適用之條約……。」❹第二次世界大戰後，聯合國憲章第十四條規定：「大會對於其所認爲足以妨害國際間公共福利或友好關係之任何情勢，不論其起源如何，包括由違反憲章所載聯合國宗旨及原則而起之情勢，得建議和平調整辦法，……。」❺本條所稱的情勢，應包括各當事國訂約所依據的情勢，如果與條約相關的情勢，「足以妨害國際間公共福利或友好關係」，則大會可以建議和平的辦法，以調整各當事國的條約

---

❹ 該條英文爲「The Assembly may from time to time advise the reconsideration by Members of the League of treaties which have become inapplicable)」。

❺ 該條英文爲「……the General Assembly may recommend measures for the peaceful adjustment of any situation, regardless of origin, which it deems likely to impair the general welfere or friendly relations among nations, including situations resulting from a violation of the provisions of the present Charter setting forth the Purposes and Principles of the United Nations.

關係。因爲無論國際聯盟或聯合國的大會，都沒有施行盟約第十九條或憲章第十四條的實例，現在不能說「和平調整辦法」是否包括終止條約或退出條約。至於情勢變遷原則是否已成爲國際法則的問題，也不能從這些規定中獲得解答。

一九六九年以前，國際法學者對於這問題的意見，頗爲紛歧。例如羅特拍認爲，這原則只是國內法官的立法（Judge-made law），旨在謀求契約權利義務的公平，國際法庭未曾承認這原則爲實證法則 ❶ 。持其他理由反對這原則者，亦大有人在。但是贊成者則另有其說法。例如賀爾說：「契約任何一方，依其意願，都不能使其在訂約時所知以外的條件下受拘束；另一方面，訂約時有義務性效力的任何東西實質改變時，契約立刻喪失拘束力。」❷ 范維克（Fenwick）也說：「一切國際契約都在一些隱含的條件下簽訂，隱含的條件連同明列的條件，全是構成契約要素的值得考慮的相等部分；公法學者說這原則是實證法的規則，似是正確的」❸ 。其他學者雖然承認這原則不夠明確，易被濫用，又沒有具強制管轄權的司法機關監督其適用，弊端叢生，卻也主張這原則的價值應受重視，因爲在無國際監督的情形下，國際法體系已存在多年，所以這原則也可以在無國際司法監督下存

❶ Hersch Lauterpacht, "Spinoza and International Law", *British Yearbook of International Law*, 1927, p. 99.

❷ William E. Hall, *A Treatise on International Law*, 8th ed. by A. P. Higgins, Oxford, 1924, §116.

❸ Charles G. Fenwick, *International Law*, 4th ed., 1965, p. 545.

在；其次，任何法則都可能被濫用，各國不應該因怕它被濫用而否定它的存在。

　　一九六〇年代，儘管多數學者承認這已是國際法原則，對於訂約時的情勢涵義，則各家意見不同。只限於當時確定的情勢？包含當時預知將來可能變成的情勢？僅以實質關係的情勢為限？連同心理上的因素？情勢變到什麼程度才可以援引這原則？非嚴重到妨害國家發展的程度不得援引？誰判斷情勢已發生這樣的變遷？這些都是爭論不休的理論問題。

　　現代公法學者，鑒於這些問題不易解答，一則承認「重大情勢變遷原則」是國際法則，再則主張置這原則於很小的範圍內，定下援引這原則的嚴格條件，尤其在仍無強制管轄的一般制度時，更須預防這原則威脅條約安全的危險；他們同時警告，居今日，國際情勢常變，每當小變的時候，會被別有用心者假定為已變到條約不能適用的程度。

　　另一方面，常設國際法院和現在的國際法院，都未曾正面肯定這原則，更未正式適用[19]，所以不能引據實例以證明這原則的功用。但是無論如何，現在已廣泛接受了下列意見，就是情況的基本改變，可以使終止條約和修改條約的要求為合法，雖然這改變並不賦予當事國片面終止條約的權利。也就是說，當事國可以援引情況已變為理由，以要求修改或終止條約，卻不可以藉情況已變以自行終止條約。

　　從以往的許多實例可知，條約可以連續存在多年久載，其中

---

[19]　*P. C. I. J., Series* A/B, No. 46 (1932), pp. 156-8.

規定可能因情況的基本改變而使某當事國受過度的束縛，或因其他當事國十分固執，對於已變的情況視而不見，無顧該當事國的損害，則該約的功用必受嚴重考驗。在這情形下，假如國際法硬性規定，非另訂新約不得終止條約，不准以其他方法終止或修改條約，則必使各當事國間的關係過度緊張，會迫使受害國採取法外途徑以解脫困厄。因為直到一九五〇年代，仍然沒有緩和這類緊張的明確法則，所以這年代以前的許多條約，或規定較短的效期，或規定若干年一次的循環期限（Recurrent terms），附上各期屆滿時的廢約權，或明定（或默示）准許通知廢約，以使條約終止，或訂明有廢約權的當事國得要求其他當事國同意廢約。沒有這類規定的條約，縱使已不合時宜，而且造成某當事國的不合理損害，該國也不能依法獲得紓解，非援引重大情勢變遷原則，就不能爭取其他當事國的某種妥協，以解脫悖理的全部或部分束縛。

以往許多不定期限的條約，常被視為載有隱含的條件，准許條約於情勢有基本的變遷時自動失效，和「條約必須遵守」原則牴觸。現在要調和這兩個原則，幾乎是不可能的事情，所以多數條約不顧情勢變遷原則，只求條約的穩定和安全，如果顧及情勢變遷，便列明文加以規定，以避免主觀的解釋和權利的濫用。也因此，本條不照用舊詞「重大情勢變遷原則」，改用新詞「情況之基本改變」，以表示和舊原則不同，脫離舊原則的含義。

從前很多公法學者，認為「無限期的」條約——不訂明效期終了的條約，可以適用「重大情勢變遷原則」，現在他們明白，從寬適用這原則，總是弊多利少，因為效期定為九十九年的條

約，固然不用說了，就是效期定爲十年或五年的條約，在效期內發生情況的基本改變，也不能預先排除，所以本條列載新原則「情況之基本改變」，不應限其只適用於永久性條約，而應訂明其可適用於長期性和短期性的條約，也就是不分條約爲短期的和長期的，都可援引這新原則。

　　由於這新原則的適用應從嚴，本條第一項便定下五種適用上的限制：(一)發生變化的原情況必須是締約時存在的；(二)這改變必須是基本的，不是細端末節的；(三)這改變必須是各當事國未預料到的；(四)原情況的存在已構成各當事國同意承受條約拘束的實質基礎；(五)這改變對於按照條約尚待履行的義務範圍有根本性的影響。本條第一項定下這五種限制外，又用「不得援引……除非……」的消極語氣，以免鼓勵援引這新原則。

　　因爲情況的一般性改變，牽動締約時存在的情況改變，這改變又是基本的。例如國家政策改變，導致訂約時存在的情況改變，這是不是本條所指的改變？答案可以是肯定的，也可是否定的，隨各案的相關細節而定。

　　已經畫定的國家疆界，必須固定不變，以維持國際秩序，並且穩定國際關係，如果國與國間的邊界可以隨情況的基本改變而改變，則這秩序不能維持，有關國家間的關係不能安定融洽，自非人類之福，因而本條第二項規定，確定邊界的條約，任何當事國都不得援引情況的基本改變爲理由，宣告退出，或予以終止。這一規定，不是新制，而是傳統國際法則 —— 處分性條約 (Executed treaty) 所造成的法律狀態，非另訂新約，不得改變。畫界條約就是典型的處分性條約。

　　情況的基本改變，如果是某當事國所造成，造成時違反條約義務，或違反該國對條約任何其他當事國所承擔的國際義務，則該國不得援引這改變爲理由，以終止或退出條約，因爲所有國家都不得從違反條約或任何國際義務中獲得利益，要是准其獲得利益，便是鼓勵或默許各國違反這些義務。所以本條第二項(乙)款特別作禁止的規定。

　　本條第三項的主旨，在減少終止條約和退出條約的當事國。爲了達到這一主旨，便准許條約當事國作選擇，於其可以援引情況的基本改變爲理由時，選擇較溫和的作法，只暫停施行條約，不終止或退出條約，若干時日後，於情況另有改變時，才恢復施行。這樣一來，條約的當事國數就不因適用這新原則而減少了。

　　暫停施行條約的當事國，必須符合本條第一項和第二項的規定，可以援引情況的基本改變爲理由，以終止條約或退出條約，其暫停施行條約才是合法的，如果不能援引這理由，貿然停止施行條約，則是違反本條的規定，亦不符合本條減少廢約國和退約國的意旨。

第六十三條　斷絕外交或領事關係

　　條約當事國間斷絕外交或領事關係不影響彼此間由條約確定之法律關係，但外交或領事關係之存在爲適用條約所必不可少者，不在此限。

　　雙邊條約所確定的法律關係，例如上述畫界條約所定的法律狀態，多邊條約所確定的法律關係，例如殘害人羣罪防止及懲治

公約所定的法律關係，都不因當事國間斷絕外交或領事關係而受影響，可以在這些關係停止後繼續存在，不予改變。其他法律關係，例如雙邊條約所定的友好同盟關係，多邊條約所定的共同防禦關係，各當事國須有外交關係才可以履行條約義務，一旦外交關係斷絕了，原有條約所確定的法律關係，就不能不變了。

　　依照國際慣例，兩國間斷絕外交關係時，並不當然同時斷絕領事關係，在某些情形下，有外交和領事關係的兩個國家，於斷絕外交關係後，繼續維持領事關係，以保障兩國的僑民和經濟利益，所以這兩國間條約所確定的僑民法律地位，於其領事關係斷絕後，純按法律來說，可以改變，雖然兩國基於政治經濟的原因可以不予變更。

　　兩國間外交關係的斷絕，不當然影響國際法的適用。一九六三年維也納領事關係公約第二條第三項已訂明：「斷絕外交關係並不當然斷絕領事關係。」一九六一年維也納外交關係公約第四十五條規定，兩國斷絕外交關係時，」(甲)接受國務應尊重並保護使館館舍以及使館財產與檔案，縱有武裝衝突情事，亦應如此辦理；(乙)派遣國得將使館館舍以及使館財產與檔案委託接受國認可之第三國保管；(丙)派遣國得委託接受國認可之第三國代為保護派遣國及其國民之利益。」這些規定表示，兩國斷絕外交關係後，其原有的領事關係不一定受影響，其他法律關係不是全受影響，一般國際法則繼續適用，完全不改變。

　　現在必須指出，本條所稱的「法律」關係，不是政治、經濟、文化、軍事之類的關係。法律關係的涵義很廣，不能盡述，諸如相互給予對方外交官員和政府首長特權和豁免、尊重對方的

國家行為、承認對方的國際法人資格和地位、承認對方法院判決的效力等是。

　　本條所規定的，只及於斷絕外交或領事關係的事實，不及於發生這情事的原因。其原因是兩國或多國交惡，或是兵戎相見，或是嚴重誤會，都在所不問。條約當事國間斷絕外交或領事關係，無論是由於什麼原因，本條的規定一律適用。

第六十四條　一般國際法新強制規律（絕對法）之產生

　　遇有新一般國際法強制規律產生時，任何現有條約之與該項規律牴觸者，即成為無效而終止。

　　本公約第五十三條已規定：「條約在締結時與一般國際法強制規律牴觸者無效。」上文析論該條時，已敍明一般國際法強制規律的涵義，這裏用不着贅述。

　　現在必須假定，在當代的一般國際法中，維持國際公共秩序的一些基本規律，不應准許或容忍任何國家破壞，任何國際法人都不得以訂約或其他方式加以損抑。這些基本規律，通稱為強制規律或絕對法，已為各國公認、接受、遵行。

　　本條規定，現行的和未來的條約，牴觸絕對法的「即成為無效而終止」，所牽涉的行為和情勢便被取銷，給予當事國的權利消滅，課予當事國的義務作罷，例如以前管制販賣奴隸的條約，因為牴觸禁止販賣奴隸的公約，都變為無效了，終止了，在該類條約下享受權利的當事國不得繼續享受，擔負義務的當事國毋需繼續擔負，該類條約所造成的情勢應即消失。

　　本條所稱的規律，是一般國際法的新絕對法，所以應注意下述兩點：第一、絕對法以一般國際法的爲限，不包括區域國際法的，更不含特別國際法的；第二、絕對法以新的爲限，舊的和現在的絕對法屬於第五十三條範圍內。因此，任何條約如果在簽訂時牴觸絕對法，就自始無效，如果在簽訂後牴觸新的絕對法，就不是自始無效，而是自牴觸時「成爲無效而終止」，因爲它於簽訂時不違反任何法律，到新的絕對法出現時才有牴觸，才由於牴觸而無效。

　　依照本條的眞義，現行的和將來的任何條約，只要牴觸了一般國際法的新強制規律，便全約無效，不是約中某（些）規定與絕對法牴觸的無效，也就是說，本條不認可條約各條款的可分性，不承認絕對法的溯往效力。本條條文中「遇有新一般國際法強制規律產生時」等字，表示了不溯既往的意思。本條又採用「任何現有條約」等字，不像在其他條文中使用「……條約之規定……」⑳，又足以顯示：牴觸絕對法的條約，是全約無效，不只是約中某（些）規定無效。

第四節　程　　序

第六十五條　關於條約失效、終止、退出條約或停止施行
　　　　　　條約應依循之程序

---

⑳　第六十四條的英文是：If a new preemptory norm of general internationel law emerges, any existing treaty which is in conflict with that norm becomes void and terminates.

一、當事國依照本公約之規定援引其承受條約拘束之同意有誤為理由，或援引非難條約效力、終止、退出或停止施行條約之理由者，必須將其主張通知其他當事國。此項通知應載明對條約所提議採取之措施及其理由。

二、在一非遇特別緊急情形不得短於自收到通知時起算三個月之期間屆滿後，倘無當事國表示反對，則發出通知之當事國得依第六十七條規定之方式，實施其所提議之措施。

三、但如有任何其他當事國表示反對，當事國應藉聯合國憲章第三十三條所指之方法以謀解決。

四、上列各項絕不影響當事國在對其有拘束力之任何關於解決爭端之現行規定下所具有之權利或義務。

五、以不妨礙第四十五條為限，一國未於事前發出第一項所規定之通知之事實並不阻止該國為答覆另一當事國要求其履行條約或指稱其違反條約而發出此種通知。

一般說來，如果在其他當事國反對下，准許某當事國自擬理由，以使條約失效、終止條約或暫停施行條約，則一定有妨礙條約安全的眞正危險，該當事國如果以另一個（些）當事國違反條約為理由，或以情況的基本改變為理由，宣告終止條約，或宣告退出條約，則這種危險尤其嚴重。所以為防止這種危險起見，立法時必須定下很仔細客觀的可以援引的理由。有了規定的理由以後，任何當事國所援引的理由是不是合法的問題，便常常是事實問題，也可能成為當事國間的爭端。本條因而規定，有關各當事國應依解決爭端的程序，以避免任何當事國利用遁辭來擺脫條約義務。本條的規定，也防止反對國任意為反對而反對，故意刁

難，使受困當事國不能依法卸下其認為不當的義務。

條約當事國間發生爭端後，依照本條的意旨，無論是關於條約失效、終止條約、退出條約或暫停施行條約的爭端，都並非送請現在的聯合國國際法院解決不可，因為本條不授予該院處理這類爭端的強制管轄權，除非爭端當事國事前或臨時同意由該院論斷，該院便無緣置喙。本條只規定，爭端應依聯合國憲章第三十三條所定的方法，以謀求解決。該條所定的方法，包括談判、調查、調停、和解、公斷、司法解決、區域機關之利用、區域辦法之利用等，所以這類爭端也可以送請國際法院處理。又依聯合國憲章精神和第二條第三款，爭端當事國負有一般國際法的義務，必須「……以和平方法解決其國際爭端，俾免危及國際和平、安全及正義。」可見本條的精神，是崇高遠大的，是配合聯合國憲章而擬定的。

本條第一項訂明，要使條約失效的當事國，要援引正當理由以終止條約、退出條約或暫停施行條約的當事國，必須先把其主意通知其他當事國，以發起正常的程序。通知時應敍明提議的事項，例如終止條約或暫停施行條約，並且說明作這提議的理由。顯然的，通知的目的，在使其他當事國知道其主意，敍明事項的用意，在表示通知的主旨，說明理由是辯護其所援引的理由為正當。

本條第二項要求發通知國給予其他當事國一個合理的期間，俾便它們針對通知作反應。除有特別緊急的情形外，這期間不得短於三個月，也就是不得限制作反應的時間為三個月以下。在三個月內，如果沒有任何當事國表示反對，該國就可以正式實施其

主張。

在發出通知後的三個月內，如果有當事國表示反對，則依本條第三項的規定，爭端當事國須遵照聯合國憲章第三十三條所定的方法，以求得爭端的解決。假如遵照辦理，仍不能解決，有關當事國仍應按誠信原則進行，無論是不是聯合國會員國，都可以提請聯合國某一適當機關處理。如前文所說，並不排除國際法院。

本條第四項的形式意義多於實質意義，因為它說本條的規定，不影響各當事國彼此間解決爭端的現行條約規定的地位，也就是說，各當事國可以依照那些規定，以解決因適用本條而來的爭端，而不必遵照本條的規定。這是常理，即令沒有本條第四項，也是一樣。

依照本條第五項，一當事國縱使未於事前發出第一項所規定的通知，若不妨礙本公約第四十五條，仍可於另一當事國要求其履行條約，或指稱其違反條約時，提出答覆，並發出本條第一項所規定的通知。這樣就保障了它發通知的權利，它可以援引不能履行條約為理由，或以情況已有基本的改變為理由，以達到其終止、退出或暫停施行條約的目的。

第六十六條　司法解決、公斷及和解之程序

倘在提出反對之日後十二個月內未能依第六十五條第三項獲致解決，應依循下列程序··

(甲)關於第五十三條或第六十四條之適用或解釋之爭端之任一當事國得以請求書將爭端提請國際法院裁決之，但各當事國同意將爭端

　　提交公斷者不在此限；

　　(乙)關於本公約第五編任一其他條文之適用或解釋之爭端之任一當事

　　　國得向聯合國秘書長提出請求，發動本公約附件所定之程序。

　　如本條標題所示，本條訂明解決爭端的程序，以便爭端當事國遵循。

　　關於終止條約、退出條約和暫停施行條約的爭端，如果拖延很久不能解決，則對有關當事國會產生不良的影響。本條爲防止爭端久懸不決起見，要求有關當事國於反對意見提出後，最遲應在十二個月內解決。關於本公約第五十三條或第六十四條的適用或解釋的爭端，應送請國際法院判決，關於本公約第五編（就是本編）任何其他條文（就是第四十二條至第七十二條，本條除外）的適用或解釋的爭端，則應請聯合國秘書長發動解決的程序（就是本公約附件所定的程序），速謀解決。

　　本條使用「應依循下列程序」（…the following procedures shall be followed）等字，表示各當事國必須依循，都有遵守所定程序的義務，如不遵守，便是違反本公約下的義務，可以依照聯合國憲章或其他條約的規定，要求遵守。

　　送請國際法院判決的爭端，應是或多數是法律性的，或是法律性多於政治性的，只要送達法院，法院應予裁決，依往例推測，法院必定裁決，一經裁決，爭端應可消除或緩和了。

　　本公約附件所定的程序大致如下：本公約各當事國委派夠格法學家國民和解員二人，列成名冊，聯合國秘書長接到請求時，從冊中挑選各爭端當事國國民一人第三國國民二人，以組成和解

委員會，由這四人從上述名册選聘第五位和解員擔任主席。委員
會自定其程序，經各爭端當事國同意後，得邀請條約任何當事國
提口頭或書面意見，經和解委員會過半數委員同意，得作成決定
或建議，並得促請各爭端當事國注意可能促成友好解決的任何措
施。委員會聽悉各爭端當事國的意見後，應提出友好解決爭端的
建議，又應於委員會成立後十二個月內提出報告書。報告書存放
聯合國秘書處，並分送各爭端當事國。委員會的建議沒有拘束
力。秘書長應提供委員會需要的協助和便利。委員會的費用由聯
合國負擔。

　　送請聯合國秘書長推動解決程序以求解決的爭端，往往是政
治性的，或者是政治性多於法律性的，所以不像法律性的爭端，
未必於程序開始後，當然獲得解決，因爲和解委員會不一定能夠
作成建議，建議即令作成了，也沒有法律拘束力，很可能被爭端
當事國拒絕接受。

　　然而無論如何，本條的規定能不能達到預期的目的，都會有
或多或少的指引作用，當本條所稱的爭端發生時，已有明確的途
徑可供當事國遵行，無需臨時找尋或設計了，爭端解決的時間或
可縮短了。

　　從上可見，本公約擬訂者多麼重視退約等爭端的解決，聯合
國又多麼願意協助解決這類爭端。至於適用本條約的實例，則至
今仍付闕如，所以還不能評論本條約的功能。

第六十七條　宣告條約失效、終止、退出或停止施行條約之文書
　　一、第六十五條第一項規定之通知須以書面爲之。

二、凡依據條約規定或第六十五條第二項或第三項規定宣告條約失效、終止、退出或停止施行條約之行爲，應以文書致送其他當事國爲之。倘文書未經國家元首、政府首長或外交部長簽署，得要求致送文書國家之代表出具全權證書。

　　本條所列的三項規定，正如字面意義所示，意思十分明顯確定。第一項要求本公約第六十五條第一項規定的通知以書面作成，不得用口頭或其他行爲代替，以示正式、隆重、莊嚴。以前有一些國家，廢約時只作片面的聲明，曾引起不少困擾。本項的要求，便是針對這類惡例。第二項訂明，所有宣告條約失效的行爲，宣告退出終止或暫停施行條約的行爲，必須以書面通知其他當事國，通知後行爲才算完成了，不遵辦便視爲未發出通知，未發出通知就不發生終止、退出或暫停施行條約的效力。以前有一些國家，不正式通知其他當事國，便自行認定並且辯稱已發生這種效力。這是惡劣的做法，應予禁止。本項鑑於這種事實，便作禁止的規定，並且要求如下：通知所用的文書應由國家元首、政府首長或外交部長簽署，如果不經其中一人簽署，則有關的任何一個當事國得要求，要求致送文書的國家代表提出其所奉的全權證書。這正和本公約第七條的意旨相吻合，國家代表從事拘束其國家的行爲，必須獲得授權，才能發生法律效力。

　　簡單說來，本條的目的，在使終止、退出和暫停施行條約的行爲正式、隆重、莊嚴，以加強條約安全的保障。

第六十八條　撤銷第六十五條及第六十七條所規定之通知及文書

第六十五條或第六十七條所規定之通知或文書得在其發生效力以前隨時撤銷之。

　　一般說來，一份條約締結後，無論效期是多麼的長，都以沒有任何當事國使它失效、或宣告終止、退出或暫停施行為最佳，最能符合締約國的初衷，因而不幸偶有這種宣告，又以文書作正式的通知後，最好是准許隨時撤銷已發出的通知。

　　本公約第六十五條和第六十七所規定的通知，必須以書面作成，並且須等到其他當事國收到通知所用的文書三個月屆滿時，才能發生通知的效力。這一規定，是為了給予其他當事國考慮的時間，以決定是否反對，並且讓其他當事國作條約終止前的必要準備，俾其能夠及時作適度的調整，所以這三個月的期間是不可少的。

　　依照本條規定，上述通知和文書發生效力以前，發出通知的當事國得隨時撤銷，不受任何限制，也就是在通知經其他當事國收到後三個月內，可以無條件的撤回，無需履行條約義務以外的國際義務。這就符合上文所說的意思，准許隨時撤銷的意思。

　　准許隨時撤銷通知，似乎失之過寬，但深入推敲後，又覺得並無缺失，因為通知須經三個月後才能生效的規定，已隱含一種權利 —— 撤銷通知的權利，而這權利的行使，常對各當事國有益而無害，所以如果各締約國認為不許撤銷為較佳，仍可在所訂條約中作不許的規定。此外，在准許撤銷通知的情形下，其他當事國收到這類通知時，知道非到某日通知不生效，應即開始作調整的準備，並且考慮這期間的時日因素，少有不及調整適應的情

形。因而從遠大處着眼，本條規定便利撤銷這類通知，可以說是暗中鼓勵或引誘發通知的當事國採取撤銷的行爲。

第五節　條約失效、終止或停止施行之後果

第六十九條　條約失效之後果

一、條約依本公約確定失效者，無效。條約無效者，其規定無法律效力。

二、但如已有信賴此種條約而實施之行爲，則：

(甲)每一當事國得要求任何其他當事國在彼此關係上儘可能恢復未實施此項行爲前原應存在之狀況；

(乙)在援引條約失效之理由前以善意實施之行爲並不僅因條約失效而成爲不合法。

三、遇第四十九條、第五十條、第五十一條或第五十二條所稱之情形，第二項之規定對應就詐欺、賄賂行爲或强迫貢責之當事國不適用之。

四、遇某一國家承受多邊條約拘束之同意成爲無效之情形，上列各項規則在該國與條約當事國之關係上適用之。

本條所稱的後果，是指法律效果。

本條只訂明條約失效 (Invalidity) 的法律效果，不涉及使條約失效的行爲，不過問那行爲引起的國際責任，更不規定詐欺、賄賂、强迫等行爲所引起的救濟（賠償）問題。關於這類問題，本公約第四十九條、第五十條、第五十一條和第五十二條已有規定，應可適用，所以本條不適用於這類問題。

根據本公約第五編第二節規定的理由以確定的條約失效，是條約自始無效，不是自確定之日起無效。依本公約第五編第三節第六十五條而變成無效的條約，是自確定時起無效，不是自始無效。無論條約自何時起無效，其規定自條約無效時起都沒有法律效力。

本條第二項第一款規定，儘管某條約自始無效，但是某一（些）當事國由於無過失的原因，信賴該約，在一個時段內，已依約實施了一些行為，才援引該約失效的理由，以使條約失效。這時候，其行為的法律地位雖然是問題，而就條約失效的原因看，卻不能把詐欺、賄賂或強迫的責任歸屬該（等）國家，不可視其為過失者，只好從條約自始無效和當事國善意兩方面考慮，以決定其行為的法律地位。於是規定，每一個當事國得要求任何其他當事國，要求它們盡可能恢復那行為實施前原應存在的狀況，以進行彼此間的關係。這就表示了一種承認，即在原則上，條約雖然自締結時起無效，卻容許條約有完全的法律效果，任何當事國因而可以要求盡力確定原來存在的狀況。

本條第二項第二款的用意，是強化第一款的力量，規定當事國在援引條約失效的理由之前，善意實施了的行為，不因為條約的失效而變成不合法。換句話說，如果那行為不是出自善意的，或那行為是不合法的，則在條約失效前和失效後，那行為都是不合法的。

本條第三項訂明，要為詐欺、賄賂或強迫行為負責任的國家，本條第二項的規定不對其適用。如上文所說，對於這類國家，本公約已另作規定。

本條第四項說，多邊條約當事國承受條約拘束的同意失效時，上列各項規則適用於該國與條約當事國的關係。一般說來，各當事國間的條約關係，是以那同意爲基礎，當那同意失效，彼此間的條約關係便喪失了基礎，不能存在了。

第七十條　條約終止之後果

一、除條約另有規定或當事國另有協議外，條約依其規定或依照本公約終止時：

(甲)解除當事國繼續履行條約之義務；

(乙)不影響當事國在條約終止前經由實施條約而產生之任何權利、義務或法律情勢。

二、倘一國廢止或退出多邊條約，自廢止或退出生效之日起，在該國與條約每一其他當事國之關係上適用第一項之規定。

當事國使條約終止的某種行爲，諸如破壞條約、無端的片面宣告廢約等行爲，可以引起國際責任的問題，跟着可能發生賠償的問題。本條不規範這類問題，只規範條約終止的法律效果。

多數條約不訂明當事國終止或退出條約的後果，只有少數條約訂明。例如一九六二年五月二十五日在布魯塞爾簽訂的核子船操作人責任公約 (Convention on the Liability of Operators of Nuclear Ships)，於其第十九條訂明：卽令在公約終止後，於公約有效運作期間核准的船舶所負的核子事件責任，仍繼續存在一段期間。又如歐洲人權及基本自由公約 (European Convention on Human Rights and Fundamental Freedoms)，於其第六十五條規定：當事國終止條約並不解除其在公

約施行期間的行為責任。雖然有這些實例，這裏仍應贅述：實例
是極稀少的。

當條約卽將終止前夕，當一個當事國聲明退出條約時，如
果各當事國進行談判，並且就終止條約或退出條約的條件達成協
議，則其協議必比本公約的規定優先；如果條約列有關於終止條
約或退出條約的規定，規定也優先於本公約的條款。這是本條第
一項首先表示的意思。

條約終止了，就解除各當事國繼續履行條約的義務。

在條約終止前，當事國實施條約所產生的權利、義務或法律
情勢，仍然繼續存在，不受條約終止的影響。權利和義務 (Rights and obligations) 是指依法律規定可以享有的利益和應
負擔的責任。所謂法律情勢 (Legal situation)，則是法律規
定的狀況，所以不受條約終止影響的權利、義務和法律情勢，全
是法律規定的，法律未規定的（就是條約未規定的）是否受影
響，則要按各案相關事實而定。至於個人的旣得利益 (Vested
interest)，則非本條所稱的權利，難免要受條約終止的影響。

條約終止時，可能造成損害。如不造成損害，則引發的問
題，也許較少而較易解答，如造成損害，條約又有關於損害賠償
的規定，當可據以請求賠償或其他救濟，如無此種規定，就要臨
時經由談判或其他方法以解決問題了。本條未對這種情形作任何
規定，因而受損害國唯有援引「條約必須遵守」、「善意履行國
際義務」等原則，以爭取補救或滿足了。

本條第二項的目的無他，在把第一項的規定也適用於多邊條
約，訂明終止和退出條約的當事國與其他當事國的條約關係，自

終止或退出條約的行為生效日起，便適用第一項的規定。

　　本條規定的條約終止，當然和第六十四條所提的強制規律相關，閱讀本條時，應回顧該條，才能前後貫通。依該條的規定而終止的條約，無疑的，也發生本條所列的後果。又本條和第四十三條亦有密切關係，因為該條已規定，由於適用本公約或相關條約以致該約失效或終止，並不妨礙當事國履行其在條約外國際法下的義務。所以於條約沒有規定關於損害賠償事宜時，受害國仍可依一般國際法請求救濟。

第七十一條　條約因與一般國際法強制規律相牴觸而失效之後果
　　一、條約依第五十三條無效者，當事國應：
　　　　(甲)儘量消除依據與任何一般國際法強制規律相牴觸之規定所實施行為之後果；及
　　　　(乙)使彼此關係符合一般國際法強制規律。
　　二、遇有條約依第六十四條成為無效而終止之情形，條約之終止：
　　　　(甲)解除當事國繼續履行條約之義務；
　　　　(乙)不影響當事國在條約終止前經由實施條約而產生之任何權利、義務或法律情勢；但嗣後此等權利、義務或情勢之保持僅以與一般國際法新強制規律不相牴觸者為限。

　　條約於締結時牴觸當時一般國際法強制規律，是不可常見的事情，因為有這種牴觸而自始無效，則是條約無效的稀有特例。依本公約第六十四條的與新強制規律牴觸而無效的情形（不是自始無效），也是條約無效的罕見特例。條約自始無效所衍生的問題，是各當事國如何消除實施條約已獲致的結果，以及如何調整

地位以使彼此關係符合強制規律。本公約第六十九條所定的條約失效的後果，雖然在原則上可以適用於本條所定的情形，但是仍應顧及在新的強制規律下，經由實施條約而產生的權利、義務或法律情勢，究竟還可以繼續維持到何種程度。本公約第五十三條訂明一般國際法強制規律的定義，規定牴觸這種規律的條約無效。本公約第六十四條說：與一般國際法新強制規律牴觸的條約無效。本條把條約依這兩條而失效的法律效果並列，使讀者比較容易看出兩者的差別，也可藉以知道兩者都沒有追溯既往的效力。

本條分列兩項，第一項要求各當事國在條約自始無效的情形下，首先盡力消除已依條約規定的行為後果，使後果不復牴觸強制規律，其次是調整彼此的關係，調整到完全符合強制規律的程度。至於各當事國間的相互利益，本條則未要求各當事國調整，留給各當事國自行考量。這就表示，本條期望的，是各當事國遵守強制規律，不涉及其利益關係。

本條第二項針對着條約牴觸新強制規律而失效的情形，要求自新規律出現時起牴觸規律的條約無效，但是，因實施條約已產生的權利、義務和法律情勢，在符合新規律的範圍內，得繼續維持。這樣規定，凸顯了新規律的最高地位和強制性質，表示新規律在同性質的一切規則之上，卻不使它有溯及既往的效力。

第七十二條　條約停止施行之後果

一、除條約另有規定或當事國另有協議外，條約依其本身規定或依照本公約停止施行時：

　　(甲)解除停止施行條約之當事國於停止施行期間在彼此關係上履
　　　　行條約之義務；

　　(乙)除此以外，並不影響條約所確定當事國間之法律關係。

　二、在停止施行期間，當事國應避免足以阻撓條約恢復施行之行為。

　　本條直接訂明暫停施行條約的法律效果，不涉及暫停施行條
約的當事國的國際責任 —— 在「條約必須遵守」等原則下的國際
責任。

　　條約各當事國可於約中規定，也可以經由協議，共同決定暫
停施行條約的相關事項。有這種規定或協議，就必須依照規定或
協議，以暫停施行條約。若無這種規定，便要臨時達成這種協
議。如果既無這種規定，又無這種協議，則當事國片面的決定暫
停施行條約時，難免惹起爭端，須負國際責任。

　　當事國暫停施行條約，只有一種法律效果，就是解除了該國
「於停止施行期間在彼此關係上履行條約之義務」。但是，這不
等於說「該國在一切關係上免除了履行條約的義務」，因為該國
在其他方面仍須履行條約義務。例如甲乙丙三國訂約，規定甲乙
兩國各於十五年內提供丙國十五億元經濟援助，每年一億元；現
在甲國依條約規定暫停施行該約，雖然解除了其與乙國關係上履
行條約的義務，卻仍須履行其與丙國關係上的條約義務，繼續提
供經濟援助。誠然甲國與丙國，為了這種經濟援助，很可能彼此
另行訂約，要求甲國繼續援助，使兩國的權利義務關係更明確，
但是即令沒有新約，甲國依照其與乙國間條約的規定，還是應該
履行該條約。可見暫停施行條約的當事國，不能免除履行一切關

係上的條約義務。

　　本條第一項(乙)款規定，暫停施行條約，並不影響條約所確定的各當事國間的法律關係。也就是說，各當事國仍是該約的當事國，暫停施行前依約產生的一切事實、情況等，一律維持不變，直到條約恢復施行時止。當然，無論是何種情況，非因人為原因而變的，自屬例外。

　　暫停施行條約期間，各當事國，尤其是策動暫停施行的當事國，應避免任何足以妨礙條約恢復施行的事情，以便於暫停施行的原因消失後，條約可以順利於一定時間內恢復施行。這是一般法律原則，是國際法的「條約必須遵守」、「誠信和善意」等原則所隱含的，所以縱使本條第二項不以明文規定，各當事國也應明白而自動遵守。

第六編　雜項規定

第七十三條　國家繼承、國家責任及發生敵對行爲問題

本公約之規定不妨礙國家繼承或國家所負責任或國家間發生敵對行爲所引起關於條約之任何問題。

本編標題是「雜項規定」（Miscellaneous provisions），表示編內所列各條文，不涉及本公約的主旨，也不觸及任何條約的本體，只規定一些與條約有關的廣泛而零星的事項，使本公約的構想完整。

本條列載三點，就是國家繼承所引起的條約問題、國家責任所引起的條約問題、國家間發生敵對行爲所引起關於條約的任何問題。國家繼承、國家所擔負的國際責任、國家間發生敵對行爲，都可能牽涉本公約以及公約以外相關的國際法則。其中法則，規範這三個問題的，都非常複雜，如果在本公約列載，就會犯掛一漏萬、語而不詳、不妥善、不周延的毛病，非由國家繼承法❶、國家責任法、國家間敵對行爲法等公約分別規定不可，所以本公約未予列入。本公約只作這一籠統概括性的規定，也許是草擬者爲了使本公約略具完整性，並且避免讀者誤解他們未注意

---

❶　一九七八年八月二十三日，聯合國召開的國際會議締結了「關於國家在條約方面的繼承的維也納公約」。

這些問題的存在和複雜性。

本條對於「國家間發生敵對行為」所引起的關於條約的任何問題，不加以規定，或是深思的結果，因為條約當事國間發生敵對行為時，實際的情況會阻止條約的履行，而不履行條約，便引起責任問題。自聯合國憲章生效施行以來，國家間發生敵對行為，固然已是違法，而且被視為完全異常的情事，適用國家間正常關係的國際法則來處理，才可以獲致合理的解決，因為違反條約所引起的責任，唯有在有關各國都希望維持彼此正常關係的情形下，才能夠依法處理。所以雖然一九六一年的外交關係公約，一九六三年的領事關係公約，分別於其第四十四條和第二十六條，提及武裝衝突事項，卻不規定武裝衝突的後果。本公約也不規定當事國間發生敵對行為所引起的關於條約的問題，避免越出本公約性質所應包括的範圍。

總之，本條沒有積極性的規定，只作消極性的保留或排除，用意無他，在使本公約符合邏輯的推理，並求公約的完整，免被誤為思考不周而已。

第七十四條　外交及領事關係與條約之締結

兩個以上國家之間斷絕外交或領事關係或無此種關係不妨礙此等國家間締結條約。條約之締結本身不影響外交或領事關係方面之情勢。

一般說來，在正常情形下，兩個以上的國家（或國際組織）或一個國家和一個國際組織，都有締結條約的意願和決心時，可

以開始談判訂約事宜；談判結果，如果能夠就條約內容和文字達成協議，就可以進行簽署；所簽的條約如果訂明須經批准才能夠生效，則雙邊條約經兩國批准後，多邊條約經某數目的國家批准後，自某日起生效施行。這些訂約程序的進行，完全毋需以談判國間、簽署國間、接受國間、贊同國間或加入國間有外交關係為前提，也不以它們有領事關係為基礎。這些國家間要是有外交或領事關係，一旦這種關係斷絕了，亦不妨礙其締結條約。中華民國和美國自一九七九年起，中止了外交和領事關係，仍然簽訂了彼此外交人員特權與豁免協定等文件，便是近例。就以往實例看，中華民國與日本國間的外交和領事關係，因日本發動侵略戰爭，由中華民國宣告斷絕了，民國四十一年，在臺北簽訂中日和平條約，隨和約的簽訂，兩國的外交和領事關係才恢復了。其他和平條約簽訂的實例，不勝枚舉。在戰爭進行期間，兩個或兩個以上的敵對國家，在沒有邦交的情形下，簽訂停火協定、交換戰俘協定、交換死者傷者病者協定、停戰協定等，曾是屢見的事實。可見各國訂約時，絕對毋需以彼此有外交或領事關係為基礎。

　　外交關係公約第二條規定：「國與國間外交關係及常設使館之建立，以協議為之。」領事關係公約第二條訂明：「國與國間領事關係之建立，以協議為之。三、斷絕外交關係並不當然斷絕領事關係。」這兩份公約，都說國家間外交和領事關係的建立，須基於協議。毫無疑問的，兩國於達成這種協議之前，這些關係還沒有建立，於建立之前沒有外交關係，或者也沒有領事關係。這也表示，國家間的協議，是建立外交或領事關係所不可或缺

的。而協議本身，雖然可以用口頭作成，但在絕大多數的情形下，都是以文書簽訂。這類文書，當然是本公約所包括的條約。這又充分說明，缺乏或斷絕了外交或領事關係，兩國可以締結條約，不會有一般國際法或本公約所設的阻礙。

另一方面，兩國間如果從來沒有外交或領事關係，或者斷絕了這種關係，則縱使現在締結了和這種關係無關的條約，仍然未改變其無這種關係的事實。換句話說，兩國締結的如果不是建立這種關係的協議，彼此間依舊沒有外交或領事關係，或沒有外交和領事關係。兩國間如果有外交和領事關係，其締結的條約如果和這些關係無直接關連，亦不影響這些關係。因而本條第二句說：條約的締結行為和事實，和外交或領事關係方面的情勢沒有任何瓜葛。

第七十五條　侵略國問題

本公約之規定不妨礙因依照聯合國憲章對侵略國之侵略行為所採措施而可能引起之該國任何條約義務。

條約非經甲國同意不對甲國發生拘束力。這已於前文析論條約與第三國的關係時，予以敘明。但這一原則並非毫無例外，侵略國行為所引起的條約義務，便是一個例外，最明顯的例外。

本公約第五十二條已訂明，違反聯合國憲章原則以使用武力或威脅，以強迫簽訂的條約，自始無效。反過來看，依照聯合國憲章的規定，以強迫侵略國簽訂的條約，即令曾經使用了武力或威脅以強迫，仍是有效的，並不違反本公約第五十二條的規定。

　　本條勾畫的，是一個概括式的保留，旨在防止侵略國被摒棄於條約法之外，並且便利侵略國重返國際社會，希望其再和國際社會各成員發生正常關係。

　　本條所稱的措施❷，應包括聯合國憲章第四十一條的「經濟關係、鐵路、海運、航空、郵、電、無線電、及其他交通工具之局部或全部停止，以及外交關係之斷絕」，甚至第四十二條的「空海陸軍示威、封鎖及其他軍事舉動」。此外，還包括強迫侵略國簽訂停戰協定、和平條約等。這些措施既是憲章所准許的，便是本公約所認可的。這些措施所引起的侵略國的條約義務，跟著不受本條的限制。

　　爲了防止條約當事國以某國已在侵略爲藉口，以終止對自己不利的條約，本公約於是規定，禁止使用的，以違反聯合國憲章原則的武力或威脅的使用爲限；不違反憲章原則的和憲章不禁止的使用，不在此限。這意味各當事國雖然得在憲章授權下，強迫侵略國承受條約的拘束，卻不得因某國依法使用武力或威脅，便斷言該國已有侵略行爲，而自行終止其與該國間的現行條約。

　　因此，本條只訂明，依聯合國憲章對侵略國的侵略行爲採取措施後，可能引起該侵略國的某（些）條約義務問題。有關國家遇有這些（類）問題（如強令侵略國簽約承諾於某期限內撤出全部武裝人員），處理時應免受本公約前列的限制。

　　至於侵略行爲的定義，在本公約簽署時（一九六九年）正在

---

❷　第七十五條條文中的「措施」，是英文的 measures，而聯合國
　　憲章第四十一條和第四十二條的 measures，中文譯本則譯爲「辦
　　法」。譯爲「措施」或「辦法」，都可達意，亦無錯誤，應順此指出。

討論中，還沒有決定，所以本條不載明何爲侵略國或略侵行爲。
一九七四年，聯合國大會通過第三三一四（貳捌）號決議案，爲
侵略下了定義❸。這定義儘管不是本書討論的主題，卻可增加對
侵略行爲的了解，讀者仍請注意詳閱。

❸ 一九七四年十二月十四日，聯合國大會通過決議案，爲「侵略」一詞
所下的定義如下：

第一條　侵略是指一個國家使用武力侵犯另一個國家的主權領土完整或政治
　　　　獨立，或以本「定義」所宣示的與聯合國憲章不符的任何其他方式
　　　　使用武力。
　　　　解釋性說明：本「定義」中「國家」一詞：
　　　　(a) 其使用不影響承認問題或一個國家是否爲聯合國會員國的問
　　　　　　題；
　　　　(b) 適當時包括「國家集團」的概念在內。
第二條　一個國家違反憲章的規定而首先使用武力，就構成侵略行爲的顯見
　　　　證據，但安全理事會得按照憲章的規定下論斷：根據其他有關情
　　　　況，包括有關行爲或其後果不甚嚴重的事實在內，沒有理由可以確
　　　　定已經發生了侵略行爲。
第三條　在遵守並按照第二條規定的情況下，任何下列情形，不論是否經過
　　　　宣戰，都構成侵略行爲：
　　　　(a) 一個國家的武裝部隊侵入或攻擊另一個國家的領土；或因此種
　　　　　　侵入或攻擊而造成的任何軍事佔領，不論時間如何短暫；或使
　　　　　　用武力吞併另一個國家的領土或其一部分；
　　　　(b) 一個國家的武裝部隊轟炸另一國家的領土；或一個國家對另一
　　　　　　國家的領土使用任何武器；
　　　　(c) 一個國家的武裝部隊封鎖另一國家的港口或海岸；
　　　　(d) 一個國家的武裝部隊攻擊另一國家的陸、海、空軍或商船或民
　　　　　　航機〔隊〕；
　　　　(e) 一個國家違反其與另一國家訂立的協定所規定的條件使用其根
　　　　　　據協定在接受國領土內駐紮的武裝部隊，或在協定終止後，延
　　　　　　長該項武裝部隊在該國領土內的駐紮期間；
　　　　(f) 一個國家以其領土供另一國家使用讓該國來對第三國進行侵略
　　　　　　行爲；
　　　　(g) 一個國家以其名義派遣武裝小隊、武裝團體非正規軍或僱用
　　　　　　兵，對另一國家進行武力行爲，其嚴重性相當於上述所列各項
　　　　　　行爲；或該國實際捲入了這些行爲。
第四條　以上列舉的行爲並非詳盡無遺；安全理事會得斷定其他行爲亦構成
　　　　憲章規定下的侵略行爲。（以上譯文係聯大中文紀錄稿。本決議案
　　　　第五至第八條不介紹侵略，這裏從略。）

第七編　保管機關、通知、更正及登記

第七十六條　條約之保管機關

一、條約之保管機關得由談判國在條約中或以其他方式指定之。保管機關得爲一個以上國家或一國際組織或此種組織之行政首長。

二、條約保管機關之職務係國際性質，保管機關有秉公執行其職務之義務。條約尚未在若干當事國間生效或一國與保管機關間對該機關職務之行使發生爭議之事實，尤不應影響該項義務。

　　雙邊條約經兩造批准並且互換批准書後，兩造各執條約原本一份，自行保管，沒有條約保管問題，無需指定保管機關，可以不提及保管機關，所以本條所定的保管機關，顯然只適用於多邊條約，純以多邊條約爲考慮對象。

　　條約保管機關，在多邊條約的順利運作方面，扮演程序上的重要角色。這一角色通常由國家或國際組織擔任，不交付任何人擔任。在甲國境內談判簽署的條約，如果沒有特殊情形，必指定甲國爲保管機關，例如在美國舊金山簽訂的聯合國憲章，於第一百十一條訂明：「本憲章應留存美利堅合衆國政府之檔案。」這是籠統的指定。較精確的指定，則是指定某國外交部。在國際組織內或在國際組織主持下簽訂的條約，通常指定組織內的適當機

關爲保管機關。一九六一年的外交關係公約，規定在聯合國秘書
處存放，一九六六年的消除一切形式種族歧視國際公約，也訂明
應交存聯合國檔庫，便是一些實例。但這只是一般性的說明，不
一定完全符合事實，無論依法或依理，都可以由另一個國家或另
一個國際組織負責保管。

由國家保管也好，由國際組織保管也好，只要談判國協議，
就可以決定了，所以本條第一項規定，談判國得在條約內或以其
他方式，指定保管機關。

這裏應請注意，保管機關依本條規定以保管的，是條約正
本（Original copy, 又稱爲原本），不是條約副本（Certified
copy）。當然，爲了便利達成保管者的職務起見，依照正本以
製作並且保管正式副本，也確是經常辦理的事情。

本條第二項表示，條約保管者的職務，是國際性質，不是國
內事項，更不是私人職務、責任、權利或權力。保管機關必須公
正的執行職務，不得有所偏袒。公正不偏的執行職務，是保管機
關的義務，如果不執行或執行不公正，就是違反條約所定的法律
義務。縱使當事國間發生了爭執，條約已否對那些國家生效、保
管機關應否受責備等爭執，都不應影響這義務。

一九四八年十二月九日，聯合國大會通第二六〇（叁）號決議
案，批准「殘害人羣罪防止及懲治公約」。公約規定，聯合國各
會員國都可以成爲當事國，其他國家經邀請簽署批准公約後成爲
當事國，或經由加入程序而成爲當事國，於第二十份批准書（連
同加入書計算）送達聯合國秘書長後第九十日起，公約開始生
效。一九五〇年十月十四日，秘書長收到第二十份批准書，公約

因而可於一九五一年一月十二日生效，但是因爲其中一些批准書和加入書附有對公約規定的保留，公約又未訂明關於保留的效力，而且一些國家表示反對已提出的保留，於是公約可否於上述日期生效的問題，便告發生了。秘書長把事實和問題報告大會，一九五〇年十一月十六日，大會決議送請國際法院就公約保留案發表諮詢意見，一九五一年五月二十八日，法院發表意見，意見後經大會決議接受，才消除了秘書長的疑惑。

　　這一實例，雖然和本條第二項沒有顯著的直接關係，對於本公約草擬者的思考難說有所影響，但是本項列入「條約尚未在若干當事國間生效或一國與保管機關間對該機關職務之行使發生爭議之事實，尤不應影響該項義務」後，再遇有類似殘害人羣罪公約的留保，或當事國間發生爭議時，秘書長便可依例照常秉公執行條約保管的職務，毋需猶豫了，持異議的當事國，由於本條第二項的規定是這麼樣的明確，也許不會再有爭議的藉口了。至於怎樣才算公正的問題，本條未加訂明，必需按個案的實情才可以斷定並且解答。

第七十七條　保管機關之職務

一、除條約內另有規定或締約國另有協議外，保管機關之職務主要爲：

　　(甲)保管條約約文之正本及任何送交保管機關之全權證書；

　　(乙)備就約文正本之正式副本及條約所規定之條約其他語文本，並將其分送當事國及有權成爲條約當事之國家；

　　(丙)接收條約之簽署及接收並保管有關條約之文書、通知及公文；

（丁）審查條約之簽署及有關條約之任何文書、通知或公文是否妥
　　善，如有必要並將此事提請關係國家注意；

（戊）將有關條約之行為、通知及公文轉告條約當事國及有權成為
　　條約當事國之國家；

（己）於條約生效所需數目之簽署或批准書、接受書、贊同書或加
　　入書已收到或交存時，轉告有權成為條約當事國之國家；

（庚）向聯合國秘書處登記條約；

（辛）擔任本公約其他規定所訂明之職務。

二、倘一國與保管機關間對該機關職務之執行發生爭議時，保管機關
　　應將此問題提請簽署國及締約國注意，或於適當情形下提請關係
　　國際組織之主管機關注意。

　　本條把保管機關的主要職務作綜合的規定，雖然沒有詳細盡
列，卻已列載了一般多邊條約的保管機關應該做的事情。

　　第一項說，保管機關的職務，由締約國在條約內規定，或以
協議決定，如果沒有規定，又沒有協議，則依照以下規定。

　　（甲）保管條約約文的正本和送交保管機關的全權證書。原來
有些條約約文的正本，由條約簽署地國永久保管（例如聯合國憲
章），有些在國際組織主持下簽訂的條約約文的正本，由該組織
擔任保管機關。至於條約有關的全權證書，只要一經送達，保管
機關就應該收受並且保管，自不在話下。所以（甲）款是針對事的
規定。

　　（乙）款訂明：備妥約文正本的正式副本後，分送給已經批
准、接受、贊同或加入條約的各當事國，也分送給有權成為當事
國的國家。如果條約規定其他語文約本（就是條約所用文字以外

的文字本），也須備妥其副本，作同樣的分送，因爲某（些）國際組織往往規定其正式語文有一種以上，所以條約保管機關備妥其他文字本的副本，常常是必要的工作。

(丙)款訂明：條約保管機關負責收受簽署書、負責收受並且保管有關條約的文書、通知和公文(Instruments、notifications and communications)。其中通知，無疑是包括同意承受條約拘束的確定、對條約的保留、反對保留、退出條約、終止條約等等。

(丁)款要求保管機關負責審查條約的簽署是否妥善，還要求其審查有關條約的文書、通知和公文是否妥善，又要求其檢查這些書件是否符合條約或本公約的規定，於其認爲必要時，應把事實提請關係國注意，但其權責以此爲限，書件和保留是否有效的問題，不屬於其權責範圍。於提請關係國後，如果其認爲仍未妥善，最後只可以把欠妥的事實通知其他國家。

(戊)款要求保管機關把有關條約的文書等轉告各當事國和有權成爲當事國的國家。但是本款並不要求趕快轉告。這是否表示保管機關可以延遲轉告？不，依照本公約第七十六條第二項的規定，保管機關應秉公行使職務。所以保管機關必須盡速轉告，不得拖延辦理。

(己)款訂明：保管機關收到條約生效所需數目的簽署或批准書時，應通知有權成爲條約當事國的國家。簽署或批准書已否達到條約生效所需的數目？往往是不易確定的問題。保管機關遭遇這問題時，雖然可以作初步審查，卻無權斷定條約已生效並且開始拘束有關國家，縱使其判斷獲得某（些）國接受，其他國家仍

可以拒絕接受，保管機關於是應該依照本條第二項的規定，與所有其他關係國會商，以求得問題的解決。

（庚）款因襲國際聯合會盟約第十八條所創立的先例，仿照聯合國憲章第一百零二條第一項的規定。該項規定是：「本憲章發生效力後，聯合國任何會員國所締結之一切條約及國際協定應盡速在秘書處登記，並由秘書處公佈之」。所以條約保管機關向聯合國秘書處登記條約的職務，不是在本公約生效後才由本公約授予，而是在聯合國憲章生效時已經確定，因為憲章已規定，只要是聯合國會員國締結的條約，就必須登記，而登記條約的工作又是條約保管機關應盡的義務。現在非聯合國會員國間的條約，確是鳳毛麟角了。國際組織間的條約，則為數不少，雖然不必向聯合國秘書處登記，但在事實上都於締結後依上述規定登記了。可見本款的規定，毫無新義。

（辛）款說，保管機關應擔任本公約其他條款所定的職務。這是在列舉式規定後的概括式規定，以防遺漏，並避免本條施行時遭遇意外困難。究竟本公約還有涉及條約保管機關職務的其他什麼規定？顯然的，第六十五條關於條約失效、終止、退出、暫停施行等問題的答詢，第七十九條關於條約約文或正式副本的錯誤更正，第八十一條關於條約簽署場所的提供，都很可能需要保管機關辦理。本款有了概括性規定，便無需重提這些以及其他有關的規定。

本條第二項的要義，已於說明（己）款時提及，無需贅及了。

第七十八條　通知及公文

除條約或本公約另有規定外，任何國家依本公約所提送之通知或
公文，應：

(甲)如無保管機關，直接送至該件所欲知照之國家，或如有保管機關
　　則送至該機關；

(乙)僅於受文國家收到時，或如有保管機關，經該機關收到時，方視
　　爲業經發文國家提送；

(丙)倘係送至保管機關，僅於其所欲知照之國家經保管機關依照第七
　　十七條第一項(戊)款轉告後，方視爲業經該國收到。

當條約列有保管機關必須發出通知或公文的規定時，當然應
依規定辦理。如果條約或本公約都沒有相關的規定，則任何國
家依照本公約而發出的通知或公文，在沒有條約保管機關的情形
下，就應該直接送到要被知照的國家，於有保管機關時，則送到
保管機關。這是本條(甲)款的明確意旨。

通知或公文，何時才算是依法發出或收到了？這問題可能常
常發生，所涉的法律後果也可能很嚴重，所以本條(乙)款和(丙)
款解答這問題。

依照這兩款的規定，非至文件經被知照的國家收到了，不能
視爲提送文件的國家已經完成提送手續，又非至收到的時刻，不
能視爲那被知照的國家已經完成收件手續。

通知或公文，先送給保管機關，然後由保管機關轉送給被知
照的國家，就會有時差（溝）問題，因爲提送國把文件送達保管
機關，需要一段時日，保管機關內部處理那文件，難免要耗費時
光，處理妥善後把文件轉送到被知照的國家，又一定躭擱日子，
這樣一來，文件提送的日期和被知照國收到文件的日期，便有一

段距離了。因此，也許有人會問：可不可以視保管機關爲被知照
國的當然代理者，於其收到時，便算是被知照國已經收到了？答
案應該是「不可以」。旣然不可以，則保管機關可能因疏忽而拖
延了轉送，以致被知照國不能及時採取必要的行動，例如因不及
時知情，而未於限期內對某國的保留表示反對，或於通知已送給
保管機關後，被知照國從事侵犯通知提送國的權利。這固然在理
論上是可能發生的情事，就是在實際情況下也並非不可能發生。
果有這種情事時，該怎樣救濟？本公約對於這種情事未作規定，
所以遇有這種情事時，唯有視個別細節，依善意原則處理。

依照（乙）款的規定，反對保留和終止條約的通知，通知時間
的起算日，是受件國的收件日，通知內所定的期限，應從收件日
起算。這和國家同意承受條約拘束的表示不同，也和國家依國際
法院規約任選條款所作聲明的存放行爲有別，因爲這兩種行爲，
當表示意思的文件交存保管機關時便告完成，並且在其後某一固
定日發生效力，而拘束意思表示國和各關係國，例如外交關係公
約第五十一條訂明：「一「本公約應於第二十二件批准或加入文
件送交聯合國秘書長存放之日後第三十日發生效力。二、對於在
二十二件批准或加入文件存放後批准或加入本公約之國家，本公
約應於各該國存放批准或加入文件後第三十日起發生效力」。領
事關係公約第七十七條也有相同的規定。這兩份公約的規定，
都使意思表示的生效時日確定，就是某情況出現後第三十日起生
效，而依本條（丙）款所存放的文件，其生效日期則不確定，無法
預料。所以本條只規範通知和公文有關事項，不涉及批准、接
受、贊同或加入條約的文件。

第七十九條　條約約文或正式副本錯誤之更正

一、條約約文經認證後，倘簽署國及締約國僉認約文有錯誤時，除各
　　該國決定其他更正方法外，此項錯誤應依下列方式更正之：

　　(甲)在約文上作適當之更正，並由正式授權代表在更正處草簽；

　　(乙)製成或互換一項或數項文書，載明應作之更正；或

　　(丙)按照原有約文所經之同樣程序，製成條約全文之更正本。

二、條約如設有保管機關，該機關應將此項錯誤及更正此項錯誤之提
　　議通知各簽署國及締約國，並應訂明得對提議之更正提出反對之
　　適當期限。如在期限屆滿時：

　　(甲)倘無反對提出，則保管機關應卽在約文上作此更正加以草
　　　　簽，並製成關於訂正約文之紀事錄，將紀事錄一份遞送各當
　　　　事國及有權成爲當事國之國家；

　　(乙)已有反對提出，則保管機關應將此項反對遞送各簽署國及締
　　　　約國；

三、遇認證約文有兩種以上之語文，而其中有不一致之處，經簽署國
　　及締約國協議應予更正時，第一項及第二項之規則亦適用之。

四、除簽署國及締約國另有決定外，更正約文應自始替代有誤約文。

五、已登記條約約文之更正應通知聯合國秘書處。

六、遇約文之正式副本上發現錯誤時，保管機關應製成一項紀事錄載
　　明所作之訂正，並將該紀事錄一份遞送各簽署國及締約國。

　　在條約約文中，有時候或有錯誤，或在同一條約的相同條文
上各種文字本的意義不同。這種錯誤和意義岐異，無疑的，應該
完全消除。所以爲了更正錯誤，又爲了使條約各種文字本的意義
一致，本條確有其必要性和重要性。

　　約文的錯誤，不同文字本的同一條文的意差，可能是由於書寫者、抄錄者、打字者或排字者的疏忽，或是因為誤述或誤解的結果。無論是出於什麼原因，卽令只是標點的漏誤，亦可能影響已經認證的約文的實質意義。所以發現錯誤或意差後，應該及時更正。

　　約文究竟有沒有錯誤？不同文字本的相同條文的意義究竟是不是相同？如果對於這些問題有意見上的紛岐，便不是單純的更正問題，而是一項爭端，會變成本公約第四十八條所規定的錯誤，應該依照該條的規則處理，因為本條只規範沒有爭執的更正，不重複該條規範的事項。

　　本條第一項訂明，條約約文經認證後，簽署國和締約國都認為有錯誤時，除決定採用其他更正方法外，應依照本項所列三種方式予以更正，其中第一種和第二種，在普通情形下使用，遇有許多錯誤時，才使用第三種，重新作成條約全文的更正本。顯然的，作成全文的更正本，事較繁，非有絕對必要不應進行。

　　本條第二項的主旨，在規範設有保管機關的多邊條約的更正事宜。取得各關係國的同意，以更正約文，其程序受許多國家影響，更正的方式又隨保管機關而不同。本條為了使程序簡化和方式固定，特規定保管機關必須把錯誤和更正錯誤的提議，通知各簽署國和締約國，並且由保管機關定下反對那提議的表示期限，於期限屆滿時，如果沒有國家提出反對，便在約文上作更正，加上負責人的草簽，然後作成更正約文的紀事錄，分送給當事國和有權成為條約當事國的國家各一份；如果有任何國家提出反對，則應把反對意見分送給簽署國和締約國各一份。這裏應該提及，

依照本項規定，保管機關只須通知簽署國和締約國，無需通知談判國，因為約文文義不一致或錯誤，和簽署國與締約國才有法律意義的關係，和談判國沒有法律的關係，只有國際政治上的關係，談判國於談判結束後，或不願簽署，或未能簽署，或索性置身於條約之外，所以如果通知談判國，就是徒勞無益的作為。

　　本條第三項關涉條約譯文的錯誤。譯文有誤時，各關係國同意只更正譯文本，不更動作準文字本，那麼，只把譯文更正就行了。這時候，可以適用本條第一項和第二項的規則，適用後就可以處理了。

　　本條第四項規定，更正本自作成時起便代替被更正的約文本。這樣才可以避免適用時或解釋時，不知以那一份約文本為基準的問題。當然的，這雖然是顯而易明的道理，又是容易遵循的原則，但各關係國另有決定時，自當別論。

　　本條第五項規定，曾在聯合國秘書處登記的條約，其更正本應送到該處，以便公布周知。這時候應請注意，本項所稱的更正本，是業經登記的條約的更正本，未經登記的條約，縱使已有更正本，也不必送到該處，因為還沒有登記的條約，如果要登記之前已經更正了，則登記時只登記條約就可以了，用不著登記更正本。

　　各關係國所持有的多邊條約，是條約的正式副本，正式副本在多邊條約的處理程序上很重要。但是因為正式副本是按照經認證的約文本作成，所以更正約文副本時，只製成和經更正的約文本相符的正式副本就行了。可是本條第六項並不要求製作更正後的約文副本，僅要求保管機關作成一項紀事錄（Procés-verbal），

在紀事錄上載明已作成的更正，然後把紀事錄分送給簽署國和締約國各一份。這樣就算是更正了正式副本，無需經過本條第二項所定的冗長程序。

第八十條　條約之登記及公佈

一、條約應於生效後送請聯合國秘書處登記或存案及紀錄，並公佈之。

二、保管機關之指定，即為授權該機關實施前項所稱之行為。

本條分列兩項，第一項要求聯合國會員國締結條約後，於條約生效時送聯合國秘書處登記。這一要求，顯然是為了執行並且貫徹憲章第一百零二條的規定。本條雖然不用「儘速」送的字樣，憲章第一百零二條卻用了，所以聯合國會員國締結條約後，只要條約生效了，就必須趕快辦理登記手續，以克盡其在憲章下的義務。至於非聯合國會員國，如果不是本公約當事國，則於簽訂條約後，沒有登記條約的法定義務。但在事實上，自有了憲章以來，無論是或不是聯合國會員國，都在其所締結的條約生效後，向聯合國秘書處登記。

憲章和本公約要求登記的條約，是已開始發生效力的，不是僅正式簽署在等待批准的。其中道理，很易明白。條約經簽署後，累月積年不能生效的，比比皆是，永不生效的也為數可觀。未生效的條約，其命運如何，無法預卜，如果送到聯合國秘書處登記，雖然也許有供研究者參考的價值，卻無供任何人援引的功用，所以應暫緩登記，等到它生效後才登記較佳。

一九四六年十二月十四日，聯合國大會通過「條約與國際協定登記及出版規程」（The Regulations concerning the Registration and Publication of Treaties aud International Agreements），訂明條約登記手續，並准許非聯合國會員國和聯合國專門機關登記其條約。規程第十條使用「存案及紀錄）（Filing and recording）等字，以表示非聯合國會員國登記條約，是存案及紀錄，實則這只是自願的登記，與有義務的登記意義相同，法律效果也大致相若，因而本條第一項把登記（Registering）、存案及紀錄兩詞並列，以便聯合國會員國、非聯合國會員國、國際組織等所締結的條約，一律於生效後送請聯合國秘書長登錄。

秘書長登錄條約後，予以公佈。所謂公佈，從英文字 Publication 可知，是印行的意思，不是指張貼以便周知。

秘書處怎樣登錄和印行條約呢？這是屬於該處內部作業的問題，本條不作規定。該處所定細則，各條約當事國應該遵守，自不在話下。

本條第二項，由於各條約當事國須遵守細則而顯得重要，又由於條約越來越多而變得十分需要，所以特別標示：條約指定保管機關，就是授權給該機關，使其有權從事本條第一項所定的行為──把條約送請聯合國秘書長登記。誠然，保管機關如果是聯合國秘書處，則秘書長應主動自行登記。

第八編　最後規定

第八十一條　簽　署

本公約應聽由聯合國或任何專門機關或國際原子能總署之全體會員國或國際法院規約當事國，及經聯合國大會邀請成為本公約當事國之任何其他國家簽署，其辦法如下：至一九六九年十一月三十日止，在奧地利共和國聯邦外交部簽署，其後至一九七○年四月三十日止，在紐約聯合國會所簽署。

　　本條規定以下三項。第一項是可以簽署的國家，第二項是簽署的地方，第三項是簽署的期間。

　　可以簽署的國家，包括聯合國的、專門機關的和原子能總署的全體會員國，國際法院規約的各當事國以及被邀請的任何國家。到一九九一年底止，聯合國會員國共一六六個，幾乎容納了全球的所有國家。大韓民國（南韓）和朝鮮民主主義人民共和國（北韓）(The Republic of Korea and The Democratic People's Republic of Korea)、愛沙尼亞、拉脫維亞、立陶宛、密克羅尼西亞和馬紹爾羣島 (Estonia、Latvia、Lithuania、Micronesia and the Marshall Islands) 等七國，已於一九九一年九月十七日，經聯合國安全理事會推薦及大會批准，分別加入了，使會員國總數變為一六六個。專門機關和原子能總

署的全體會員國都是聯合國會員國。因為加入聯合國為會員的國家，必須於申請加入前批准憲章，而批准憲章又非同時批准國際法院規約不可，所以現在的規約當事國中，除瑞士、利克添士坦和聖馬利諾 (Leichtenstein and San Marino) 外，全是聯合國會員國。一九九一年，把最小的獨立國合計，全球有一七八國，所以聯合國大會縱使有意邀請，可被邀請簽署本公約的國家，為數已很少了。

這裏應該注意，本條簽署本公約者，以國家為限，不包含國際組織，雖然提及專門機關和國際原子能總署等國際組織，但是國際組織本身不得簽署，得簽署者是其會員國。只要是其會員國，就符合本條的規定。

簽署本公約的地方有兩處，也只有兩處，就是維也納的奧國外交部和紐約的聯合國會所。

簽署本公約的期間頗長，自一九六九年五月二十三日本公約由會議通過時起，到一九七〇年四月三十日止，共三百四十二天，除星期日和其他休息日假日外，天天都可由各國代表簽署。

既然定了簽署的地方，便不可以在其他地方簽署，簽署代表非親到上述兩處的一處就不能簽妥。既然定了簽署期限，便不可以在期限後簽署，要簽署的國家就必須令其代表在期限內簽妥。不於期限內完成簽署的國家，如果有意變成本公約當事國，仍然可以採用批准的程序，以達到其意願。

第八十二條　批　准

本公約須經批准。批准書應送請聯合國秘書長存放。

「本公約須經批准」的意思是：承受本公約拘束的同意，不能以簽署、接受、贊同、交換構成條約的文書或任何其他方式表示，非以批准的方式表示不可。依第八十三條的規定，以加入表示同意承受本公約的拘束，也須先行批准。批准是國內程序，各國可依其憲法規定或習慣，並且參酌各種因素，以進行批准事宜。

本條不提及批准本公約時可否附上保留，因而閱讀本條者，難免心存疑問。不過如果細察本公約的精神、宗旨和目標，顧及全約的整體內容，參酌本公約第二節各條款關於保留的規定，便可體會本公約容許符合其宗旨和目標的保留。至於怎麼樣的保留符合這要求，則須依具體的保留個案來判斷。現在只可以說，各國批准本公約時，可以提出保留。

任何國家批准本公約後，應備妥批准書。批准書沒有固定的形式和內容，只要正確的充分表示同意承受本公約的拘束就行了。因為聯合國秘書處是本公約唯一的保管機關，批准書就必須由批准國直接送該處存放。存放和登記不同，存放的是批准書而已，置於秘書處就行了，用不着公佈，而登記的是條約，登記後還要印行，才符合規定。

第八十三條　加　入

本公約應聽由屬於第八十一條所稱各類之一之國家加入。加入書應送請聯合國秘書處存放。

本公約第八十一條所稱的各類國家，已於紋析該條時說明

了，用不着再說。

任何國家準備加入本公約時，是不是必須經過其國內憲法的或習慣的程序？這是國內事項，一般國際法不加以規範，本公約亦不過問。按上文敍析批准事項所陳明的作類推，則加入國也可以提出保留，只要保留符合本公約的宗旨和目標，就不應遭受反對；加入國也要備妥加入書，把加入書送請聯合國秘書處存放。

第八十四條　發生效力

一、本公約應於第三十五件批准書或加入書存放之日後第三十日起發生效力。

二、對於第三十五件批准書或加入書存放後批准或加入本公約之國家，本公約應於各該國存放批准書或加入書後第三十日起發生效力。

依照本條第一項的規定，向聯合國秘書處交存的三十五件，無論全是批准書，或全是加入書，或是批准書連同加入書，都是自第三十五件交存日後第三十日起，本公約開始發生效力。

又依本條第二項的意旨，本公約生效後才批准或加入本公約的國家，須於其批准書或加入書交存日後第三十日起，本公約才對其開始發生效力。

原來條約開始生效的理論不一，實例各殊。就理論說，條約可於各締約國協議的任何時間和情況下開始生效。在實例上，有於各締約國簽署時，有於正式換文時，有於某種情況出現時，有於若干數目的國家批准或加入時開始生效的。國際法從不設定條約生效的條件或期限，完全留給各談判國設定，所以談判國的決

定具最後的權威性，無需他人或其他機關再加斟酌，他人和其他機關也絕對無權改變。

聯合國憲章第一百一十條第三項規定：「一俟美利堅合眾國政府通知已有中華民國、法蘭西、蘇維埃社會主義共和國聯邦、大不列顛及北愛爾蘭聯合王國、與美利堅合眾國、以及其他簽字國之過半數將批准書交存時，本憲章卽發生效力。」同條第四項又規定：「本憲章簽字國於憲章發生效力後批准者，應自其各將批准書交存之日起為聯合國之創始會員國。」

一九五八年的四份海洋法公約都分別訂明：「一、本公約應於第二十二件批准或加入文件送交聯合國秘書長存放之日後第三十日起發生效力。」

一九八二年的聯合國海洋法公約第三〇八條則定下下列不同的規則：「一、本公約應自第六十份批准書或加入書存放之日後十二個月生效。二、對於在第六十份批准書或加入書交存以後批准或加入本公約的每一國家，在第一款〔按這款字應為項字〕限制下，本公約應在該國將批准書或加入書交存後第三十天起生效。」

從上列三例可見，各條約開始發生效力的規則，沒有定型，可由談判國選擇決定，本條所列的發生效力的規則，只適用於本公約而已，甚至沒有供其他條約談判者參考的價值。

第八十五條　作準文本

本公約之原本應送請聯合國秘書長存放，其中文、英文、法文、俄文及西班牙文各本同一作準。

條約的原本 (The original of a treaty)，中文又稱爲正本，就是約文經過認證並且已由各代表簽署的文字本，不同於按正本製成的正式副本 (Certified copy)。依照本條的規定，本公約的原本應送請聯合國秘書長存放。本條只說存放 (Deposit)，不說登記或公佈，所以秘書長只負責保存就行了，無需製成正式副本分送給任何國家或機關，也不必公佈。至於他是否把本公約印行，那就是秘書處內部的事項了，不印行，絕無不可。

條約的作準文字，向無定規或習慣，可由各談判國決定。本公約以中文、英文、法文、俄文、西班牙文作準，或者是因爲聯合國憲章已經以這五種文字作準，或者是因爲聯合國活動時以這五種爲官方語文，無論如何，一定是本公約制訂會議中各國妥協的結果。

本公約既以這五種文字本同一作準，則適用和解釋本公約時，可依據中文本、英文本、法文本、俄文本或西文本，換句話說，可依據其中任何文字本，雖然因爲習慣或偏愛的緣故，也許以英文和法文本爲準的人較多，但是這種事實不能改變任何一種文字本的地位和權威。

最後文字

爲此，下列全權代表各秉本國正式授予簽字之權，謹簽字於本公約，以昭信守。

公曆一千九百六十九年五月二十三日於維也納。

以上文字，全是例行套語，毫無新義，因為老生常談如下：訂約代表簽字後，條約締結的初步程序才能完成，代表簽字時須經其本國政府正式授權，其簽字才有法律效力，才可以希望有關國家信守。

一九六九年五月二十三日，在維也納簽署本公約者，包括下列三十二國的代表：

阿富汗、阿根廷、巴貝多、玻利維亞、巴西、柬埔寨、智利、剛果（布拉薩市）、哥斯達黎加、厄瓜多、芬蘭、迦納、瓜地馬拉、蓋亞納、宏都拉斯、伊朗、牙買加、肯亞、賴比瑞亞、馬達加斯加、墨西哥、摩洛哥、尼泊爾、奈及利亞、秘魯、菲律賓、蘇丹、千里達、烏拉圭、南斯拉夫、尚比亞（中華民國、美國、英國、法國和蘇聯的代表都不簽署。）

第九編　結　　論

　　世界各地的人羣，如果都像桃花源裏的一樣，「鷄犬之聲相聞，老死不相往來」，便不會形成一個社會。大家不相往來，各做各的事，各走各的路，沒有接觸、沒有相互的關係，無需互讓互助，亦無物質的或精神的利益衝突，就不需要交往的行爲規範，不會經由習慣養成彼此遵守的規矩，更不會使用文字來訂明強制性的法則，所以這一個人羣不可能有習慣法，更不可能有制訂法。

　　全球各國，如果都和十九世紀以前的中國，閉關自守，故步自封，夜郎自大，排斥外邦，就不會有國際的商品交易，不會有人民互訪或文敎交流，以致沒有貿易競爭、聲譽比較、地位角逐、力量競賽或領土搶奪，因而用不着國家行爲規範，無需共守的準則，也就不會經由習慣以養成法則，更不會經由立法以制定國際法則。

　　可是人類畢竟是羣居的動物，做不到「鷄犬之聲相聞，老死不相往來」的境界。由人羣構成的國家，也做不到永遠閉關自守，永久排斥外邦，尤其自從交通工具發達以來，訊息傳遞迅速以後，國家和國家交往的方式五花八門，接觸的頻率日萬夜千，已出人意料之外，沒有任何方法可以阻擋，縱使若干人有意暫停交往，也必徒費心機，何況絕大多數生靈仍繼續渴望進步，增加

交往，力求發展。

凡是人，必有與生俱來的兩個基本慾望，一是求生存，二是求發展。凡是人，也都有一種潛在的本性，那就是自私心。大人物的自私行為，受潛在的天良抑制，可能是利己同時利衆，小人物的自私活動，往往是利己害人，或只利己而不害人。人羣的本性，和個人的本性並無差別。由人羣構成的國家，自然的，既要求生存，也要求發展，爭取未得的利益，固守既得的利益，減少利益的損失，並且增加利益的累積。這是天經地義，古今中外各國一樣，絕無例外。

人類的慾望無窮，國家的慾海無涯，宇宙間可得的東西卻有限，以有限的東西，滿足無窮無涯的慾望，於是有粥少僧多的情形，常常發生供應不足的事實。假如世上有一個權威性的機關或組織，把地球上的東西，作妥善的分配，分配給所有國家，就不會有強國多佔弱國被毀的惡劣情勢。很可惜，也甚令人失望，現在還沒有這種機關或組織。各國為了取得其所希望的東西，便發生利益衝突，晝夜明爭暗鬥，事事爾虞我詐，個個渾身解數，樣樣務求必得。這樣一來，世界便沒有安寧的日子了。

好在國家和個人一樣，除了從事上述的奪取行為以外，也有互助的互利的禮讓的睦誼的行為。採取相同的行為，日子久了，次數多了，國家也多了，便養成這相同行為的習慣性法則。洞燭機先的善心人士，欲利天下後世，乃鼓吹倡導，發起邀集，聚會各國代表於一堂，制定一些禁止或限制國家的某類行為的規則，並且要求大家遵守，藉以減少損害，增加福祉，等到有關國家相信遵守有益違反有害的時候，又願意遵守的時候，制定的國際法

便告產生了。

　　如上所說，國際法規則無論是一般（普通）的或特別的，都可以經由習慣和立法程序而確立，戰時不得殺害或扣留投降的敵國使臣；戰時豎白旗者，是表示投降，他方應卽停火，不得繼續射殺。這兩者都是由習慣養成的一般規則。不得販賣奴隸婦幼，不得販賣毒品淫刊，不得從事海盜行為，不得在空中刦持航空器，都是經由立法程序而確立的一般性規則。甲乙兩國簽訂條約，以畫定國界、訂明雙方人民入境免辦簽證手續、引渡普通罪犯等事項，則是確立兩國共同遵守的規則，也就是國際法院規約第三十八條所指的「特別國際協約」(Particular conventions)，通稱為國際法的特別規則。

　　無論是一般國際法規則或特別國際法規則，只要有關國家承認為法律，又願意遵守，便不問其起源為何，可以發生法律的效力，源自習慣的法律，和源自立法程序的法律，其效力並無差別。

　　在世界朝夕萬變一躍千里的今天，在國家交往極端頻繁的時代，習慣性的國際法則，固然仍然有用，而且不可少，卻已不足以供應新情勢的需要，如果仍然等待習慣養成新情勢所需的法則，會有遠水救不了近火的缺點，甚至有「急驚風偏遇慢郎中」的弊病。所以當兩個國家認為有緊急需要時，就締結雙邊條約，訂立只適用於彼此間某事項的特別規則；當若干國家認為有必要時，就締結多邊條約，確定各國間某事項的一般規則。確立特別的和一般的規則的條約，自古至今，不可勝數，在國際上解決紛爭、預防衝突、減少摩擦、維持秩序諸方面，確有很大的貢獻。

這貢獻雖然不能以升斗計量，卻是無人可以否認的，而是所有識者都承認的。

然而儘管這是事實，多年以來，各國締結雙邊條約也好，締結萬國公約也好，都沒有成文的法定程序可資遵循，締約各國談判、簽署、批准條約時採用的程序，或是稀有的習慣，或是臨時的協議，或於沒有先例可循時才臨時商定，直到一九六九年，本書析論的公約締結後，才有一套可視爲完備的條約法。

這一套條約法，是空前的一般的程序性的，可以協助國際立法，也有利於各國分別締結條約。修習國際法者，固然非研究不可，從事國際活動者、參與涉外事務者、甚至偶然出國旅遊者，也應該相當注意。

中國早在春秋戰國時代，西洋在紀元以前，都有國家和國家締結條約的事實，十八世紀以後，簽訂條約的行爲，如恒河沙數，因而至今已有經驗的累積，有若干習慣的養成，有一些模式的確定，諸如締約代表必須有充分的權力才能爲其本國表示意思；代表被詐欺而作的意思表示，無效；條約當事國必須信守條約等，都成了習慣的規則。因此，聯合國國際法委員會研究條約法時，曾有委員主張說，這一套法律應以法典 (A code) 的形態作成，認爲法典所載的都是現行法 (Lege lata) 的規則，不是理論法 (Lege ferenda) 的意見，法典一經編纂完成，便可通行全球，普遍適用，各國便應遵守，跟着可以免除批准程序。可是這只是少數委員的主張，未能成爲委員會的決定，因爲多數委員認爲，根據下列考慮，這一套法律不應採用法典的形態：第一、委員會即將擬訂的法律，不僅包含習慣的規則，還要列入新

創的規則；第二、自從第二次世界大戰後，已有許多新興的國家，這些新興國家未曾參與現行國際法的訂立或確定，其中若干國家，甚至懷疑現行國際法則的正當性和可適用性；第三、為求條約法能夠普遍適用起見，應該給予新興國家參與編訂的機會，唯有採用締結條約的方式，才能夠給予這種機會。這些理由比較周延，又是多數委員的共識，所以一九六二年以後，草擬條約法時，放棄了法典形態的念頭，完全以訂立公約為考慮的起點。

　　果然不出多數委員所料，一九六九年簽訂的條約法公約，確是一份預期中的公約，涵蓋舊的和新的法則。公約第六條訂明，「每一國家皆有締結條約之能力」；第七條規定國家元首、政府首長和外交部長由於所任職務，毋需出具全權證書，就可以代表其國家或政府表示意思，其他人員以其國家或政府名義從事國際行為時，必須出具全權證書；第四十九條和第五十條分別規定，使用詐欺或賄賂國家代表所締結的條約，該代表的本國可以撤銷受條約拘束的同意；第五十一條明訂國家代表受強迫簽訂的條約無法律效果；第五十二條說：「以威脅或使用武力對一國施行強迫」所訂立的條約無效；以及第五十三條訂明「與一般國際法強制規律牴觸之條約」自始無效。這些就是舊法則的部分實例。公約第十九條、第二十條、第二十一條、第二十二條和第二十三條，分別詳予訂明條約保留的相關事項；第六十二條以「情況之基本改變」取代「重大情勢變遷原則」；第六十三條正式宣示：「斷絕外交或領事關係」不當然斷絕條約關係；以及第六十四條確切提示，與一般國際法新的強制規律牴觸的條約無效。這些又是新法則的部分實例。這些實例，毫無疑問的，記載了國際法委

員會多數委員的智慧。

公約第七十三條說：「本公約之規定不妨礙國家繼承或國家所負國際責任或國家間發生敵對行為所引起關於條約之任何問題。」這句話包含了三個問題：第一、國家繼承和條約相關的問題，或簡稱為條約繼承問題；第二、由於條約關係而有的國際責任問題，或簡稱為違反條約所引起的國際責任問題；第三、國家間發生敵對行為所引起的關於條約的問題。本條說，「本公約之規定不妨礙」這三個問題，就等於說，有關國家可以按其協議以處理這些問題，可以不受本公約的影響。本條這樣說，是因為這些問題和條約法有不可分的密切關係，本公約應加以規定，但是，其中任何一個，都十分複雜，不能在本公約中作詳盡的規定，必須另訂三份條約，才可以包括深入周延的條款，如果由本公約作掛一漏萬的處理，便可能削減本公約的價值和可適用性，所以本公約對於這些問題，只作籠統的交代，不列具體的法則。這種交代，是一種嘗試，表示公約擬訂者雖有慧眼，仍然不能制訂一份全無缺漏的條約法。

公約第七十五條說：「本公約之規定不妨礙因依聯合國憲章對侵略國之侵略行為所採措施而可能引起之該國任何條約義務」。這一條的用意，和第七十三條的用意一樣，在排除本公約應予規定而不規定的事宜，撇開本公約不能詳細妥善解答的問題，儘管侵略國的條約義務，和本公約所定的一般條約義務有關，本公約仍是不加以規定，而留給聯合國或關係國家處理，處理時不受本公約規定的限制。這也是不得已的廣泛交代，是公約擬訂者苦心孤詣的表現。

　　就本約整體看，關於條約事宜的規定，不但有新的觀念，顧及許多可能發生的情況，列載了防患於未然的條文，而且澄清了存在多年的若干模糊概念，確定了一些可東可西的原則，排除了解釋條約的嚴重障礙。爲本公約的一些平常用語下定義，便是新觀念中的一個。條約失效、條約終止、條約暫停施行、條約因牴觸一般國際法強制規律而無效等等，其後果如何？都在第五編第五節的四個條文中作了詳細的規定。這是顧及了可能發生的幾種情況。第六十六條定下司法解決、公斷及和解條約爭端的程序，則是防患於未然。界定了「談判國」、「締約國」、「當事國」等名詞的涵義，就是澄清了這等名詞的籠統概念。第二十六條說「條約必須遵守」，第二十七條訂明國家不得因國內法阻止而不履行條約，第二十八條稱「條約不溯既往」，都使這類原則更確定了。第三十一條列述解釋條約的通則，第三十二條簡敍在什麼情形下可以使用條約解釋的補充資料，第三十三條闡明「以兩種以上文字認證之條約之解釋」，這樣一來，應可消除了條約解釋的重大障礙了。所以本公約頗具前瞻性和完整性，已有普遍適用的價值和條件。

　　一九五一年以前，關於條約的保留問題，沒有任何權威機關或人員給予解答。這是一個重要的大問題，若不解答，國際法委員會就不能擬妥本公約草案。解答了這問題後，大疑難才算消除了。好在國際法院在殘害人羣罪防止及懲治公約保留案中，消除了大部分的疑難。本公約的草擬者，接納了法院宣告的原則和規則後，加以補充改進，使關於條約保留的法則更周延妥善了。原來法院曾說，在條約不禁止的情形下，不違反條約宗旨和目標

的保留，應予容許，接受保留的當事國得視保留國爲當事國，反對保留的當事國得視保留國不是當事國。本公約則進一步訂明如下：(一)在上述限制下，國家得「於簽署、批准、接受、贊同或加入條約時提具保留」。(二)依條約明示准許而提具的保留，無需其他締約國表示接受；保留只要經另一個締約國接受，保留國就可以成爲條約當事國；條約不因保留遭受反對而不在保留國和反對國間生效，反對國明白表示相反的意思時，自當別論；各當事國都希望條約全部對全體當事國適用時，保留就需經全體當事國接受；對國際組織約章的保留，需經組織的主管機關接受；保留於另一締約國接受後發生效力；保留於提出後十二個月內不表示反對者，視爲接受保留。(三)保留國與接受保留國間的條約關係，縮小了範圍；其他當事國間的關係不變；被保留的規定，不能適用於保留國和反對保留國間的關係上。(四)得隨時撤回保留，得隨時撤回反對，都無需經他國同意；兩種撤回都自被通知的國家收到通知時發生效力。(五)保留、明示接受保留、反對保留，都要用書面作成，並且要致送有關各國；於簽署須經批准、接受或贊同的條約時提出的保留，必須於事後加以確認，才能有效。從上可見，本公約接受了權威機關的意見後，補充了改進了那意見，爲日後處理條約保留者提供了具體的可適用的法則。

回顧全約，確應給予頗高的評價。

然而再三推敲後，認爲本公約還有可以補充改進的地方。下文姑且略提幾點，以就教於高明：

第一、本公約第一條規定：「本公約適用於國家間之條約」。第三條訂明：「本公約不適用於國家與其他國際法主體間所締結

之國際協定、或此種國際法主體間之國際協定或非書面國際協定……。」也就是說，本公約不適用於國家與國際組織（例如聯合國。按國際法院於一九四九年「聯合國服務人員損害賠償案」中，確認聯合國為國際法主體）間、國際組織與國際組織間以及國際組織與其他國際法（卽國家以外的）主體間的條約。可是第五條卻說，本公約適用於為國際組織約章的條約和在國際組織內議定的條約。這是第一條規定的延伸。為什麼說是延伸？因為作為國際組織約章的條約，是國家與國家間的條約，不是相關國際組織與國家間的條約，在國際組織內議定的條約（例如殘害人羣罪防止及懲治公約），也是國家與國家間的條約，不是國際組織締結的本身為當事國的條約，和第一條所稱的國家間的條約並無差別，只是因為第一條所指的條約宗旨，多在規範國家間的事宜，第五條所指的約章條約，則在釐訂國際組織本身的事項，所以第五條的規定，勉強可視為第一條規定的延伸，旣是延伸，則應把第五條全文列為第一條的但書內容，用示本公約的適用，以國家間的條約為主，以國際組織約章和國際組織自行擬定通過的條約為輔。這樣排列條文順序，才更符合一般習慣。

　　本公約第三十四條規定：「**條約非經第三國同意，不為該國創設義務或權利**」。這一規定，只是以法律文句標示早已公認的國際法原則。這原則的例外，也早已發生，那就是聯合國憲章第二條第六款的規定。該款要求非聯合國會員國遵守憲章所列原則，也就是為非聯合國會員國創設了義務（遵守憲章原則的義務），已課予第三國條約（卽憲章）義務，至今未曾採用任何方式徵求第三國同意，該款也沒有等到第三國同意就對所有第三國

生效了。憲章生效在先，本公約締結在後，後法對於在先的位階較高的法律應予回顧，現在卻沒有回顧。其次，本公約於第三十五條訂明，課予第三國義務時，須經該國明示接受；又於第三十六條訂明，賦予第三國權利時，經該國默示接受卽可，都沒有表示在什麼情況下可有例外，以配合憲章的規定。憲章的適用範圍比本公約的廣，憲章的法律位階比本公約的高，現在的公約制訂，顯然的，應該顧及這一事實。

第三、本公約第七十三條說：「本公約之規定不妨礙……所引起關於條約之任何問題」（The provisions of the present Convention shall not prejudge any question that may rise in regard to a treaty from a succession of states or from……。）這條文的 prejudge 一字，如果中譯爲「預判」，是不是比「妨礙」恰當些？如果在本條加一但書，模仿國際法院規約第六十八條說：「倘此等問題之解決須適用本公約之規定時，以經認爲可以適用之範圍爲限。」是不是會使本條規定較有彈性？

第四、筆者析論各條條文時，曾指出若干問題有待解答，認爲公約的規定雖然相當詳細具體，仍遺漏小節細枝，需要補充，例如第八十四條訂明，於第三十五份批准書或加入書交存秘書處後第三十三日，本公約開始生效，卻未訂明：因爲退出條約而使當事國少於三十五國時，本公約是不是適用第五十五條？

以上淺見，略提公約美中不足的小節。現在，縱使發現本公約的重大缺失，也難求得改進了，甚至不可能了。實則就實用觀點看，關於條約事宜，過去曾有的缺點，不在法則的缺乏或模

糊，而在當事國的欠缺誠信。各國依照習慣的規則締結了無數的
條約，從中獲得了極大的利益，今後的問題，也許仍和以前的一
樣，當事國不願承擔違約的國際責任。預防違約、使違約國擔負
應盡的國際責任，才是今後應努力的方向，但這不是公約擬訂者
所能爲力的事情，須由政治家隨時努力以爲。

附錄一

VIENNA CONVENTION ON THE LAW OF TREATIES[1]

*Open for signature at Vienna May 23, 1969, until Nov. 30, 1969;
and at United Nations Headquarters after Nov. 30 1969,
until April 30, 1970*

The States Parties to the present Convention,

Considering the fundamental role of treaties in the history of international relations,

Recognizing the ever-increasing importance of treaties as a source of international law and as a means of developing peaceful co-operation among nations, whatever their constitutional and social systems,

Noting that the principles of free consent and of good faith and the *pacta sunt servanda* rule are universally recognized,

Affirming that disputes concerning treaties, like other international disputes, should be settled by peaceful means and in conformity with the principles of justice and international law,

Recalling the determination of the peoples of the United Nations to establish conditions under which justice and respect for the obligations arising from treaties can be maintained,

Having in mind the principles of international law embodied in the Charter of the United Nations, such as the principles of the equal rights and self-determination of peoples, of the sovereign equality and independence of all states, of non-interference in the domestic affairs of states, of the prohibition of the threat or use of force and of universal respect for, and observance of, human rights and fundamental freedoms for all,

Believing that the codification and progressive development of the law of treaties achieved in the present Convention will promote the purposes of the United Nations set forth in the Charter, namely, the maintenance of international peace and security, the development of friendly relations and the achievement of co-operation among nations,

Affirming that the rules of customary international law will continue to govern questions not regulated by the provisions of the present Convention,

Have agreed as follows:

PART I

INTRODUCTION

ARTICLE 1

Scope of the present Convention

The present Convention applies to treaties between states.

[1] U.N. Doc. A/CONF. 39/27, May 23, 1969.

ARTICLE 2

Use of terms

1. For the purposes of the present Convention :

(a) "treaty" means an international agreement concluded between states in written form and governed by international law, whether embodied in a single instrument or in two or more related instruments and whatever its particular designation ;

(b) "ratification," "acceptance," "approval" and "accession" means in each case the international act so named whereby a state establishes on the international plane its consent to be bound by a treaty ;

(c) "full powers" means a document emanating from the competent authority of a state designating a person or persons to represent the state for negotiating, adopting or authenticating the text of a treaty, for expressing the consent of the state to be bound by a treaty, or for accomplishing any other act with respect to a treaty ;

(d) "reservation" means a unilateral statement, however phrased or named, made by a state, when signing, ratifying, accepting, approving or acceding to a treaty, whereby it purports to exclude or to modify the legal effect of certain provisions of the treaty in their application to that state ;

(e) "negotiating state" means a state which took part in the drawing up and adoption of the text of the treaty ;

(f) "contracting state" means a state which has consented to be bound by the treaty, whether or not the treaty has entered into force ;

(g) "party" means a state which has consented to be bound by the treaty and for which the treaty is in force ;

(h) "third state" means a state not a party to the treaty ;

(i) "international organization" means an intergovernmental organization.

2. The provisions of paragraph 1 regarding the use of terms in the present Convention are without prejudice to the use of those terms or to the meanings which may be given to them in the internal law of any state.

ARTICLE 3

International agreements not within the scope of the present Convention

The fact that the present Convention does not apply to international agreements concluded between states and other subjects of international law or between such other subjects of international law, or to international agreements not in written form, shall not affect:

(a) the legal force of such agreements ;

(b) the application to them of any of the rules set forth in the present

Convention to which they would be subject under international law independently of the Convention;

(c) the application of the Convention to the relations of states as between themselves under international agreements to which other subjects of international law are also parties.

ARTICLE 4

Non-retroactivity of the present Convention

Without prejudice to the application of any rules set forth in the present Convention to which treaties would be subject under international law independently of the Convention, the Convention applies only to treaties which are concluded by states after the entry into force of the present Convention with regard to such states.

ARTICLE 5

Treaties constituting international organizations and treaties adopted within an international organization

The present Convention applies to any treaty which is the constituent instrument of an international organization and to any treaty adopted within an international organization without prejudice to any relevant rules of the organization.

PART II

CONCLUSION AND ENTRY INTO FORCE OF TREATIES

SECTION 1: CONCLUSION OF TREATIES

ARTICLE 6

Capacity of states to conclude treaties

Every state possesses capacity to conclude treaties.

ARTICLE 7

Full powers

1. A person is considered as representing a state for the purpose of adopting or authenticating the text of a treaty or for the purpose of expressing the consent of the state to be bound by a treaty if:

(a) he produces appropriate full powers; or

(b) it appears from the practice of the states concerned or from other circumstances that their intention was to consider that person as representing the state for such purposes and to dispense with full powers.

2. In virtue of their functions and without having to produce full powers, the following are considered as representing their state:

(a) Heads of State, Heads of Government and Ministers for Foreign Affairs, for the purpose of performing all acts relating to the conclusion of a treaty;

(b) heads of diplomatic missions, for the purpose of adopting the text of a treaty between the accrediting state and the state to which they are accredited;

(c) representatives accredited by states to an international conference or to an international organization or one of its organs, for the purpose of adopting the text of a treaty in that conference, organization or organ.

ARTICLE 8

Subsequent confirmation of an act performed without authorization

An act relating to the conclusion of a treaty performed by a person who cannot be considered under Article 7 as authorized to represent a state for that purpose is without legal effect unless afterwards confirmed by that state.

ARTICLE 9

Adoption of the text

1. The adoption of the text of a treaty takes place by the consent of all the states participating in its drawing up except as provided in paragraph 2.

2. The adoption of the text of a treaty at an international conference takes place by the vote of two-thirds of the states present and voting, unless by the same majority they shall decide to apply a different rule.

ARTICLE 10

Authentication of the text

The text of a treaty is established as authentic and definitive:

(a) by such procedure as may be provided for in the text or agreed upon by the states participating in its drawing up; or

(b) failing such procedure, by the signature, signature ad referendum or initialling by the representatives of those states of the text of the treaty or of the Final Act of a conference incorporating the text.

ARTICLE 11

Means of expressing consent to be bound by a treaty

The consent of a state to be bound by a treaty may be expressed by signature, exchange of instruments constituting a treaty, ratification, acceptance, approval or accession, or by any other means if so agreed.

ARTICLE 12

Consent to be bound by a treaty expressed by signature

1. The consent of a state to be bound by a treaty is expressed by the signature of its representative when:
   (a) the treaty provides that signature shall have that effect;
   (b) it is otherwise established that the negotiating states were agreed that signature should have that effect; or
   (c) the intention of the state to give that effect to the signature appears from the full powers of its representative or was expressed during the negotiation.
2. For the purposes of paragraph 1:
   (a) the initialling of a text constitutes a signature of the treaty when it is established that the negotiating states so agreed;
   (b) the signature *ad referendum* of a treaty by a representative, if confirmed by his state, constitutes a full signature of the treaty.

ARTICLE 13

*Consent to be bound by a treaty expressed by an
exchange of instruments constituting a treaty*

The consent of states to be bound by a treaty constituted by instruments exchanged between them is expressed by that exchange when:
   (a) the instruments provide that their exchange shall have that effect; or
   (b) it is otherwise established that those states were agreed that the exchange of instruments should have that effect.

ARTICLE 14

*Consent to be bound by a treaty expressed
by ratification, acceptance or approval*

1. The consent of a state to be bound by a treaty is expressed by ratification when:
   (a) the treaty provides for such consent to be expressed by means of ratification;
   (b) it is otherwise established that the negotiating states were agreed that ratification should be required;
   (c) the representative of the state has signed the treaty subject to ratification; or
   (d) the intention of the state to sign the treaty subject to ratification appears from the full powers of its representative or was expressed during the negotiation.
2. The consent of a state to be bound by a treaty is expressed by acceptance or approval under conditions similar to those which apply to ratification.

ARTICLE 15

Consent to be bound by a treaty expressed by accession

The consent of a state to be bound by a treaty is expressed by accession when:

(a) the treaty provides that such consent may be expressed by that state by means of accession;

(b) it is otherwise established that the negotiating states were agreed that such consent may be expressed by that state by means of accession; or

(c) all the parties have subsequently agreed that such consent may be expressed by that state by means of accession.

ARTICLE 16

Exchange or deposit of instruments of ratification, acceptance, approval or accession

Unless the treaty otherwise provides, instruments of ratification, acceptance, approval or accession establish the consent of a state to be bound by a treaty upon:

(a) their exchange between the contracting states;

(b) their deposit with the depositary; or

(c) their notification to the contracting states or to the depositary, if so agreed.

ARTICLE 17

Consent to be bound by part of a treaty and choice of differing provisions

1. Without prejudice to Articles 19 to 23, the consent of a state to be bound by part of a treaty is effective only if the treaty so permits or the other contracting states so agree.

2. The consent of a state to be bound by a treaty which permits a choice between differing provisions is effective only if it is made clear to which of the provisions the consent relates.

ARTICLE 18

Obligation not to defeat the object and purpose of a treaty prior to its entry into force

A state is obliged to refrain from acts which would defeat the object and purpose of a treaty when:

(a) it has signed the treaty or has exchanged instruments constituting the treaty subject to ratification, acceptance or approval, until it shall have made its intention clear not to become a party to the treaty; or

(b) it has expressed its consent to be bound by the treaty, pending the entry into force of the treaty and provided that such entry into force is not unduly delayed.

ARTICLE 19

Formulation of reservations

A state may, when signing, ratifying, accepting, approving or acceding to a treaty, formulate a reservation unless:
(a) the reservation is prohibited by the treaty;
(b) the treaty provides that only specified reservations, which do not include the reservation in question, may be made; or
(c) in cases not falling under sub-paragraphs (a) and (b), the reservation is incompatible with the object and purpose of the treaty.

ARTICLE 20

Acceptance of and objection to reservations

1. A reservation expressly authorized by a treaty does not require any subsequent acceptance by the other contracting states unless the treaty so provides.

2. When it appears from the limited number of the negotiating states and the object and purpose of a treaty that the application of the treaty in its entirety between all the parties is an essential condition of the consent of each one to be bound by the treaty, a reservation requires acceptance by all the parties.

3. When a treaty is a constituent instrument of an international organization and unless it otherwise provides, a reservation requires the acceptance of the competent organ of that organization.

4. In cases not falling under the preceding paragraphs and unless the treaty otherwise provides:
(a) acceptance by another contracting state of a reservation constitutes the reserving state a party to the treaty in relation to that other state if or when the treaty is in force for those states;
(b) an objection by another contracting state to a reservation does not preclude the entry into force of the treaty as between the objecting and reserving states unless a contrary intention is definitely expressed by the objecting state;
(c) an act expressing a state's consent to be bound by the treaty and containing a reservation is effective as soon as at least one other contracting state has accepted the reservation.

5. For the purposes of paragraphs 2 and 4 and unless the treaty otherwise provides, a reservation is considered to have been accepted by a state if it shall have raised no objection to the reservation by the end of a period of twelve months after it was notified of the reservation or by

the date on which it expressed its consent to be bound by the treaty,
whichever is later.

ARTICLE 21

Legal effects of reservations and of objections to reservations

1. A reservation established with regard to another party in accordance
with Articles 19, 20 and 23:
  (a) modifies for the reserving state in its relations with that other
      party the provisions of the treaty to which the reservation re-
      lates to the extent of the reservation; and
  (b) modifies those provisions to the same extent for that other party
      in its relations with the reserving state.
2. The reservation does not modify the provisions of the treaty for the
other parties to the treaty *inter se*.
3. When a state objecting to a reservation has not opposed the entry
into force of the treaty between itself and the reserving state, the provisions to which the reservation relates do not apply as between the two
states to the extent of the reservation.

ARTICLE 22

Withdrawal of reservations and of objections to reservations

1. Unless the treaty otherwise provides, a reservation may be withdrawn
at any time and the consent of a state which has accepted the reservation is not required for its withdrawal.
2. Unless the treaty otherwise provides, an objection to a reservation
may be withdrawn at any time.
3. Unless the treaty otherwise provides, or it is otherwise agreed:
  (a) the withdrawal of a reservation becomes operative in relation
      to another contracting state only when notice of it has been re-
      ceived by that state;
  (b) the withdrawal of an objection to a reservation becomes opera-
      tive only when notice of it has been received by the state which
      formulated the reservation.

ARTICLE 23

Procedure regarding reservations

1. A reservation, an express acceptance of a reservation and an objection to a reservation must be formulated in writing and communicated to
the contracting states and other states entitled to become parties to the
treaty.
2. If formulated when signing the treaty subject to ratification, acceptance or approval, a reservation must be formally confirmed by the
reserving state when expressing its consent to be bound by the treaty.

In such a case the reservation shall be considered as having been made on the date of its confirmation.

3. An express acceptance of, or an objection to, a reservation made previously to confirmation of the reservation does not itself require confirmation.

4. The withdrawal of a reservation or of an objection to a reservation must be formulated in writing.

SECTION 3: ENTRY INTO FORCE AND PROVISIONAL APPLICATION OF TREATIES

ARTICLE 24

Entry into force

1. A treaty enters into force in such manner and upon such date as it may provide or as the negotiating states may agree.

2. Failing any such provision or agreement, a treaty enters into force as soon as consent to be bound by the treaty has been established for all the negotiating states.

3. When the consent of a state to be bound by a treaty is established on a date after the treaty has come into force, the treaty enters into force for that state on that date, unless the treaty otherwise provides.

4. The provisions of a treaty regulating the authentication of its text, the establishment of the consent of states to be bound by the treaty, the manner or date of its entry into force, reservations, the functions of the depositary and other matters arising necessarily before the entry into force of the treaty apply from the time of the adoption of its text.

ARTICLE 25

Provisional application

1. A treaty or a part of a treaty is applied provisionally pending its entry into force if:

(a) the treaty itself so provides; or

(b) the negotiating states have in some other manner so agreed.

2. Unless the treaty otherwise provides or the negotiating states have otherwise agreed, the provisional application of a treaty or a part of a treaty with respect to a state shall be terminated if that state notifies the other states between which the treaty is being applied provisionally of its intention not to become a party to the treaty.

PART III

OBSERVANCE, APPLICATION AND INTERPRETATION OF TREATIES

SECTION 1: OBSERVANCE OF TREATIES

ARTICLE 26

Pacta sunt servanda

Every treaty in force is binding upon the parties to it and must be performed by them in good faith.

ARTICLE 27

Internal law and observance of treaties

A party may not invoke the provisions of its internal law as justification for its failure to perform a treaty. This rule is without prejudice to Article 46.

SECTION 2: APPLICATION OF TREATIES

ARTICLE 28

Non-retroactivity of treaties

Unless a different intention appears from the treaty or is otherwise established, its provisions do not bind a party in relation to any act or fact which took place or any situation which ceased to exist before the date of the entry into force of the treaty with respect to that party.

ARTICLE 29

Territorial scope of treaties

Unless a different intention appears from the treaty or is otherwise established, a treaty is binding upon each party in respect of its entire territory.

ARTICLE 30

Application of successive treaties relating to the same subject-matter

1. Subject to Article 103 of the Charter of the United Nations, the rights and obligations of states parties to successive treaties relating to the same subject-matter shall be determined in accordance with the following paragraphs.

2. When a treaty specifies that it is subject to, or that it is not to be considered as incompatible with, an earlier or later treaty, the provisions of that other treaty prevail.

3. When all the parties to the earlier treaty are parties also to the later treaty but the earlier treaty is not terminated or suspended in operation under Article 59, the earlier treaty applies only to the extent that its provisions are compatible with those of the later treaty.

4. When the parties to the later treaty do not include all the parties to the earlier one:

(a) as between states parties to both treaties the same rule applies as in paragraph 3;

(b) as between a state party to both treaties and a state party to only one of the treaties, the treaty to which both states are parties governs their mutual rights and obligations.

5. Paragraph 4 is without prejudice to Article 41, or to any question of the termination or suspension of the operation of a treaty under Article 60 or to any question of responsibility which may arise for a state from the conclusion or application of a treaty the provisions of which are incompatible with its obligations towards another state under another treaty.

SECTION 3: INTERPRETATION OF TREATIES

ARTICLE 31

General rule of interpretation

1. A treaty shall be interpreted in good faith in accordance with the ordinary meaning to be given to the terms of the treaty in their context and in the light of its object and purpose.

2. The context for the purpose of the interpretation of a treaty shall comprise, in addition to the text, including its preamble and annexes:

(a) any agreement relating to the treaty which was made between all the parties in connexion with the conclusion of the treaty;

(b) any instrument which was made by one or more parties in connexion with the conclusion of the treaty and accepted by the other parties as an instrument related to the treaty.

3. There shall be taken into account, together with the context:

(a) any subsequent agreement between the parties regarding the interpretation of the treaty or the application of its provisions;

(b) any subsequent practice in the application of the treaty which establishes the agreement of the parties regarding its interpretation;

(c) any relevant rules of international law applicable in the relations between the parties.

4. A special meaning shall be given to a term if it is established that the parties so intended.

ARTICLE 32

Supplementary means of interpretation

Recourse may be had to supplementary means of interpretation, including the preparatory work of the treaty and the circumstances of its conclusion, in order to confirm the meaning resulting from the application of Article 31, or to determine the meaning when the interpretation according to Article 31:

(a) leaves the meaning ambiguous or obscure; or

(b) leads to a result which is manifestly absurd or unreasonable.

ARTICLE 33

Interpretation of treaties authenticated in two or more languages

1. When a treaty has been authenticated in two or more languages, the text is equally authoritative in each language, unless the treaty provides or the parties agree that, in case of divergence, a particular text shall prevail.

2. A version of the treaty in a language other than one of those in which the text was authenticated shall be considered an authentic text only if the treaty so provides or the parties so agree.

3. The terms of the treaty are presumed to have the same meaning in each authentic text.

4. Except where a particular text prevails in accordance with paragraph 1, when a comparison of the authentic texts discloses a difference of meaning which the application of Articles 31 and 32 does not remove, the meaning which best reconciles the texts, having regard to the object and purpose of the treaty, shall be adopted.

SECTION 4: TREATIES AND THIRD STATES

ARTICLE 34

General rule regarding third states

A treaty does not create either obligations or rights for a third state without its consent.

ARTICLE 35

Treaties providing for obligations for third states

An obligation arises for a third state from a provision of a treaty if the parties to the treaty intend the provision to be the means of establishing the obligation and the third state expressly accepts that obligation in writing.

ARTICLE 36

Treaties providing for rights for third states

1. A right arises for a third state from a provision of a treaty if the parties to the treaty intend the provision to accord that right either to the third state, or to a group of states to which it belongs, or to all states, and the third state assents thereto. Its assent shall be presumed so long as the contrary is not indicated, unless the treaty otherwise provides.

2. A state exercising a right in accordance with paragraph 1 shall comply with the conditions for its exercise provided for in the treaty or established in conformity with the treaty.

ARTICLE 37

Revocation or modification of obligations or rights of third states

1. When an obligation has arisen for a third state in conformity with Article 35, the obligation may be revoked or modified only with the consent of the parties to the treaty and of the third state, unless it is established that they had otherwise agreed.

2. When a right has arisen for a third state in conformity with Article 36, the right may not be revoked or modified by the parties if it is established that the right was intended not to be revocable or subject to modification without the consent of the third state.

ARTICLE 38

Rules in a treaty becoming binding on third states
through international custom

Nothing in Articles 34 to 37 precludes a rule set forth in a treaty from becoming binding upon a third state as a customary rule of international law, recognized as such.

PART IV

AMENDMENT AND MODIFICATION OF TREATIES

ARTICLE 39

General rule regarding the amendment of treaties

A treaty may be amended by agreement between the parties. The rules laid down in Part II apply to such an agreement except in so far as the treaty may otherwise provide.

ARTICLE 40

Amendment of multilateral treaties

1. Unless the treaty otherwise provides, the amendment of multilateral treaties shall be governed by the following paragraphs.

2. Any proposal to amend a multilateral treaty as between all the parties must be notified to all the contracting states, each one of which shall have the right to take part in:

    (a) the decision as to the action to be taken in regard to such proposal;

    (b) the negotiation and conclusion of any agreement for the amendment of the treaty.

3. Every state entitled to become a party to the treaty shall also be entitled to become a party to the treaty as amended.

4. The amending agreement does not bind any state already a party to the treaty which does not become a party to the amending agreement; Article 30, paragraph 4(b), applies in relation to such state.

5. Any state which becomes a party to the treaty after the entry into force of the amending agreement shall, failing an expression of a different intention by that state:

(a) be considered as a party to the treaty as amended, and

(b) be considered as a party to the unamended treaty in relation to any party to the treaty not bound by the amending agreement.

ARTICLE 41

Agreements to modify multilateral treaties between certain of the parties only

1. Two or more of the parties to a multilateral treaty may conclude an agreement to modify the treaty as between themselves alone if:

(a) the possibility of such a modification is provided for by the treaty; or

(b) the modification in question is not prohibited by the treaty and:

(i) does not affect the enjoyment by the other parties of their rights under the treaty or the performance of their obligations;

(ii) does not relate to a provision, derogation from which is incompatible with the effective execution of the object and purpose of the treaty as a whole.

2. Unless in a case falling under paragraph 1(a) the treaty otherwise provides, the parties in question shall notify the other parties of their intention to conclude the agreement and of the modification to the treaty for which it provides.

PART V

INVALIDITY, TERMINATION AND SUSPENSION OF THE OPERATION OF TREATIES

SECTION 1: GENERAL PROVISIONS

ARTICLE 42

Validity and continuance in force of treaties

1. The validity of a treaty or of the consent of a state to be bound by a treaty may be impeached only through the application of the present Convention.

2. The termination of a treaty, its denunciation or the withdrawal of a party, may take place only as a result of the application of the provisions of the treaty or of the present Convention. The same rule applies to suspension of the operation of a treaty.

ARTICLE 43

Obligations imposed by international law independently of a treaty

The invalidity, termination or denunciation of a treaty, the withdrawal of a party from it, or the suspension of its operation, as a result of the application of the present Convention or of the provisions of the treaty, shall not in any way impair the duty of any state to fulfil any obligation embodied in the treaty to which it would be subject under international law independently of the treaty.

ARTICLE 44

Separability of treaty provisions

1. A right of a party, provided for in a treaty or arising under Article 56, to denounce, withdraw from or suspend the operation of the treaty may be exercised only with respect to the whole treaty unless the treaty otherwise provides or the parties otherwise agree.

2. A ground for invalidating, terminating, withdrawing from or suspending the operation of a treaty recognized in the present Convention may be invoked only with respect to the whole treaty except as provided in the following paragraphs or in Article 60.

3. If the ground relates solely to particular clauses, it may be invoked only with respect to those clauses where:

   (a) the said clauses are separable from the remainder of the treaty with regard to their application;

   (b) it appears from the treaty or is otherwise established that acceptance of those clauses was not an essential basis of the consent of the other party or parties to be bound by the treaty as a whole; and

   (c) continued performance of the remainder of the treaty would not be unjust.

4. In cases falling under Articles 49 and 50 the state entitled to invoke the fraud or corruption may do so with respect either to the whole treaty or, subject to paragraph 3, to the particular clauses alone.

5. In cases falling under Articles 51, 52 and 53, no separation of the provisions of the treaty is permitted.

ARTICLE 45

Loss of a right to invoke a ground for invalidating, terminating, withdrawing from or suspending the operation of a treaty

A state may no longer invoke a ground for invalidating, terminating, withdrawing from or suspending the operation of a treaty under Articles 46 to 50 or Articles 60 and 62 if, after becoming aware of the facts:

   (a) it shall have expressly agreed that the treaty is valid or remains in force or continues in operation, as the case may be; or

(b) it must by reason of its conduct be considered as having acquiesced in the validity of the treaty or in its maintenance in force or in operation, as the case may be.

ARTICLE 46

Provisions of internal law regarding competence to conclude treaties

1. A state may not invoke the fact that its consent to be bound by a treaty has been expressed in violation of a provision of its internal law regarding competence to conclude treaties as invalidating its consent unless that violation was manifest and concerned a rule of its internal law of fundamental importance.

2. A violation is manifest if it would be objectively evident to any state conducting itself in the matter in accordance with normal practice and in good faith.

ARTICLE 47

Specific restrictions on authority to express the consent of a state

If the authority of a representative to express the consent of a state to be bound by a particular treaty has been made subject to a specific restriction, his omission to observe that restriction may not be invoked as invalidating the consent expressed by him unless the restriction was notified to the other negotiating states prior to his expressing such consent.

ARTICLE 48

Error

1. A state may invoke an error in a treaty as invalidating its consent to be bound by the treaty if the error relates to a fact or situation which was assumed by that state to exist at the time when the treaty was concluded and formed an essential basis of its consent to be bound by the treaty.

2. Paragraph 1 shall not apply if the state in question contributed by its own conduct to the error or if the circumstances were such as to put that state on notice of a possible error.

3. An error relating only to the wording of the text of a treaty does not affect its validity; Article 79 then applies.

ARTICLE 49

Fraud

If a state has been induced to conclude a treaty by the fraudulent conduct of another negotiating state, the state may invoke the fraud as invalidating its consent to be bound by the treaty.

ARTICLE 50

Corruption of a representative of a state

If the expression of a state's consent to be bound by a treaty has been procured through the corruption of its representative directly or indirectly by another negotiating state, the state may invoke such corruption as invalidating its consent to be bound by the treaty.

ARTICLE 51

Coercion of a representative of a state

The expression of a state's consent to be bound by a treaty which has been procured by the coercion of its representative through acts or threats directed against him shall be without any legal effect.

ARTICLE 52

Coercion of a state by the threat or use of force

A treaty is void if its conclusion has been procured by the threat or use of force in violation of the principles of international law embodied in the Charter of the United Nations.

ARTICLE 53

Treaties conflicting with a peremptory norm of general international law (jus cogens)

A treaty is void if, at the time of its conclusion, it conflicts with a peremptory norm of general international law. For the purposes of the present Convention, a peremptory norm of general international law is a norm accepted and recognized by the international community of states as a whole as a norm from which no derogation is permitted and which can be modified only by a subsequent norm of general international law having the same character.

SECTION 3: TERMINATION AND SUSPENSION OF THE
OPERATION OF TREATIES

ARTICLE 54

Termination of or withdrawal from a treaty under its provisions or by consent of the parties

The termination of a treaty or the withdrawal of a party may take place:
  (a) in conformity with the provisions of the treaty; or
  (b) at any time by consent of all the parties after consultation with the other contracting states.

ARTICLE 55

Reduction of the parties to a multilateral treaty below the number necessary for its entry into force

Unless the treaty otherwise provides, a multilateral treaty does not terminate by reason only of the fact that the number of the parties falls below the number necessary for its entry into force.

ARTICLE 56

Denunciation of or withdrawal from a treaty containing no provision regarding termination, denunciation or withdrawal

1. A treaty which contains no provision regarding its termination and which does not provide for denunciation or withdrawal is not subject to denunciation or withdrawal unless:
   - (a) it is established that the parties intended to admit the possibility of denunciation or withdrawal; or
   - (b) a right of denunciation or withdrawal may be implied by the nature of the treaty.

2. A party shall give not less than twelve months' notice of its intention to denounce or withdraw from a treaty under paragraph 1.

ARTICLE 57

Suspension of the operation of a treaty under its provisions or by consent of the parties

The operation of a treaty in regard to all the parties or to a particular party may be suspended:
   - (a) in conformity with the provisions of the treaty; or
   - (b) at any time by consent of all the parties after consultation with the other contracting states.

ARTICLE 58

Suspension of the operation of a multilateral treaty by agreement between certain of the parties only

1. Two or more parties to a multilateral treaty may conclude an agreement to suspend the operation of provisions of the treaty, temporarily and as between themselves alone, if:
   - (a) the possibility of such a suspension is provided for by the treaty; or
   - (b) the suspension in question is not prohibited by the treaty and:
       - (i) does not affect the enjoyment by the other parties of their rights under the treaty or the performance of their obligations;
       - (ii) is not incompatible with the object and purpose of the treaty.

2. Unless in a case falling under paragraph 1(a) the treaty otherwise provides, the parties in question shall notify the other parties of their intention to conclude the agreement and of those provisions of the treaty the operation of which they intend to suspend.

ARTICLE 59

Termination or suspension of the operation of a treaty implied by conclusion of a later treaty

1. A treaty shall be considered as terminated if all the parties to it conclude a later treaty relating to the same subject-matter and:

(a) it appears from the later treaty or is otherwise established that the parties intended that the matter should be governed by that treaty; or

(b) the provisions of the later treaty are so far incompatible with those of the earlier one that the two treaties are not capable of being applied at the same time.

2. The earlier treaty shall be considered as only suspended in operation if it appears from the later treaty or is otherwise established that such was the intention of the parties.

ARTICLE 60

Termination or suspension of the operation of a treaty as a consequence of its breach

1. A material breach of a bilateral treaty by one of the parties entitles the other to invoke the breach as a ground for terminating the treaty or suspending its operation in whole or in part.

2. A material breach of a multilateral treaty by one of the parties entitles:

(a) the other parties by unanimous agreement to suspend the operation of the treaty in whole or in part or to terminate it either:

(i) in the relations between themselves and the defaulting state; or

(ii) as between all the parties;

(b) a party specially affected by the breach to invoke it as a ground for suspending the operation of the treaty in whole or in part in the relations between itself and the defaulting state;

(c) any party other than the defaulting state to invoke the breach as a ground for suspending the operation of the treaty in whole or in part with respect to itself if the treaty is of such a character that a material breach of its provisions by one party radically changes the position of every party with respect to the further performance of its obligations under the treaty.

3. A material breach of a treaty, for the purposes of this article, consists in:

(a) a repudiation of the treaty not sanctioned by the present Convention ; or

(b) the violation of a provision essential to the accomplishment of the object or purpose of the treaty.

4. The foregoing paragraphs are without prejudice to any provision in the treaty applicable in the event of a breach.

5. Paragraphs 1 to 3 do not apply to provisions relating to the protection of the human person contained in treaties of a humanitarian character, in particular to provisions prohibiting any form of reprisals against persons protected by such treaties.

ARTICLE 61

Supervening impossibility of performance

1. A party may invoke the impossibility of performing a treaty as a ground for terminating or withdrawing from it if the impossibility results from the permanent disappearance or destruction of an object indispensable for the execution of the treaty. If the impossibility is temporary, it may be invoked only as a ground for suspending the operation of the treaty.

2. Impossibility of performance may not be invoked by a party as a ground for terminating, withdrawing from or suspending the operation of a treaty if the impossibility is the result of a breach by that party either of an obligation under the treaty or of any other international obligation owed to any other party to the treaty.

ARTICLE 62

Fundamental change of circumstances

1. A fundamental change of circumstances which has occurred with regard to those existing at the time of the conclusion of a treaty, and which was not foreseen by the parties, may not be_invoked as a ground for terminating or withdrawing from the treaty unless :

(a) the existence of those circumstances constituted an essential basis of the consent of the parties to be bound by the treaty; and

(b) the effect of the change is radically to transform the extent of obligations still to be performed under the treaty.

2. A fundamental change of circumstances may not be invoked as a ground for terminating or withdrawing from a treaty :

(a) if the treaty establishes a boundary; or

(b) if the fundamental change is the result of a breach by the party invoking it either of an obligation under the treaty or of any other international obligation owed to any other party to the treaty.

3. If, under the foregoing paragraphs, a party may invoke a fundamental change of circumstances as a ground for terminating or withdraw-

ing from a treaty it may also invoke the change as a ground for suspending the operation of the treaty.

ARTICLE 63

Severance of diplomatic or consular relations

The severance of diplomatic or consular relations between parties to a treaty does not affect the legal relations established between them by the treaty except in so far as the existence of diplomatic or consular relations is indispensable for the application of the treaty.

ARTICLE 64

Emergence of a new peremptory norm of general international law (jus cogens)

If a new peremptory norm of general international law emerges, any existing treaty which is in conflict with that norm becomes void and terminates.

SECTION 4: PROCEDURE

ARTICLE 65

Procedure to be followed with respect to invalidity, termination, withdrawal from or suspension of the operation of a treaty

1. A party which, under the provisions of the present Convention, invokes either a defect in its consent to be bound by a treaty or a ground for impeaching the validity of a treaty, terminating it, withdrawing from it or suspending its operation, must notify the other parties of its claim. The notification shall indicate the measure proposed to be taken with respect to the treaty and the reasons therefor.

2. If, after the expiry of a period which, except in cases of special urgency, shall not be less than three months after the receipt of the notification, no party has raised any objection, the party making the notification may carry out in the manner provided in Article 67 the measure which it has proposed.

3. If, however, objection has been raised by any other party, the parties shall seek a solution through the means indicated in Article 33 of the Charter of the United Nations.

4. Nothing in the foregoing paragraphs shall affect the rights or obligations of the parties under any provisions in force binding the parties with regard to the settlement of disputes.

5. Without prejudice to Article 45, the fact that a state has not previously made the notification prescribed in paragraph 1 shall not prevent it from making such notification in answer to another party claiming performance of the treaty or alleging its violation.

ARTICLE 66

*Procedures for judicial settlement, arbitration
and conciliation*

If, under paragraph 3 of Article 65, no solution has been reached within a period of 12 months following the date on which the objection was raised, the following procedures shall be followed:

(a) any one of the parties to a dispute concerning the application or the interpretation of Article 53 or 64 may, by a written application, submit it to the International Court of Justice for a decision unless the parties by common consent agree to submit the dispute to arbitration;

(b) any one of the parties to a dispute concerning the application or the interpretation of any of the other articles in Part V of the present Convention may set in motion the procedure specified in the Annex to the Convention by submitting a request to that effect to the Secretary-General of the United Nations.

ARTICLE 67

*Instruments for declaring invalid, terminating, withdrawing
from or suspending the operation of a treaty*

1. The notification provided for under Article 65 paragraph 1 must be made in writing.

2. Any act declaring invalid, terminating, withdrawing from or suspending the operation of a treaty pursuant to the provisions of the treaty or of paragraphs 2 or 3 of Article 65 shall be carried out through an instrument communicated to the other parties. If the instrument is not signed by the Head of State, Head of Government or Minister for Foreign Affairs, the representative of the state communicating it may be called upon to produce full powers.

ARTICLE 68

*Revocation of notifications and instruments
provided for in Articles 65 and 67*

A notification or instrument provided for in Articles 65 or 67 may be revoked at any time before it takes effect.

SECTION 5: CONSEQUENCES OF THE INVALIDITY, TERMINATION
OR SUSPENSION OF THE OPERATION OF A TREATY

ARTICLE 69

Consequences of the invalidity of a treaty

1. A treaty the invalidity of which is established under the present Convention is void. The provisions of a void treaty have no legal force.

2. If acts have nevertheless been performed in reliance on such a treaty:
   (a) each party may require any other party to establish as far as possible in their mutual relations the position that would have existed if the acts had not been performed;
   (b) acts performed in good faith before the invalidity was invoked are not rendered unlawful by reason only of the invalidity of the treaty.

3. In cases falling under Articles 49, 50, 51 or 52, paragraph 2 does not apply with respect to the party to which the fraud, the act of corruption or the coercion is imputable.

4. In the case of the invalidity of a particular state's consent to be bound by a multilateral treaty, the foregoing rules apply in the relations between that state and the parties to the treaty.

ARTICLE 70

Consequences of the termination of a treaty

1. Unless the treaty otherwise provides or the parties otherwise agree, the termination of a treaty under its provisions or in accordance with the present Convention:
   (a) releases the parties from any obligation further to perform the treaty;
   (b) does not affect any right, obligation or legal situation of the parties created through the execution of the treaty prior to its termination.

2. If a state denounces or withdraws from a multilateral treaty, paragraph 1 applies in the relations between that state and each of the other parties to the treaty from the date when such denunciation or withdrawal takes effect.

ARTICLE 71

Consequences of the invalidity of a treaty which conflicts with a peremptory norm of general international law

1. In the case of a treaty which is void under Article 53 the parties shall:
   (a) eliminate as far as possible the consequences of any act performed in reliance on any provision which conflicts with the peremptory norm of general international law; and
   (b) bring their mutual relations into conformity with the peremptory norm of general international law.

2. In the case of a treaty which becomes void and terminates under Article 64, the termination of the treaty:
   (a) releases the parties from any obligation further to perform the treaty;
   (b) does not affect any right, obligation or legal situation of the parties created through the execution of the treaty prior to its termination; provided that those rights, obligations or situations

may thereafter be maintained only to the extent that their maintenance is not in itself in conflict with the new peremptory norm
of general international law.

ARTICLE 72

Consequences of the suspension of the operation of a treaty

1. Unless the treaty otherwise provides or the parties otherwise agree,
the suspension of the operation of a treaty under its provisions or in accordance with the present Convention:
   (a) releases the parties between which the operation of the treaty is
       suspended from the obligation to perform the treaty in their
       mutual relations during the period of the suspension;
   (b) does not otherwise affect the legal relations between the parties
       established by the treaty.
2. During the period of the suspension the parties shall refrain from
acts tending to obstruct the resumption of the operation of the treaty.

PART VI

MISCELLANEOUS PROVISIONS

ARTICLE 73

*Cases of state succession, state responsibility
and outbreaks of hostilities*

The provisions of the present Convention shall not prejudge any question that may arise in regard to a treaty from a succession of states or
from the international responsibility of a state or from the outbreak of
hostilities between states.

ARTICLE 74

Diplomatic and consular relations and the conclusion of treaties

The severance or absence of diplomatic or consular relations between two
or more states does not prevent the conclusion of treaties between those
states. The conclusion of a treaty does not in itself affect the situation
in regard to diplomatic or consular relations.

ARTICLE 75

Case of an aggressor state

The provisions of the present Convention are without prejudice to any
obligation in relation to a treaty which may arise for an aggressor state
in consequence of measures taken in conformity with the Charter of the
United Nations with reference to that state's aggression.

PART VII

DEPOSITARIES, NOTIFICATIONS, CORRECTIONS AND REGISTRATION

ARTICLE 76

Depositaries of treaties

1. The designation of the depositary of a treaty may be made by the negotiating states, either in the treaty itself or in some other manner. The depositary may be one or more states, an international organization or the chief administrative officer of the organization.

2. The functions of the depositary of a treaty are international in character and the depositary is under an obligation to act impartially in their performance. In particular, the fact that a treaty has not entered into force between certain of the parties or that a difference has appeared between a state and a depositary with regard to the performance of the latter's functions shall not affect that obligation.

ARTICLE 77

Functions of depositaries

1. The functions of a depositary, unless otherwise provided in the treaty or agreed by the contracting states, comprise in particular:

   (a) keeping custody of the original text of the treaty and of any full powers delivered to the depositary;

   (b) preparing certified copies of the original text and preparing any further text of the treaty in such additional languages as may be required by the treaty and transmitting them to the parties and to the states entitled to become parties to the treaty;

   (c) receiving any signatures to the treaty and receiving and keeping custody of any instruments, notifications and communications relating to it;

   (d) examining whether the signature or any instrument, notification or communication relating to the treaty is in due and proper form and, if need be, bringing the matter to the attention of the state in question;

   (e) informing the parties and the states entitled to become parties to the treaty of acts, notifications and communications relating to the treaty;

   (f) informing the states entitled to become parties to the treaty when the number of signatures or of instruments of ratification, acceptance, approval or accession required for the entry into force of the treaty has been received or deposited;

   (g) registering the treaty with the Secretariat of the United Nations;

   (h) performing the functions specified in other provisions of the present Convention.

2. In the event of any difference appearing between a state and the depositary as to the performance of the latter's functions, the depositary shall bring the question to the attention of the signatory states and the contracting states or, where appropriate, of the competent organ of the international organization concerned.

ARTICLE 78

Notifications and communications

Except as the treaty or the present Convention otherwise provide, any notification or communication to be made by any state under the present Convention shall:
- (a) if there is no depositary, be transmitted direct to the states for which it is intended, or if there is a depositary, to the latter;
- (b) be considered as having been made by the state in question only upon its receipt by the state to which it was transmitted or, as the case may be, upon its receipt by the depositary;
- (c) if transmitted to a depositary, be considered as received by the state for which it was intended only when the latter state has been informed by the depositary in accordance with Article 77, paragraph 1(e).

ARTICLE 79

Correction of errors in texts or in certified copies of treaties

1. Where, after the authentication of the text of a treaty, the signatory states and the contracting states are agreed that it contains an error, the error shall, unless they decide upon some other means of correction, be corrected:
- (a) by having the appropriate correction made in the text and causing the correction to be initialled by duly authorized representatives;
- (b) by executing or exchanging an instrument or instruments setting out the correction which it has been agreed to make; or
- (c) by executing a corrected text of the whole treaty by the same procedure as in the case of the original text.

2. Where the treaty is one for which there is a depositary, the latter shall notify the signatory states and the contracting states of the error and of the proposal to correct it and shall specify an appropriate time-limit within which objection to the proposed correction may be raised. If, on the expiry of the time-limit:
- (a) no objection has been raised, the depositary shall make and initial the correction in the text and shall execute a *procès-verbal* of the rectification of the text and communicate a copy of it to the parties and to the states entitled to become parties to the treaty;

(b) an objection has been raised, the depositary shall communicate the objection to the signatory states and to the contracting states.

3. The rules in paragraphs 1 and 2 apply also where the text has been authenticated in two or more languages and it appears that there is a lack of concordance which the signatory states and the contracting states agree should be corrected.

4. The corrected text replaces the defective text *ab initio*, unless the signatory states and the contracting states otherwise decide.

5. The correction of the text of a treaty that has been registered shall be notified to the Secretariat of the United Nations.

6. Where an error is discovered in a certified copy of a treaty, the depositary shall execute a *procès-verbal* specifying the rectification and communicate a copy of it to the signatory states and to the contracting states.

ARTICLE 80

Registration and publication of treaties

1. Treaties shall, after their entry into force, be transmitted to the Secretariat of the United Nations for registration or filing and recording, as the case may be, and for publication.

2. The designation of a depositary shall constitute authorization for it to perform the acts specified in the preceding paragraph.

PART VIII

FINAL PROVISIONS

ARTICLE 81

Signature

The present Convention shall be open for signature by all States Members of the United Nations or of any of the specialized agencies or of the International Atomic Energy Agency or parties to the Statute of the International Court of Justice, and by any other state invited by the General Assembly of the United Nations to become a party to the Convention, as follows: until 30 November 1969, at the Federal Ministry for Foreign Affairs of the Republic of Austria, and subsequently, until 30 April 1970, at United Nations Headquarters, New York.

ARTICLE 82

Ratification

The present Convention is subject to ratification. The instruments of ratification shall be deposited with the Secretary-General of the United Nations.

ARTICLE 83

Accession

The present Convention shall remain open for accession by any state belonging to any of the categories mentioned in Article 81. The instruments of accession shall be deposited with the Secretary-General of the United Nations.

ARTICLE 84

Entry into force

1. The present Convention shall enter into force on the thirtieth day following the date of deposit of the thirty-fifth instrument of ratification or accession.

2. For each state ratifying or acceding to the Convention after the deposit of the thirty-fifth instrument of ratification or accession, the Convention shall enter into force on the thirtieth day after deposit by such state of its instrument of ratification or accession.

ARTICLE 85

Authentic texts

The original of the present Convention, of which the Chinese. English, French, Russian and Spanish texts are equally authentic, shall be deposited with the Secretary-General of the United Nations.

IN WITNESS WHEREOF the undersigned Plenipotentiaries, being duly authorized thereto by their respective governments, have signed the present Convention.

DONE AT VIENNA, this twenty-third day of May, one thousand nine hundred and sixty-nine.

[The convention was signed on May 23, 1969, on behalf of: Afghanistan, Argentina, Barbados, Bolivia, Brazil, Cambodia, Chile, Colombia, Congo (Brazzaville), Costa Rica, Ecuador, Finland, Ghana, Guatemala, Guyana, Honduras, Iran, Jamaica, Kenya, Liberia, Madagascar, Mexico, Morocco, Nepal, Nigeria, Peru, Philippines, Sudan, Trinidad and Tobago, Uruguay, Yugoslavia and Zambia.]

ANNEX

1. A list of conciliators consisting of qualified jurists shall be drawn up and maintained by the Secretary-General of the United Nations. To this end, every state which is a Member of the United Nations or a party to the present Convention shall be invited to nominate two conciliators, and the names of the persons so nominated shall constitute the list. The term of a conciliator, including that of any conciliator nominated to fill a casual vacancy, shall be five years and may be renewed. A conciliator whose term expires shall continue to fulfil any function for which he shall have been chosen under the following paragraph.

2. When a request has been made to the Secretary-General under Article 66, the Secretary-General shall bring the dispute before a conciliation commission constituted as follows:

The state or states constituting one of the parties to the dispute shall appoint:

(a) one conciliator of the nationality of that state or of one of those states, who may or may not be chosen from the list referred to in paragraph 1; and

(b) one conciliator not of the nationality of that state or of any of those states, who shall be chosen from the list.

The state or states constituting the other party to the dispute shall appoint two conciliators in the same way. The four conciliators chosen by the parties shall be appointed within sixty days following the date on which the Secretary-General receives the request.

The four conciliators shall, within sixty days following the date of the last of their own appointments, appoint a fifth conciliator chosen from the list, who shall be chairman.

If the appointment of the chairman or of any of the other conciliators has not been made within the period prescribed above for such appointment, it shall be made by the Secretary-General within sixty days following the expiry of that period. The appointment of the chairman may be made by the Secretary-General either from the list or from the membership of the International Law Commission. Any of the periods within which appointments must be made may be extended by agreement between the parties to the dispute.

Any vacancy shall be filled in the manner prescribed for the initial appointment.

3. The Conciliation Commission shall decide its own procedure. The Commission, with the consent of the parties to the dispute, may invite any party to the treaty to submit to it its views orally or in writing. Decisions and recommendations of the Commission shall be made by a majority vote of the five members.

4. The Commission may draw the attention of the parties to the dispute to any measures which might facilitate an amicable settlement.

5. The Commission shall hear the parties, examine the claims and objections, and make proposals to the parties with a view to reaching an amicable settlement of the dispute.

6. The Commission shall report within twelve months of its constitution. Its report shall be deposited with the Secretary-General and transmitted to the parties to the dispute. The report of the Commission, including any conclusions stated therein regarding the facts or questions of law, shall not be binding upon the parties and it shall have no other character than that of recommendations submitted for the consideration of the parties in order to facilitate an amicable settlement of the dispute.

7. The Secretary-General shall provide the Commission with such assistance and facilities as it may require. The expenses of the Commission shall be borne by the United Nations.

附錄二

VIENNA CONVENTION ON SUCCESSION OF STATES IN
RESPECT OF TREATIES °

The States Parties to the present Convention,

Considering the profound transformation of the international community brought about by the decolonization process,

Considering also that other factors may lead to cases of succession of States in the future,

Convinced, in these circumstances, of the need for the codification and progressive development of the rules relating to succession of States in respect of treaties as a means for ensuring greater juridical security in international relations,

Noting that the principles of free consent, good faith and *pacta sunt servanda* are universally recognized,

Emphasizing that the consistent observance of general multilateral treaties which deal with the codification and progressive development of international law and those the object and purpose of which are of interest to the international community as a whole is of special importance for the strengthening of peace and international co-operation,

Having in mind the principles of international law embodied in the Charter of the United Nations, such as the principles of the equal rights and self-determination of peoples, of the sovereign equality and independence of all States, of non-interference in the domestic affairs of States, of the prohibition of the threat or use of force, and of universal respect for, and observance of, human rights and fundamental freedoms for all,

Recalling that respect for the territorial integrity and political independence of any State is required by the Charter of the United Nations,

Bearing in mind the provisions of the Vienna Convention on the Law of Treaties of 1969,

Bearing also in mind article 73 of that Convention,

Affirming that questions of the law of treaties other than those that may arise from a succession of States are governed by the relevant rules of international law, including those rules of customary international law which are embodied in the Vienna Convention on the Law of Treaties of 1969,

Affirming that the rules of customary international law will continue to govern questions not regulated by the provisions of the present Convention,

Have agreed as follows:

PART I

GENERAL PROVISIONS

Article 1—Scope of the present Convention

The present Convention applies to the effects of a succession of States in respect of treaties between States.

° UN Doc. A/CONF. 80/31. This convention was adopted on August 23, 1978 by a vote of 82 in favor with 2 abstentions (France and Switzerland) at the United Nations Conference on Succession of States in Respect of Treaties, Vienna. The Final Act of the conference is UN Doc. A/CONF. 80/32.

Article 2—Use of terms

1. For the purposes of the present Convention:

(a) "treaty" means an international agreement concluded between States in written form and governed by international law, whether embodied in a single instrument or in two or more related instruments and whatever its particular designation;

(b) "succession of States" means the replacement of one State by another in the responsibility for the international relations of territory;

(c) "predecessor State" means the State which has been replaced by another State on the occurrence of a succession of States;

(d) "successor State" means the State which has replaced another State on the occurrence of a succession of States;

(e) "date of the succession of States" means the date upon which the successor State replaced the predecessor State in the responsibility for the international relations of the territory to which the succession of States relates;

(f) "newly independent State" means a successor State the territory of which immediately before the date of the succession of States was a dependent territory for the international relations of which the predecessor State was responsible;

(g) "notification of succession" means in relation to a multilateral treaty any notification, however phrased or named, made by a successor State expressing its consent to be considered as bound by the treaty;

(h) "full powers" means in relation to a notification of succession or any other notification under the present Convention a document emanating from the competent authority of a State designating a person or persons to represent the State for communicating the notification of succession or, as the case may be, the notification;

(i) "ratification," "acceptance" and "approval" mean in each case the international act so named whereby a State establishes on the international plane its consent to be bound by a treaty;

(j) "reservation" means a unilateral statement, however phrased or named, made by a State when signing, ratifying, accepting, approving or acceding to a treaty or when making a notification of succession to a treaty, whereby it purports to exclude or to modify the legal effect of certain provisions of the treaty in their application to that State;

(k) "contracting State" means a State which has consented to be bound by the treaty, whether or not the treaty has entered into force;

(l) "party" means a State which has consented to be bound by the treaty and for which the treaty is in force;

(m) "other State party" means in relation to a successor State any party, other than the predecessor State, to a treaty in force at the date of a succession of States in respect of the territory to which that succession of States relates;

(n) "international organization" means an intergovernmental organization.

2. The provisions of paragraph 1 regarding the use of terms in the present Convention are without prejudice to the use of those terms or to the meanings which may be given to them in the internal law of any State.

Article 3—Cases not within the scope of the present Convention

The fact that the present Convention does not apply to the effects of a succession of States in respect of international agreements concluded between States and other subjects of international law or in respect of international agreements not in written form shall not affect:

    (a) the application to such cases of any of the rules set forth in the present Convention to which they are subject under international law independently of the Convention;

    (b) the application as between States of the present Convention to the effects of a succession of States in respect of international agreements to which other subjects of international law are also parties.

Article 4—Treaties constituting international organizations and treaties adopted within an international organization

The present Convention applies to the effects of a succession of States in respect of:

    (a) any treaty which is the constituent instrument of an international organization without prejudice to the rules concerning acquisition of membership and without prejudice to any other relevant rules of the organization;

    (b) any treaty adopted within an international organization without prejudice to any relevant rules of the organization.

Article 5—Obligations imposed by international law independently of a treaty

The fact that a treaty is not considered to be in force in respect of a State by virtue of the application of the present Convention shall not in any way impair the duty of that State to fulfil any obligation embodied in the treaty to which it is subject under international law independently of the treaty.

Article 6—Cases of succession of States covered by the present Convention

The present Convention applies only to the effects of a succession of States occurring in conformity with international law and, in particular, the principles of international law embodied in the Charter of the United Nations.

Article 7—Temporal application of the present Convention

1. Without prejudice to the application of any of the rules set forth in the present Convention to which the effects of a succession of States would be subject under international law independently of the Convention, the Convention applies only in respect of a succession of States which has occurred after the entry into force of the Convention except as may be otherwise agreed.

2. A successor State may, at the time of expressing its consent to be bound by the present convention or at any time thereafter, make a declaration that it will apply the provisions of the Convention in respect of its own succession of States which has occurred before the entry into force of the Convention in relation to any other contracting State or State Party to the Convention which makes a declaration accepting the declaration of the successor State. Upon the entry into force of the Convention as between the States making the declarations or upon the making of the declaration of acceptance, whichever occurs later, the provisions of the Convention shall apply to the effects of the succession of States as from the date of that succession of States.

3. A successor State may at the time of signing or of expressing its consent to be bound by the present Convention make a declaration that it will apply the provisions of the Convention provisionally in respect of its own succession of States which has occurred before the entry into force of the Convention in relation to any other signatory or contracting State which makes a declaration accepting the declaration of the successor State; upon the making of the declaration of acceptance, those provisions shall apply provisionally to the effects of the succession of States as between those two States as from the date of that succession of States.

4. Any declaration made in accordance with paragraph 2 or 3 shall be contained in a written notification communicated to the depositary, who shall inform the Parties and the States entitled to become Parties to the present Convention of the communication to him of that notification and of its terms.

Article 8—Agreements for the devolution of treaty obligations or rights from a predecessor State to a successor State

1. The obligations or rights of a predecessor State under treaties in force in respect of a territory at the date of a succession of States do not become The obligations or rights of the successor State towards other States parties to those treaties by reason only of the fact that the predecessor State and the successor State have concluded an agreement providing that such obligations or rights shall devolve upon the successor State.

2. Notwithstanding the conclusion of such an agreement, the effects of a succession of States on treaties which, at the date of that succession of States, were in force in respect of the territory in question are governed by the present Convention.

Article 9—Unilateral declaration by a successor State regarding treaties of the predecessor State

1. Obligations or rights under treaties in force in respect of a territory at the date of a succession of States do not become the obligations or rights of the successor State or of other States parties to those treaties by reason only of the fact that the successor State has made a unilateral declaration providing for the continuance in force of the treaties in respect of its territory.

2. In such a case, the effects of the succession of States on treaties which, at the date of that succession of States, were in force in respect of the territory in question are governed by the present Convention.

Article 10—Treaties providing for the participation of a successor State

1. When a treaty provides that, on the occurrence of a succession of States, a successor State shall have the option to consider itself a party to the treaty, it may notify its succession in respect of the treaty in conformity with the provisions of the treaty or, failing any such provisions, in conformity with the provisions of the present Convention.

2. If a treaty provides that, on the occurrence of a succession of States, a successor State shall be considered as a party to the treaty, that provision takes effect as such only if the successor State expressly accepts in writing to be so considered.

3. In cases falling under paragraph 1 or 2, a successor State which establishes its consent to be a party to the treaty is considered as a party from

the date of the succession of States unless the treaty otherwise provides or it is otherwise agreed.

Article 11—Boundary régimes

A succession of States does not as such affect:

(a) a boundary established by a treaty; or
(b) obligations and rights established by a treaty and relating to the régime of a boundary.

Article 12—Other territorial régimes

1. A succession of States does not as such affect:

(a) obligations relating to the use of any territory, or to restrictions upon its use, established by a treaty for the benefit of any territory of a foreign State and considered as attaching to the territories in question;

(b) rights established by a treaty for the benefit of any territory and relating to the use, or to restrictions upon the use, of any territory of a foreign State and considered as attaching to the territories in question.

2. A succession of States does not as such affect:

(a) obligations relating to the use of any territory, or to restrictions upon its use, established by a treaty for the benefit of a group of States or of all States and considered as attaching to that territory;
(b) rights established by a treaty for the benefit of a group of States or of all States and relating to the use of any territory, or to restrictions upon its use, and considered as attaching to that territory.

3. The provisions of the present article do not apply to treaty obligations of the predecessor State providing for the establishment of foreign military bases on the territory to which the succession of States relates.

Article 13—The present Convention and permanent sovereignty over natural wealth and resources

Nothing in the present Convention shall affect the principles of international law affirming the permanent sovereignty of every people and every State over its natural wealth and resources.

Article 14—Questions relating to the validity of a treaty

Nothing in the present Convention shall be considered as prejudging in any respect any question relating to the validity of a treaty.

PART II

SUCCESSION IN RESPECT OF PART OF TERRITORY

Article 15—Succession i.. respect of part of territory

When part of the territory of a State, or when any territory for the international relations of which a State is responsible, not being part of the territory of that State, becomes part of the territory of another State:

(a) treaties of the predecessor State cease to be in force in respect of the territory to which the succession of States relates from the date of the succession of States; and
(b) treaties of the successor State are in force in respect of the territory to which the succession of States relates from the date of the succession

of States, unless it appears from the treaty or is otherwise established that the application of the treaty to that territory would be incompatible with the object and purpose of the treaty or would radically change the conditions for its operation.

PART III

NEWLY INDEPENDENT STATES

SECTION 1. GENERAL RULE

Article 16—Position in respect of the treaties of the predecessor State

A newly independent State is not bound to maintain in force, or to become a party to, any treaty by reason only of the fact that at the date of the succession of States the treaty was in force in respect of the territory to which the succession of States relates.

SECTION 2. MULTILATERAL TREATIES

Article 17—Participation in treaties in force at the date of the succession of States

1. Subject to paragraphs 2 and 3, a newly independent State may, by a notification of succession, establish its status as a party to any multilateral treaty which at the date of the succession of States was in force in respect of the territory to which the succession of States relates.

2. Paragraph 1 does not apply if it appears from the treaty or is otherwise established that the application of the treaty in respect of the newly independent State would be incompatible with the object and purpose of the treaty or would radically change the conditions for its operation.

3. When, under the terms of the treaty or by reason of the limited number of the negotiating States and the object and purpose of the treaty, the participation of any other State in the treaty must be considered as requiring the consent of all the parties, the newly independent State may establish its status as a party to the treaty only with such consent.

Article 18—Participation in treaties not in force at the date of the succession of States

1. Subject to paragraphs 3 and 4, a newly independent State may, by a notification of succession, establish its status as a contracting State to a multilateral treaty which is not in force if at the date of the succession of States the predecessor State was a contracting State in respect of the territory to which that succession of States relates.

2. Subject to paragraphs 3 and 4, a newly independent State may, by a notification of succession, establish its status as a party to a multilateral treaty which enters into force after the date of the succession of States if at the date of the succession of States the predecessor State was a contracting State in respect of the territory to which that succession of States relates.

3. Paragraphs 1 and 2 do not apply if it appears from the treaty or is otherwise established that the application of the treaty in respect of the newly independent State would be incompatible with the object and purpose of the treaty or would radically change the conditions for its operation.

4. When, under the terms of the treaty or by reason of the limited number of the negotiating States and the object and purpose of the treaty, the participation of any other State in the treaty must be considered as requiring the consent of all the parties or of all the contracting States, the newly independent State may establish its status as a party or as a contracting State to the treaty only with such consent.

5. When a treaty provides that a specified number of contracting States shall be necessary for its entry into force, a newly independent State which establishes its status as a contracting State to the treaty under paragraph 1 shall be counted as a contracting State for the purpose of that provision unless a different intention appears from the treaty or is otherwise established.

Article 19—Participation in treaties signed by the predecessor State subject to ratification, acceptance or approval

1. Subject to paragraphs 3 and 4, if before the date of the succession of States the predecessor State signed a multilateral treaty subject to ratification, acceptance or approval and by the signature intended that the treaty should extend to the territory to which the succession of States relates, the newly independent State may ratify, accept or approve the treaty as if it had signed that treaty and may thereby become a party or a contracting State to it.

2. For the purpose of paragraph 1, unless a different intention appears from the treaty or is otherwise established, the signature by the predecessor State of a treaty is considered to express the intention that the treaty should extend to the entire territory for the international relations of which the predecessor State was responsible.

3. Paragraph 1 does not apply if it appears from the treaty or is otherwise established that the application of the treaty in respect of the newly independent State would be incompatible with the object and purpose of the treaty or would radically change the conditions for its operation.

4. When, under the terms of the treaty or by reason of the limited number of the negotiating States and the object and purpose of the treaty, the participation of any other State in the treaty must be considered as requiring the consent of all the parties or of all the contracting States, the newly independent State may become a party or a contracting State to the treaty only with such consent.

Article 20—Reservations

1. When a newly independent State establishes its status as a party or as a contracting State to a multilateral treaty by a notification of succession under article 17 or 18, it shall be considered as maintaining any reservation to that treaty which was applicable at the date of the succession of States in respect of the territory to which the succession of States relates unless, when making the notification of succession, it expresses a contrary intention or formulates a reservation which relates to the same subject-matter as that reservation.

2. When making a notification of succession establishing its status as a party or as a contracting State to a multilateral treaty under article 17 or 18, a newly independent State may formulate a reservation unless the reservation is one the formulation of which would be excluded by the provisions of sub-paragraph (a), (b) or (c) of article 19 of the Vienna Convention on the Law of Treaties.

3. When a newly independent State formulates a reservation in conformity with paragraph 2, the rules set out in articles 20 to 23 of the Vienna Convention on the Law of Treaties apply in respect of that reservation.

Article 21—Consent to be bound by part of a treaty and choice between differing provisions

1. When making a notification of succession under article 17 or 18 establishing its status as a party or contracting State to a multilateral treaty, a newly independent State may, if the treaty so permits, express its consent to be bound by part of the treaty or make a choice between differing provisions under the conditions laid down in the treaty for expressing such consent or making such choice.

2. A newly independent State may also exercise, under the same conditions as the other parties or contracting States, any right provided for in the treaty to withdraw or modify any consent expressed or choice made by itself or by the predecessor State in respect of the territory to which the succession of States relates.

3. If the newly independent State does not in conformity with paragraph 1 express its consent or make a choice, or in conformity with paragraph 2 withdraw or modify the consent or choice of the predecessor State, it shall be considered as maintaining:

(a) the consent of the predecessor State, in conformity with the treaty, to be bound, in respect of the territory to which the succession of States relates, by part of that treaty; or
(b) the choice of the predecessor State, in conformity with the treaty, between differing provisions in the application of the treaty in respect of the territory to which the succession of States relates.

Article 22—Notification of succession

1. A notification of succession in respect of a multilateral treaty under article 17 or 18 shall be made in writing.

2. If the notification of succession is not signed by the Head of State, Head of Government or Minister for Foreign Affairs, the representative of the State communicating it may be called upon to produce full powers.

3. Unless the treaty otherwise provides, the notification of succession shall:

(a) be transmitted by the newly independent State to the depositary, or, if there is no depositary, to the parties or the contracting States;
(b) be considered to be made by the newly independent State on the date on which it is received by the depositary or, if there is no depositary, on the date on which it is received by all the parties or, as the case may be, by all the contracting States.

4. Paragraph 3 does not affect any duty that the depositary may have, in accordance with the treaty or otherwise, to inform the parties or the contracting States of the notification of succession or any communication made in connection therewith by the newly independent State.

5. Subject to the provisions of the treaty, the notification of succession or the communication made in connection therewith shall be considered as received by the State for which it is intended only when the latter State has been informed by the depositary.

Article 23—Effects of a notification of succession

1. Unless the treaty otherwise provides or it is otherwise agreed, a newly independent State which makes a notification of succession under article 17 or article 18, paragraph 2, shall be considered a party to the treaty from the date of the succession of States or from the date of entry into force of the treaty, whichever is the later date.

2. Nevertheless, the operation of the treaty shall be considered as suspended as between the newly independent State and the other parties to the treaty until the date of making of the notification of succession except in so far as that treaty may be applied provisionally in accordance with article 27 or as may be otherwise agreed.

3. Unless the treaty otherwise provides or it is otherwise agreed, a newly independent State which makes a notification of succession under article 18, paragraph 1, shall be considered a contracting State to the treaty from the date on which the notification of succession is made.

SECTION 3. BILATERAL TREATIES

Article 24—Conditions under which a treaty is considered as being in force in the case of a succession of States

1. A bilateral treaty which at the date of a succession of States was in force in respect of the territory to which the succession of States relates is considered as being in force between a newly independent State and the other State party when:

(a) they expressly so agree; or
(b) by reason of their conduct they are to be considered as having so agreed.

2. A treaty considered as being in force under paragraph 1 applies in the relations between the newly independent State and the other State party from the date of the succession of States, unless a different intention appears from their agreement or is otherwise established.

Article 25—The position as between the predecessor State and the newly independent State

A treaty which under article 24 is considered as being in force between a newly independent State and the other State party is not by reason only of that fact to be considered as being in force also in the relations between the predecessor State and the newly independent State.

Article 26—Termination, suspension of operation or amendment of the treaty as between the predecessor State and the other State party

1. When under article 24 a treaty is considered as being in force between a newly independent State and the other State party, the treaty:

(a) does not cease to be in force between them by reason only of the fact that it has subsequently been terminated as between the predecessor State and the other State party;
(b) is not suspended in operation as between them by reason only of the fact that it has subsequently been suspended in operation as between the predecessor State and the other State party;
(c) is not amended as between them by reason only of the fact that it has subsequently been amended as between the predecessor State and the other State party.

2. The fact that a treaty has been terminated or, as the case may be, suspended in operation as between the predecessor State and the other State party after the date of the succession of States does not prevent the treaty from being considered to be in force or, as the case may be, in operation as between the newly independent State and the other State party if it is established in accordance with article 24 that they so agreed.

3. The fact that a treaty has been amended as between the predecessor State and the other State party after the date of the succession of States does not prevent the unamended treaty from being considered to be in force under article 24 as between the newly independent State and the other State party, unless it is established that they intended the treaty as amended to apply between them.

SECTION 4. PROVISIONAL APPLICATION

Article 27—Multilateral treaties

1. If, at the date of the succession of States, a multilateral treaty was in force in respect of the territory to which the succession of States relates and the newly independent State gives notice of its intention that the treaty should be applied provisionally in respect of its territory, that treaty shall apply provisionally between the newly independent State and any party which expressly so agrees or by reason of its conduct is to be considered as having so agreed.

2. Nevertheless, in the case of a treaty which falls within the category mentioned in article 14, paragraph 3, the consent of all the parties to such provisional application is required.

3. If at the date of the succession of States, a multilateral treaty not yet in force was being applied provisionally in respect of the territory to which the succession of States relates and the newly independent State gives notice of its intention that the treaty should continue to be applied provisionally in respect of its territory, that treaty shall apply provisionally between the newly independent State and any contracting State which expressly so agrees or by reason of its conduct is to be considered as having so agreed.

4. Nevertheless, in the case of a treaty which falls within the category mentioned in article 17, paragraph 3, the consent of all the contracting States to such continued provisional application is required.

5. Paragraphs 1 to 4 do not apply if it appears from the treaty or is otherwise established that the application of the treaty in respect of the newly independent State would be incompatible with the object and purpose of the treaty or would radically change the conditions for its operation.

Article 28—Bilateral treaties

A bilateral treaty which at the date of a succession of States was in force or was being provisionally applied in respect of the territory to which the succession of States relates is considered as applying provisionally between the newly independent State and the other State concerned when:

(a) they expressly so agree; or
(b) by reason of their conduct they are to be considered as having so agreed.

Article 29—Termination of provisional application

1. Unless the treaty otherwise provides or it is otherwise agreed, the provisional application of a multilateral treaty under article 27 may be terminated:

(a) by reasonable notice of termination given by the newly independent State or the party or contracting State provisionally applying the treaty and the expiration of the notice; or

(b) in the case of a treaty which falls within the category mentioned in article 17, paragraph 3, by reasonable notice of termination given by the newly independent State or all of the parties or, as the case may be, all of the contracting States and the expiration of the notice.

2. Unless the treaty otherwise provides or it is otherwise agreed, the provisional application of a bilateral treaty under article 28 may be terminated by reasonable notice of termination given by the newly independent State or the other State concerned and the expiration of the notice.

3. Unless the treaty provides for a shorter period for its termination or it is otherwise agreed, reasonable notice of termination shall be twelve months' notice from the date on which it is received by the other State or States provisionally applying the treaty.

4. Unless the treaty otherwise provides or it is otherwise agreed, the provisional application of a multilateral treaty under article 27 shall be terminated if the newly independent State gives notice of its intention not to become a party to the treaty.

SECTION 5. NEWLY INDEPENDENT STATES FORMED FROM TWO
OR MORE TERRITORIES

Article 30—Newly independent States formed from two or more territories

1. Articles 16 to 29 apply in the case of a newly independent State formed from two or more territories.

2. When a newly independent State formed from two or more territories is considered as or becomes a party to a treaty by virtue of article 17, 18, or 24 and at the date of the succession of States the treaty was in force, or consent to be bound had been given, in respect of one or more, but not all, of those territories, the treaty shall apply in respect of the entire territory of that State unless:

(a) it appears from the treaty or is otherwise established that the application of the treaty in respect of the entire territory would be incompatible with the object and purpose of the treaty or would radically change the conditions for its operation;

(b) in the case of a multilateral treaty not falling under article 17, paragraph 3, or under article 18, paragraph 4, the notification of succession is restricted to the territory in respect of which the treaty was in force at the date of the succession of States, or in respect of which consent to be bound by the treaty had been given prior to that date;

(c) in the case of a multilateral treaty falling under article 17, paragraph 3, or under article 18, paragraph 4, the newly independent State and the other States parties or, as the case may be, the other contracting States otherwise agree; or

(d) in the case of a bilateral treaty, the newly independent State and the other State concerned otherwise agree.

3. When a newly independent State formed from two or more territories becomes a party to a multilateral treaty under article 19 and by the signa-

ture or signatures of the predecessor State or States it had been intended that the treaty should extend to one or more, but not all, of those territories, the treaty shall apply in respect of the entire territory of the newly independent State unless:

(a) it appears from the treaty or is otherwise established that the application of the treaty in respect of the entire territory would be incompatible with the object and purpose of the treaty or would radically change the conditions for its operation;

(b) in the case of a multilateral treaty not falling under article 19, paragraph 4, the ratification, acceptance or approval of the treaty is restricted to the territory or territories to which it was intended that the treaty should extend; or

(c) in the case of a multilateral treaty falling under article 19, paragraph 4, the newly independent State and the other States parties or, as the case may be, the other contracting States otherwise agree.

PART IV

UNITING AND SEPARATION OF STATES

Article 31—Effects of a uniting of States in respect of treaties in force at the date of the succession of States

1. When two or more States unite and so form one successor State, any treaty in force at the date of the succession of States in respect of any of them continues in force in respect of the successor State unless:

(a) the successor State and the other State party or States parties otherwise agree; or

(b) it appears from the treaty or is otherwise established that the application of the treaty in respect of the successor State would be incompatible with the object and purpose of the treaty or would radically change the conditions for its operation.

2. Any treaty continuing in force in conformity with paragraph 1 shall apply only in respect of the part of the territory of the successor State in respect of which the treaty was in force at the date of the succession of States unless:

(a) in the case of a multilateral treaty not falling within the category mentioned in article 17, paragraph 3, the successor State makes a notification that the treaty shall apply in respect of its entire territory;

(b) in the case of a multilateral treaty falling within the category mentioned in article 17, paragraph 3, the successor State and the other States parties otherwise agree; or

(c) in the case of a bilateral treaty, the successor State and the other State party otherwise agree.

3. Paragraph 2(a) does not apply if it appears from the treaty or is otherwise established that the application of the treaty in respect of the entire territory of the successor State would be incompatible with the object and purpose of the treaty or would radically change the conditions for its operation.

Article 32—Effects of a uniting of States in respect of treaties not in force at the date of the succession of States

1. Subject to paragraphs 3 and 4, a successor State falling under article 31 may, by making a notification, establish its status as a contracting State

to a multilateral treaty which is not in force if, at the date of the succession of States, any of the predecessor States was a contracting State to the treaty.

2. Subject to paragraphs 3 and 4, a successor State falling under article 31 may, by making a notification, establish its status as a party to a multilateral treaty which enters into force after the date of the succession of States if, at that date, any of the predecessor States was a contracting State to the treaty.

3. Paragraphs 1 and 2 do not apply if it appears from the treaty or is otherwise established that the application of the treaty in respect of the successor State would be incompatible with the object and purpose of the treaty or would radically change the conditions for its operation.

4. If the treaty is one falling within the category mentioned in article 17, paragraph 3, the successor State may establish its status as a party or as a contracting State to the treaty only with the consent of all the parties or of all the contracting States.

5. Any treaty to which the successor State becomes a contracting State or a party in conformity with paragraph 1 or 2 shall apply only in respect of the part of the territory of the successor State in respect of which consent to be bound by the treaty had been given prior to the date of the succession of States unless:

(a) in the case of a multilateral treaty not falling within the category mentioned in article 17, paragraph 3, the successor State indicates in its notification made under paragraph 1 or 2 that the treaty shall apply in respect of its entire territory; or

(b) in the case of a multilateral treaty falling within the category mentioned in article 17, paragraph 3, the successor State and all the parties or, as the case may be, all the contracting States otherwise agree.

6. Paragraph 5(a) does not apply if it appears from the treaty or is otherwise established that the application of the treaty in respect of the entire territory of the successor State would be incompatible with the object and purpose of the treaty or would radically change the conditions for its operation.

Article 33—Effects of a uniting of States in respect of treaties signed by a predecessor State subject to ratification, acceptance or approval

1. Subject to paragraphs 2 and 3, if before the date of the succession of States one of the predecessor States had signed a multilateral treaty subject to ratification, acceptance or approval, a successor State falling under article 31 may ratify, accept or approve the treaty as if it had signed that treaty and may thereby become a party or a contracting State to it.

2. Paragraph 1 does not apply if it appears from the treaty or is otherwise established that the application of the treaty in respect of the successor State would be incompatible with the object and purpose of the treaty or would radically change the conditions for its operation.

3. If the treaty is one falling within the category mentioned in article 17, paragraph 3, the successor State may become a party or a contracting State to the treaty only with the consent of all the parties or of all the contracting States.

4. Any treaty to which the successor State becomes a party or a contracting State in conformity with paragraph 1 shall apply only in respect of the part

of the territory of the successor State in respect of which the treaty was signed by one of the predecessor States unless:

(a) in the case of a multilateral treaty not falling within the category mentioned in article 17, paragraph 3, the successor State when ratifying, accepting or approving the treaty gives notice that the treaty shall apply in respect of its entire territory; or

(b) in the case of a multilateral treaty falling within the category mentioned in article 17, paragraph 3, the successor State and all the parties or, as the case may be, all the contracting States otherwise agree.

5. Paragraph 4(a) does not apply if it appears from the treaty or is otherwise established that the application of the treaty in respect of the entire territory of the successor State would be incompatible with the object and purpose of the treaty or would radically change the conditions for its operation.

Article 34—Succession of States in cases of separation of parts of a State

1. When a part or parts of the territory of a State separate to form one or more States, whether or not the predecessor State continues to exist:

(a) any treaty in force at the date of the succession of States in respect of the entire territory of the predecessor State continues in force in respect of each successor State so formed;

(b) any treaty in force at the date of the succession of States in respect only of that part of the territory of the predecessor State which has become a successor State continues in force in respect of that successor State alone.

2. Paragraph 1 does not apply if:

(a) the States concerned otherwise agree; or

(b) it appears from the treaty or is otherwise established that the application of the treaty in respect of the successor State would be incompatible with the object and purpose of the treaty or would radically change the conditions for its operation.

Article 35—Position if a State continues after separation of part of its territory

When, after separation of any part of the territory of a State, the predecessor State continues to exist, any treaty which at the date of the succession of States was in force in respect of the predecessor State continues in force in respect of its remaining territory unless:

(a) the States concerned otherwise agree;

(b) it is established that the treaty related only to the territory which has separated from the predecessor State; or

(c) it appears from the treaty or is otherwise established that the application of the treaty in respect of the predecessor State would be incompatible with the object and purpose of the treaty or would radically change the conditions for its operation.

Article 36—Participation in treaties not in force at the date of the succession of States in cases of separation of parts of a State

1. Subject to paragraphs 3 and 4, a successor State falling under article 34, paragraph 1, may, by making a notification, establish its status as a contracting State to a multilateral treaty which is not in force if, at the date of the succession of States, the predecessor State was a contracting State

to the treaty in respect of the territory to which the succession of States relates.

2. Subject to paragraphs 3 and 4, a successor State falling under article 34, paragraph 1, may, by making a notification, establish its status as a party to a multilateral treaty which enters into force after the date of the succession of States if at that date the predecessor State was a contracting State to the treaty in respect of the territory to which the succession of States relates.

3. Paragraphs 1 and 2 do not apply if it appears from the treaty or is otherwise established that the application of the treaty in respect of the successor State would be incompatible with the object and purpose of the treaty or would radically change the conditions for its operation.

4. If the treaty is one falling within the category mentioned in article 17, paragraph 3, the successor State may establish its status as a party or as a contracting State to the treaty only with the consent of all the parties or of all the contracting States.

Article 37—Participation in cases of separation of parts of a State in treaties signed by the predecessor State subject to ratification, acceptance or approval

1. Subject to paragraphs 2 and 3, if before the date of the succession of States the predecessor State had signed a multilateral treaty subject to ratification, acceptance or approval and the treaty, if it had been in force at that date, would have applied in respect of the territory to which the succession of States relates, a successor State falling under article 34, paragraph 1, may ratify, accept or approve the treaty as if it had signed that treaty and may thereby become a party or a contracting State to it.

2. Paragraph 1 does not apply if it appears from the treaty or is otherwise established that the application of the treaty in respect of the successor State would be incompatible with the object and purpose of the treaty or would radically change the conditions for its operation.

3. If the treaty is one falling within the category mentioned in article 17, paragraph 3, the successor State may become a party or a contracting State to the treaty only with the consent of all the parties or of all the contracting States.

Article 38—Notifications

1. Any notification under articles 31, 32 or 36 shall be made in writing.

2. If the notification is not signed by the Head of State, Head of Government or Minister for Foreign Affairs, the representative of the State communicating it may be called upon to produce full powers.

3. Unless the treaty otherwise provides, the notification shall:

   (a) be transmitted by the successor State to the depositary, or, if there is no depositary, to the parties or the contracting States;
   (b) be considered to be made by the successor State on the date on which it is received by the depositary or, if there is no depositary, on the date on which it is received by all the parties or, as the case may be, by all the contracting States.

4. Paragraph 3 does not affect any duty that the depositary may have, in accordance with the treaty or otherwise, to inform the parties or the con-

tracting States of the notification or any communication made in connection therewith by the successor State.

5. Subject to the provisions of the treaty, such notification or communication shall be considered as received by the State for which it is intended only when the latter State has been informed by the depositary.

PART V

MISCELLANEOUS PROVISIONS

Article 39—Cases of State responsibility and outbreak of hostilities

The provisions of the present Convention shall not prejudge any question that may arise in regard to the effects of a succession of States in respect of a treaty from the international responsibility of a State or from the outbreak of hostilities between States.

Article 40—Cases of military occupation

The provisions of the present Convention shall not prejudge any question that may arise in regard to a treaty from the military occupation of a territory.

PART VI

SETTLEMENT OF DISPUTES

Article 41—Consultation and negotiation

If a dispute regarding the interpretation or application of the present Convention arises between two or more Parties to the Convention, they shall, upon the request of any of them, seek to resolve it by a process of consultation and negotiation.

Article 42—Conciliation

If the dispute is not resolved within six months of the date on which the request referred to in article 41 has been made, any party to the dispute may submit it to the conciliation procedure specified in the Annex to the present Convention by submitting a request to that effect to the Secretary-General of the United Nations and informing the other party or parties to the dispute of the request.

Article 43—Judicial settlement and arbitration

Any State at the time of signature or ratification of the present Convention or accession thereto or at any time thereafter, may, by notification to the depositary, declare that, where a dispute has not been resolved by the application of the procedures referred to in articles 41 and 42, that dispute may be submitted for a decision to the International Court of Justice by a written application of any party to the dispute, or in the alternative to arbitration, provided that the other party to the dispute has made a like declaration.

Article 44—Settlement by common consent

Notwithstanding articles 41, 42, and 43, if a dispute regarding the interpretation or application of the present Convention arises between two or more Parties to the Convention, they may by common consent agree to submit it to the International Court of Justice, or to arbitration, or to any other appropriate procedure for the settlement of disputes.

Article 45—Other provisions in force for the settlement of disputes

Nothing in articles 41 to 44 shall affect the rights or obligations of the Parties to the present Convention under any provisions in force binding them with regard to the settlement of disputes.

PART VII

FINAL PROVISIONS

Article 46—Signature

The present Convention shall be open for signature by all States until 28 February 1979 at the Federal Ministry for Foreign Affairs of the Republic of Austria, and subsequently, until 31 August 1979, at United Nations Headquarters in New York.

Article 47—Ratification

The present Convention is subject to ratification. The instruments of ratification shall be deposited with the Secretary-General of the United Nations.

Article 48—Accession

The present Convention shall remain open for accession by any State. The instruments of accession shall be deposited with the Secretary-General of the United Nations.

Article 49—Entry into force

1. The present Convention shall enter into force on the thirtieth day following the date of deposit of the fifteenth instrument of ratification or accession.

2. For each State ratifying or acceding to the Convention after the deposit of the fifteenth instrument of ratification or accession, the Convention shall enter into force on the thirtieth day after deposit by such State of its instrument of ratification or accession.

Article 50—Authentic texts

The original of the present Convention, of which the Arabic, Chinese, English, French, Russian and Spanish texts are equally authentic, shall be deposited with the Secretary-General of the United Nations.

IN WITNESS WHEREOF the undersigned Plenipotentiaries, being duly authorized thereto by their respective Governments, have signed the present Convention.

DONE at Vienna, this twenty-third day of August, one thousand nine hundred and seventy-eight.

ANNEX

1. A list of conciliators consisting of qualified jurists shall be drawn up and maintained by the Secretary-General of the United Nations. To this end, every State which is a Member of the United Nations or a Party to the present Convention shall be invited to nominate two conciliators, and the names of the persons so nominated shall constitute the list. The term of a conciliator, including that of any conciliator nominated to fill a casual vacancy, shall be five years and may be renewed. A conciliator whose term

expires shall continue to fulfil any function for which he shall have been chosen under the following paragraph.

2. When a request has been made to the Secretary-General under article 42, the Secretary-General shall bring the dispute before a conciliation commission constituted as follows:

The State or States constituting one of the parties to the dispute shall appoint:

(a) one conciliator of the nationality of that State or of one of those States, who may or may not be chosen from the list referred to in paragraph 1; and

(b) one conciliator not of the nationality of that State or of any of those States, who shall be chosen from the list.

The State or States constituting the other party to the dispute shall appoint two conciliators in the same way. The four conciliators chosen by the parties shall be appointed within sixty days following the date on which the Secretary-General receives the request.

The four conciliators shall, within sixty days following the date of the appointment of the last of them, appoint a fifth conciliator chosen from the list, who shall be chairman.

If the appointment of the chairman or of any of the other conciliators has not been made within the period prescribed above for such appointment, it shall be made by the Secretary-General within sixty days following the expiry of that period. The appointment of the chairman may be made by the Secretary-General either from the list or from the membership of the International Law Commission. Any of the periods within which appointments must be made may be extended by agreement between the parties to the dispute.

Any vacancy shall be filled in the manner prescribed for the initial appointment.

3. The Conciliation Commission shall decide its own procedure. The Commission, with the consent of the parties to the dispute, may invite any Party to the present Convention to submit to it its views orally or in writing. Decisions and recommendations of the Commission shall be made by a majority of the five members.

4. The Commission may draw the attention of the parties to the dispute to any measures which might facilitate an amicable settlement.

5. The Commission shall hear the parties, examine the claims and objections, and make proposals to the parties with a view to reaching an amicable settlement of the dispute.

6. The Commission shall report within twelve months of its constitution. Its report shall be deposited with the Secretary-General and transmitted to the parties to the dispute. The report of the Commission, including any conclusions stated therein regarding the facts or questions of law, shall not be binding upon the parties and it shall have no other character than that of recommendations submitted for the consideration of the parties in order to facilitate an amicable settlement of the dispute.

7. The Secretary-General shall provide the Commission with such assistance and facilities as it may require. The expenses of the Commission shall be borne by the United Nations.

附錄三

UNITED NATIONS: VIENNA CONVENTION ON THE LAW OF TREATIES
BETWEEN STATES AND INTERNATIONAL ORGANIZATIONS
OR BETWEEN INTERNATIONAL ORGANIZATIONS*
[Done at Vienna, March 21, 1986]

UNITED NATIONS
GENERAL
ASSEMBLY

A/CONF.129/15
20 March 1986

ENGLISH
Original: ARABIC/CHINESE/
ENGLISH/FRENCH/
RUSSIAN/SPANISH

UNITED NATIONS CONFERENCE ON THE LAW OF
TREATIES BETWEEN STATES AND
INTERNATIONAL ORGANIZATIONS OR
BETWEEN INTERNATIONAL ORGANIZATIONS

Vienna, 18 February - 21 March 1986

VIENNA CONVENTION ON THE LAW OF TREATIES BETWEEN STATES AND INTERNATIONAL

ORGANIZATIONS OR BETWEEN INTERNATIONAL ORGANIZATIONS

The Parties to the present Convention,

Considering the fundamental role of treaties in the history of international
relations,

Recognizing the consensual nature of treaties and their ever-increasing
importance as a source of international law,

Noting that the principles of free consent and of good faith and the
pacta sunt servanda rule are universally recognized,

---

*[Reproduced from U.N. General Assembly Document A/CONF.129/15 of
March 20, 1986.   The Annex on arbitration and conciliation procedures
established in application of Article 66 appears at I.L.M. page 589.
[On March 21, 1986, the following countries signed the Convention:
Austria, Brazil, Burkina Faso, Ivory Coast, Egypt, Mexico, Morocco,
Sudan, Yugoslavia, Zaire and Zambia.]

Affirming the importance of enhancing the process of codification and progressive development of international law at a universal level,

Believing that the codification and progressive development of the rules relating to treaties between States and international organizations or between international organizations are means of enhancing legal order in international relations and of serving the purposes of the United Nations,

Having in mind the principles of international law embodied in the Charter of the United Nations, such as the principles of the equal rights and self-determination of peoples, of the sovereign equality and independence of all States, of non-interference in the domestic affairs of States, of the prohibition of the threat or use of force and of universal respect for, and observance of, human rights and fundamental freedoms for all,

Bearing in mind the provisions of the Vienna Convention on the Law of Treaties of 1969,

Recognizing the relationship between the law of treaties between States and the law of treaties between States and international organizations or between international organizations,

Considering the importance of treaties between States and international organizations or between international organizations as a useful means of developing international relations and ensuring conditions for peaceful co-operation among nations, whatever their constitutional and social systems,

Having in mind the specific features of treaties to which international organizations are parties as subjects of international law distinct from States,

Noting that international organizations possess the capacity to conclude treaties which is necessary for the exercise of their functions and the fulfilment of their purposes,

Recognizing that the practice of international organizations in concluding treaties with States or between themselves should be in accordance with their constituent instruments,

Affirming that nothing in the present Convention should be interpreted as affecting those relations between an international organization and its members which are regulated by the rules of the organization,

Affirming also that disputes concerning treaties, like other international disputes, should be settled, in conformity with the Charter of the United Nations, by peaceful means and in conformity with the principles of justice and international law,

Affirming also that the rules of customary international law will continue to govern questions not regulated by the provisions of the present Convention.

Have agreed as follows:

PART I

INTRODUCTION

Article 1
Scope of the present Convention

The present Convention applies to:

(a) treaties between one or more States and one or more international organizations, and

(b) treaties between international organizations.

Article 2
Use of terms

1. For the purposes of the present Convention:

(a) "treaty" means an international agreement governed by international law and concluded in written form:

(i) between one or more States and one or more international organizations; or

(ii) between international organizations,

whether that agreement is embodied in a single instrument or in two or more related instruments and whatever its particular designation;

(b) "ratification" means the international act so named whereby a State establishes on the international plane its consent to be bound by a treaty;

(b bis) "act of formal confirmation" means an international act corresponding to that of ratification by a State, whereby an international organization establishes on the international plane its consent to be bound by a treaty;

(b ter) "acceptance", "approval" and "accession" mean in each case the international act so named whereby a State or an international organization establishes on the international plane its consent to be bound by a treaty;

(c) "full powers" means a document emanating from the competent authority of a State or from the competent organ of an international organization designating a person or persons to represent the State or the organization for negotiating, adopting or authenticating the text of a treaty, for expressing the consent of the State or of the organization to be bound by a treaty, or for accomplishing any other act with respect to a treaty;

(d) "reservation" means a unilateral statement, however phrased or named, made by a State or by an international organization when signing, ratifying, formally confirming, accepting, approving or acceding to a treaty, whereby it purports to exclude or to modify the legal effect of certain provisions of the treaty in their application to that State or to that organization;

(e) "negotiating State" and "negotiating organization" mean respectively:

(i) a State, or

(ii) an international organization,

which took part in the drawing up and adoption of the text of the treaty;

(f) "contracting State" and "contracting organization" mean respectively:

(i) a State, or

(ii) an international organization,

which has consented to be bound by the treaty, whether or not the treaty has entered into force;

(g) "party" means a State or an international organization which has consented to be bound by the treaty and for which the treaty is in force;

(h) "third State" and "third organization" mean respectively:

(i) a State, or

(ii) an international organization,

not a party to the treaty;

(i) "international organization" means an intergovernmental organization;

(j) "rules of the organization" means, in particular, the constituent instruments, decisions and resolutions adopted in accordance with them, and established practice of the organization.

2.   The provisions of paragraph 1 regarding the use of terms in the present Convention are without prejudice to the use of those terms or to the meanings which may be given to them in the internal law of any State or in the rules of any international organization.

Article 3
International agreements not within the
scope of the present Convention

The fact that the present Convention does not apply:

(i) to international agreements to which one or more States, one or more international organizations and one or more subjects of international law other than States or organizations are parties;

(ii) to international agreements to which one or more international organizations and one or more subjects of international law other than States or organizations are parties;

(iii) to international agreements not in written form between one or more States and one or more international organizations, or between international organizations; or

(iv) to international agreements between subjects of international law other than States or international organizations;

shall not affect:

(a) the legal force of such agreements;

(b) the application to them of any of the rules set forth in the present Convention to which they would be subject under international law independently of the Convention;

(c) the application of the Convention to the relations between States and international organizations or to the relations of organizations as between themselves, when those relations are governed by international agreements to which other subjects of international law are also parties.

Article 4
Non-retroactivity of the present Convention

Without prejudice to the application of any rules set forth in the present Convention to which treaties between one or more States and one or more international organizations or between international organizations would be subject under international law independently of the Convention, the Convention applies only to such treaties concluded after the entry into force of the present Convention with regard to those States and those organizations.

Article 5
Treaties constituting international organizations
and treaties adopted within an
international organization

The present Convention applies to any treaty between one or more States and one or more international organizations which is the constituent instrument of an international organization and to any treaty adopted within an international organization, without prejudice to any relevant rules of the organization.

PART II

CONCLUSION AND ENTRY INTO FORCE OF TREATIES

SECTION 1. CONCLUSION OF TREATIES

Article 6
Capacity of international organizations to conclude treaties

The capacity of an international organization to conclude treaties is governed by the rules of that organization.

Article 7
Full powers

1. A person is considered as representing a State for the purpose of adopting or authenticating the text of a treaty or for the purpose of expressing the consent of the State to be bound by a treaty if:

(a) that person produces appropriate full powers; or

(b) it appears from practice or from other circumstances that it was the intention of the States and international organizations concerned to consider that person as representing the State for such purposes without having to produce full powers.

2. In virtue of their functions and without having to produce full powers, the following are considered as representing their State:

(a) Heads of State, Heads of Government and Ministers for Foreign Affairs, for the purpose of performing all acts relating to the conclusion of a treaty between one or more States and one or more international organizations;

(b) representatives accredited by States to an international conference, for the purpose of adopting the text of a treaty between States and international organizations;

(c) representatives accredited by States to an international organization or one of its organs, for the purpose of adopting the text of a treaty in that organization or organ;

(d) heads of permanent missions to an international organization, for the purpose of adopting the text of a treaty between the accrediting States and that organization.

3. A person is considered as representing an international organization for the purpose of adopting or authenticating the text of a treaty, or expressing the consent of that organization to be bound by a treaty if:

(a) that person produces appropriate full powers; or

(b) it appears from the circumstances that it was the intention of the States and international organizations concerned to consider that person as representing the organization for such purposes, in accordance with the rules of the organization, without having to produce full powers.

Article 8
Subsequent confirmation of an act performed without authorization

An act relating to the conclusion of a treaty performed by a person who cannot be considered under article 7 as authorized to represent a State or an international organization for that purpose is without legal effect unless afterwards confirmed by that State or that organization.

Article 9
Adoption of the text

1. The adoption of the text of a treaty takes place by the consent of all the States and international organizations or, as the case may be, all the organizations participating in its drawing up except as provided in paragraph 2.

2. The adoption of the text of a treaty at an international conference takes place in accordance with the procedure agreed upon by the participants in that conference. If, however, no agreement is reached on any such procedure, the adoption of the text shall take place by the vote of two-thirds of the participants present and voting unless by the same majority they shall decide to apply a different rule.

Article 10
Authentication of the text

1. The text of a treaty between one or more States and one or more international organizations is established as authentic and definitive:

(a) by such procedure as may be provided for in the text or agreed upon by the States and organizations participating in its drawing up; or

(b) failing such procedure, by the signature, signature ad referendum or initialling by the representatives of those States and those organizations of the text of the treaty or of the Final Act of a conference incorporating the text.

2. The text of a treaty between international organizations is established as authentic and definitive:

(a) by such procedure as may be provided for in the text or agreed upon by the organizations participating in its drawing up; or

(b) failing such procedure, by the signature, signature ad referendum or initialling by the representatives of those organizations of the text of the treaty or of the Final Act of a conference incorporating the text.

Article 11
Means of expressing consent to be
bound by a treaty

1. The consent of a State to be bound by a treaty may be expressed by signature, exchange of instruments constituting a treaty, ratification, acceptance, approval or accession, or by any other means if so agreed.

2.　The consent of an international organization to be bound by a treaty may be expressed by signature, exchange of instruments constituting a treaty, act of formal confirmation, acceptance, approval or accession, or by any other means if so agreed.

Article 12
Consent to be bound by a treaty
expressed by signature

1.　The consent of a State or of an international organization to be bound by a treaty is expressed by the signature of the representative of that State or of that organization when:

(a)　the treaty provides that signature shall have that effect;

(b)　it is otherwise established that the negotiating States and negotiating organizations or, as the case may be, the negotiating organizations were agreed that signature should have that effect;　or

(c)　the intention of the State or organization to give that effect to the signature appears from the full powers of its representative or was expressed during the negotiation.

2.　For the purposes of paragraph 1:

(a)　the initialling of a text constitutes a signature of the treaty when it is established that the negotiating States and negotiating organizations or, as the case may be, the negotiating organizations so agreed;

(b)　the signature ad referendum of a treaty by the representative of a State or an international organization, if confirmed by his State or organization, constitutes a full signature of the treaty.

Article 13
Consent to be bound by a treaty expressed by an
exchange of instruments constituting a treaty

The consent of States or of international organizations to be bound by a treaty constituted by instruments exchanged between them is expressed by that exchange when:

(a) the instruments provide that their exchange shall have that effect; or

(b) it is otherwise established that those States and those organizations or, as the case may be, those organizations were agreed that the exchange of instruments should have that effect.

Article 14

Consent to be bound by a treaty expressed by
ratification, act of formal confirmation,
acceptance or approval

1. The consent of a State to be bound by a treaty is expressed by ratification when:

(a) the treaty provides for such consent to be expressed by means of ratification;

(b) it is otherwise established that the negotiating States and negotiating organizations were agreed that ratification should be required;

(c) the representative of the State has signed the treaty subject to ratification; or

(d) the intention of the State to sign the treaty subject to ratification appears from the full powers of its representative or was expressed during the negotiation.

2. The consent of an international organization to be bound by a treaty is expressed by an act of formal confirmation when:

(a) the treaty provides for such consent to be expressed by means of an act of formal confirmation;

(b) it is otherwise established that the negotiating States and negotiating organizations or, as the case may be, the negotiating organizations were agreed that an act of formal confirmation should be required;

(c) the representative of the organization has signed the treaty subject to an act of formal confirmation; or

(d) the intention of the organization to sign the treaty subject to an act of formal confirmation appears from the full powers of its representative or was expressed during the negotiation.

3. The consent of a State or of an international organization to be bound by a treaty is expressed by acceptance or approval under conditions similar to those which apply to ratification or, as the case may be, to an act of formal confirmation.

Article 15
Consent to be bound by a treaty expressed by accession

The consent of a State or of an international organization to be bound by a treaty is expressed by accession when:

(a) the treaty provides that such consent may be expressed by that State or that organization by means of accession;

(b) it is otherwise established that the negotiating States and negotiating organizations or, as the case may be, the negotiating organizations were agreed that such consent may be expressed by that State or that organization by means of accession; or

(c) all the parties have subsequently agreed that such consent may be expressed by that State or that organization by means of accession.

Article 16
Exchange or deposit of instruments of ratification, formal confirmation, acceptance, approval or accession

1. Unless the treaty otherwise provides, instruments of ratification, instruments relating to an act of formal confirmation or instruments of acceptance, approval or accession establish the consent of a State or of an international organization to

be bound by a treaty between one or more States and one or more international organizations upon:

    (a) their exchange between the contracting States and contracting organizations;

    (b) their deposit with the depositary; or

    (c) their notification to the contracting States and to the contracting organizations or to the depositary, if so agreed.

2. Unless the treaty otherwise provides, instruments relating to an act of formal confirmation or instruments of acceptance, approval or accession establish the consent of an international organization to be bound by a treaty between international organizations upon:

    (a) their exchange between the contracting organizations;

    (b) their deposit with the depositary; or

    (c) their notification to the contracting organizations or to the depositary, if so agreed.

Article 17
Consent to be bound by part of a treaty and choice of differing provisions

. Without prejudice to articles 19 to 23, the consent of a State or of an international organization to be bound by part of a treaty is effective only if the treaty so permits, or if the contracting States and contracting organizations or, s the case may be, the contracting organizations so agree.

. The consent of a State or of an international organization to be bound by a treaty which permits a choice between differing provisions is effective only if it s made clear to which of the provisions the consent relates.

Article 18
Obligation not to defeat the object and purpose of a treaty
prior to its entry into force

A State or an international organization is obliged to refrain from acts which would defeat the object and purpose of a treaty when:

(a) that State or that organization has signed the treaty or has exchanged instruments constituting the treaty subject to ratification, act of formal confirmation, acceptance or approval, until that State or that organization shall have made its intention clear not to become a party to the treaty; or

(b) that State or that organization has expressed its consent to be bound by the treaty, pending the entry into force of the treaty and provided that such entry into force is not unduly delayed.

SECTION 2. RESERVATIONS

Article 19
Formulation of reservations

A State or an international organization may, when signing, ratifying, formally confirming, accepting, approving or acceding to a treaty, formulate a reservation unless:

(a) the reservation is prohibited by the treaty;

(b) the treaty provides that only specified reservations, which do not include the reservation in question, may be made; or

(c) in cases not falling under sub-paragraphs (a) and (b), the reservation is incompatible with the object and purpose of the treaty.

Article 20
Acceptance of and objection to reservations

1.   A reservation expressly authorized by a treaty does not require any subsequent acceptance by the contracting States and contracting organizations or, as the case may be, by the contracting organizations unless the treaty so provides.

2.   When it appears from the limited number of the negotiating States and negotiating organizations or, as the case may be, of the negotiating organizations and the object and purpose of a treaty that the application of the treaty in its entirety between all the parties is an essential condition of the consent of each one to be bound by the treaty, a reservation requires acceptance by all the parties.

3.   When a treaty is a constituent instrument of an international organization and unless it otherwise provides, a reservation requires the acceptance of the competent organ of that organization.

4.   In cases not falling under the preceding paragraphs and unless the treaty otherwise provides:

    (a) acceptance of a reservation by a contracting State or by a contracting organization constitutes the reserving State or international organization a party to the treaty in relation to the accepting State or organization if or when the treaty is in force for the reserving State or organization and for the accepting State or organization;

    (b) an objection by a contracting State or by a contracting organization to a reservation does not preclude the entry into force of the treaty as between the objecting State or international organization and the reserving State or organization unless a contrary intention is definitely expressed by the objecting State or organization;

    (c) an act expressing the consent of a State or of an international organization to be bound by the treaty and containing a reservation is effective as soon as at least one contracting State or one contracting organization has accepted the reservation.

5.   For the purposes of paragraphs 2 and 4 and unless the treaty otherwise provides, a reservation is considered to have been accepted by a State or an international organization if it shall have raised no objection to the reservation by the end of a period of twelve months after it was notified of the reservation or by the date on which it expressed its consent to be bound by the treaty, whichever is later.

Article 21
Legal effects of reservations and
of objections to reservations

1.   A reservation established with regard to another party in accordance with articles 19, 20 and 23:

(a) modifies for the reserving State or international organization in its relations with that other party the provisions of the treaty to which the reservation relates to the extent of the reservation; and

(b) modifies those provisions to the same extent for that other party in its relations with the reserving State or international organization.

2.   The reservation does not modify the provisions of the treaty for the other parties to the treaty inter se.

3.   When a State or an international organization objecting to a reservation has not opposed the entry into force of the treaty between itself and the reserving State or organization, the provisions to which the reservation relates do not apply as between the reserving State or organization and the objecting State or organization to the extent of the reservation.

Article 22
Withdrawal of reservations and of objections to reservations

1.   Unless the treaty otherwise provides, a reservation may be withdrawn at any time and the consent of a State or of an international organization which has accepted the reservation is not required for its withdrawal.

2.   Unless the treaty otherwise provides, an objection to a reservation may be withdrawn at any time.

3.   Unless the treaty otherwise provides, or it is otherwise agreed:

(a) the withdrawal of a reservation becomes operative in relation to a contracting State or a contracting organization only when notice of it has been received by that State or that organization;

(b) the withdrawal of an objection to a reservation becomes operative only when notice of it has been received by the State or international organization which formulated the reservation.

Article 23
Procedure regarding reservations

. A reservation, an express acceptance of a reservation and an objection to a reservation must be formulated in writing and communicated to the contracting States and contracting organizations and other States and international organizations entitled to become parties to the treaty.

. If formulated when signing the treaty subject to ratification, act of formal confirmation, acceptance or approval, a reservation must be formally confirmed by the reserving State or international organization when expressing its consent to be bound by the treaty. In such a case the reservation shall be considered as having been made on the date of its confirmation.

. An express acceptance of, or an objection to, a reservation made previously to confirmation of the reservation does not itself require confirmation.

. The withdrawal of a reservation or of an objection to a reservation must be formulated in writing.

SECTION 3. ENTRY INTO FORCE AND PROVISIONAL
APPLICATION OF TREATIES

Article 24
Entry into force

. A treaty enters into force in such manner and upon such date as it may provide or as the negotiating States and negotiating organizations or, as the case may be, the negotiating organizations may agree.

. Failing any such provision or agreement, a treaty enters into force as soon as consent to be bound by the treaty has been established for all the negotiating States and negotiating organizations or, as the case may be, all the negotiating organizations.

3. When the consent of a State or of an international organization to be bound by a treaty is established on a date after the treaty has come into force, the treaty enters into force for that State or that organization on that date, unless the treaty otherwise provides.

4. The provisions of a treaty regulating the authentication of its text, the establishment of consent to be bound by the treaty, the manner or date of its entry into force, reservations, the functions of the depositary and other matters arising necessarily before the entry into force of the treaty apply from the time of the adoption of its text.

Article 25
Provisional application

1. A treaty or a part of a treaty is applied provisionally pending its entry into force if:

(a) the treaty itself so provides; or

(b) the negotiating States and negotiating organizations or, as the case may be, the negotiating organizations have in some other manner so agreed.

2. Unless the treaty otherwise provides or the negotiating States and negotiating organizations or, as the case may be, the negotiating organizations have otherwise agreed, the provisional application of a treaty or a part of a treaty with respect to a State or an international organization shall be terminated if that State or that organization notifies the States and organizations with regard to which the treaty is being applied provisionally of its intention not to become a party to the treaty.

PART III

OBSERVANCE, APPLICATION AND
INTERPRETATION OF TREATIES

SECTION 1. OBSERVANCE OF TREATIES
Article 26
Pacta sunt servanda

Every treaty in force is binding upon the parties to it and must be performed by them in good faith.

Article 27
Internal law of States, rules of international organizations
and observance of treaties

1. A State party to a treaty may not invoke the provisions of its internal law as justification for its failure to perform the treaty.

2. An international organization party to a treaty may not invoke the rules of the organization as justification for its failure to perform the treaty.

3. The rules contained in the preceding paragraphs are without prejudice to article 46.

SECTION 2. APPLICATION OF TREATIES

Article 28
Non-retroactivity of treaties

Unless a different intention appears from the treaty or is otherwise established, its provisions do not bind a party in relation to any act or fact which took place or any situation which ceased to exist before the date of the entry into force of the treaty with respect to that party.

Article 29
Territorial scope of treaties

Unless a different intention appears from the treaty or is otherwise established, a treaty between one or more States and one or more international organizations is binding upon each State party in respect of its entire territory.

Article 30
Application of successive treaties relating
to the same subject-matter

. The rights and obligations of States and international organizations parties to successive treaties relating to the same subject-matter shall be determined in accordance with the following paragraphs.

2. When a treaty specifies that it is subject to, or that it is· not to be considered as incompatible with, an earlier or later treaty, the provisions of that other treaty prevail.

3. When all the parties to the earlier treaty are parties also to the later treaty but the earlier treaty is not terminated or suspended in operation under article 59, the earlier treaty applies only to the extent that its provisions are compatible with those of the later treaty.

4. When the parties to the later treaty do not include all the parties to the earlier one:

(a) as between two parties, each of which is a party to both treaties, the same rule applies as in paragraph 3;

(b) as between a party to both treaties and a party to only one of the treaties, the treaty to which both are parties governs their mutual rights and obligations.

5. Paragraph 4 is without prejudice to article 41, or to any question of the termination or suspension of the operation of a treaty under article 60 or to any question of responsibility which may arise for a State or for an international organization from the conclusion or application of a treaty the provisions of which are incompatible with its obligations towards a State or an organization under another treaty.

6. The preceding paragraphs are without prejudice to the fact that, in the event of a conflict between obligations under the Charter of the United Nations and obligations under a treaty, the obligations under the Charter shall prevail.

SECTION 3. INTERPRETATION OF TREATIES

Article 31
General rule of interpretation

1. A treaty shall be interpreted in good faith in accordance with the ordinary meaning to be given to the terms of the treaty in their context and in the light of its object and purpose.

2. The context for the purpose of the interpretation of a treaty shall comprise, in addition to the text, including its preamble and annexes:

(a) any agreement relating to the treaty which was made between all the parties in connection with the conclusion of the treaty;

(b) any instrument which was made by one or more parties in connection with the conclusion of the treaty and accepted by the other parties as an instrument related to the treaty.

3. There shall be taken into account, together with the context:

(a) any subsequent agreement between the parties regarding the interpretation of the treaty or the application of its provisions;

(b) any subsequent practice in the application of the treaty which establishes the agreement of the parties regarding its interpretation;

(c) any relevant rules of international law applicable in the relations between the parties.

4. A special meaning shall be given to a term if it is established that the parties so intended.

Article 32
Supplementary means of interpretation

Recourse may be had to supplementary means of interpretation, including the preparatory work of the treaty and the circumstances of its conclusion, in order to confirm the meaning resulting from the application of article 31, or to determine the meaning when the interpretation according to article 31:

(a) leaves the meaning ambiguous or obscure; or

(b) leads to a result which is manifestly absurd or unreasonable.

Article 33
Interpretation of treaties authenticated
in two or more languages

1. When a treaty has been authenticated in two or more languages, the text is equally authoritative in each language, unless the treaty provides or the parties agree that, in case of divergence, a particular text shall prevail.

2. A version of the treaty in a language other than one of those in which the text was authenticated shall be considered an authentic text only if the treaty so provides or the parties so agree.

3. The terms of a treaty are presumed to have the same meaning in each authentic text.

4. Except where a particular text prevails in accordance with paragraph 1, when a comparison of the authentic texts discloses a difference of meaning which the application of articles 31 and 32 does not remove, the meaning which best reconciles the texts, having regard to the object and purpose of the treaty, shall be adopted.

SECTION 4. TREATIES AND THIRD STATES
OR THIRD ORGANIZATIONS

Article 34
General rule regarding third States
and third organizations

A treaty does not create either obligations or rights for a third State or a third organization without the consent of that State or that organization.

Article 35
Treaties providing for obligations for
third States or third organizations

An obligation arises for a third State or a third organization from provision of a treaty if the parties to the treaty intend the provision to be th means of establishing the obligation and the third State or the third organizatio expressly accepts that obligation in writing. Acceptance by the third organizatio of such an obligation shall be governed by the rules of that organization.

Article 36
Treaties providing for rights for third
States or third organizations

A right arises for a third State from a provision of a treaty if the parties the treaty intend the provision to accord that right either to the third State, to a group of States to which it belongs, or to all States, and the third State sents thereto. Its assent shall be presumed so long as the contrary is not licated, unless the treaty otherwise provides.

A right arises for a third organization from a provision of a treaty if the ties to the treaty intend the provision to accord that right either to the third anization, or to a group of international organizations to which it belongs, or all organizations, and the third organization assents thereto. Its assent shall governed by the rules of the organization.

A State or an international organization exercising a right in accordance with agraph 1 or 2 shall comply with the conditions for its exercise provided for in treaty or established in conformity with the treaty.

Article 37
Revocation or modification of obligations
or rights of third States
or third organizations

When an obligation has arisen for a third State or a third organization formity with article 35, the obligation may be revoked or modified only with t ent of the parties to the treaty and of the third State or the thi nization, unless it is established that they had otherwise agreed.

When a right has arisen for a third State or a third organization ormity with article 36, the right may not be revoked or modified by the part t is established that the right was intended not to be revocable or subject fication without the consent of the third State or the third organization.

The consent of an international organization party to the treaty or of a third nization, as provided for in the foregoing paragraphs, shall be governed by the s of that organization.

Article 38
Rules in a treaty becoming binding on third States or
third organizations through international custom

Nothing in articles 34 to 37 precludes a rule set forth in a treaty from
becoming binding upon a third State or a third organization as a customary rule of
international law, recognized as such.

PART IV

AMENDMENT AND MODIFICATION OF TREATIES

Article 39
General rule regarding the amendment of treaties

1.   A treaty may be amended by agreement between the parties. The rules laid down
in Part II apply to such an agreement except in so far as the treaty may otherwise
provide.

2.   The consent of an international organization to an agreement provided for in
paragraph 1 shall be governed by the rules of that organization.

Article 40
Amendment of multilateral treaties

1.   Unless the treaty otherwise provides, the amendment of multilateral treaties
shall be governed by the following paragraphs.

2.   Any proposal to amend a multilateral treaty as between all the parties must be
notified to all the contracting States and all the contracting organizations, each
one of which shall have the right to take part in:

    (a) the decision as to the action to be taken in regard to such proposal;

    (b) the negotiation and conclusion of any agreement for the amendment of the
treaty.

3.   Every State or international organization entitled to become a party to the
treaty shall also be entitled to become a party to the treaty as amended.

4. The amending agreement does not bind any State or international organization already a party to the treaty which does not become a party to the amending agreement; article 30, paragraph 4(b), applies in relation to such State or organization.

5. Any State or international organization which becomes a party to the treaty after the entry into force of the amending agreement shall, failing an expression of a different intention by that State or that organization:

(a) be considered as a party to the treaty as amended; and

(b) be considered as a party to the unamended treaty in relation to any party to the treaty not bound by the amending agreement.

Article 41
Agreements to modify multilateral treaties between certain of the parties only

1. Two or more of the parties to a multilateral treaty may conclude an agreement to modify the treaty as between themselves alone if:

(a) the possibility of such a modification is provided for by the treaty; or

(b) the modification in question is not prohibited by the treaty and:

(i) does not affect the enjoyment by the other parties of their rights under the treaty or the performance of their obligations;

(ii) does not relate to a provision, derogation from which is incompatible with the effective execution of the object and purpose of the treaty as a whole.

2. Unless in a case falling under paragraph 1 (a) the treaty otherwise provides, the parties in question shall notify the other parties of their intention to conclude the agreement and of the modification to the treaty for which it provides.

PART V

INVALIDITY, TERMINATION AND SUSPENSION
OF THE OPERATION OF TREATIES

SECTION 1. GENERAL PROVISIONS

Article 42
Validity and continuance in force of treaties

1.   The validity of a treaty or of the consent of a State or an international
organization to be bound by a treaty may be impeached only through the application
of the present Convention.

2.   The termination of a treaty, its denunciation or the withdrawal of a party,
may take place only as a result of the application of the provisions of the treaty
or of the present Convention. The same rule applies to suspension of the operation
of a treaty.

Article 43
Obligations imposed by international law
independently of a treaty

The invalidity, termination or denunciation of a treaty, the withdrawal of a
party from it, or the suspension of its operation, as a result of the application
of the present Convention or of the provisions of the treaty, shall not in any way
impair the duty of any State or of any international organization to fulfil any
obligation embodied in the treaty to which that State or that organization would be
subject under international law independently of the treaty.

Article 44
Separability of treaty provisions

1.   A right of a party, provided for in a treaty or arising under article 56, to
denounce, withdraw from or suspend the operation of the treaty may be exercised
only with respect to the whole treaty unless the treaty otherwise provides or the
parties otherwise agree.

2.   A ground for invalidating, terminating, withdrawing from or suspending the
operation of a treaty recognized in the present Convention may be invoked only with

respect to the whole treaty except as provided in the following paragraphs or in article 60.

3. If the ground relates solely to particular clauses, it may be invoked only with respect to those clauses where:

(a) the said clauses are separable from the remainder of the treaty with regard to their application;

(b) it appears from the treaty or is otherwise established that acceptance of those clauses was not an essential basis of the consent of the other party or parties to be bound by the treaty as a whole; and

(c) continued performance of the remainder of the treaty would not be unjust.

4. In cases falling under articles 49 and 50, the State or international organization entitled to invoke the fraud or corruption may do so with respect either to the whole treaty or, subject to paragraph 3, to the particular clauses alone.

5. In cases falling under articles 51, 52 and 53, no separation of the provisions of the treaty is permitted.

Article 45
Loss of a right to invoke a ground for invalidating, terminating, withdrawing from or suspending the operation of a treaty

. A State may no longer invoke a ground for invalidating, terminating, withdrawing from or suspending the operation of a treaty under articles 46 to 50 or rticles 60 and 62 if, after becoming aware of the facts:

(a) it shall have expressly agreed that the treaty is valid or remains in orce or continues in operation, as the case may be; or

(b) it must by reason of its conduct be considered as having acquiesced in he validity of the treaty or in its maintenance in force or in operation, as the ase may be.

2. An international organization may no longer invoke a ground for invalidating, terminating, withdrawing from or suspending the operation of a treaty under articles 46 to 50 or articles 60 and 62 if, after becoming aware of the facts:

(a) it shall have expressly agreed that the treaty is valid or remains in force or continues in operation, as the case may be; or

(b) it must by reason of the conduct of the competent organ be considered as having renounced the right to invoke that ground.

SECTION 2. INVALIDITY OF TREATIES

Article 46
Provisions of internal law of a State and rules of an international
organization regarding competence to conclude treaties

1. A State may not invoke the fact that its consent to be bound by a treaty has been expressed in violation of a provision of its internal law regarding competence to conclude treaties as invalidating its consent unless that violation was manifest and concerned a rule of its internal law of fundamental importance.

2. An international organization may not invoke the fact that its consent to be bound by a treaty has been expressed in violation of the rules of the organization regarding competence to conclude treaties as invalidating its consent unless that violation was manifest and concerned a rule of fundamental importance.

3. A violation is manifest if it would be objectively evident to any State or any international organization conducting itself in the matter in accordance with the normal practice of States and, where appropriate, of international organizations and in good faith.

Article 47
Specific restrictions on authority to express the consent
of a State or an international organization

If the authority of a representative to express the consent of a State or of an international organization to be bound by a particular treaty has been made subject to a specific restriction, his omission to observe that restriction may not be invoked as invalidating the consent expressed by him unless the restriction was notified to the negotiating States and negotiating organizations prior to his expressing such consent.

Article 48
Error

1.   A State or an international organization may invoke an error in a treaty as invalidating its consent to be bound by the treaty if the error relates to a fact or situation which was assumed by that State or that organization to exist at the time when the treaty was concluded and formed an essential basis of the consent of that State or that organization to be bound by the treaty.

2.   Paragraph 1 shall not apply if the State or international organization in question contributed by its own conduct to the error or if the circumstances were such as to put that State or that organization on notice of a possible error.

3.   An error relating only to the wording of the text of a treaty does not affect its validity;   article 80 then applies.

Article 49
Fraud

A State or an international organization induced to conclude a treaty by the fraudulent conduct of a negotiating State or a negotiating organization may invoke the fraud as invalidating its consent to be bound by the treaty.

Article 50
Corruption of a representative of a State
or of an international organization

A State or an international organization the expression of whose consent to be bound by a treaty has been procured through the corruption of its representative directly or indirectly by a negotiating State or a negotiating organization may invoke such corruption as invalidating its consent to be bound by the treaty.

Article 51
Coercion of a representative of a State
or of an international organization

The expression by a State or an international organization of consent to be bound by a treaty which has been procured by the coercion of the representative of that State or that organization through acts or threats directed against him shall be without any legal effect.

Article 52
Coercion of a State or of an international organization by the threat or use of force

A treaty is void if its conclusion has been procured by the threat or use of force in violation of the principles of international law embodied in the Charter of the United Nations.

Article 53
Treaties conflicting with a peremptory norm of general international law (jus cogens)

A treaty is void if, at the time of its conclusion, it conflicts with a peremptory norm of general international law. For the purposes of the present Convention, a peremptory norm of general international law is a norm accepted and recognized by the international community of States as a whole as a norm from which no derogation is permitted and which can be modified only by a subsequent norm of general international law having the same character.

SECTION 3. TERMINATION AND SUSPENSION OF THE OPERATION OF TREATIES

Article 54
Termination of or withdrawal from a treaty under its provisions or by consent of the parties

The termination of a treaty or the withdrawal of a party may take place:

(a) in conformity with the provisions of the treaty; or

(b) at any time by consent of all the parties after consultation with the contracting States and contracting organizations.

Article 55
Reduction of the parties to a multilateral treaty below the number necessary for its entry into force

Unless the treaty otherwise provides, a multilateral treaty does not terminate by reason only of the fact that the number of the parties falls below the number necessary for its entry into force.

Article 56
Denunciation of or withdrawal from a treaty containing no provision regarding termination, denunciation or withdrawal

1. A treaty which contains no provision regarding its termination and which does not provide for denunciation or withdrawal is not subject to denunciation or withdrawal unless:

(a) it is established that the parties intended to admit the possibility of denunciation or withdrawal; or

(b) a right of denunciation or withdrawal may be implied by the nature of the treaty.

2. A party shall give not less than twelve months' notice of its intention to denounce or withdraw from a treaty under paragraph 1.

Article 57
Suspension of the operation of a treaty under its provisions or by consent of the parties

The operation of a treaty in regard to all the parties or to a particular party may be suspended:

(a) in conformity with the provisions of the treaty; or

(b) at any time by consent of all the parties after consultation with the contracting States and contracting organizations.

Article 58
Suspension of the operation of a multilateral treaty by
agreement between certain of the parties only

1.   Two or more parties to a multilateral treaty may conclude an agreement to suspend the operation of provisions of the treaty, temporarily and as between themselves alone, if:

(a)   the possibility of such a suspension is provided for by the treaty;   or

(b)   the suspension in question is not prohibited by the treaty and:

(i)   does not affect the enjoyment by the other parties of their rights under the treaty or the performance of their obligations;

(ii)   is not incompatible with the object and purpose of the treaty.

2.   Unless in a case falling under paragraph 1(a) the treaty otherwise provides, the parties in question shall notify the other parties of their intention to conclude the agreement and of those provisions of the treaty the operation of which they intend to suspend.

Article 59
Termination or suspension of the operation
of a treaty implied by conclusion
of a later treaty

1.   A treaty shall be considered as terminated if all the parties to it conclude a later treaty relating to the same subject-matter and:

(a)   it appears from the later treaty or is otherwise established that the parties intended that the matter should be governed by that treaty;   or

(b)   the provisions of the later treaty are so far incompatible with those of the earlier one that the two treaties are not capable of being applied at the same time.

2.   The earlier treaty shall be considered as only suspended in operation if it appears from the later treaty or is otherwise established that such was the intention of the parties.

Article 60
Termination or suspension of the operation of a treaty
as a consequence of its breach

1. A material breach of a bilateral treaty by one of the parties entitles the other to invoke the breach as a ground for terminating the treaty or suspending its operation in whole or in part.

2. A material breach of a multilateral treaty by one of the parties entitles:

(a) the other parties by unanimous agreement to suspend the operation of the treaty in whole or in part or to terminate it either:

(i) in the relations between themselves and the defaulting State or international organization, or

(ii) as between all the parties;

(b) a party specially affected by the breach to invoke it as a ground for suspending the operation of the treaty in whole or in part in the relations between itself and the defaulting State or international organization;

(c) any party other than the defaulting State or international organization to invoke the breach as a ground for suspending the operation of the treaty in whole or in part with respect to itself if the treaty is of such a character that a material breach of its provisions by one party radically changes the position of every party with respect to the further performance of its obligations under the treaty.

3. A material breach of a treaty, for the purposes of this article, consists in:

(a) a repudiation of the treaty not sanctioned by the present Convention; or

(b) the violation of a provision essential to the accomplishment of the object or purpose of the treaty.

4. The foregoing paragraphs are without prejudice to any provision in the treaty applicable in the event of a breach.

5. Paragraphs 1 to 3 do not apply to provisions relating to the protection of the human person contained in treaties of a humanitarian character, in particular to provisions prohibiting any form of reprisals against persons protected by such treaties.

Article 61
Supervening impossibility of performance

1. A party may invoke the impossibility of performing a treaty as a ground for terminating or withdrawing from it if the impossibility results from the permanent disappearance or destruction of an object indispensable for the execution of the treaty. If the impossibility is temporary, it may be invoked only as a ground for suspending the operation of the treaty.

2. Impossibility of performance may not be invoked by a party as a ground for terminating, withdrawing from or suspending the operation of a treaty if the impossibility is the result of a breach by that party either of an obligation under the treaty or of any other international obligation owed to any other party to the treaty.

Article 62
Fundamental change of circumstances

1. A fundamental change of circumstances which has occurred with regard to those existing at the time of the conclusion of a treaty, and which was not foreseen by the parties, may not be invoked as a ground for terminating or withdrawing from the treaty unless:

(a) the existence of those circumstances constituted an essential basis of the consent of the parties to be bound by the treaty; and

(b) the effect of the change is radically to transform the extent of obligations still to be performed under the treaty.

2. A fundamental change of circumstances may not be invoked as a ground for terminating or withdrawing from a treaty between two or more States and one or more international organizations if the treaty establishes a boundary.

3.　A fundamental change of circumstances may not be invoked as a ground for terminating or withdrawing from a treaty if the fundamental change is the result of a breach by the party invoking it either of an obligation under the treaty or of any other international obligation owed to any other party to the treaty.

4.　If, under the foregoing paragraphs, a party may invoke a fundamental change of circumstances as a ground for terminating or withdrawing from a treaty it may also invoke the change as a ground for suspending the operation of the treaty.

Article 63
Severance of diplomatic or
consular relations

The severance of diplomatic or consular relations between States parties to a treaty between two or more States and one or more international organizations does not affect the legal relations established between those States by the treaty except in so far as the existence of diplomatic or consular relations is indispensable for the application of the treaty.

Article 64
Emergence of a new peremptory norm of
general international law (jus cogens)

If a new peremptory norm of general international law emerges, any existing treaty which is in conflict with that norm becomes void and terminates.

SECTION 4.　PROCEDURE

Article 65
Procedure to be followed with respect to invalidity,
termination, withdrawal from or suspension
of the operation of a treaty

1.　A party which, under the provisions of the present Convention, invokes either a defect in its consent to be bound by a treaty or a ground for impeaching the validity of a treaty, terminating it, withdrawing from it or suspending its operation, must notify the other parties of its claim. The notification shall indicate the measure proposed to be taken with respect to the treaty and the reasons therefor.

2. If, after the expiry of a period which, except in cases of special urgency, shall not be less than three months after the receipt of the notification, no party has raised any objection, the party making the notification may carry out in the manner provided in article 67 the measure which it has proposed.

3. If, however, objection has been raised by any other party, the parties shall seek a solution through the means indicated in Article 33 of the Charter of the United Nations.

4. The notification or objection made by an international organization shall be governed by the rules of that organization.

5. Nothing in the foregoing paragraphs shall affect the rights or obligations of the parties under any provisions in force binding the parties with regard to the settlement of disputes.

6. Without prejudice to article 45, the fact that a State or an international organization has not previously made the notification prescribed in paragraph 1 shall not prevent it from making such notification in answer to another party claiming performance of the treaty or alleging its violation.

Article 66
Procedures for judicial settlement, arbitration and conciliation

1. If, under paragraph 3 of article 65, no solution has been reached within a period of twelve months following the date on which the objection was raised, the procedures specified in the following paragraphs shall be followed.

2. With respect to a dispute concerning the application or the interpretation of article 53 or 64:

(a) if a State is a party to the dispute with one or more States, it may, by a written application, submit the dispute to the International Court of Justice for a decision;

(b) if a State is a party to the dispute to which one or more international organizations are parties, the State may, through a Member State of the United Nations if necessary, request the General Assembly or the Security Council or, where appropriate, the competent organ of an international organization which is a party to the dispute and is authorized in accordance with Article 96 of the Charter of the United Nations, to request an advisory opinion of the International Court of Justice in accordance with article 65 of the Statute of the Court;

(c) if the United Nations or an international organization that is authorized in accordance with Article 96 of the Charter of the United Nations is a party to the dispute, it may request an advisory opinion of the International Court of Justice in accordance with article 65 of the Statute of the Court;

(d) if an international organization other than those referred to in sub-paragraph (c) is a party to the dispute, it may, through a Member State of the United Nations, follow the procedure specified in sub-paragraph (b);

(e) the advisory opinion given pursuant to sub-paragraph (b), (c) or (d) shall be accepted as decisive by all the parties to the dispute concerned;

(f) if the request under sub-paragraph (b), (c) or (d) for an advisory opinion of the Court is not granted, any one of the parties to the dispute may, by written notification to the other party or parties, submit it to arbitration in accordance with the provisions of the Annex to the present Convention.

3. The provisions of paragraph 2 apply unless all the parties to a dispute referred to in that paragraph by common consent agree to submit the dispute to an arbitration procedure, including the one specified in the Annex to the present Convention. [*]

4. With respect to a dispute concerning the application or the interpretation of any of the articles in Part V, other than articles 53 and 64, of the present Convention, any one of the parties to the dispute may set in motion the conciliation procedure specified in the Annex to the Convention by submitting a request to that effect to the Secretary-General of the United Nations.

---

*[I.L.M. page 589.]

Article 67
Instruments for declaring invalid, terminating, withdrawing from or suspending the operation of a treaty

1.   The notification provided for under article 65, paragraph 1 must be made in writing.

2.   Any act declaring invalid, terminating, withdrawing from or suspending the operation of a treaty pursuant to the provisions of the treaty or of paragraphs 2 or 3 of article 65 shall be carried out through an instrument communicated to the other parties.   If the instrument emanating from a State is not signed by the Head of State, Head of Government or Minister for Foreign Affairs, the representative of the State communicating it may be called upon to produce full powers.   If the instrument emanates from an international organization, the representative of the organization communicating it may be called upon to produce full powers.

Article 68
Revocation of notifications and instruments provided for in articles 65 and 67

A notification or instrument provided for in articles 65 or 67 may be revoked at any time before it takes effect.

SECTION 5.   CONSEQUENCES OF THE INVALIDITY, TERMINATION OR SUSPENSION OF THE OPERATION OF A TREATY

Article 69
Consequences of the invalidity of a treaty

1.   A treaty the invalidity of which is established under the present Convention is void. The provisions of a void treaty have no legal force.

2.   If acts have nevertheless been performed in reliance on such a treaty:

(a)   each party may require any other party to establish as far as possible in their mutual relations the position that would have existed if the acts had not been performed;

(b) acts performed in good faith before the invalidity was invoked are not rendered unlawful by reason only of the invalidity of the treaty.

3. In cases falling under articles 49, 50, 51 or 52, paragraph 2 does not apply with respect to the party to which the fraud, the act of corruption or the coercion is imputable.

4. In the case of the invalidity of the consent of a particular State or a particular international organization to be bound by a multilateral treaty, the foregoing rules apply in the relations between that State or that organization and the parties to the treaty.

Article 70
Consequences of the termination of a treaty

1. Unless the treaty otherwise provides or the parties otherwise agree, the termination of a treaty under its provisions or in accordance with the present Convention:

(a) releases the parties from any obligation further to perform the treaty;

(b) does not affect any right, obligation or legal situation of the parties created through the execution of the treaty prior to its termination.

2. If a State or an international organization denounces or withdraws from a multilateral treaty, paragraph 1 applies in the relations between that State or that organization and each of the other parties to the treaty from the date when such denunciation or withdrawal takes effect.

Article 71
Consequences of the invalidity of a treaty which conflicts
with a peremptory norm of general international law

1. In the case of a treaty which is void under article 53 the parties shall:

(a) eliminate as far as possible the consequences of any act performed in reliance on any provision which conflicts with the peremptory norm of general international law; and

(b) bring their mutual relations into conformity with the peremptory norm of general international law.

2.   In the case of a treaty which becomes void and terminates under article 64, the termination of the treaty:

(a) releases the parties from any obligation further to perform the treaty;

(b) does not affect any right, obligation or legal situation of the parties created through the execution of the treaty prior to its termination;   provided that those rights, obligations or situations may thereafter be maintained only to the extent that their maintenance is not in itself in conflict with the new peremptory norm of general international law.

Article 72
Consequences of the suspension of the
operation of a treaty

1.   Unless the treaty otherwise provides or the parties otherwise agree, the suspension of the operation of a treaty under its provisions or in accordance with the present Convention:

(a) releases the parties between which the operation of the treaty is suspended from the obligation to perform the treaty in their mutual relations during the period of the suspension;

(b) does not otherwise affect the legal relations between the parties established by the treaty.

2.   During the period of the suspension the parties shall refrain from acts tending to obstruct the resumption of the operation of the treaty.

PART VI

MISCELLANEOUS PROVISIONS
Article 73
Relationship to the Vienna Convention on the Law of Treaties

As between States parties to the Vienna Convention on the Law of Treaties of 1969, the relations of those States under a treaty between two or more States and one or more international organizations shall be governed by that Convention.

Article 74
Questions not prejudged by the present Convention

1.   The provisions of the present Convention shall not prejudge any question that may arise in regard to a treaty between one or more States and one or more international organizations from a succession of States or from the international responsibility of a State or from the outbreak of hostilities between States.

2.   The provisions of the present Convention shall not prejudge any question that may arise in regard to a treaty from the international responsibility of an international organization, from the termination of the existence of the organization or from the termination of participation by a State in the membership of the organization.

3.   The provisions of the present Convention shall not prejudge any question that may arise in regard to the establishment of obligations and rights for States members of an international organization under a treaty to which that organization is a party.

Article 75
Diplomatic and consular relations and the conclusion of treaties

The severance or absence of diplomatic or consular relations between two or more States does not prevent the conclusion of treaties between two or more of those States and one or more international organizations. The conclusion of such a treaty does not in itself affect the situation in regard to diplomatic or consular relations.

Article 76
Case of an aggressor State

The provisions of the present Convention are without prejudice to any obligation in relation to a treaty between one or more States and one or more international organizations which may arise for an aggressor State in consequence of measures taken in conformity with the Charter of the United Nations with reference to that State's aggression.

PART VII

DEPOSITARIES, NOTIFICATIONS, CORRECTIONS
AND REGISTRATION

Article 77
Depositaries of treaties

1.   The designation of the depositary of a treaty may be made by the negotiating States and negotiating organizations or, as the case may be, the negotiating organizations, either in the treaty itself or in some other manner. The depositary may be one or more States, an international organization or the chief administrative officer of the organization.

2.   The functions of the depositary of a treaty are international in character and the depositary is under an obligation to act impartially in their performance. In particular, the fact that a treaty has not entered into force between certain of the parties or that a difference has appeared between a State or an international organization and a depositary with regard to the performance of the latter's functions shall not affect that obligation.

Article 78
Functions of depositaries

1.   The functions of a depositary, unless otherwise provided in the treaty or agreed by the contracting States and contracting organizations or, as the case may be, by the contracting organizations, comprise in particular:

    (a) keeping custody of the original text of the treaty and of any full powers delivered to the depositary;

    (b) preparing certified copies of the original text and preparing any further text of the treaty in such additional languages as may be required by the treaty and transmitting them to the parties and to the States and international organizations entitled to become parties to the treaty;

    (c) receiving any signatures to the treaty and receiving and keeping custody of any instruments, notifications and communications relating to it;

(d) examining whether the signature or any instrument, notification or communication relating to the treaty is in due and proper form and, if need be, bringing the matter to the attention of the State or international organization in question;

(e) informing the parties and the States and international organizations entitled to become parties to the treaty of acts, notifications and communications relating to the treaty;

(f) informing the States and international organizations entitled to become parties to the treaty when the number of signatures or of instruments of ratification, instruments relating to an act of formal confirmation, or of instruments of acceptance, approval or accession required for the entry into force of the treaty has been received or deposited;

(g) registering the treaty with the Secretariat of the United Nations;

(h) performing the functions specified in other provisions of the present Convention.

2.   In the event of any difference appearing between a State or an international organization and the depositary as to the performance of the latter's functions, the depositary shall bring the question to the attention of:

(a) the signatory States and organizations and the contracting States and contracting organizations; or

(b) where appropriate, the competent organ of the international organization concerned.

Article 79
Notifications and communications

Except as the treaty or the present Convention otherwise provide, any notification or communication to be made by any State or any international organization under the present Convention shall:

(a) if there is no depositary, be transmitted direct to the States and organizations for which it is intended, or if there is a depositary, to the latter;

(b) be considered as having been made by the State or organization in question only upon its receipt by the State or organization to which it was transmitted or, as the case may be, upon its receipt by the depositary;

(c) if transmitted to a depositary, be considered as received by the State or organization for which it was intended only when the latter State or organization has been informed by the depositary in accordance with article 78, paragraph 1(e).

Article 80
Correction of errors in texts or in
certified copies of treaties

1. Where, after the authentication of the text of a treaty, the signatory States and international organizations and the contracting States and contracting organizations are agreed that it contains an error, the error shall, unless those States and organizations decide upon some other means of correction, be corrected:

(a) by having the appropriate correction made in the text and causing the correction to be initialled by duly authorized representatives;

(b) by executing or exchanging an instrument or instruments setting out the correction which it has been agreed to make; or

(c) by executing a corrected text of the whole treaty by the same procedure as in the case of the original text.

2. Where the treaty is one for which there is a depositary, the latter shall notify the signatory States and international organizations and the contracting States and contracting organizations of the error and of the proposal to correct it and shall specify an appropriate time-limit within which objection to the proposed correction may be raised. If, on the expiry of the time-limit:

(a) no objection has been raised, the depositary shall make and initial the correction in the text and shall execute a procès-verbal of the rectification of the text and communicate a copy of it to the parties and to the States and organizations entitled to become parties to the treaty;

(b) an objection has been raised, the depositary shall communicate the objection to the signatory States and organizations and to the contracting States and contracting organizations.

3.   The rules in paragraphs 1 and 2 apply also where the text has been authenticated in two or more languages and it appears that there is a lack of concordance which the signatory States and international organizations and the contracting States and contracting organizations agree should be corrected.

4.   The corrected text replaces the defective text _ab initio_, unless the signatory States and international organizations and the contracting States and contracting organizations otherwise decide.

5.   The correction of the text of a treaty that has been registered shall be notified to the Secretariat of the United Nations.

6.   Where an error is discovered in a certified copy of a treaty, the depositary shall execute a _procès-verbal_ specifying the rectification and communicate a copy of it to the signatory States and international organizations and to the contracting States and contracting organizations.

Article 81

Registration and publication of treaties

1.   Treaties shall, after their entry into force, be transmitted to the Secretariat of the United Nations for registration or filing and recording, as the case may be, and for publication.

2.   The designation of a depositary shall constitute authorization for it to perform the acts specified in the preceding paragraph.

PART VIII

FINAL PROVISIONS

Article 82

Signature

The present Convention shall be open for signature until 31 December 1986 at he Federal Ministry for Foreign Affairs of the Republic of Austria, and subsequently, until 30 June 1987, at United Nations Headquarters, New York by:

(a) all States;

(b) Namibia, represented by the United Nations Council for Namibia;

(c) international organizations invited to participate in the United Nations Conference on the Law of Treaties between States and International Organizations or between International Organizations.

Article 83
Ratification or act of formal confirmation

The present Convention is subject to ratification by States and by Namibia, represented by the United Nations Council for Namibia, and to acts of formal confirmation by international organizations. The instruments of ratification and those relating to acts of formal confirmation shall be deposited with the Secretary-General of the United Nations.

Article 84
Accession

1. The present Convention shall remain open for accession by any State, by Namibia, represented by the United Nations Council for Namibia, and by any international organization which has the capacity to conclude treaties.

2. An instrument of accession of an international organization shall contain a declaration that it has the capacity to conclude treaties.

3. The instruments of accession shall be deposited with the Secretary-General of the United Nations.

Article 85
Entry into force

1. The present Convention shall enter into force on the thirtieth day following the date of deposit of the thirty-fifth instrument of ratification or accession by States or by Namibia, represented by the United Nations Council for Namibia.

2. For each State or for Namibia, represented by the United Nations Council for Namibia, ratifying or acceding to the Convention after the condition specified in

paragraph 1 has been fulfilled, the Convention shall enter into force on the thirtieth day after deposit by such State or by Namibia of its instrument of ratification or accession.

3. For each international organization depositing an instrument relating to an act of formal confirmation or an instrument of accession, the Convention shall enter into force on the thirtieth day after such deposit, or at the date the Convention enters into force pursuant to paragraph 1, whichever is later.

Article 86

Authentic texts

The original of the present Convention, of which the Arabic, Chinese, English, French, Russian and Spanish texts are equally authentic, shall be deposited with the Secretary-General of the United Nations.

IN WITNESS WHEREOF the undersigned Plenipotentiaries, being duly authorized by their respective Governments, and duly authorized representatives of the United Nations Council for Namibia and of international organizations have signed the present Convention.

DONE AT VIENNA this twenty-first day of March one thousand nine hundred and eighty-six.

ANNEX

ARBITRATION AND CONCILIATION PROCEDURES ESTABLISHED
IN APPLICATION OF ARTICLE 66

I. ESTABLISHMENT OF THE ARBITRAL TRIBUNAL
OR CONCILIATION COMMISSION

1. A list consisting of qualified jurists, from which the parties to a dispute may choose the persons who are to constitute an arbitral tribunal or, as the case may be, a conciliation commission, shall be drawn up and maintained by the Secretary-General of the United Nations. To this end, every State which is a

Member of the United Nations and every party to the present Convention shall be
invited to nominate two persons, and the names of the persons so nominated shall
constitute the list, a copy of which shall be transmitted to the President of the
International Court of Justice. The term of office of a person on the list,
including that of any person nominated to fill a casual vacancy, shall be five
years and may be renewed. A person whose term expires shall continue to fulfil any
function for which he shall have been chosen under the following paragraphs.

2. When notification has been made under article 66, paragraph 2,
sub-paragraph (f), or agreement on the procedure in the present Annex has been
reached under paragraph 3, the dispute shall be brought before an arbitral
tribunal. When a request has been made to the Secretary-General under article 66,
paragraph 4, the Secretary-General shall bring the dispute before a conciliation
commission. Both the arbitral tribunal and the conciliation commission shall be
constituted as follows:

The States, international organizations or, as the case may be, the States and
organizations which constitute one of the parties to the dispute shall appoint by
common consent:

(a) one arbitrator or, as the case may be, one conciliator, who may or may
not be chosen from the list referred to in paragraph 1; and

(b) one arbitrator or, as the case may be, one conciliator, who shall be
chosen from among those included in the list and shall not be of the nationality of
any of the States or nominated by any of the organizations which constitute that
party to the dispute, provided that a dispute between two international
organizations is not considered by nationals of one and the same State.

The States, international organizations or, as the case may be, the States and
organizations which constitute the other party to the dispute shall appoint two
arbitrators or, as the case may be, two conciliators, in the same way. The four
persons chosen by the parties shall be appointed within sixty days following the
date on which the other party to the dispute receives notification under
article 66, paragraph 2, sub-paragraph (f), or on which the agreement on the
procedure in the present Annex under paragraph 3 is reached, or on which the
Secretary-General receives the request for conciliation.

The four persons so chosen shall, within sixty days following the date of the last of their own appointments, appoint from the list a fifth arbitrator or, as the case may be, conciliator, who shall be chairman.

If the appointment of the chairman, or any of the arbitrators or, as the case may be, conciliators, has not been made within the period prescribed above for such appointment, it shall be made by the Secretary-General of the United Nations within sixty days following the expiry of that period. The appointment of the chairman may be made by the Secretary-General either from the list or from the membership of the International Law Commission. Any of the periods within which appointments must be made may be extended by agreement between the parties to the dispute. If the United Nations is a party or is included in one of the parties to the dispute, the Secretary-General shall transmit the above-mentioned request to the President of the International Court of Justice, who shall perform the functions conferred upon the Secretary-General under this sub-paragraph.

Any vacancy shall be filled in the manner prescribed for the initial appointment.

The appointment of arbitrators or conciliators by an international organization provided for in paragraphs 1 and 2 shall be governed by the rules of that organization.

II. FUNCTIONING OF THE ARBITRAL TRIBUNAL

3.   Unless the parties to the dispute otherwise agree, the Arbitral Tribunal shall decide its own procedure, assuring to each party to the dispute a full opportunity to be heard and to present its case.

4.   The Arbitral Tribunal, with the consent of the parties to the dispute, may invite any interested State or international organization to submit to it its views orally or in writing.

5.   Decisions of the Arbitral Tribunal shall be adopted by a majority vote of the members. In the event of an equality of votes, the vote of the Chairman shall be decisive.

6.   When one of the parties to the dispute does not appear before the Tribunal or fails to defend its case, the other party may request the Tribunal to continue the

proceedings and to make its award. Before making its award, the Tribunal must satisfy itself not only that it has jurisdiction over the dispute but also that the claim is well founded in fact and law.

7. The award of the Arbitral Tribunal shall be confined to the subject—matter of the dispute and state the reasons on which it is based. Any member of the Tribunal may attach a separate or dissenting opinion to the award.

8. The award shall be final and without appeal. It shall be complied with by all parties to the dispute.

9. The Secretary—General shall provide the Tribunal with such assistance and facilities as it may require. The expenses of the Tribunal shall be borne by the United Nations.

III. FUNCTIONING OF THE CONCILIATION COMMISSION

10. The Conciliation Commission shall decide its own procedure. The Commission, with the consent of the parties to the dispute, may invite any party to the treaty to submit to it its views orally or in writing. Decisions and recommendations of the Commission shall be made by a majority vote of the five members.

11. The Commission may draw the attention of the parties to the dispute to any measures which might facilitate an amicable settlement.

12. The Commission shall hear the parties, examine the claims and objections, and make proposals to the parties with a view to reaching an amicable settlement of the dispute.

13. The Commission shall report within twelve months of its constitution. Its report shall be deposited with the Secretary—General and transmitted to the parties to the dispute. The report of the Commission, including any conclusions stated therein regarding the facts or questions of law, shall not be binding upon the parties and it shall have no other character than that of recommendations submitted for the consideration of the parties in order to facilitate an amicable settlement of the dispute.

14. The Secretary—General shall provide the Commission with such assistance and facilities as it may require. The expenses of the Commission shall be borne by the United Nations.

索　引

中文索引

十二畫

十三畫

英 文 索 引

A

B

J

K

L

M

國立中央圖書館出版品預行編目資料

條約法公約析論／陳治世著.--初版-- 臺北市：臺灣
學生，民81
　面；　公分
含索引
ISBN 957-15--0331-2（精裝).--ISBN 957-15
-332-0（平裝）

1.條約

579.7　　　　　　　　　　　　　　81000615

條 約 法 公 約 析 論（全一冊）

著 作 者：陳　　　　治　　　　世
出 版 者：臺 灣 學 生 書 局
本 書 局 登
記 證 字 號：行政院新聞局局版臺業字第一一〇〇號
發 行 人：丁　　　文　　　治
發 行 所：臺 灣 學 生 書 局
　　　　　臺北市和平東路一段一九八號
　　　　　郵政劃撥帳號〇〇〇二四六六八號
　　　　　電　話：3 6 3 4 1 5 6
　　　　　FAX：(0 2) 3 6 3 6 3 3 4
印刷所：淵 明 印 刷 有 限 公 司
　　　　地　址：永和市成功路1段43巷5號
　　　　電　話：9 2 8 7 1 4 5
香港總經銷：藝 文 圖 書 公 司
　　　　地址：九龍偉業街99號連順大厦五字
　　　　樓及七字樓　電話：7959595
定價　精裝新臺幣四四〇元
　　　平裝新臺幣三八〇元
中 華 民 國 八 十 一 年 八 月 初 版

ISBN 957-15-0331-2（精裝）
ISBN 957-15-0332-0（平裝）